155.8
K54     Kiell, Norman, comp.
a            The psychodynamics of
        American Jewish life.

155.8
K54     Kiell, Norman, comp.
a            The psychodynamics of
        American Jewish life.

## Temple Israel
### Library
**Minneapolis, Minn.**

----

Please sign your full name on the above card.

Return books promptly to the Library or Temple Office.

Fines will be charged for overdue books or for damage or loss of same.

# THE PSYCHODYNAMICS
## OF
# AMERICAN JEWISH LIFE:

*An Anthology*

# The Psychodynamics

## of

## American Jewish Life:

*An Anthology*

*Edited by*

NORMAN KIELL

TWAYNE PUBLISHERS, INC.
NEW YORK, N. Y. 10003

*For*

CHARLOTTE AND HERBERT RUBEN

GOOD FRIENDS

# Preface

EVER since the advent of Sigmund Freud, psychoanalysis and the Jews have been inextricably linked. Psychoanalysis has been called, frequently and pejoratively, a "Jewish science," perhaps for three reasons. First, it was founded by a Jew. Second, except for Ernest Jones, the original coterie around Freud, and his subsequent loyal disciples, was largely Jewish. And last, psychoanalysis, in its pursuit of the curlicues and dotting of the i and crossing of the t in ferreting out the secrets of the human psyche, resembles very much the patient exploration of the Talmudic scholars, steeped as they were in certain attitudes toward sex, authority, interpersonal and family relations, which Freud found substantially compatible with his own theories.

But of course the link between Jews and psychoanalysis has long since gone beyond the tenuous relationship of the accident of one man's birth. Although Freud was not what we call today an observant Jew, he felt himself to be, as Jones describes him, "Jewish to the core, and it evidently meant a great deal to him. He had the common Jewish sensitiveness to the slightest hint of anti-Semitism, and he made very few friends who were not Jews."

The storm of protest generated by Freud's ideas on religion was prompted by several of his most controversial works: *The Future of An Illusion; Civilization and Its Discontents;* and *Moses and Monotheism.* In his psychoanalytic theory of religious behavior, Freud suggests that God was an invention of primitive man, an agent to fall back on when overwhelmed by life's inevitable woes and frustrations. In response to these difficulties, the individual repressed the wish to be a child again and could appeal and be helped by his all-powerful father. Thus emerged the concept of the omnipotent God. The father is not only a source of help and support but also, as a result of the castration

7

complex, a fear-inspiring figure. Thus, God too is both feared and loved. Moreover, Freud clearly implies that this theory is intended to explain not only the religious behavior of primitive man but also the religious behavior of all men.

Jewish life today, as it has been for several thousand years, is at a crossroads whose branches lead in traditional directions—assimilation, alienation, intermarriage, cultural pluralism, and so on. Psychoanalysis is not a new gnosis but rather an avenue by which new light can shine on old truths, illuminating the obscure and the hidden, refurbishing the antics of the wayward word, mind, and spirit. It is my hope that the articles in this collection will help toward that end.

These articles center around psychoanalytic and psychological theories of religious behavior as especially reflected in the emotional life of the American Jew. The collection has at least two functions: (1) to unearth neglected papers as well as others of merit and importance and (2) to assemble in one convenient place an array of highly regarded articles on the psychological literature of the Jew.

The scope of the book is manifest in the four section headings seen in the Table of Contents. Each topic bears on the emotional experience of the Jew in the United States. The papers are concerned with the answers five-year-olds give to the question, "Can a dog or a cat be Jewish?" and to the geriatric problems of the Jewish aged. Another paper deals with the "perfect doll," the thirty-year-old Jewish narcissistic female, found typically in the upper-middle socioeconomic class, who is all dressed up with no place to go, emotionally or spiritually. Still another paper tells us that the incidence of the Jew "on the couch" is two and a half times that above expectation as compared with the two other major faiths. On the other hand, very few Jews are either alcoholic or drug addicts, on either an absolute or comparative basis.

The primary search of every individual is the search for identity and perhaps it is nowhere more acute than for the Jew through the ages. In the United States, the fractionalization of the Jewish community into innumerable factions and ideologies makes identification a somewhat complex phenomenon. Chein enumerates some different types of Jew: the "out of pocket" Jew who feels that he has fulfilled his Jewishness by giving to charity; the "cardiac" Jew who experiences his Jewishness in the heart; and the "gastronomic" Jew who feels Jewish when he has a Jewish meal. On the other hand, he says, there are many Jews who, while identifying themselves as Jews, do not care about anything Jewish.

Jewish identification consists of a number of potentially independent axes or subtypes of identification. The most relevant among them, according to Rinder, are general, religious, racial, national, and cultural feelings of Jewishness. These expressions of Jewish identity are evident, in their most overt form, in the rites and ceremonies practiced by orthodox and conservative Jews and to a more limited extent by reform Jews.

Rituals give the individual the opportunity to act out his sublimated or repressed libidinal urgings. The almost continual round of ritualistic performance in the daily life of the devout Jew is a defense against the collapse of aggressive impulses. "These impulses," writes Wolfenstein, "were to a large extent turned inward. The Jews underwent endless sufferings which they accepted in a spirit of exalted masochism as inflicted by a God who loved them above all others. This submission to external authority was haunted by rebellious impulses which appeared as doubts about religious rules to which exceptions could always be found; and the doubts were in turn fought back by even more refined formulations of the rules. The Jewish religion concentrated on regulating relations between men; between a sole father-god and his sons. There are covert indications of sadistic impulses of children toward mothers which also have to be held in check. Thus the motive behind the taboo against eating meat and milk may have been a defense against the impulse of the infant to bite and eat the milk-giving breast."

The articles in the book are drawn from such journals as the *Psychoanalytic Review, International Journal of Psycho-Analysis, Psychiatry, American Imago, International Journal of Social Psychiatry, Journal of Genetic Psychology, Journal of the Hillside Hospital,* and the *Journal of Jewish Community Service.* The authors are psychoanalysts, clinical and social psychologists, an anthropologist, a sociologist, and a rabbi who is also a psychiatrist. The eclectic approach gives the reader an opportunity to review areas of Jewish life and expression from a variety of disciplines. It is the editor's hope that the papers presented here will offer thoughtful stimulation to professional people in the clergy, in the fields of psychology, teaching and social work, and to lay people.

NORMAN KIELL

*Merrick, N. Y.*

9

# Acknowledgments

The editor wishes to acknowledge, with grateful thanks, the permission he has received from the following journals and authors for use of the materials in this book.

Ruth Landes and Mark Zborowski, Hypotheses concerning the Eastern European Jewish family, *Psychiatry*, 1950, 13:447-464. Copyright and reprinted by special permission of the William Alanson White Psychiatric Foundation, Inc.

Abraham N. Franzblau, M.D., A new look at the psychodynamics of Jewish family living, *Journal of Jewish Communal Service*, 1958, 35:57-71.

Kenneth B. Clark, Jews in contemporary America. Problems in identification, *Jewish Social Service Quarterly*, 1954, 31:12-22.

Maurice E. Linden, M.D., Emotional problems in living, *Journal of Jewish Communal Service*, 1954, 31:80-89.

Jerold S. Heiss, Premarital characteristics of the religiously intermarried in an urban area, *American Sociological Review*, 1960, 25:47-55. Reprinted by permission of the American Sociological Review.

Alexander Grinstein, M.D., Profile of a "Doll"—a female character type, *Psychoanalytic Review*, 1963, 50(2):161-174. Reprinted through the courtesy of the editors and the publisher, National Psychological Association for Psychoanalysis, Inc.

Henry Raphael Gold, M.D., Can we speak of Jewish neuroses? In, Novick, Simon (ed.), *Judaism and Psychiatry*, New York: United Synagogue of America, 1956, pages 155-160. Reprinted by permission of the publisher, the National Academy for Adult Jewish Studies of the United Synagogue of America.

11

# Table of Contents

13

# Contributors

RENATO J. ALMANSI, M.D., is a diplomate of the American Board of Psychiatry and Neurology and Associate Psychiatrist at Hillside Hospital and Kings County Hospital, New York.

GERDA G. BARAG, M.D., is a psychoanalyst in Tel Aviv, Israel.

KENNETH B. CLARK is professor of psychology at City College of the City University of New York. Professor Clark received his doctoral degree from Columbia, has taught at Hampton University and was resident director of the Northside Center for Child Development. Dr. Clark helped to prepare the draft for the famous United States Supreme Court decision on desegregation.

MONTAGUE D. EDER, M.D., was one of the earliest analysts to practice in London.

DAVID ELKIND obtained his doctorate at the University of California at Los Angeles and after stints of duty in the East at such institutions as the Austin Riggs Center, Wheaton College and the Beth Israel Hospital of Boston, he returned to the West, serving in the Department of Psychiatry of UCLA's School of Medicine and more recently at the University of Denver.

DR. SANDOR S. FELDMAN is Clinical Professor of Psychiatry in the School of Medicine and Dentistry at University of Rochester. Of more than passing interest is the fact that his brother is Rabbi Arthur Feldman and his brother-in-law was formerly Chief Rabbi of Hungary.

ABRAHAM N. FRANZBLAU has both Ph.D. and M.D. degrees and for many years has headed up the pastoral counseling program at the Hebrew Union College of the Jewish Institute of Religion. He is also Associate Psychiatrist at Mount Sinai Hospital, New York City.

17

HENRY R. GOLD, M.D., was a practicing rabbi for many years and now is a practicing psychoanalyst and psychiatrist. He has frequently published articles on the psychological values of Judaism.

ALEXANDER GRINSTEIN, M.D., a psychoanalyst from Detroit, Michigan, is the editor of the monumental ten volume bibliography, *Index to Psychoanalysis*.

NELSON G. HANAWALT, PH. D., is professor and chairman of the Department of Psychology at Douglass College of Rutgers University, New Brunswick, N.J.

JEROLD S. HEISS is on the faculty of the Department of Sociology at the University of Connecticut and is a frequent contributor to the sociological journals on problems relating to interfaith courtship and marriage.

RUTH LANDES received her Ph.D. in anthropology from Columbia University as well as a Master's Certificate from the New York School of Social Work. She has taught at Columbia, Brooklyn College and Fisk University. She served on the staff of the Myrdal Study of the American Negro and the President's Committee on Fair Employment Practices.

DR. BORIS M. LEVINSON is Director of the Psychological Center and professor of psychology at the Graduate School of Education of Yeshiva University.

MAURICE E. LINDEN, M.D., is associated with the Norristown (Pa.) State Hospital and has long been concerned with psychogeriatric problems.

ARNOLD MEADOW has his Ph. D. from Harvard University, has taught at the University of Buffalo, was a Fulbright lecturer at the University of Bordeaux and is presently professor of psychology at the University of Arizona.

IRWIN D. RINDER is professor of psychology at the University of Wisconsin (Milwaukee).

VICTOR D. SANUA, PH. D., was with the O.S.S. in the Middle East and served with the United Nations Relief for Palestine Refugees. He was a Fellow at the Payne Whitney Psychiatric Clinic, taught at Michigan State University and Harvard and is now on the faculty of the Wurzweiler School for Social Work of Yeshiva University. He is also Research Director for the YM-YWHA.

DR. M. WOOLF practised psychoanalysis in Tel Aviv, Israel.

MARK ZBOROWSKI has several degrees from the University of Paris. He

18

has been a consultant to the Army Services Forces, a staff member of the Yiddish Scientific Institute and the Department of Scientific Research of the American Jewish Committee. He is the author of *Life Is with People.*

# I.  THE AMERICAN SCENE

# INTRODUCTION

**M**OST of the fore forebears of the present first and second generation American Jews emigrated from the Ukraine, Galicia, Russian Poland, Lithuania, Bessarabia, Bukovina, Hungary, and Carpatho-Russia. It has been estimated that roughly 90 per cent of the Jews in the United States today have parents or grandparents who originally came from these geographical areas. Thus it would seem logical that, in order to understand the American Jew, one must first understand the East European Jew and his family. This is why the section on the American scene begins with an empirical paper on the form and function of the now-destroyed Eastern European small town, or *shtetl*.

In their observations, Dr. Landes and Mr. Zborowski note that among Eastern European Jews, the home was the only area where women had status, where they symbolized emotionality, and where they were frequently the breadwinners. The father's preferred sphere of activity was outside the home in the synagogue. The most dynamic relationships existed between husband and wife, mother and son, and father and daughter, with considerable tension displayed between parents and children of the same sex. Here we can see some evidence for the powerful role the mother plays in American Jewish life; and, although there has been some acculturation with the dominant Protestant family system, the common denominator of the Oedipal complex is still pervasive.

The family system and values the Jewish immigrants brought to the New World persist in their basic forms. Dr. Abraham N. Franzblau's "New Look at the Psychodynamics of Jewish Family Living" points out the emotional integrity of the family, the attitude of sanctity toward human life, the origin of religious impulses in the Oedipus Complex, the status of the mother, the high standards of sexual morality, and the pleasurable and robust Jewish attitude toward sex. The continuity of

19

these characteristics, transplanted, with modifications, from one culture to another, is apparent and self-evident, steeped as they are in Judaic values.

One of the ways in which Jewish tradition in the United States is being eroded is through the increased incidence of intermarriage. Fourteen per cent of the Jews today marry outside the faith. This phenomenon has aroused considerable anxiety among the rabbinate and some lay people as a threat to Jewish survival and has prompted a number of studies on the subject.

Most of the studies have approached the problem from a sociological, statistical, or religious point of view, centering on the limited variables of religious training, generation, or socioeconomic status. The paper by Dr. Jerold S. Heiss, included in this volume, differs from previous research in that its main interest lies in the premarital characteristics of the intermarried. The author's goal was to learn how it was possible for people to intermarry despite what seems to be general disapproval of such marriages. The findings, based on the Midtown Mental Health Project carried out in New York City, support the hypotheses that the intermarried are characterized by (1) nonreligious parents; (2) greater dissatisfaction with parents when young; (3) greater early family strife; (4) less early family integration; and (5) greater emancipation from parents at the time of marriage.

The attempt to assimilate in order to escape from the effects of contemporary American attitudes toward Jews is dealt with by Dr. Kenneth B. Clark. He shows that prejudice in our society has almost inevitable effects on personality development and behavior. With the rare exception of some Jewish groups who live religiously and socially secluded lives, most Jews are exposed to the contrasts between themselves and non-Jews. Kurt Lewin has noted, and Dr. Clark reasserts, that the ability to assimilate into the dominant group serves to intensify the individual's conflict and ambivalence. As social and physical boundaries break down between a minority and majority group, the individual's tie to his own minority group may weaken. The accessibility and allure of the majority group invite him to cross the line. The Jew's struggle is whether to maintain his identity as a Jew or to assimilate. No matter what his choice, Dr. Clark states, he will not escape conflict, ambivalence, and anxiety.

This search for identity is seen in its tragic manifestations in "The Profile of a Doll," by Dr. Alexander Grinstein. The perfect "doll" is described as a first-generation American female between the ages of thirty and thirty-five, born of immigrant Jewish parents during the Depression and who now belongs in the upper-middle socioeconomic class. She is overdressed, overly made up and coiffured, sexually frigid, extremely narcissistic and aloof, and conceals behind these traits a bewildered, frightened child.

The virulency of the Oedipal conflict becomes apparent in Dr. Grinstein's delineation of the mother-daughter relationship from the daughter's infancy to her marriage. The kind of characterological defenses this type of woman develops lies in the quality of the mother-daughter relationship. In the article by Landes and Zborowski, the dominant role of the East European Jewish mother and the shadowy figure cast by the father was spelled out. Dr. Grinstein shows the effect of these roles, where such parents were transplanted, on their American-born daughter. The primitive characteristic of many of these mothers has a profound effect on the entire psychosocial development of these girls, with the resulting disturbance in identity and values.

Chapter 1

# Hypotheses Concerning the Eastern European Jewish Family

RUTH LANDES AND MARK ZBOROWSKI

𝕿HE present discussion is directed towards phrasing hypotheses about the form and functioning of the Jewish family in the now destroyed Eastern European small town known in Yiddish as the *shtetl*. The shtetl life, organized into characteristic, richly detailed patterns of behavior, was destroyed under the German occupation of World War II. Persons reared in shtetl culture, however, constituted the bulk of the East European Jewish migration to the United States; in the absence of exact figures, there is a belief among authorities that it constituted 90 per cent or even more of the total, in the aggregate.

Our hypotheses are drawn from a mass of data collected by the Columbia University Project, Research in Contemporary Cultures, inaugurated by the late Dr. Ruth Benedict. The data were assembled during two years of work in New York City which included intensive interviewing of 128 informants who had migrated to New York from the shtetl, and of 10 more born here of shtetl parentage,[1] besides the combing of a variety of literature relevant to shtetl culture. Research in Contemporary Cultures based its general picture on conditions in Ukrainian Jewish communities before the Russian Revolution of 1917 and in the Polish, Hungarian, and Romanian villages or small towns before their destruction in the years 1939-1945. The data were not collected for the purposes of this paper, however, but in order to yield a rounded picture of the total life.

Our purpose, reported in this paper, is to develop enough understanding of Eastern European Jewish family life to provide us with a theoretical base line from which to start field inquiries among American Jewish families descended from this tradition. The Research in Contemporary Cultures data, for our particular purpose, left lacunae that we have tried to span with our hypotheses, testing them against facts in the literature, against our own scattered interviews, and against Eastern European Jewish films which we have analyzed. Having blocked out these hypotheses rather completely, we offer them now with two objectives: for the insights they may provide the sociocultural, psychological, and psychiatric specialties; and for critical appraisal as tools for our own proposed field research into American Jewish family life. It came as a surprise to all of the researchers to realize the seemingly considerable per- severance of traditional European modes in American surround- ings, even in the third generation, despite some evidence of important changes or, at least, of shifts of emphasis. Shtetl Jews themselves expect perseverance, and in orthodox religious circles decry any of the changes in family life.

## I.  FAMILY RELATIONSHIPS

Though there were two major ranked groups of high social mobility in the shtetl, called *sheyne* (Yiddish, beautiful, fine) and *proste* (Yiddish, common), our hypotheses of family life appear to apply to both, except for situational details. This is because the family behavior of traditional Jews everywhere has been painstakingly guided for centuries by written codes that standardized conduct. The ideals of the codes held for all, though they were often ignored in practice.

This family of our hypotheses obviously belongs to Western civilization. In its general outlines, it is patrilineal, even patriarchal, fostering obligations among members of the biolo- gical family, weakening them with more distant kin. Within these outlines, however, there are developments which we may call institutional, and behavioristic emphases and nuances which vary markedly and consistently enough to make this family distinct among the others in the European tradition, including Jewish families of central and western Europe[2].

There are three dynamic relationships within the shtetl family that constitute an institutional universe and a field of tensions. These are: the bonds between man and wife, between mother and son, and between father and daughter. Other blood and kin ties flow from, support, and otherwise are consequences of these three.

A man and woman marry primarily to have offspring, and their duties and roles are carefully detailed by tradition. The Schulchan Aruch, or Jewish Code of Law[3], covers the subject precisely, as do many portions of the Talmud and many folk sayings. Our informants carried these injunctions clearly in their minds, both the regular ones and those covering special individual cases like sterility and quarrelsomeness, and special social cases like defined *mésalliances*[4].

We differentiated three aspects of behavior: prescribed conduct as formulated in the Jewish Code of Law; customary behavior which varies with social position and geographical area, and which is manifest in folklore, folk sayings, proverbs, institutions; and behavior not verbalized by the inhabitants of the shtetl, but manifest to the scientific observer. Thus, we distinguished between "formalized" and "unformalized" family behavior to facilitate our understanding of the dynamics of both equilibrium and change within the family. By formalized, we mean the codified and customary conduct of relatives. By unformalized, we mean the motivations and emotions of persons occupying the different roles, which are often unconscious or unverbalized, and often not evident in behavior; these are deeply intertwined with the formal structures, giving them fresh connotations, producing tensions and resolving them, but all contained within the confines of an equilibrium-directed logic termed *Sholem Bayis* (Hebrew, domestic peace).

The formal structuring of the husband's role places upon the man the responsibility for propagating the family, which carries his name, but attributes the failure to the wife; so that after ten years of barren marriage, the man is enjoined by Jewish law to request a divorce that will enable him to remarry fruitfully, though he and his wife may care deeply for each other[5]. The husband should study sacred literature and promote the book learning tradition of Israel, and this is so heavily stressed that devotion to study is the one condition allowed by the Schulchan Aruch for delaying marriage[6]. A scholar is expected to delegate the family's economic responsibilities to his wife; she is secondary to him in the spiritual or intellectual sphere, but is expected to be fully responsible in mundane affairs. However, the ideal, sometimes realized, is for a man to be both learned and successful in business. The husband is responsible for certain important domestic rituals, such as the Kiddush prayers said over wine on the Sabbath and holidays, the feast of the Passover, the pinning of the mezuzah on the house door-jam[7]. And always he is responsible for his wife's general well-being, an injunction which was often so interpreted as to allow the Eastern European Jewish woman latitude and opportunities for movement, to conduct business, seek employment, and visit relatives in other parts.

The wife's role, from a legalistic point of view, is regarded as complementary to her husband's. From a functional point of view, it is subordinated to and dependent upon her husband's. This is perhaps symbolized by the belief that a woman enters heaven at her husband's footstool regardless of her possibly superior virtue and despite the fact that theoretically she enters heaven just as her husband does because "every Jew has his share in the world to come[8]." The fear of infertility threatens a Jewish woman with a heavy penalty of shame, producing anxieties, and may lead to social subterfuges like the adoption of children. A wife serves her husband and children in prescribed ways, and she is trained to be ready to assume the economic burdens of the family. In emergencies, like illness, her husband will carry out the duties, and one informant even told of a Jewish father giving the breast to his motherless infant to stop his crying. The wife shares responsibility for the Kashruth ritual[9] with her husband, but bears the burden of its correct functioning within the home; and she is responsible for fulfilling her own female ritual bearing on the family's well-being, such as observing the Mikvah[10] bath, lighting and blessing the Sabbath candles, offering God a portion of the dough from the Sabbath loaf.

This clear-cut understanding of the specialized functions of a husband and a wife, with its emphatic suggestion of male and female worlds of acts and values, does not preclude overlapping and interchange in specific situations of need. In time of need,

women may carry out a large part of the sacred activity normally assigned to men, and this is permissible because they are far less completely covered by regulations than are men; that is, when necessary, women may do anything unforbidden to them, even if normally it is bidden only to men.  It is the universal obligation of all Jews to fulfill the obligations of the Jewish way of living, and in emergencies formal specializations of sex-typed roles are largely ignored.

A couple fulfills its Jewish mission by raising its offspring, hopefully numerous and favored with sons, in traditional detailed ways.  Both parents support the children, educate them, and provide for the "crisis rites" of circumcision, confirmation, marriage, even death and apostasy.  The male child is officially preferred by both parents, and the eldest boy (Hebrew, *B'chor*) is singled out as his father's legal heir, to receive respect from the younger siblings all of his life[11].  Birth of a son is announced joyously by the father in the synagogue, in contrast with the flat announcement of a daughter's birth; the son carries the responsibility of the mourning prayers for the parents, called Kaddish.  However, a boy, like his sister, develops relationships with each parent that are culturally characteristic, and qualitatively different, partly in consequence of the different roles of the sexes in the community and of the differently structured ties with the parent of either sex, partly in consequence of the unformalized developments around the structuring.  The father supervises the son's education.  A daughter is not encouraged in advanced study but may teach herself from any available source.  The mother is the representative and administrator of the father's wishes, as she is the effective disciplinarian; her daughters, however, are her own full responsibility.  She is always in or near the home with her sons and daughters, tending their physical needs, while the father is usually out of the home, studying in the synagogue or occupied with business.  The father's presence and interests are remote from domestic concerns.  But the mother prepares the food and serves it; she is always associated with the tangibles of existence. The father has the further obligation of supporting his married daughter and her husband in his home during the first few years of marriage, if his son-in-law is a promising scholar; this is known as supporting the young couple in *kest*, and is regarded by the bride's parents as an ideal arrangement. A divorcee or widow may return to her parents, but this is not expected of a son.

The reciprocally correct conduct of children is to respect and obey the parents unconditionally. This has many manifestations, prescribed in the Schulchan Aruch; symbolically, the son is obliged to rise whenever his father enters the room. The daughter serves her father, and helps and serves her mother, and the daughter is expected to influence her husband to support her parents when necessary. When mature, that is, married, all children are officially expected to support parents, though proverbs indicate how distasteful this can be to both parties since it connotes frailty or deficiency of the parents.

Relationships among siblings are guided by the parents, systematized along the lines of sex difference or identity, and of relative age. It appears that children introject parental standards successfully, and much of their behavior can be understood as modeled after that of the parent of the same sex. This does not of course preclude rebellion, or introjection of other ideals or adult models such as the teacher; priority of the teacher is even enjoined by law[12].

Parents discourage opposite-sex siblings from playing together by reminding them of their sex differences, and attaching to these implications of prestige. Thus, a boy attending cheder, Hebrew school, is told it is beneath him to play girls' games, if he is found playing with his sister.

Siblings are prohibited as sex partners by the Levitical code. In the shtetl, the prohibition is realized by avoidance devices which include full body covering and segregated seating of the sexes except on rare formal occasions. Avoidance seems to increase with the maturity of brother and sister, as does the tension between them. Communication between them is fostered by the mother, when she initiates matters of interest to them but insists on functioning as their intermediary in such a way as to maintain their avoidance.

Parents are frequent intermediaries in the cross-sex sibling relationship, either on their own initiative or at the call of the children. Consistent with the indoctrinated habits of avoidance, mutual aid among these siblings is expected, and is often initiated by the parents. A practice of third-party mediation is in fact a feature of other aspects of the culture, notably in marriage and business arrangements.

Any sibling can develop into a parent-substitute as need arises. This adds to the strains in all sibling relationships, for authority, avoidances, and intimacies are differently organized between the parents and children. Siblings do not participate in each other's private lives until one assumes the role of substitute parent. Males and females are equally responsible for maintaining a traditionally prescribed standard of respectability and integrity that is contained in the word *yiddishkeit* (lit. "Jewishness," roughly analogous to the United States' "our own way of life").

Brothers do not maintain avoidance in the sense cultivated by opposite-sex siblings, but it seems to us they manifest only a slight amount of interest in each other except when forcibly called upon in a family crisis. Then, after having raised requested funds, or provided for needy youngsters, they are likely to relapse into their distant ways. Even quarrels do not bring them together, as they do sisters, for angry men characteristically withdraw into sulky silences.

All women are presumed to quarrel more violently than men, in speech and act. This release of expression actually serves to bring sisters close together, at least socially, into a community little known to brothers.

A convention stresses marriage for siblings in their age sequence; this is emphasized for sisters, because, as rationalized by informants, it serves to minimize envy and quarrels, and to stress the authority of age.

The structuring of roles within this small biological family, the traditional allowances accorded each—either explicitly or by oversight—and the interrelationships among them result in role functions peculiar to this Eastern European Jewish culture. The functions or uses of the roles appear to be affected less by necessities of the family structure itself than by the ethos of the people[13], by their "prevalent tone of sentiment"[14], or collective "emotional emphases" [15].

The most striking instance of ethological variation is the behavior of the woman as mother, particularly in relations with her son; she behaves similarly, however, as wife, and as sister in relationships with her brother.   In other words, it is in association with these three relatives of the opposite sex that she most fully evolves her emotional or sentimental potentialities. Our data suggest that it is the woman who initiates these opposite-sex interactions, who arouses them and conditions them.   It was a practice, in the time of arranged marriages, for a mother to select a wife for her son; in memoirs written by Jewish men recording marriages, it was often the woman who instigated the negotiations and "had her way"[16]; in folk and published stories, and in films, a sister assumes the role of mother when necessary. There is a saying that domestic harmony rests with the wife, and another that "a wife sets you on your feet, or knocks you off them[17]."   It often happens that the mother's relatives are the ones best known to her children, even, in cases, to the entire ignorance of the father's kin.   Informants born and reared in the shtetl area have told us of never having met paternal grandparents, especially the paternal grandfather, until the age of thirteen or fourteen.   On male informant explained that the "mother's side was closer [because] first of all the very word *mameh* [Yiddish, mother] is closer to you than the word *tateh* [Yiddish, father]."   And a proverb declares, "A son always takes after his mother's brother[18]."   Indeed, the wife is the actual head of the household, and responsible for its "Jewish way of life."

The house is the place for rearing the children.   "She kills herself," people say of a good mother, in order to bring up her children.   The father too becomes like a child to her in the home, except when he is studying or performing ritual acts; only outside of the home, in the synagogue or in business, does he enter upon a fully adult role.   Mother is frequently described as "a loving despot"[19], always busy, always nagging, "the last and highest court af appeal"[20].   Generally her conduct is understood, tolerated, loved.   In retrospect it is idealized, as shown in the published memoirs of Jewish men.   Levin says[21], recalling his childhood, ". . . One figure emerges . . . my mother.   In that image I recognize the beginning of my life and feel the first pulse beat of my being . . . My mother was in my eyes the personification of all that is loveliest and most lovable. . . . In my eyes she was a saint. . . . Though my head was drawn toward [my] father, [my] heart [was drawn] toward [my] mother, and I was forever swinging like a pendulum between these two forces." A folk tale that has even crept into American lore tells of a mother's devotion: A young man begs his mother for her heart, which his betrothed has demanded as a gift; having torn it out of his mother's proffered breast, he races away with it; and as he stumbles, the heart falls to the ground, and he hears it question protectively, "Did you hurt yourself, my son?"

The woman in the home personifies emotionality—the mother most of all. A young son often sleeps with her, unlike her husband who is prohibited by sacred law from remaining in her bed. In one memoir a boy slept with his mother until he was 13, that is, ritually a man. Although displays of endearment between husband and wife are frowned upon, regarded as vulgar whether in speech or gesture, a great deal of demonstrativeness is allowed between mother and son, which mothers encourage. The father is also unwontedly demonstrative to his daughter, but less so than the mother to her son.

It seems to us that though the marital obligations are fulfilled with the husband, the romance exists with the son. In the *New York Times* of October 29, 1949, an Associated Press story from Capetown, South Africa, reports "A mother who had traced her missing sailor son around the globe fell dead of shock here when she faced him. The story was related today by the woman's husband as last rites were said at her grave. . . . Mrs. R. Levi of Aden saw her 19-year-old son early in World War II when he kissed her good-bye and left to join the Royal Navy. After several months she was advised that his ship had been torpedoed and all hands lost. . . . She refused to believe her son dead and wandered through Mediterranean ports seeking him. Mrs. Levi visited Britain, the United States and Australia in her weary search. . . . Then, in an asylum at Observatory, near Capetown, she found her son. He was a human wreck who could only mutter 'shalom, shalom,'—the Hebrew word for 'peace.' She looked at him, fell to the floor, and died." The same theme appeared in a Polish Jewish film, "Long Is the Road," where mother and son, separated by the Nazi occupation of Warsaw, sought each other after the Nazi defeat, searching devastated cities and concentration camps of Central Europe, until eventually the son located his mother in a hospital to which she had been taken in a state of breakdown. In the film, the woman's acceptance of her husband's murder by the Nazis contrasts with her agonized search for her son. Again, in the film "The Eternal Song" is depicted a Polish woman's tragic love and desperate search for her son, ending in her own death. Another Polish Jewish film, "Bar Mitzvah," dramatically depicts the attachment between mother and son in another setting, and here too it causes all other relationships to pale[22].

In actuality, a boy avoids[23] his sister, especially if she is a coeval, the avoidance increasing as they age; among most orthodox Jews, especially the very numerous Chassidic sect, a man avoids all women except his wife, mother, and daughter[24]. The interest in the sister however is powerful, revealed in indirect ways: in the Talmud[25] where dreams of incest with mother and sister are described coolly as "opening the way to wisdom," and where another dream symbol of incest with sister is to see one eye kiss another; in European Jewish films—"I Want To Be a Mother," "Bar Mitzvah," "Mamele"—brother-sister interest ranged from violent horseplay to one suggestion of romance and another of marriage, where however the siblings were unaware of their biological kinship.

There is no avoidance between mother and son, except that intercourse is forbidden. Mother is the embodiment of warmth, intimacy, food, unconditional love, security, practical reality. This inclusive libidinal character, of which the sisters partake to a lesser extent—the coeval sister partaking the least so that she is as much a stranger as a relative—is in complete contrast with the spiritualized, remote character of the father. Father's life is as dedicated to the study of the Law as mother's is to material comforts for the family; he is remote from his son physically and emotionally, being mentor and guide rather than comforter and nurse, and occupied outside of the home. Insofar as is possible to a living creature, a father's personality is delibidinized. Levin[26] observes, "Toward my father my attitude was one of the deepest respect, but in that respect there was not lacking an element of fear. ... I would say that my father's influence was to intellectualize me, my mother's to inspire me:

From my father streamed a cool, clear light: from my mother, warmth and emotion. . . ." Yet the father and son bear a similar relationship to the wife and mother, except that the woman owes respect to the husband because such is her defined obligation, and the son owes respect to the mother because that is his obligation. Indeed, rivalry between father and son is a familiar theme, expressed in large and small ways, privately and publicly. It is a commonplace that a man prefers his son-in-law to his son, and a proverb says, "Every son-in-law has in him something of his father-in-law[27]." Partly for this reason, it is proverbial that a man, though legally his father's heir, feuds with his sister's husband who stands to inherit his father-in-law's goodwill and perhaps his property; this is particularly striking in the history of some noted Chassidic "courts" or "dynasties"[28].

The mother-son relationship does not run smoothly, with all of the woman's high feeling. The Jewish mother of our informants is known for nagging, quarreling, worrying, and hypochondria. She overstresses her concern and her criticism, and offers or so manipulates the serving of the food as to indicate which[29]. Her husband and son are used to this. When she becomes too difficult, the man withdraws psychologically, silently picking up a book, or bodily, silently leaving for the synagogue; sometimes he deserts the family. By her conduct the woman manipulates her traditionally subordinate status to win some advantages: in many directions, she thus persuades her husband and her son to do her will [30].

We have found the involvements between mother and son to be so far-reaching and intense as to approximate a kind of adoration. The mother is extremely jealous or resentful of her son's interest in another woman, even though she wants him to marry, for that is a Jew's obligation, and to have children, for that is also his duty and will besides bring her the joy, the *nakhes*, of grandmotherhood. Even though she may choose his wife, the feeling of treason is such that there is a folk saying, "When the son marries, he gives the wife a contract and the mother a divorce[31]." The bitterest mother-in-law stories are told by Jewish women, and here we see one element determining the greater closeness with the mother's kin.

What enters into the son's adoration of his mother? It appears to us that fundamentally there is her great concentraion of loving, admiring attention on him, creating an interacting libidinal universe of two. To no one else will he ever be so desirable and important, nowhere else will he receive the indulgences shown a helpless child. If the son does not know this, the mother and the whole tradition so inform him. Besides, we think, the son early experiences the threat of being deprived of her. This happens when his parents start training him for adulthood. At three or four years of age, a "man" ready for study, he is carried in his father's arms away from the all-permissive home to the Hebrew school, or cheder, where he meets a harsh, indifferent teacher. He is sent away from home to the accompaniment of his mother's heartbroken sobs, to spend ten hours daily in the cold company of books and scholars, eating scantily whereas before he had overeaten, obliged in these surroundings to be "a man." If at home he now complains to mother about his teacher's whippings, she does not sympathize, but supports the brutal teacher. She steadily reminds him that in the area of Jewish studies he stands on his own as a man. Levin[32] recalls, ". . . at the age of four I was treated like a big boy. Whenever I forgot to put on my *Arba Kanfoth* [ritual male body-garment], my mother would speak to me seriously, as to a grownup, and tell me how shameful it was for an adult Jew to be running about like a heathen without the reminder of his Jewishness hung about his body." Such recollections are repeated in the memoirs of Eastern European Jewish men.

From this time on, the son is subject to continuing uncertainties of the same sort. We hear of boys of nine and ten being sent off to other cities to study with famous teachers, living with relatives or friends and dreaming of the indulgent mother far away. One informant, now a rabbi, said he actually dreaded returning home for the holidays, knowing how he would suffer when it came time to leave his mother's endless love and attentions and return to school. Sometimes one parent would die, necessitating distributing the children among relatives. Here enters the miserable state of orphanhood. Charney[33] describes the tragic parting from his widowed mother at the age of 13, when she left for another city to marry. She had been even more thoughtful than other mothers in waiting until he reached legal manhood before leaving. They both wept over the separation, and the boy said courageously, "If it will be good for you —it will be good for me. You will see." His feeling of loss and of personal helplessness come clearly to the reader. And it appears characteristic of Jewish males to regard the mother as a retreating figure of shelter, a most desirable warm figure always just out of reach, a poignant symbol of tenderness. Morris Raphael Cohen writes thus of his mother and his wife[34]. Indeed we believe that the Jewish man hopes to find a mother again in his wife, and is happiest in his marriage when this search is fulfilled[35]. Besides, the culture aids him, for in the time of arranged marriages his mother selected his wife, and a proverb states, "Every daughter-in-law has something of her mother-in-law[36]."

A girl's place in the family is a reflection of her mother's, but her truly affectionate tie is with her father. She is peculiarly his; when she is little, her father calls her his "queen" and "princess." At all ages she is the one family member in whose company he can relax; and when she marries, he finds joy in her husband[37] that he cannot find in his own son. If, as the people say, "a man sees himself in his son-in-law," they understand why he takes particular pleasure in his daughter's children. The mother observes all this and complains that the father spoils his daughter, though he may be severe to his son; she herself nags her daughter, especially before marriage, but conveys none of the overtones of affection and play that temper her nagging of husband and son.

The daughter responds readily to these highly specialized interpersonal situations. In all respects she follows her mother's example. In case of need, she takes over her mother's duties[38]. In *proste*, or "common" families, that do not maintain the highest Jewish standards, the father may be harsher and ruder with his family, including his daughter.

This easy relationship between father and daughter is comparable to the mother-son bond only in its selective coupling. Just as the mother imbues her activities with powerful emotion, the father gives his the culturally standardized spiritual and intellectual leanings demanded of a male. With his daughter, the father is indulgent and undemanding; his daughter is the only female other than his wife and mother with whom he may remain alone[39], for to him she is not sexual. Real intimacy is not expected of a Jewish father, especially of *sheyne* class or aspirations, but he shows his daughter a unique affection and comradeship[40].

Actually, short of incest, there are no norms prescribed in the Codes or elsewhere in tradition to guide a father in relations with his daughter; and he appears to follow a need to cultivate in this rather overlooked relationship a haven fairly free of tension[41]. This is in contrast with his prescribed relationships with his son, which are authoritarian and didactic, for a father represents all of traditional Law and is the personal model for his son to emulate. Comfortable as the father-daughter bond is, it lacks the obvious drama belonging to the mother-son and the muted tension—often expressed in rivalry and rebellion in adulthood—inherent in the father-son[42]. However, the content of a film, based on a classic Yiddish play[43], indicates the powerful emotional current that possibly underlies relations of father and daughter, threatening to draw them together and to displace the mother from her wifely status. It was reported to us that occasional instances of this sort actually occurred among Eastern European Jewish immigrants. Perhaps in daily life, the mother, unaware, anticipates this eventuality when she repeatedly attacks her unmarried daughter; indeed a monotonous theme in her nagging is her articulated anticipatory refusal to be supplanted in any capacity by her daughter. We suggest that the interchangeability of any individual's role in shtetl society functions in a woman's life as a threat of replaceability that may color her total personality with anxiety and tension. Since her status is defined in terms of her domestic roles, she expresses her anxieties in this area.

The mother-daughter relationship contains more rivalry and even hostility than do the other family couplings. The mother cues this development as clearly as she does her different relationship with her son. Though she nags at all members of the family, in her special woman's idiom of communication, she nags at her daughter in a consistently hostile manner, while her husband and her son can be nagged at with affectionate purposes apparent to everyone. The mother knows she must rear her daughter to be like herself, but she is determined to keep the daughter in her place as a junior female as long as the latter lives in the parental home.   Informants indicate that the mother does not really wish to teach the daughter cooking or any other skill that might replace her own services, and so she rails, for example, "Keep out of my kitchen!   This is *my* kitchen!   You don't know how to cook!   You just waste time and food[44]." Her negativism is a striking contrast to the emphasis of many other cultures, where girlhood also is the mandatory period of training for housewifely responsibilities.   And in fact the Jewish girl's goals in life are precisely to function as wife and mother[45]. However, the Jewish mother confines her daughter to the role of unskilled assistant.   When the daughter makes a household suggestion or any other suggestion touching upon the mother's sphere of influence, the mother may react as to a challenge and strive to confine her.   This can be interpreted as the mother's jealous protection of the adult status she acquired by marriage; it is consistent with a probable predisposition of the women to react defensively or hostilely.   Upon the daughter's marriage there is an important shift in the interaction, from authoritarian to egalitarian, since the daughter's new status approaches that of her mother, and since she may for the first time leave the home if she does not remain on kest.

The relations between siblings of opposite sex are polarized about regulations of avoidance and incest, and, depending upon the relative age of the two siblings, are characterized by avoidance-quarrelsomeness or by permissiveness. Actually there appears to be a gradient of these attitudes.   Much tension is frequently found between opposite-sex siblings of about the same age, expressed in quarrelsome or silent hostility; our film analyses suggest that we regard this conduct as possibly a barrier to incest.   As age differences between such siblings increase, permissiveness is allowed increasingly by the elder along the lines of permissiveness between mother-son, father-daughter; as age differences between the siblings decrease, avoidance increases. The role of mother-substitute need not be adopted by the chronologically senior sister, though that is the expectation; as is commonly known, and as is illustrated in the film "Mamele," a less senior sister whose personality is more congenial to the role can actually function as mother-substitute. (The adaptability of personality to the traditionally sex-typed roles appears in all aspects of Eastern European Jewish culture.) Considering males of the family from the viewpoint of a girl, one might say that there is maximum permissiveness with the father, although the incest taboo is always observed; with the elder brother there is considerable permissiveness, and some degree of avoidance; with the coeval brother there is more avoidance than permissiveness; the relationship with the younger brother is a mirror-image of the father-daughter relationship, since here is displayed a maximum permissiveness following the mother-son pattern, and a minimum of avoidance, barring incest. The same gradient behavior patterns a boy's relationships with his mother and sisters within the poles of parental permissiveness and sibling avoidance.

Behavior among siblings of the same sex follows a gradient that is comparable in extent but different in qualities. Thus among brothers, the father represents ritual and statutory authority, in which the older brother shares; between coevals there is a mutual ignoring of this authority, but in the relationship with the younger brother, authority must reappear. Among sisters, the mother enforces her authority over her daughters largely through generation-linked attributes; the elder sister partakes of this authority, but coeval sisters quarrel over any manifestations of privilege or even of equality; the generation-bred authority reappears in the relationship with the younger sister. All of these relationships become more equalized after marriage, since the status of the women is then referred not to the parental authority but to the conjugal role.

Parents distinguish between the eldest child who, if male, is the heir, and the youngest, who is the beloved baby. Beyond these two, singled out by traditional appellations, the various children are often indicated by affectionate, somewhat ironical appellations descriptive of personal qualities like beauty, brains, skills, idiosyncracies. Daughters employ these identifications in their rivalrous quarrels, especially when the identifications derive from the father. Sons however tend to substitute sulky silences and ignoring for quarrels and thus drive themselves further apart.

## II. AFFINAL BEHAVIOR

Affinal behavior is intelligible as a function of the behavior of the blood kin, especially as functions of the mother-son, father-daughter, and brother-sister relationships. In the period of arranged marriages[46], a woman chose her prospective daughter-in-law carefully, appraising the social and financial standing of her parents, demanding dowry and kest to correspond to her son's intellectual talents, examining the future bride's housewifely abilities, and generally measuring her by severe personal and role specifications. As informants said half-humorously, a prospective mother-in-law "knows" no girl is good enough for her boy, yet Jewish law obliges each man to marry. Even after marriages by personal choice were accepted—and today in this country—a woman impresses her son with her caustic opinions, and in informal ways subjects his prospective mate to examination. One woman raised in the shtetl but now living in New York told us with real chagrin, "I can't find anything wrong with my son's girl! But I've got to criticize her! All her buttons are sewed on right, the seams of her stockings are straight, there are no tears or holes in her clothing even when she doesn't expect to see me!"

The relationship between a woman and her daughter-in-law is expected to be one of tension despite the hopeful proverb that "a woman sees herself mirrored in her daughter-in-law," for in effect she has chosen her. At the wedding ceremony itself the two dance the *broiges tants*, or "angry dance." Tradition has stressed the son's marriage as the mother's divorce[47]. And the people love to tell a comical story, in many variations, having the point that whatever the daughter-in-law has, does, or enjoys is an exploitation of the son in the eyes of the doting mother; whereas the same circumstances in the life of the daughter are testimony to the virtues of the son-in-law.

Not until a young matron gives birth to a child can she face her mother-in-law with something like equality, when the older woman must admit that the marriage has been justified and that she has been blessed with grandmotherhood. Nevertheless she is ever alert to comment that her daughter-in-law does not cook or indulge or otherwise take care of the son as adequately as she did[48]; and an angry husband will rebuke his wife as though in his mother's behalf, saying, "You can't cook as well as she did![49]" Soon too a woman becomes highly critical of her daughter-in-law's methods of rearing the grandchild, her son's child, the more so as the harassed daughter-in-law turns to her own mother for help, and avoids or excludes her possessive mother-in-law. This may be one reason why the maternal kin are closer than the paternal. The son is caught between the complaints of mother and wife. The father-in-law has a fairly conventional, formal relationship with his daughter-in-law, growing out of sex avoidance and tension with the son.

It is some relief to the strain between a woman and her mother-in-law if the former begins her married life at a distance, if possible taking her husband to live in kest with her own parents. The typical mother-daughter rivalry in the wife's family is now moderated by the accomplishment of marriage, which elevates the status of all parties, and which introduces a new and much desired member into the family circle. Father and mother both welcome the son-in-law with open arms. We suggest that this welcome contains nuances that differ with the mother and with the father, growing out of their differing relationships to their daughter. It appears to us as a possibility that the mother's characteristically rivalrous relationship with her daughter employs the entrance of the son-in-law into the family as a situation offering additional potentialities for expressing or cultivating her well-established feeling of rivalry. For example, a woman will belittle her daughter in conversation with her son-in-law, even at the risk of arousing his antagonism. The son-in-law comes to resent his mother-in-law because she disparages and nags his wife, for his wife is *his*, and she is not his mother-in-law's property any longer. A man may scold his wife, saying for example, that she doesn't run the house as well as his own mother, but he will quarrel with his mother-in-law when she scolds his wife. Thus, a woman's relationship with her son-in-law contains elements that derive in part from her characteristic relationship with her daughter, since her rivalrous relationship with her daughter-in-law derives in part from her special relationship with her son. On the other hand, the father employs the entrance of his son-in-law into the family as an additional opportunity for expressing his habitual affection for his daughter. We have no unequivocal documentary evidence for this interpretation, but we offer it because it seems to us consistent with the other family relationships and suggests those roots in the filial bonds out of which are elaborated details in affinal behavior.

The father, in the days of arranged marriages, chose the son-in-law after testing him for family and personal qualities, stressing scholarly accomplishments over physical and economic qualifications. The mother welcomed the son-in-law as a kind of son, with a warmth that the young man often found objectionable and in conflict with his mother-son bond. He often rejected her as a "witch" (Yiddish, *machasheifeh*) telling her so and quarreling with her, unlike her silent, often resigned husband and son. The special, poorly reciprocated fondness of a woman for her son-in-law is a familiar matter among the people. It is equally understood that real affection and camaraderie exist between a man and his son-in-law—if the son-in-law fulfills expectations—when the relationship assumes an ease and warmth foreign to the relationship of father and son[50].

However, this unusually amiable tie, prettily consistent with the amiable father-daughter relationship, is sensed with hostility by the unmarried brothers-in-law who see in the newcomer a competitor for everybody's affections[51] and an unjustified beneficiary of the family's goods, since the son-in-law receives a dowry and kest support. Ordinarily the brothers-in-law operate with the distance characteristic of males, but after the father's death they are likely to quarrel over his estate, such as his seat in the synagogue, or the loyalty of his followers, should he be a Chassidic leader. The unmarried sisters-in-law behave differently however, prevented by inter-sex avoidance from manifesting fully the parental attitude of welcome. Siblings-in-law come into their true importance as aunt and uncle, potential guardians of the children.

However, an unmarried girl is predisposed to dislike strongly her coeval brother's wife, considering her inferior, unattractive, stupid, thus supporting her mother's feelings about her daughter-in-law. When sisters-in-law first meet however, before or after the marriage, they greet each other with a show of kindness that may conceal hostile anticipations, even from their own conscious thoughts. The formal kindness is related to the recurring admonition in the Schulchan Aruch, "You must receive [everybody] with a friendly countenance and joyful feeling[52]." The mother-in-law and daughter-in-law also meet thus, the former being very "kind" to her son's wife, cooking special dishes, serving elaborately, keeping the young woman from domestic chores. However, friction soon develops, which the mother-in-law initiates with ironical remarks that grow more stinging, alternating with prolonged silences (*broiges*, Yiddish, angry), continuing in noisy quarrels and arguments about any detail of everyday life but especially over the inadequate care that the daughter-in-law gives her husband. It is probably the "kind" period that produces behavior reflected in the folk saying (woman speaking) "Scold your daughter, but mean your daughter-in-law." The saying also reveals some of the pressure that is placed on the unmarried daughter at this time.

It appears to us that in the relations between the sisters-in-law, it is the unmarried girl who originates the hostilities. She complains in idioms taken from her mother that her sister-in-law does not feed her brother properly, and that she acts as though she were more important than the sister. Thus family ranking is introduced between the sisters-in-law to establish their interacting roles. The sister feels sincerely that her brother's wife's family is not as good as her own, and that her brother's intellectual and other attainments are superior to his wife's.

We infer that where avoidance characterizes the relationship between sister and brother, the marriage of the brother may prod the sister to displace her concealed feelings about him onto his wife in the form of resentment. Thus from one point of view, affinal behavior is determined by sibling avoidance: the sister is driven by unconscious jealousy of the advantages which the wife possesses in her relationship with her husband. The wife responds by stressing her enviable married status. These interactions produce a mounting tension, eventually relieved for the sister through the channel of affection for her brother's children. Nonetheless the sister in one way or another puts the scornful question, "Why should anyone want to marry my brother?" This seems to reflect the Jewish family's habit of belittling the son in comparison with his father, and to be also an expression of sibling avoidance.

Our data suggest that the marriage of the sister leads to a lessening of her resentment against the sister-in-law. This is attributable not to any change in the relationship with the brother but to the equalization of the statuses of the two young matrons. Rivalry continues however on the new level of common married interests. It is voiced through quarrels and nagging, which are a recognized style of communication by women —although men should quarrel only about important matters, such as business, or points of learning. With time, the sisters-in-law drift apart, as each family tends to cultivate its own flesh-and-blood maternal kin and to overlook its more indifferent paternal kin [53].

### III. THE CHARACTER OF MARRIAGES

It seems to us that the distinct kinship roles cultivated by members of the small two-generation family guide and even determine the character of the marriages into which the children enter. Traditional law contains few indicators for the choice of partner; mainly the chief restriction is that from among his kin a man may marry only in collateral lines of descent, that is, nieces, and that an unmarried man must honor the obligation of the levirate[54] within specified limits. Actually when marriage was by parental arrangement, the preference of the opposite-sexed parent allowed little or no choice.

We think that this preference in fact matched, and still matches, needs in the child of opposite sex. If one examines the nature of marriages taking place through free personal choice, it seems that a young woman is guided in these private relations with men by two male models from within her own family universe: her father and her brother[55]. As already shown, she behaves quite differently with each. Roughly, one is a permissive, secure situation, the other is tense and uncertain. We suggest that father is the model for "husband," in which relationship the woman ideally expects security, status, unconditional affection, spiritual and intellectual qualities, a minimizing of youthful traits however these are defined locally, and a certain kinship feeling of "belonging." We suggest that brother is the model for "lover" in extramarital experience, a relationship which holds for the woman libidinal attractions, nonintellectual interests (in keeping with the father's lower valuation of his son), physical appeals of youthfulness and play, and the quality of being a "stranger" (which probably roots in coeval avoidance) instead of kin.

Similarly, a young man is guided in his private relations with women by two female models from within his family universe: his mother and his sister.  With the first there is great permissiveness, with the second there is avoidance.  We suggest that mother is the model for "wife," with whom the man ideally expects security, protection, warmth, unconditional affection, practical support, and the kinship quality of "belonging."  We suggest that sister is the model for "lover," containing expectations of libidinal appeals, physical characteristics of youth, independence, and an aspect of "strangeness" instead of kinship; it is in this context that we understand the affair with the gentile girl.

Under the system of arranged marriage, the father selected his son-in-law, the mother chose her daughter-in-law.  As the proverbs quoted earlier indicate[56], the bride is married to someone expected to be like her father, the groom is married to someone expected to be like his mother.  Hence, the bride responds to the groom somewhat as to her father; the groom responds to the bride somewhat as to his mother.  One of our scholarly informants was of the opinion that those marriages succeeded where the husband really did find mother-qualities in his wife: he thought that the frequent desertions by men[57] could be related to the inability of the wife to function in the mother-role; for instance an extramarital affair usually would not of itself lead to desertion or divorce.  Thus, it seems to us that the arranged marriage, in its selection of the young couple, corresponds to the successful marriage by free choice.  Shtetl marriages were usually regarded as successful, despite the ease of divorce.  Also, couples often considered themselves happy. This shtetl saying offered pertinent advice:   "First marry, then love."

## IV.  FAMILY OBLIGATIONS

When the Jew speaks of his family, he means the biological family of parents, children, and siblings. Ancient codes prescribe specifically the reciprocal obligations within it and override completely personal preferences. The informal, ethologically influenced aspects still function within the condified framework. The only codified behavior outside of the biological family is the incest taboo extended to grandparents and grandchildren. As relationships move out from the biological famly, personal perferences operate with increased freedom and variety, filling a vacuum otherwise occupied by institutional prescriptions. In this area the only codifications are those covering the behavior of the total society, such as deference and respect toward older people and scholars, as well as general avoidance of women.

The shtetl Jews consider all members of the Jewish community to be related to each other through kinship ties, a belief expressed formally in the collective term *B'nai Israel*, Children of Israel, and in the acceptance of the three Biblical patriarchs as the ancestors of all Jews. In actual practice, two Jews who meet try to identify themselves in the expectation of establishing some kin connection, no matter how remote or indirect. This is regarded as a pleasurable circumstance and holds the assurance of mutual aid. It is considered good Jewish behavior to refer social interests to the framework of family thinking.

The interaction of family roles produces a field of tensions whose balance is a goal periodically striven for, but regularly disturbed by the complications of the mother-son, father-daughter, and opposite-sex sibling relationships. This goal of balanced tensions, domestic harmony, is termed *Sholem Bayis*. Within its dynamics, of striving and of briefly-held fulfillment, are patterned the differentiated effects of being cared for reliably and intensively by mother, and of being disciplined or loved irregularly and distantly by father. It is a pattern offering all participants comfort, excitement, and security; but it is also tyrannical and in its strong demands promotes much individual strain and often revolt. For the boy, the filial role provides the prototypes of adult relationships, since he will act with his wife much as he acts with his mother, and with older men much as he acts with his father.  The filial role is somewhat different for the girl, since she must early learn to accept her obligation to be a mother, and will discover her widest opportunities in this sex-typed function only after her marriage.  Modifications of these relationships are practiced and fixed in the sibling interrelationships, and from here carried out in the contacts outside the home.

Traditional family rearing lays great emphasis on sex differences, defining social functions in terms of sex.  Tradition views the differentiation as complementary, but in actuality there are frequent implications of male status-superiority and of female status-inferiority.  Ritual and learning are honorific male occupations; and homely family duties including economic responsibility and childbearing and physical child-care are less exalted female pursuits.  There is thus a complete dichotomy between the intellectual burdens and opportunities charged to men, and the earthy ones charged to women.  This is true under the ordinary circumstances of living, but under stress, practically without restriction, a person can carry out needed functions of the other sex[58]; this adaptive elasticity obtains also in other aspects of the culture, enjoined by traditional law. Our data suggest that women, being the less honorifically placed and as such neglected by the codified prescriptions, found widening opportunities exactly under conditions of stress.  They took on the responsibilities brought to them, and we have no record of large-scale female rebellion in the traditional communities[59].  But history is replete with rebellions led by men and composed of men.  These range from simple open rivalry between father and son, noted even in folk sayings, to great social movements[60].

Within the traditional community, where almost all values and ideals and honorific activities are cast in male terms and references, and are understood to be such when not explicit, the private life of the family emerges as the responsibility of women and is largely dominated by them.  A man, busy outside the home with holy study or his livelihood, often appears as a guest[61] on the domestic scene, as his wife orders space and quiet for his rest and study. This is the complement to the place of the woman in the synagogue which, as a community house for studious men, reserves a place for her in a separated section. However, there is considerable understanding and cooperation between the sex-separated functions of shtetl society, both in the family and outside in the general community; no secrets exist between them; the two spheres of male and female activities are welded into interdependent wholes by severe bonds of ritual and of specialized responsibility.

## V. SUMMARY

Our hypotheses concern the form and functioning of the Jewish family in the recently destroyed Eastern European small town containing the indigenous Jewish culture. We emphasize that these are not definitive findings, nor can these hypotheses ever be tested in the field, since the Jewish communities no longer exist. We risk the additional conjecture that this was a distinct culture, and therefore a distinct set of family phenomena, since it employed its own common language, Yiddish, and its own sacred language, Hebrew; it boasted of its ancient and special history and its religious and scholarly traditions, known to all the Western world; and it always functioned under highly precarious conditions among hostile peoples.

Within the space and objectives of this article, we cannot attempt sytematically to compare Jewish and other European and American cultures. We can illustrate important differences, however, by pointing out that whereas among Eastern European Jews no man hopes to be outstripped by his son, the opposite is often described as true in middle-class urban American life. This may be a value adopted by Jewish immigrants. Again, Eastern European Jewry stresses the superiority of the arranged durable marriage, and the attendant responsibilities of the elder generations; the opposite is known to obtain widely in the United States where romantic and rather impermanent unions are standard. And again, the authority of the Eastern European Jewish father rests ideally and primarily upon his status as an exponent of the religious and scholarly tradition, and only secondarily upon his reliability as an earner; but in the United

States no man escapes the primary pressure to provide economically for his family, and failure can be punished by state law.

In the recently flourishing Eastern European Jewish family, the traditionally codified standards underwent local and temporal modifications, and among certain kin were often interpreted or acted out unexpectedly under the pressures of living. Its most dynamic relationships were those between husband-wife, mother-son, and father-daughter; other blood and kin ties flowed from, supported, and otherwise were consequences of these three. All the relationships were keyed to operate under conditions of high psychological tension that often threatened to break down, but peace-making machinery was set in motion at the point of rupture; thus family harmony or balance, *Sholem Bayis,* was restored. In the overcrowded shtetl where there could be no privacy within the home, or among the homes, where all men attended synagogue daily, all boys attended cheder daily, and the women met at their work, the community was always reckoned with in connection with *Sholem Bayis:* each family felt it important to maintain a respectable front in the face of public opinion.

In the family, as throughout the culture, there are provisions for male and female worlds of acts and values. But this does not preclude overlapping and interchange in specific situations of need. Women may sense this interchangeability as a threat of replacement in spouse relations, against which they see a principal safeguard in fecundity.

Relationships among siblings are patterned after those between parents and children especially where age differences exist, but a stressed avoidance separates opposite-sexed coeval siblings. Patterned avoidance appears with variations among all family kin of opposite sex, and also among men and women in the general community. After the spouses, the least avoidance obtains between mother and son, and then between father and daughter. Considerable tension exists between parents and children of the same sex. Important aspects of relationships among affinal kind appear as functions of the behavior of the blood kin. Consistent with the avoidance practices, parents are frequent intermediaries in the cross-sibling relationships; besides, third-party mediation is a feature of other aspects of the culture, notably in marriage and business arrangements.

The functions or uses of the family roles appear to be strongly influenced by ethological emphases of the people. This is strikingly so in the behavior of women within the family; the home is traditionally specified as the only area where they possess status. Legalistically, men have higher status everywhere; actually, as scholars, their preferred sphere lies outside the home in the synagogue. Women are often the effective breadwinners and adapt better to necessity than their husbands, but this does not confer status on them. Women symbolize emotionality, men symbolize spirituality.

Marriage marks the complete adulthood of men and women, and leads to changed relationships with the families of origin. Marriage should be arranged by the parents, who keep in mind traditional criteria as well as personal preferences. The institution of kest roots here, where a young scholar is supported by his father-in-law during the first years of marriage. Generally families try to live separately. Modern marriages by free choice may actually correspond in values to the arranged marriage.

# References

1. Informants included 74 women and 64 men, ranging in age from the 20's to the 90's, of different social classes and degrees of education.

2. Within it we find reminders of Freud's familial formulations, but embedded among relationships and values that were unrealized by him.

3. For references dealing with "prescribed" behavior, the following sources are used, if not specified otherwise: A. Cohen, *Everyman's Talmud;* New York, E. P. Dutton & Co., 1949 (abbr. Talmud). Salomon Ganzfried, *Code of Jewish Law (Kitzur Schulchan Aruch;* Hyman E. Goldin, tr.); New York, Hebrew Publishing Co., 1927 (abbr. Schulchan Aruch).

4. Marriage is seen as a legal outlet for man's sexual desire, which is given to man in order to procreate. (Schulchan Aruch CL, 9.) This desire, if not satisfied, handicaps a man's prescribed study of sacred law. Therefore, man must find a legal sexual partner as soon as possible; and early marriages between the ages of eighteen and twenty are highly recommended. (Schulchan Aruch CXLV, 1.)

   Procreation, however, is not the only reason for marriage. The Code insists upon the obligation to marry even when the man or woman is unable to procreate. The Law states that it is not good for a man to be alone. (Schulchan Aruch CXLV, 3; cf. Talmud, p. 162.)

   Striking physical and age differences should be avoided in marriage, and the partners should have the same social background. (Schulchan Aruch CXLV, 6, 8; Talmud, pp. 163-164.) The most highly recommended partner for a girl is a learned man; and for a boy, the daughter of a learned father. Romantic love is ignored by the Code. Relationships between husband and wife are phrased exclusively in terms of mutual duties and obligations. (Schulchan Aruch CXLV, 10; Talmud, p. 165.)

5. Schulchan Aruch CXLV, 4; Talmud, p. 168.

6. Schulchan Aruch CXLV, 1.

7. Maybaum, Ignatz. *The Jewish Home.* London: Clarke & Co., 1945, pp. 45, 27.

8. *Mishna Aboth Pirke Aboth (Sayings of the Fathers).* 4th Ed. NY: Bloch, 1929.

9. The Kashruth observances are dietary prohibitions and regulations, without which the functioning of a Jewish traditional household is inconceivable. They were elaborated over centuries by generations of Jewish sages, on the basis of an original set of dietary regulations stated in the Pentateuch. The observances of Kashruth are prime criteria in the orthodox definition of a household as

"Jewish." Although the traditional theory of Kashruth is studied by the men, its application belongs mainly to the women, who are responsible for the handling of food. Any doubts which may arise in connection with the application of Kashruth laws are to be referred for decision to the religious authority in the community, the Rabbi.

10. Mikvah is the ritual bath which every Jewish wife must take after the menstruation period. During this period all physical contact between husband and wife is prohibited, and by extension avoided between all members of opposite sex. Deformed children are regarded as divine punishment for violation of the taboo. Detailed rules govern the relationship between husband and wife during the impure period; the responsibility for the observances rests with the married women. An unmarried girl is not subject to these prohibitions.

11. Schulchan Aruch CXLIII, 20.

12. Schulchan Aruch CXLIII, 1.

13. Landes, Ruth. The abnormal among the Ojibwa Indians. *Journal of Abnormal and Social Psychology,* 1938, 33:14-33; and Bateson, Gregory. *Naven.* London: Cambridge University Press, 1936, p. 32.

14. *Oxford English Dictionary.*

15. Bateson, *op. cit.*

16. Horwich, Bernard. *My First Eighty Years.* Chicago: Argus Books, 1939, p. 5.

17. Ausubel, Nathan. *A Treasury of Jewish Folklore.* NY: Crown Publications, 1948, p. 638.

18. Bernstein, Ignatz. *Yiddishe Sprichwerter.* Warsaw, 1912, p. 97. Cf. Bava Bathra 100, 1; in the Talmud.

19. Horwich, *op. cit.,* p. 9.

20. Levin, Shmarya. *Childhood in Exile.* NY: Harcourt, Brace, 1920, p. 6.

21. Levin, *op. cit.,* pp. 3-7.

22. Cf. the Talmud, where pouring olive oil on olives is a dream symbol of incest with the mother; this is interpreted by us as symbolizing in part a "return to the source." Berachoth 56.

23. Avoidance appears in alternating forms of silence and of nagging and quarrels.

24. Schulchan Aruch CLII, 10. The ancient Teachers emphasize the sexual desirability of woman as well as her dangerous character. She is considered sexually aggressive and therefore is to be strictly avoided. She is considered unreliable and generally possesses undesirable traits of character. Talmud, p. 160.

25. Berachoth 56.

26. Levin, *op. cit.,* pp. 6-7.

27. Bernstein, *op. cit.,* p. 11. Proverb 4, p. 96, expresses the same idea: "One's son is given, but one's son-in-law is chosen."

28. Chassidism was a socioreligious movement which arose in Poland in the eighteenth century and spread over all of Eastern Europe. It was characterized by the intense belief of the followers in the personality of the leader, called the *tsaddik*. The followers centered about "courts" composed of the leader, his family, and servants. The leadership became hereditary.

29. Food as a social control is the monopoly of women, as learning is the monopoly of men.

30. The intellectual interest of the husband and his "childish" helplessness in domestic affairs often lead the wife to decry his practical abilities; thus she calls him "my breadwinner" with an ironical intonation. But she always admires his intellectual abilities and boasts of them to outsiders.

31. Bernstein, *op. cit.*, p. 96.

32. Levin, *op. cit.*, p. 14.

33. Charney, Daniel. *Barg Arof*. Warsaw: Uphill, 1935, p. 65.

34. Cohen, Morris R. *A Dreamer's Journey*. Boston: Beacon Press, 1949, pp. 15-62 *passim*.

35. An informant aptly states that, "From the moment the boy is taken from the maternal environment into school, he is considered an adult in study, synagogue, and community; but he is always a child in the area of physical needs. His mother, his sister, and his wife consider him a child even when he is old, though he was considered a man intellectually by the age of three."

36. Ausubel, *op. cit.*, p. 638.

37. Tchernowitz, Chaim. Grandfather Mendele as I remember him. *Commentary*, 1948, 6:436-443.

38. Cf. film *Mamele* (Poland); Lang, Lucy R. *Tomorrow Is Beautiful*. NY: Macmillan, 1948, p. 16; Antin, Mary. *The Promised Land*. NY: Houghton Mifflin, 1941.

39. Schulchan Aruch CLIII, 1.

40. The daughter may utilize her father's indulgence to advance herself beyond the limitations of her status, as when she secures permission to share in her brother's studies.

41. "When father returned home after work, he would embrace me tenderly for my day's work and after dinner, when the dishes were washed and the house put in order, he would braid my hair." Lang, *op. cit.*, p. 7.

42. "We live in a generation which has rebelled against the father.... We possess a whole literature full of complaints of sons against the father. Psychology and literature united in order to voice the oppressed son's complaints." Maybaum, *op. cit.*, p. 27.

43. *God, Flesh and the Devil*, New York City, 1949. In this drama, a pious, childless couple rears the orphaned daughters of the wife's sister. When the elder ward reaches marriageable age, her foster father proposes marriage to her, saying that he will divorce his wife, whom the girl addresses as "second mother"; legally he may

divorce his wife because she is still barren after twenty years. The foster daughter accepts the proposal, and her "second mother" resigns herself to the situation.

44. On the other hand, informants indicate that mother enjoys showing her son how to cook as he assists her in the kitchen. She wants his company and is flattered by his interest.

45. Intellectual training is presented to her as of secondary importance, and is often completely neglected. Folk sayings belittle women's mental capacities.

46. Romantic love was considered "un-Jewish" by the better families, though songs and stories show it interested young people. Parents chose marital partners for their children of opposite sex, often aided by a professional matchmaker, and without consulting the children's preferences.

47. Bernstein, *op. cit.,* p. 96.

48. After the period of the kest, if the husband continues to devote himself to study, his wife is expected to take over all the burden of providing subsistence for the family. A wife who supports her learned husband, who is devoted to the correct functioning of the household, who sacrifices herself for the well-being of her husband and children, is highly praised in the community, and is expected to be rewarded after death by sharing her husband's life in heaven. The ideal arrangement is achieved when two people of more or less similar backgrounds live together, fulfilling their culturally expected roles—the man devoting most of his time to intellectual pursuits and conjugal duties, the woman devoting her life to husband, children, and household, and providing the material support of the family.

    Where the husband is not a learned man but is engaged in some business, his work is nevertheless considered "mental," and his relationship to his wife is similar to that of a learned man. But an ignoramus who is dependent upon his wife is despised by the community and is considered a parasite.

49. When pleased with his wife, the husband may tell her that she is "almost as good as mother," according to some informants.

50. Anton, *op. cit.,* p. 65.

51. A man may be jealous of his sister's husband partly because of the stranger's sudden claim upon his sister and upon his mother, but also because of the formality and stereotyped tension in his relations with his father. According to a saying, "Great men have lesser sons." But a man's traditional attitude is that his son-in-law whom he chose in the arranged marriage is "smarter" or more desirable than his son. The Lubavitcher Rabbi in his *Memoirs* (Joseph I. Schneersohn. *Lubavitcher Rabbis's Memoirs.* Brooklyn: Otzer Hachassidim, 1949), p. 79, quotes a smith in the Russian town of Dobramysl thusly: "I must say that I am more than satisfied with my daughters. . . . They are married to fine, well-

learned men and are nicely settled in a house I had built for them. My sons-in-law spend their time in study, but as for my son, Samuel Nahum, I have to admit he is a great disappointment to me. I had hoped he too would be a scholar, but unfortunately he has no talent whatsoever for studying." This is a conventional statement of the situation, and suggests how forlorn the unmarried man can feel in the father-son relationship. Relief may come when he marries, leaving the parental home, and in his turn shining forth as the beloved son, perhaps supported by his father-in-law on kest. But even after marriage, resentment of the father can persist a life long, having its roots in the didactic demands laid down in early childhood.

52. This attitude connotes expectations of aid, analogous to ceremonies in other cultures where greetings are expressed with offerings of tobacco, food, drink, baths.

53. "We inherited from Momma and Poppa two sets of *tantehs* and uncles, who produced in turn an abundance of cousins, who got hitched to other people's cousins and uncles and *tantehs,*—and they all came to our house. And, as usually happens, Momma's side of the family was favored—the Chosen People." Sammy Levenson, *Meet the Folks.* N.Y.: Citadel Press, 1948, p. 24.

54. That is, the Jewish man must marry his brother's widow if she is childless.

55. The plots of Yiddish language films—for example, "I Want To Be a Mother," "Bar Mitzvah," "Mamele"—include these themes.

56. They follow the form: A man (woman) sees himself (herself) in his (her) son-in-law (daughter-in-law).

57. In New York City the National Desertion Bureau, a Jewish Community agency established in 1914, devotes itself exclusively to this problem. Miriam Shomer Zunser, in *Yesterday* (N.Y.: Stackpole Sons, 1939), suggests other factors in desertion among Eastern European Jewish men, such as sheer displeasure with the ugliness or age of the bride. One informant said *sheyne* men deserted less often than *proste,* for they were more sensitive to public opinion. Pp. 64-74; 160-179 *passim.*

58. For example, in Sabbath and holiday ritual, and in child rearing.

59. Individual women occasionally rebelled by repudiating the unattractive spouse arranged for them, but only after the marriage ceremony. There were also some suicides by married women who felt trapped. Men acted similarly much more often. Cf. Zunser, reference footnote 65; pp. 64-74; pp. 160-179 *passim.* Folk songs and stories reflect conflicts over arranged marriages.

60. It sems to us, for example, that these elements played an important role in the history of eighteenth-century mystical Chassidism which developed out of traditional rational Judaism, and in the secularized Socialist labor movement of the nineteenth and twentieth centuries

which scorned the religious tradition and advocated assimilation with the non-Jewish world.

61.   "He is a guest in his own house," is a popular turn of phrase.

Chapter 2

# A New Look at the Psychodynamics of Jewish Family Living

ABRAHAM N. FRANZBLAU, Ph.D., M.D.

**I**N a recent paper on "Family Diagnosis," the late Dr. Robert Gomberg traced how, beginning with the therapy of the individual, the realization steadily evolved that the family constellation was an inseparable part of the psyche of each of its members, and that the whole was, indeed, greater than the sum of its parts. We are all familiar with the profound implications of this realization, and the effect which it is exerting in certain quarters on the concepts, modalities, techniques and procedures of psychoanalytically oriented psychotherapy.

Dr. Gomberg says, in the same paper, "The whole concept of role theory, small group theory, culture value orientation and its influence on personality is a complex and not simply digested, understood and used theory. In addition, the need to develop an inter-relatedness between inner psychological factors and social role and cultural values with respect to etiology, motivation and character formation, is again a complex task to be worked out."

One of these culture values, which he was taking a fresh delight in exploring at the period of his untimely death, was religion, especially Judaism. He was following the rabbinic dictum, "Let thy house be open wide" and was perceiving a wider entity than either the individual or the family, in his people, its culture, its beliefs and its practices. He was reaching out for something great and deep, and greeting it, when he found it, with the joy of discovery or re-discovery.

We had many discussions on the essence of liberal Jewish thought in theological matters like the meaning of life, the problem of evil, sin and guilt, the motivation of behavior, reward and punishment, and many others, as well as on many ethical, sociological and even political Jewish themes. He was fascinated by comparison of the Jewish point of view with that of other religions, particularly Christianity, and would glow with pleasure at the recognition of a point of uniqueness or excellence, or the discovery of an area where the wisdom of the ancient sages adumbrated an insight of modern depth psychology. Not only the ideology of Judaism attracted him strongly in recent years, but its practices as well. Our families often celebrated Sabbath and festivals together. He spent a whole summer, along with his family, at our "Camp for Living Judaism," in California. From all this he seemed to be acquiring a *Neshomah Yesayrah*, an added soul.

In this, I like to feel that he was symbolizing the quest of many Jews in the fields of the medical and social sciences for roots, for rediscovery of the ancient truths, which have for millennia fructified Jewish life, and which may perhaps again be reinterpreted and applied for the enrichment of our own experience. Judaism came to be for Dr. Gomberg not a substitute for anything, but an interdigitating entity which strengthened, inspired and integrated his personal life.

I imagine that we all, at times, seek a unifying principle in our work and our world. We need not blush for it. Einstein sought such a principle. This genius who unlocked the unimaginable power of the atom, posited, in his Unified Field Theory, one formula, one law, for the microcosm, the world of atoms too small to comprehend, and for the macrocosm, the world of heavens too great to encompass. Is it wrong for us to strive to include also the anthropocosm, the world of man and his works?

It is in line with this thought that I have chosen to discuss a few of the larger issues related to Jewish family living. I would like to explore some of the inter-relationships of religion and psychoanalysis as they bear upon the Christian and Jewish family situations and to draw some inferences, if possible, about the etiology of the differences which are still so widely found between our own patterns and those of our neighbors. It would be important to note whether, and if so, to what extent they stem from religious or cultural differences and to trace, if possible, the psychodynamics of the process.

That differences in the findings as to quality of social behavior have always existed barely requires proof. Yet, since so many of us deal daily with disturbed Jews or with Jewish families of marginal emotional adjustment and maturity, it may be appropriate to sound the note of caution, that our clients or patients are perhaps the exception rather than the rule among the Jewish group. The comparative studies of Jews and other groups roll up an impressive testimonial whether the factual material presented be on juvenile delinquency, adult criminality, prison populations, family desertion and non-support, separation and divorce rates, alcoholism and alcoholic psychoses, venereal disease rates, commitments to mental hospitals for the tertiary manifestations of syphilis, or whatever. As a most recent example, the Yale Center of Alcoholic Studies reports first admissions of alcoholic psychotics in New York State Hospitals which shows that such admissions are 50 times as numerous among the Irish as among the Jews (25.6% vs. 0.5%), fifteen times as many among the Scandinavians, ten times among the Italians, nine times among the English and eight times among the Germans.

The simple finding in the alcohol study seems to need no explanation. And yet it does. If it is true, as it seems to be, that Jewish home and family life are even today endowed with some mysterious extra safeguards against the disintegrative forces of the environment, how can we account for this fact? As scientists, we must seek causes as well as describe phenomena.

While it has not been fashionable for people in such professions as psychiatry, psychology and the social services to concern themselves too greatly with religion as a force in the psychodynamics of family life, the Jewish religious profession has been insisting with ardor and conviction that the kind of findings we are discussing here are due to the Jewish concept of *Kiddush Hachayim*, the sanctification of life, which, they claim, introduces emotional integrity into the family, strengthens what we call "reciprocal role adaptation," "complementarity," etc., and underlies all of Jewish family dynamics. The sanctification of life in the family is the only gateway, they claim, to *Kiddush*

*Hashem*, the sanctification of God. It is this "secret weapon" also, they say, operating through both favorable and unfavorable periods of Jewish history, through golden eras of culture and enlightenment and dark centuries of persecution and pogrom, which has safeguarded the individual, and assured the moral integrity, survival and growth of Jewry and Judaism.

The lines of alienation are growing less hard and fast, and we now are not entirely surprised to find some psychoanalysts who concern themselves, to some degree, with what goes on in churches, synagogues and temples. There was a time in the beginning, when psychoanalysis did not concern itself particularly with values, morals and religion, *per se*. However, Freud soon began to play the spotlight of his brilliant perceptions in this direction. In 1919 he published *Totem and Taboo;* then *The Future of an Illusion;* and after that, *Moses and Monotheism,* all of which deal with various aspects of religion.

Freud has suggested that there are three basic reasons why religion evolves. First, Nature is cruel and capricious, showing man no favor. He feels weak and fearful and alone, like a child. He must battle for his existence or perish. If the benevolent or malevolent forces in his environment become personified as deities, he can attribute the praise or blame for successes and windfalls, failures and disasters to them alone, and he can propitiate the malevolent deities and flatter those that are benevolent, with the conviction that he is thereby averting evil and attracting good. By peopling the universe with gods, even though some of them are conceived as hostile, man does not feel so alone.

Second, Freud says, as far as man can possibly know, death is the inescapable end of life. There is no shred of evidence to the contrary. But this, man cannot bring himself to accept. He cannot conceive of his own non-existence, nor of leaving or being left by his loved ones. So he invents immortality and the hereafter as a means of thwarting the inexorable and equalizing the inexplicable inequities of life. The gods whom he has invented, he appoints as keepers of the accounts which will consign him to some kind of Heaven or Hell.

Third, man cannot face the hazards of living, all by himself. He needs the help of his fellow men for his own survival and that of his loved ones. But to gain it he must yield some of his own pleasures when they conflict with theirs. This is the price he must pay for the benefits of civilization, however much he may resent the paying. Since the strong might take advantage of their strength and oppress the weak, the basic commandments of communal living are given divine origin and sanction. The likelihood of obedience is thus enhanced, with the result that the strong are controlled and the weak protected. Obedience to his deity and the divine commands gives primitive man the feeling of "being good" and therefore of earning divine favor, as he earned parental favor in childhood.

Thus, to Freud, religion is a neurotic substitute for a mature resolution of the problems and conflicts of living. He feels it is the "universal obsessional neurosis of humanity"[1]. This neurosis, "like the child's, originated in the Oedipus Complex, the relation to the father." Ernest Jones puts this point of view succinctly: "The religious life represents a dramatization on a cosmic plane of the emotions, fears and longings which arose in the child's relations to his parents[2]."

Freud was a keen, though critical student of religion, hence his contributions cannot be dismissed lightly, even by religionists. If, as he maintains, religion has no sound basis, then, from our point of view, the word Jewish is superfluous in our theme, and the dynamics and logistics of Jewish family living must become essentially a study in pathology.

The truth is that among the primitive religions, we find almost complete confirmation of his formulations. The primitive deities are the personification of the benevolent and malevolent forces of their environment, and primitive religion consists mainly of the propitiation or flattery of these deities. The afterlife, as they conceive it, is largely a continuation of their existence, with the pain subtracted and the pleasure multiplied. Family and communal behavior, motivated and controlled by divine injunction, is interpreted for the masses by highly privileged, consecrated religious functionaries, who are accepted as representatives of the gods. To proceed with even the simplest functions, without consulting the will of the gods, is to risk disaster. Since disaster was the constant companion of man before civilization multiplied his defenses, the sway of the religious functionary was great.

The psychoanalytic study of religion has also shown us the large role played by the awesome mystery of sex in primitive religious belief and ritual, epitomized in the primitive puberty rites, which, in whatever time or clime we may examine them, are almost identical everywhere in form and content. They have one common pattern: the privilege of sex is granted by the elders, provided the taboos of the community (especially those relating to incest) are accepted by the initiates. The solemn and mettle-testing rituals attending initiation of the young adults into the community of their elders were usually climaxed by wildly orgiastic rites.

The mixture of the sacred and the sexual, which we find so crudely expressed here, is also characteristic of many of the later religions. Sacred prostitution, as one example, played a large role in some of the ancient religions, and various actual or symbolic castration ceremonials were practiced in others. The priests of Cybele, often self-castrated, would hold a recurrent festival in which on the third day, Attis, the son of the Goddess, who had died, is brought to life again through the ministrations and intercession of his mother. In the Egyptian religion, similarly, Isis periodically restores Serapis-Osiris to life. In Mithraism, the young Son-God opposes and finally slays the father and becomes the master of his own fate. Similarly, in the Greek and Roman religions we find the human sexual conflict intertwined with the relations which the gods reflect in their behavior, relations which are often abhorrent to our sense of morality. Their family morality, in turn, reflected the patterns of the gods.

From the dynamic point of view Christianity represents, in many ways, a compromise between primitive and more advanced religious and psycho-sexual concepts, which is reflected in many ways in attitudes and behavior in the family. The contrast between Christianity and Judaism in this respect is so striking, as I shall point out in detail, that the more one studies this subject, the more one wonders what meaning the term "Judeo-Christian," which is so commonly used today, can actually have.

The creed of Christianity, and in this we must include Protestantism as well as Catholicism, for only a few deny the Divinity of Jesus, is that Jesus is God's only-begotten Son, who came to earth in the flesh to take upon Himself man's sins and atone for them by His death upon the Cross, and who then was resurrected and returned to Heaven.  This dogma, which represents in some ways a pathway for escape from personal responsibility for untoward behavior, contains primitive elements present in earlier religions hundreds of years before Christianity. The myth of a son born of a divine being and a human, who dies and is reborn, occurs again and again in early literature. In tne Vedic literature, almost five thousand years old, there is an almost exact parallel to the Jesus story.

Ubiquitous, too, in primitive ritual, was the custom of eating the God.  It was related to fertility rites and stems from cannibalistic fantasies (perhaps even practices) about the father, later substituting the totem animal and finally the ritual meal. The Mass, or Holy Communion, is a symbolic residual of this same primitive rite of eating the God.  Dogmas like the Virgin Birth and practices like chastity vows of the religious orders testify to the depth of the sexual conflict, of which these are attempted, though unsuccessful, resolution.  The father authority principle is at once accepted, by the inclusion of God in the Trinity, and rejected, by the central role which Jesus, the Son, comes to play.  The virile masculine principle, or procreative male, is not permitted to function in the conception of Jesus, but instead an abstract, asexual principal, the Holy Ghost, is the fecundating agency.  Similarly, the female, in contradistinction to all her other earthly sisters, does not accept the full boon of her femininity as wife, by accepting a male sexually, but is impregnated asexually.  Yet her loving mother-function, once the child Jesus is born, is acceptable in this religious system, and receives full adoration in the majority of the churches, and some adoration in all.

An analysis of the psychodynamic roots of this aspect of Christianity is given by Bunker.  He says in part: "... the Christian religion asks, What shall a man do to be saved? ... The answer to this crucial question we see acted out in every initiation ceremony, while at the same time we find it verbalized in the Christian canon as: 'Except ye be circumcised ... ye cannot be saved.' (Acts, 15:1.) ... only if one first suffers the talion – punishment (of symbolic castration) for incestuous wishes for the mother and death wishes against the father, only then is it permitted to see the Kingdom of God, to be 'saved,' to be received into the father-generation as an equal, to achieve adult sexuality; 'castration' is the price of immortality[3]."

The contrasts with Jewish doctrine are striking. Circumcision is placed at the eighth day of life when all of its Oedipal struggle connotations are sublimated in the highest degree and tied, not to a competitive struggle with the father, but to the tender and protective parental impulses. The Bar Mitzvah rites in Judaism, the counterpart of the primitive initiation rites, channelize sexual and aggressive energies into study and the acquisition of power through knowledge, as Arlow points out. "This is a particularly favorable way out, consistent with the demands of a society in which there is a considerable time lag between sexual maturity and sanctioned heterosexuality[4]." This love of Torah, which incidentally is usually put in the feminine gender (*Etz Chayim Hee*—"She is a tree of life"), continues all through the life of the Jew and affords a sublimated ideal, while the tenacious clinging to the concepts of love of Jesus or of Mary, the mother of God, which is characteristic of Christianity, may delay or interfere with such sublimation. Arlow says of the Bar Mitzvah boy, "The initiate renounces remnants of his Oedipal wishes for the demands of the developing superego, namely, group loyalty and studiousness[5]." The ordeal through which he passes is standing up before the multitudes and making an oral communication, reading the blessings or the Torah and Haftorah, and making a speech. His gift, as the many-level quip, "Today I am a fountain pen," highlights, is symbolic, but sublimated.

The evidences of deep unresolved sexual conflicts in the roots of original New Testament Christian theological dogma, the implications of which for family life are obvious, crop up continuously also in the writings of many of the church fathers and church leaders through the centuries. St. Paul's famous statement in I Corinthians VII, 7-9, is significant: ". . . I say therefore to the unmarried and widows, it is good for them if they abide even as I. But if they cannot contain, let them marry; for it is better to marry than to burn."

Marriage is placed in the third and lowest scale of Christian purity, the next higher being celibacy voluntarily adopted after marriage or after the death of a spouse, and the highest being absolute virginity. As zealous as St. Augustine was for virgins before he became a monk, so ardent was he for virginity afterward. His example is instructive: one either yields to sin, or renounces it—there is no middle course—as there is no such thing as slightly pregnant. The celibacy of the Church's highest functionaries, the religious orders of priests and nuns, speaks for itself. Contrast this view with that of Judaism that teachers and religious functionaries are unfit to serve unless they are married. The High Priest could not perform the service in the Holy of Holies, unless he had a wife. The Rabbis said (*Yebamoth*, 62b), "He who is without a wife is without joy, blessing or good." It is interesting to note, as Rabbi Maybaum has pointed out in his article entitled "Tradition that is Living," that while some of the great men who have influenced European culture spent their lives without wife or child (including Descartes, Kant, Leibnitz, Schopenhauer, and Nietzsche), of over 2,000 rabbis of the Talmud whose teachings have come down to us, only one, Ben Azzai, is reported to have been unmarried.

On the position of women, St. Paul is clear: they are inferior. "They are commanded to be under obedience." "Let them be silent, and at home consult their own husbands." (I Corinthians, XIV, 34.) Tertullian actually rails against them: "You are the Devil's gateway . . . On account of your desert— that is, death—even the Son of God had to die[6]." What a tender contrast is the statement (in *Ketuboth*, 62a), "A man must not cause his wife to weep, for God counts her tears," or another (in *Baba Metziah*, 59a), "If your wife is small, bend down and listen to her."

Who of us can doubt that the guilt feelings about sex which Christianity inculcates both directly by its teachings and indirectly by the unconscious perception of the sexual conflict symbolized in the Godhead, are not conducive to the achievement of the best possible sexual adjustment in marriage for the couple or in family life for the children. The conflict is, in turn, projected onto the Godhead, and is readmitted as a force to distort and disturb personal behavior and attitudes in home and family life, in which it is rooted. Hence, there is created a vicious circle, a reflexive, self-perpetuating, endless pattern, like when we stand between two facing mirrors in a hallway. Can this possibly be without effect?

Also to be a spiritual shuttlecock, thrown back and forth endlessly in the grip of the desires of the flesh which are styled by the church and felt by the individual to be both infinitely tempting and infinitely sinful, is a fate under which only the most stoical can stand up for long. There can be no middle ground between the two, not even in holy matrimony, for guilt forms a canopy over every Christian bed. As Nietzsche has so well put it, "Christianity poured a drop of poison into the cup of Eros."

The robust attitude toward sex, on the other hand, which is found in the Bible,—"Rejoice in the wife of thy youth," "Be thou ravished with her love," and countless other examples in Proverbs, Song of Songs and other books, is continued in rabbinic literature, and exemplified in Jewish family life down through the ages. In *Marriage and the Jewish Tradition*[7], the rabbinic references are quoted abundantly. A succinct summary is also available in Mihaly's article[8]. For example, the great Rabbi Meir (*Niddah*, 31b) says the ideal is for the sex act not to be perfunctory and dutiful but as exciting and fresh as the first union on the wedding night. In *Moed Katan*, 9b, the wife is urged to use cosmetics and wear ornaments so that she may be attractive to her husband, not only in her youth, but also in her old age. In the Pentateuch we find it stated boldly that a man, on the other hand, may not diminish his wife's "food, raiment, or conjugal rights." (Exodus, 21:10).

It is interesting to note, when we look into the personal history of some of the leaders of the pessimistic neo-Calvinist movement in modern Christian theology, how often it has been their lot to have unhappy family relations in childhood, particularly with their earthly fathers. This seems to color their marital experience and their concepts of man and of the relations between God and man. It is as though their unhappy relationships and their gloomy theology spring like twin geysers out of the depths of the seething miseries of their childhood and youth.

Soren Kierkegaard is a classic example. He was engaged

to Regina Olsen, a lovely girl, but broke the engagement after four years, unable to face marriage. Bruenner, one of the outstanding spokesmen of Christendom, says, "We cannot think of our Lord as married, although we are not in the least jarred by the fact that he ate and drank[9]." Sex seems to be the "original sin." To turn one's back on it is alone deemed worthy. To be what Kierkegaard calls a "single one," a solitary man whose contact with the world is broken, is, to him, the only way to salvation. He says, "In order to come to love, I had to remove the object." Martin Buber, commenting on this, says: "God wants us to come to him by means of the Reginas he has created, and not by renunciation of them." This is what the rabbis meant when they said in *Mishna Berachot*, IX, 5, "You shall love God with all your inclinations"—even with the *Yezer Ha-rah*, the sexual urge. Note that while it is commonly termed the "evil inclination," its use in the loving service of God belies the designation. The rabbis so cherished the institution of marriage that they pictured God as occupying himself in Heaven, since the completion of the creation of the world, mainly with matching couples.

The doctrine of salvation by withdrawal from life reaches its absurd extreme in Heidigger, the German theologian: man can discover his true being and become himself, he says, only through death.

What is the origin of such ideas, dynamically? We must remember that the Son of God, who is, for man, the sole gateway to salvation and to whom prayers for addressed "In the name of our Lord, Jesus Christ, Amen!" came to outrank the Father, God, only at the cost of death, the greatest of all possible punishments. Only after suffering death on the cross could he be redeemed, rise again and rule. Such dogmas have their roots, as we all know, in the time-old unconscious Oedipal struggle of the rising son and the declining father. Must not the ever-present crucifix, symbolizing the rebellion, the punishment and the triumph, have its unconscious influence upon this same struggle as it takes place even today, in all Christian homes where adolescents are moving toward adulthood?

Compulsory submission to parental authority is required of children, while the adult voluntarily subjects himself to authority on many fronts; he obeys the law, honors his contracts, conforms to custom and convention, complies with moral codes, and the like. He can achieve this new status healthily during adolescence and after, not by rebelling against the authority of his father and triumphing over him, but by a growth process which the emotionally healthy father aids in every way possible, and in which he takes pride. Thus in healthy Oedipal resolution, each succeeding generation may stand on the shoulders, not on the neck, of its predecessors.

If ethical sanctions cannot be rooted effectively in rebelliousness, neither can they be formed in fear, whether it be fear of divine, or of temporal or parental authority, whether of pain or deprivation in this world, or of Hellfire in the next. In Jewish thought the "fear of God" was not defined in terms of a reaction to a threat of punishment. Its proper definition has always been recognized to be "awe of God." Fear cannot accomplish the miracle of the creation of a mature and noble human. Only love can.

This does not, of course, imply that a child must be reared fearless. There are fears rooted in reality which are the benevolent tutors of the ego and help conform the child's id-impulses to reality. Artificially engendered fears, however, become tyrannical martinets over the superego. The pressure of such fears is resented and evokes hostility against those who create or impose them, often followed by feelings of guilt. Through fear a person may be controlled, but he can never learn through this means to control himself. On the other hand, when the suppression of impulses by parentally or artificially engendered theological or sexual guilt and fear fails, it may foster rebellion against all authority, even that which operates for one's own advancement or which is necessary for one's own survival. We can then become rebels against ourselves, divided souls with no resting place, neither in Heaven nor in Hell.

In the dynamics and logistics of the conversion experience within Christianity, we may explore another manifestation of the influence of its all-pervading guilt load and may perhaps gain further insights. Not only non-Christians become converts to Christianity, but also many good Christians undergo a religious "conversion," a unique experience, unlike any other in their prior religious life. They are suffused with a feeling of at-one-ness with their Savior and freedom from sin, and they move in a mood of exultation, sublimely confident that they have been "saved." They become, in the metaphor of William James, "twice-born souls."

Dynamically, the background for the Christian conversion experience is found in the harnessing of both the normal self-deprecatory inferiority feelings and the compensating omnipotence fantasy of infancy to a two-pronged religious hypothesis —first, that sinfulness is the natural unredeemed state of man and dooms him to eternal damnation, and second, that redemption can come only through Christ.

It is evident that acceptance of the first hypothesis prolongs and builds up the infantile guilt tensions *ecclesiogenically*, that is, wholly and solely through church teachings. It is well-known that an individual may carry a great burden of such guilt regardless of exemplary ethical and moral behavior in reality. Starbuck points out how this may be a retarding factor in character formation. He says, "Conversion is a process of struggling away from sin, rather than of striving toward righteousness[10]."

I believe further, that the exultant feeling of being "saved," like the guilt feelings which preceded it, is also *ecclesiogenic*, that is, it grows wholly and solely out of church teachings. It derives its power from unresolved residuals of the infantile omnipotence fantasy. It is somewhat akin to the phenomenal exultation accompanying the feeling of being "in love," which I have elsewhere traced to the same source[11].

It is, incidentally, very different from the closest parallel to it which exists in Judaism, the exultation of the Hasidim in their worship. The reason is that they have no antecedent depression to provide the trigger-tension for the release, but believe that, through joy and fervor, man reaches the highest religious insights. Cohen puts it succinctly in his book on Buber: "The holiness of God, according to Hasidism, was wherever man chose to find it and open himself to its greeting[12]."

The first Christian hypothesis, about the innate sinfulness of man, leads to depression and despair. The second hypothesis, about the exclusive saving power of Jesus, leads to exultation and release. Clearly, if the dynamics of the process are not accepted, the logistics will be destined to fail. Non-believers will remain unmoved. In Franz Werfel's *Song of Bernadette*, Lafite says, "There are no conversions to belief. There is only a return to it." I think it is safe to conclude that Heaven cannot really be harvested at a baptismal font, nor ripe fruit of the spirit from the Golden Bough.

Needless to say these dogmas are a sidelong factor and do not alone determine, even though they may greatly influence, behavior. There are millions of excellent marriages, made by good Christians, who rear fine children in happy homes. The question I am raising is whether this is because of or in spite of dogmas which denigrate man, which afford him easy escape from the responsibility for his behavior, which surround sex with guilt, and which control him by threat of Hellfire or promise of Heaven. Where ethics has little relationship to behavior and grows out of doctrine rather than experience, where the difference between guilt rooted in reality and that which is ecclesiogenic becomes fuzzy, and where absolution may be granted rather than earned in relation to the injured party or the offense, we remain cautious as to the strength of the character traits which result.

How can limits be set? On what basis does reality testing take place and how firm are its results? What kind of ego-boundaries result from this pattern of child rearing? If character is not firmly rooted, may it not be swaying structure, built on quicksand, which can overturn under the stress of temptation or adversity? The live branch withstands the storm; the rotted bough may break and fall.

What about Judaism in these respects? There are within it, undoubtedly, relics of the primitive. Are these characteristic or marginal? Has Judaism developed to maturity over the ages? Can we find any relation between the theological concepts of Judaism and the home and family life of Jews? Is there an explanation for the unique and excellent family situation to which we have alluded?

Analyzing the primitive elements in Judaism Rosenfeld admits that, ". . . in the horns of Moses are haunting memories of the wild god Pan, as well as of the immovable Yahveh[13]." She maintains that monotheism brings organization into the chaos and enables science and intellect, rather than primitive emotions, to attain a commanding position. She says: "The development of monotheism was, like the formation of the superego, a gradual process in which each phase retained traces of the epoch which preceded it." It would seem that only in a dynamic faith could such growth occur. The resistance of the rabbis to the completion of the canon of the Bible, or even to commit the Talmud to writing shows a stubborn refusal to undergo fossilization, such as that of which Toynbee accuses us. In the life of the individual this keeps the mind open for new insights, new revelations, and it gives democratic responsibility to each generation, as Maimonides urged, to advance our understandings. It makes for "continuity through change," as Honor called it, or as the theologians call it, "progressive revelation."

Brenner states, ". . . a voluntary mutual covenant would be entered into by God . . . only with a people who possess a sense of responsibility, i.e., a super-ego . . . Hebraism therefore arrives at a mature means of identification with the father God—by internalization, not of His symbolized flesh, but His authority, His law, His moral standards[14]." Clearly, what can be accomplished by a whole people can be accomplished by individuals in the Jewish family.

The unique agency in Jewish history, in fact, in the total history of all mankind, which accomplished this internalization of God's "authority, His law, His moral standards," rather than "of His symbolized flesh," is unquestionably the institution of prophecy. What was it that made and moved the prophets?

Arlow has given an answer to this question: "The prophet . . . regarded himself as a mere instrumentality in the service of a greater cause . . . he transcended the barrier of reason and played on the unconscious emotions of his listeners, exhorting them to participate in his exultation and to share with him his vision of glory . . . Toward his master, the prophet is the passive 'rod of his wrath' but in so doing he is permitted to share in God's omnipotence. He exhorts the multitudes, berates Kings and High Priests, and proclaims God's will . . . It was Freud who demonstrated the feeling for God is derived from the feeling for the father. Upon this emotional basis is founded the relationship between the prophet and God . . . This is what distinguishes the true prophet from the false prophet . . . the true prophet is one who correctly divines and expresses the emergent, but still inarticulate dreams and aspirations of his people. In this respect prophecy is like great art and both survive for the same reason. . . . At the threshold of the ages," concludes Arlow, "stands the prophet, midwife of humanity's dreams[15]."

If the prophet was the midwife of humanity's dreams, the rabbis and teachers of later generations were the wet-nurses, nourishing and sustaining them after the prophets had helped them to birth. They led them by the hand and guided their faltering footsteps. They embodied the ethical ideal in a way of life for the home and family, the market place and the wider outer world, which stood the test of time. It survived the hammer-blows of adversity and the temptations of favored eras, because while it remained dynamic and flexible, changing its dogmas and its rituals, changing even the face of God as its insights grew, it afforded a solid base for the intimate sphere of family relations, which did not fluctuate or vacillate.

Freud's assertion that religious impulses originate in the Oedipus Complex is undoubtedly true. But this does not necessarily stigmatize religion as neurotic. We speak of "the infantile neurosis," yet we recognize that the Oedipus Complex is not a sickness, but supplies the crucial building materials out of which adult sexuality is constructed. Out of the child's infantile desire for exclusive possession of his mother grows the mature desire for exclusive possession of his mate, the foundation of fidelity in family life, and out of his infantile hostile impulses toward his father grow the healthily aggressive traits which enable a man to win a place for himself in the world and provide for and protect his family. So it is with the primitive impulses of religion. In Judaism they do not remain primitive, but can serve as building materials for adult morality and as a springboard from which man's spirit can leap to great heights. Their origin in the Oedipus is not necessarily fatal.

If the Godhead in Christianity projects unresolved sexual conflicts, and may, in turn, adversely affect the sexual adjustment of couples in marriage, the God concept in Judaism should have the opposite effect. In Jewish theology, God is the undivided unity ruling the universe. He is the *El Ehaddai*, the epitome of masculine strength and power, yet the *El Rachum*, who tempers justice with mercy, as must any human father who wishes to rear his children healthily. He rules by law, not by whim, and His law is immutable—it has no exceptions. There is thus a fundamental discipline in the universe, as there must be in the world of man.

The acceptance of law as a principle thus places the individual, in his own private life, in harmony with the universe. The child's security as he learns about life lies in this very fact, that there is a vast preponderance of certainty and justice which he can trust, pitted against the occasional capriciousness of the world and the people around him. The certainties need not always be pleasant. The child can face and accept hunger, physical suffering, pain, sorrow, privation, even persecution, if they are merely unpleasant realities, instead of barbed accusations of personal worthlessness and inferiority.

In this same fact lies, perhaps, one of the secrets of Jewish survival. The acceptance of the dynamic concept of God as a just and loving ruler in a moral universe, with whom the Jew could identify, lent the same strength to the entire Jewish group as the individual child's acceptance of his mother as his partner in his world. Having "swallowed" the loving God, in the same sense as the child introjects the loving mother, and being filled, as the prophets were in their theophanies, with a sense of being saturated with divine love and elevated by a feeling of original worth rather than of original sin, the Jews can withstand persecution and move forward to ever greater maturity. We saw this during the London blitz, when children held in their mothers' arms through the seemingly unending terrors of the air raids, in bleak underground shelters, were safe and unharmed emotionally, while children separated from their mothers' loving and protecting arms languished despite luxurious surroundings and the finest personnel[16].

I believe it is in *this* kind of psychodynamic explanation, rather than in that of moral masochism, that the phenomenon of the absence of hate against our detractors and persecutors lies. The emotionally mature Jew accepts anti-Semitism and prejudice realistically. He does not conclude, because the outside world may be prejudiced and may manifest discrimination

against him, that the fault lies within him. Rather, he sees
prejudice as the problem of the prejudiced. He tries to teach
this point of view to his children in his home. It would be
unrealistic, however, to ignore the undertow of resentment or
even rebellion which is engendered in some by this behavior on
the part of the outside world, against the fate of being a Jew
and which leads to lesser or greater forms of escapism or even
apostasy. The problem is somewhat similar to that which
preventive medicine encounters in combating an epidemic
disease; one can either combat the causing organism or immunize
the individual. Our Jewish defense organizations attempt the
first; the second can best be done in a home with Jewish self-
appreciation in a setting of emotional maturity.

In Jewish theology the mother figure does not rule in heaven
as part of the God-company, but reigns on earth as the high-
priestess of the home, loved, revered, and respected by her
family, and accorded rights far beyond those which any other
civilization accorded its women for thousands of years afterward, in fact, not until the emancipation of women in the
modern era. In addition to her rights to property, protection,
divorce, etc., think of a statement like the one in *Leviticus Rabba*
(IX, 9): "A groom must not enter the bride's chamber without
first asking her consent," in the light of the life-and-death power
which husbands had over their wives and children in other
cultures for millennia afterward.

A Jewish mother in the pattern of her faith cherishes and
never rejects her femininity both as a wife and as a mother.
Jewish literature is full of examples of all of the excellent
qualities which have characterized her and made her home
a secure fortress for her loved ones. Proverbs 32, the *Ashet
Chayil,* A Woman of Valor, was written over 2000 years ago.
She has always cried out with her matriarch mother Rachel to
her own Jacob, "Give me children, or else I die." (Genesis,
30:1) She has felt, as the rabbis said in *Kiddushin* (30b), "God,
father and mother are partners in man's creation," and as for
her children, she has treated them as though in truth the dictum
"You cannot see God's face and live" were abrogated for
them. . . . "Little ones look upon the face of the Shechinah."
*(Masseket Kallah Rabbati,* 11,8.) She gives her husband the

respect and veneration which are due him for the support and protection, as well as for loving guidance which he gives his family. And he reciprocates.

The absence from the Jewish home of venereal disease, syphilitic psychoses, alcoholism and a host of similar weaknesses which have their roots in the moral realm are not accidental, for the standards of sexual morality are high, for good reason. In a "good" marriage—where the needs of the couple meet and match on both the conscious and unconscious levels—we also have a lasting marriage and a satisfying one.

The attitude of Judaism toward sex is a robust one as well as a moral one. The pleasures of the marital bed are to be enjoyed to the full, without shame or guilt. In fact, the Talmud gives full recognition to the need and desire for foreplay and the normal variations of sexual activity and the right of both partners for gratification. It also approves contraception in certain situations. The pull of infidelity is, under these circumstances, bound to be lessened even if it were not as abhorrent as it is to the Jewish ideal.

In this, the Jewish home stands at the very pinnacle of the ladder of evolution. For the latest achievement of the human race biologically, which marks us off from all of the rest of creation, is the capacity of the human female to enjoy pleasure in sexual intercourse. In the rest of the animal kingdom, the female is driven by "heat," which is seasonal, cyclic and based on biochemical secretions. The human female is driven, instead, by what is in many ways the most powerful force in the universe —love. This places her in a state of continuous latent capacity, which can become intense on stimulation, and she seeks something higher than mere erotic excitement (which is the easy way, open to anyone and everyone), namely, a setting in which meaning and purpose can enrich both her pleasure and her soul. It is in a loving home, with a loving husband, rearing well-loved children that she finds it, as all other daughters of Eve could, too. The absence of guilt feelings and shame enables her to strive for and often actually reach the heights to which this new-found evolutionary skill entitle her. The Jewish home by its very nature must achieve this goal more frequently than that of its neighbors. And the fruit of it is a high order of character, by all comparative standards, in both the parents and the children.

The son of Jewish creed and deed does not identify himself consciously or unconsciously with a rebellious divine Son upon whom he may cast the guilt of his own desires and rebelliousness and thus achieve a vicarious redemption. But he accepts his divine Father in reverence and love, as he accepts his human father. In Judaism the son is regarded and treated as a worthy individual and as he matures, he acquires his entitlement of worth and dignity, and also of responsibility, in his own right. Thus he becomes capable of standing side by side with his father, and of assuming parental authority himself, later, in his own familial relationships. Reared by loving parents who accept themselves as personalities, he can accept himself, his gender and his potency. He can, in a realistic fashion, accept the fact that he has both excellencies and shortcomings, utilizing the one and striving to remedy the other in building a good life. He can resolve his authority-conflict healthily under the guidance of loving parents, who see him through the turbulence of his adolescence with patience and understanding, and respected outsiders, who can serve as "authority bridges" over the chasm between the infantile and the adult concepts. With siblings and rivals of his own generation, he is able to handle both cooperation and competition healthily. And toward his subordinates and inferiors, he is able to show respect and consideration, appreciation and fairness, sufficient to earn him loyalty and devotion from them.

This is the probable source of the manifold excellence of the findings about Jewish family life. For myself, I cannot separate the faith of the Jew from the patterns of his home life, for the evidence would seem to indicate that where there is a diminution in the strength of the one, the strength of the other also declines.

From a dynamic point of view, too, there seems to me to be correlation between this faith and the principles and criteria which we have set up for emotional maturity. Judaism is man-fostering, not man-flagellating. It attributes to man original worth, not original sin. It approves a robust rather than a puritanical sexual life, but insists that it be characterized by fidelity and integrity. Its ethics are deed-centered, rather than creed-centered. It is healthily aggressive, in the face of evil, rather than passive or permissive and does not turn the other cheek to sadism. It insists that guilt feelings must be related to untoward behavior, rather than to violations of ecclesiastic principles. It eschews the use of fear as a deterrent or the promise of rewards in the hereafter as a motivation, in compensation for good deeds. (Ben Azzai said, "The reward of a *mitzvo* |good deed| is a *mitzvo;* and the reward of an *averah* (transgression) is an *averah.*") It favors sublimation and gratification of id-impulses, rather than blanket renunciation or repression. It is this-worldly, rather than other-worldly, progressivistic, rather than perfectionistic, centrifugal, moving constantly outward from the individual to society, from the "I" to the "Thou," rather than centripetal, concerning itself with the salvation of the individual and his soul alone. It is reality centered, rather than myth and mystery centered. It is melioristic as to the future of man rather than messianic or pessimistic. It is God-seeking, rather than God-fawning. It leans on reason rather than revelation in its questing for truth. It is universal, rather than parochial. It is democratic, rather than sacerdotal, and it is dynamic, rather than static.

In a recent article, Salisbury sums it up, as though for this paper. He says, "Judaism is characterized by the noticeable extent to which the highest religious feeling is identified with family relationship and experience. The stability and solidarity of both institutions are thereby enhanced by this fusion of religious and familial functions[17]." The Jewish home is, perhaps, as the rabbis said, a *Mikdash M'at*, a small sanctuary.

# References

1. Freud, Sigmund. *The Future of an Illusion.* NY: Liveright, 1928, p. 76.
2. Jones, Ernst. The psychology of religion. In *Essays in Applied Psycho-Analysis.* Vol. II. London: International Psychoanalytic Press, 1923, p. 195.
3. Bunker, Henry A. Psychoanalysis and religion. In Muensterberger, W., & Ayelrad, S. (eds.), *Psychoanalysis and the Social Sciences.* Vol. III. NY: International Universities Press, 1954, p. 30.
4. Arlow, Jacob A. A psychoanalytic study of a religious initiation rite—Bar Mitzvah. In Eissler, R.S., *et al.* (eds.), *The Psychoanalytic Study of the Child.* Vol. VI. NY: International Universities Press, 1951, p. 372.
5. *Op. cit.,* p. 373.
6. Tertullian. On family dress. In *Ante-Nicene Fathers.* Vol. XI, p. 305.
7. Brav, Stanley R. (ed.). *Marriage and the Jewish Tradition.* NY: Philosophical Library, 1951.
8. Mihaly, Eugene. The Jewish view of marriage. *Central Conference of American Rabbis Journal,* 1954 (Oct.), 32-38.
9. Bruenner, H. Emil. *Man in Revolt.* Phila.: Westminister Press, 1947, p. 348.
10. Starbuck, E.D. *The Psychology of Religion: An Empirical Study of the Growth of Religious Consciousness.* NY: Scribner's, 1899, p. 64.
11. Franzblau, Abraham N. Why Cupid is an infant. In *The Road to Sexual Maturity.* NY: Simon Schuster, 1954, Ch. 4.
12. Cohen, Arthur. *Martin Buber.* NY: Hillary House, 1957, p. 84.
13. Rosenfeld, Eva M. The Pan-headed Moses—a parallel. *International Journal of Psycho-Analysis,* 1951, 32:83.
14. Brenner, Arthur B. The convenant with Abraham. *Psychoanalytic Review,* 1952, 39:34.
15. Arlow, Jacob A. The consecration of the prophet. *Psychoanalytic Quarterly,* 1951, 20:374.
16. Freud, Anna, & Burlingham, Dorothy T. *War and Children.* NY: Medical War Books, 1943.
17. Salisbury, W. Seward. Faith, ritualism, charismatic leadership and religious behavior. *Social Forces,* 1956, 34:241.

Chapter 3

# Profile of a "Doll"—A Female Character Type

### ALEXANDER GRINSTEIN, M.D.

ALTHOUGH I have been mulling over the observations contained in this paper for a considerable period of time, I finally decided to write them down when a colleague described the following incident. He and a friend had gone to eat at a neighborhood restaurant. After they had been there a while, his companion remarked that the *same woman seemed* to be going through the door repeatedly! Although this seemed ridiculous, it contained enough truthful elements to warrant a serious study.

Many people have commented upon this type of woman, found in all large cities of this country. However, to my knowledge, no study of her has been made.

This 'doll' is between the ages of 30 and 35, very well-dressed in the height of fashion. Her grooming is impeccable and her hair is styled in the latest vogue. Her jewelry, of which there is a good deal, is likely to be heavy and noisy. She tends to be overdressed for the "ordinary" occasion. During the day, she uses a good deal of makeup, including eye shadow, mascara, etc., which also seems striking and inappropriate. Perhaps one would not be quite so struck by her appearance at a cocktail party as one is in seeing her attired in her customary fashion in the neighborhood shops. In an effort to maintain the highest level of fashion, current styles are copied so slavishly that she strongly resembles her counterparts with the result that the man in the restaurant could not distinguish one woman from another.

Socio-economically, these women's husbands, either business or professional men, are comfortable financially. They live in rather large houses in the better middle class neighborhoods and have two or three children. There is at least one maid, with additional help for the "heavy cleaning." The maids are usually colored; the women themselves, Jewish.

These women are usually fairly well educated. The large majority are high school graduates and in many instances are college trained as well. Usually they have not completed their college education nor have they pursued a career. They may *appear* uneducated and one is struck by the relative impoverishment of their expressed interests. Although the *exceptions* have pursued further study, e.g., extension courses in music, "great books," etc., the majority have not. They appear to have little in the way of genuine cultural interests or understanding. They go to the theatre or concerts more because it is "the thing to do," than because of their own genuine interest. After their children have gone off to school, they spend their mornings in sleeping late, talking to their friends on the telephone, doing some marketing, and taking care of their shopping and beauty needs. Their afternoons are spent in bridge, canasta, mah jong, and at clubs of various kinds. Some will take the trouble to transport their children to the various after-school activities in which their children participate: music lessons, dancing lessons, Hebrew school, etc. Others cannot wait to relegate this chore to someone else so that they "can be free." They seldom drink cocktails during the afternoon since this is not a regular part of their cultural pattern as it is with the non-Jewish women of a similar economic status.

Most of these women do not get up to make breakfast for their husbands—especially if the latter leave for work somewhat early. Few of them cook dinner as this function is relegated to the maid. Several times a week they go out with their husbands after dinner. The entertainment is usually socializing with friends or relatives. There is a good deal of card playing but little drinking. They frequently go out to restaurants to be seen and to "table hop." They may appear to be flirtatious but very often this behavior is more teasing than it is real. One man, in describing his contact with a woman of this type, recounted a flirtatious incident. They had begun to dance, and she moved her body very close to him in an obviously seductive manner. Since she was so close, he reached over to kiss her and was met with a prompt rebuff: "Don't muss my hair!" The way the remark was made successfully ended the whole episode.

In social groups, these women spend a good deal of time with other women rather than mixing with the men. Their shallow conversation centers around clothes, gossip and food. They compare their material possessions with such seriousness as to hardly befit even a small child. They usually brag about their material acquisitions and their husbands' income. One woman, for example, spoke disparagingly of another's mink coat to a "friend," referring to it as "nothing but a cheap dog" and boasting that the amount she paid for hers wholesale was more than the retail price of the other's. Such comparisons in dresses and household furnishings of all kinds are discussed at great length. They brag about their affluence, or more properly speaking, of their acquired affluence. In their remarks and actions one clearly sees a strong competitive element. Emphasis is placed upon who is the first with a certain type of possession, especially clothes.

One gets the impression that many of the comments are made in an effort to impress their audience with their own virtues and their self-importance. Thus they may describe the bargains which they made in a shopping expedition to demonstrate their shrewdness and cleverness. Or, they may seek pity from their listeners by lamenting about their unfortunate chain of maids, a conversation that frequently brings many of their listeners to tell similar tales of incompetence. Sometimes they spend their time narrating stories of their children's exploits, especially if the children are in the "cute stage." Superficially at least, some of them seem to have an interest in their children's problems. Many have a reading knowledge of Spock and read the columns on child care in the various magazines and newspapers. There is a kind of pseudo-sophistication in this respect and a shallow glibness with concepts that is somewhat jarring to a professional person. In their relationship with their children one detects a note of harshness but not cold indifference.

A profile of this woman, to be meaningful, must include a description for her background. In most instances she is first generation American, born of immigrant Jewish parents during the depression years. In many cases, the parents were poor and struggled hard to make a good living and sacrificed a good deal to provide for the physical needs of their children. The philosophy of the home dictated that the boys be educated to prepare them for the highly valued professional life or business, and the girls were to marry, as soon as possible, young men in the professions or those who would do well financially. Education for these girls was definitely not stressed. It was often discouraged as a goal in itself, as being unnecessary training for a housewife. One girl, for instance, was told, "You don't have to go to college to learn to wash dishes or to clean diapers."

Generally, these women do not seek professional help as their characterological makeup keeps them symptom-free. However, when this type of woman does seek help, her appeal occurs at a time when emotional difficulties become manifest to herself.

In the initial interview with these dolled-up women, one is struck by some emptiness in their expression. It is not, however, the affectlessness of the schizoid individual. Everything about them is "just right" but there is something missing. One has the impression that these women are difficult to approach or to be close to, as there is somehow an impenetrable wall that exists between them and the person they are with. They are very narcissistic in their appearance and their manner, so that the appeal for help is somewhat incongruent with this picture.

The complaints which she makes are vague: "Things don't seem to be going quite well. I don't know what is wrong. I love my husband but ... He is a good husband, a good father to my children, but ... " One gets some obscure references to mild psychosomatic disturbances, but in the main it is the impression of a general feeling of an underlying unrest which is so important.

Viewed from a dynamic standpoint the presenting complaints which these women make may be subsumed under a general heading of a loss or a threatened loss of a love object. Their narcissistic defenses had been maintained by the supplies which they received from those about them. When there was a possibility that these would no longer be forthcoming, and that these defenses were in danger of collapsing, these women came for help. At times they complained that their children had reached an age where they no longer required their attention as formerly, and they themselves felt that they did not want to have any more children. Sometimes they remark that they are getting old and may lose their appeal (in their 30's!). Sometimes they seem to be vaguely aware that their husbands are dissatisfied with things at home, that they have begun to lose interest in them as love objects and may even have begun an extramarital liaison. Under these circumstances these women, usually very moral in their sexual lives, may sometimes express the fear that they may act out sexually. They may seize upon the idea that such a proposed relationship will provide them with a gratification of some of their unfulfilled longings. At times these women express the concern that their parents, especially their mothers, are getting old and they are afraid that they may die. In all these instances, varied as they may be, the present threat of withdrawal of supplies or of love privation seems to suggest the possibility of an impending depression.

With the beginning of their psychoanalytic treatment, certain of their characterological defenses become manifest. These women demonstrate a kind of childish confusion and bewilderment. They have a hard time in "getting going" as they have no clear-cut symptoms such as anxiety, depression or sexual problems which they can start to work out in their treatment. They try to be likeable and even attempt to "charm" the analyst. They ask questions or volunteer analytic constructions that have a striking naïveté about them. Not infrequently, they talk about their children, raising questions and problems related to their management. In this way, they act like the *child* who appeals to the parent for help, the parent being generally the mother. One quickly gets the impression that the whole overdressed makeup and manner, the extreme narcissism and aloofness represent a characterological defense, concealing behind it a bewildered frightened child.

The transference which is established is, from the very beginning, that of a child to her mother. This, of course, is in no way unusual for young women with infantile tendencies. One soon begins to see a strong tendency toward a repression of the feelings that have to do with affectional feelings for the mother. As the picture of the transference unfolds, one is struck by the repeated tendency to deny such feelings toward the mother, or to isolate them from other feelings that are expressed. Whereas the intensity of their emotional involvement in the transference may be seen to be great from the study of the dream material and associations, these patients see it, if at all, only intellectually. When they approach a recognition of its existence, flight to familiar defenses is promptly effected. For a long time the infantile picture persists, and the feelings of deep dependency are more evident to the therapist than to the analysand.

As time goes on, and movement in these patients is very slow, one is able to see the gradual unfolding of some rather striking similarities which in the main seem to center around the core theme of a struggle for a sense of identity. This identity, which normally derives from the girl's identification with her mother, is in these cases pathetically confused. It is fraught with considerable conflict and the emotions toward the mother remain perpetually in a state of ambivalence.

What are some of the characteristics of the mothers of these women? Their mothers were rather harsh, primitive, loud, aggressive women who did not fit in well with the American way of life, and who maintained many of the prejudices and fears deriving from old world deprivation and persecution. At times there was little love between the parents. Marriages were arranged, or the parents were separated at the time of their emigration to America. As these mothers themselves felt out of place in this country, they presented to their daughters a model of being maladjusted and misfit. Furthermore, wishing the best for their daughters, the mothers literally pushed them to be unlike themselves, to be better than they were. They frequently expressed the hope that their daughters would not have to slave away in their adult years as they had to do. They reiterated the refrain that what they were doing was for the welfare of their children. "I am doing this for you so that *you* won't have to!" These mothers, on the one hand, pushed their daughters to be different and unlike themselves, to have a better life than they had and indicated by their own commands that an identification with the slavish aspects of the mother's personality was neither necessary nor desirable. Nonetheless on the other hand, they interfered with their development along these lines by badgering them and cursing them in their own inimitable primitive fashion when they strove in the direction of independence and difference. This presented a woefully confusing state of affairs for these girls: a struggle against their identification with their mothers. The girls maintained a façade of enforced and exaggerated difference from their mothers. However, it did not fit them. As so often happens, they retained within their makeup many of the old identifications. They became neither wholly American nor wholly foreign like their mothers, neither modern nor old-fashioned. Their own crudeness and inappropriateness in their dress, the excrescence of harshness in their behavior toward their children, the loudness in their manner, the lack of accepted values—all speak for an identification with some of their mothers' striking primitive characteristics. Their sense of identity is thus seriously disturbed and they are constantly dissatisfied with themselves in the role that they are playing. They wanted to rebel against their heritage but inwardly they retained the old identification. It is as though one can see the middle European ghetto community living within the "modern personality" of these women, like Williamsburg in the middle of the New York metropolis. Exploration into this area of their psychic life reveals superstition and ignorance, magical thinking and beliefs quite different in character from those of women raised in different backgrounds. Their infantile theories, quite normal in all children, took on a quality of reality because they were given a credence by their mothers' infantile personalities.

Insofar as the girls had difficulty in selecting a real model with which to identify, they gravitated in their thinking and fantasy life to an identification with alluring idealized figures of various kinds such as movie stars and heroines of magazine stories. Pictures of the models in ads came to have more meaning to these girls, as reality was so bewildering to them. They strove valiantly to repress the early model of their mothers, as such a figure was completely unadaptable to their coveted way of life in their "new world" environment. In secret they attempted to identify with the girls of the "unreal" world. But, being a fantasy type of model, the identification was in itself something *unreal*. As these idealized figures did not provide anything in return for the identification, the search which the girls carried out for a love object with whom to identify remained unfulfilled.

The relationship to the mother was further complicated by the extreme amount of aggression which was present toward her. Because of the lack of permission for any normal discharge of aggression and the mother's own intense aggression, the rebellious tendencies of these girls in childhood and even adolescence accumulated and were internalized into a highly intra-punitive agency. It should be emphasized that with all the aggression, these girls' mothers did show them a good deal of care and in the earliest years, gave them a great deal of affection. This certainly was of great value to them, but it also made for much more conflict in their relationship with their mother and made the ultimate separation from her much more difficult. From this one may understand that in those instances where the presenting complaints dealt with the mother's condition directly, the anxiety of the women stemmed from the triggering of a flood of guilt feelings, stemming from the long-standing aggression toward the mother.

No one who has ever treated this type of woman can fail to recognize her manner of speech. There may be an effort to maintain a kind of cultured accent. Yet one hears a childlike whine, a kind of petulant clamoring, punctuated at times with the traces of foreign accent or a Jewish expression. During the course of therapy, one may see transient phases during which there is an increase in vulgarity with a preponderance of anal terms, Jewish curses and expressions. The aggressive quality of the productions (easily recognized in the beginning by the therapist) becomes progressively more obvious in character as time goes on. Coincident with this, the true affective character of the rages against the mother (and against the therapist) become apparent in the transference. The patient comes to her analytic appointments carelessly dressed without makeup and may even emphasize that she has interrupted her housework. Thereby she gives further clues to her early identification. Anxiety in the analysis, stemming from the fears that the analyst will punish, beat, hit, curse, condemn, or reject her as a consequence of this inner hatred, clearly portray the dynamics of the childhood emotional constellations. The picture of the mother that emerges in the course of treatment is primitive indeed; her primitive character was an important factor in maintaining the level of anxiety in these girls.

As might well be expected, the primitive character of these mothers had a profound effect upon the entire psychosexual development of these girls as usually fixations occur on a pregenital level. The oral stage, so particularly important in character development, is usually seen to have been without too much frustration. These girls have usually been breast fed and from what one gathers, for a considerable period of time. Evidently, from various descriptions, the earliest period was not especially traumatic. Interestingly enough, the mothers of these girls emphasized feeding a great deal, and there were constant exhortations throughout their development to eat. This general lack of early deprivation may perhaps account for the absence of schizophrenic tendencies in these women.

Difficulties appear to have begun somewhat beyond the early oral stage. The tendency which these women have toward depressive reactions indicates that the point of fixation in their psychosexual development lies in the oral-sadistic phase and beyond. It would be well within our expectation that, barraged by the oral aggressive personality of the types of mothers which these girls have, they themselves would develop fixations in this area. The anal phase, too, is usually traumatic in these girls, leading to fixations in this area as well. One gets the impression that, in the main, toilet training was rather harsh and early. The emphasis on cleanliness quickly instilled sharp reaction formations, albeit anal-sadistic talk and expressions are common. Masturbation was strictly prohibited and no sexual enlightenment was offered. What knowledge these girls picked up was from the street, from older sisters, and from friends.

These girls have to contend with special difficulties which highly color their reactions of penis envy as well as sibling rivalry. They come from homes which culturally place a high value upon the male members of the family, especially the sons. The European and Jewish tradition of the importance of the male, perpetuated in the daily prayers of the Orthodox Jew, dominate the attitude in the household. Boys are to be educated, and the goal of "my son, the doctor" is no myth in its importance to the self-esteem of the hardworking and self-sacrificing mother. In their mother's unconscious the son was frequently equated with the mother's phallus. The consequence of the mother's ambition for her sons and preferential treatment of them often results in a bitter sacrifice of the daughter's personality. The obeisance demanded of the daughters to their brothers' expected accomplishments serves to perpetuate a feeling of repressed aggression and secret contempt within these girls. Specific defenses must then be erected to cope with these emotions. Their excessive preening and exhibitionism in which they make unconscious use of the familiar equation body-phallus, represents one way in which these girls attempt to solve their problem of intensified penis envy, as well as their extreme jealousy of their brothers who were so much more valued by their mothers than they were.

One such woman described how well she looked when she was made up, saying to me, "You know, I look like a *living doll* and everyone looks at me when I walk into a room full of people." Her perception of herself with all its vanity revived an expression her mother had used years before to describe her. When she "dolled herself up" to gain the favorable attention of her women friends, she was actually trying to recapture the attention and love from her mother which, as a child, she felt she had never really gotten since the mother's affection was directed so much more to her brothers. The brothers were educated and were prepared to inherit their father's business. She, on the other hand, was only valuable as someone who by her looks would be able to attract a man to marry her.

This woman, as a highly self-adored doll, who maintained a kind of stiff appearance, represented by her treatment of her body an identification with the highly prized and highly desired male genital. The highly overvalued regard for her body reflected in its essence her mother's overvaluation of the male members of her family. She succeeded in treating herself with the identical wished-for preferential treatment that she felt her mother lavished upon her brothers. This process of taking her own body as a highly prized object led to an intensification of narcissism in her makeup and created a difficulty in the establishment of healthy object relations.

The most important libidinal object of these women is, as one would expect, the mother. Because of the intense aggressiveness and phallic quality of the mothers, the girls' homosexual ties to them were never completely resolved. The tremendous anxiety referable to their mothers, however, protected them against homosexual entanglements in their adult life—that is, insofar as any acting out is concerned. However, the existence of their homosexual feelings, albeit in an aim-inhibited sense, may be seen clearly in the relationships with the women who take care of them (their maids, hairdressers, masseuses) as well as their girl friends. A great deal of the dressing and making up is directed more to their girl friends than to the men for whom they claim to be glamorous. One such woman, at a party, turned sarcastically to one of the men who had commented somewhat disapprovingly on her "overdone" makeup and said, "The trouble with you men is that you don't appreciate glamor when you see it!" With this remark she turned promptly to a woman standing next to her, and blinking her eyelids at her, in a most affected manner said to *her*, "Don't you agree, doll, that men don't really appreciate glamor?" The tie to their women friends is clearly libidinal but stops short of any sexual expression.

Very often one may learn a great deal about their relationship to their mothers by the information which they give about their relations to their maids. The personality of the maids they select, their complaints about them, their emphasis upon the kind of care the maids provide them as well as their children, etc., all serve to reveal much as to the original mother-daughter relationship. At times these women demonstrate a state of near panic when their maids do not show up for work. Such reactions occur in situations where there is no real inconvenience to the woman, betraying in this way the neurotic elements of the relationship.

In the transference situation with a male therapist, similar impulses prevail. They often want to dress to impress him, not as a man, but as another woman. Frustrated at not being accepted in this light, they turn upon him with aggression. It is very striking how, in the course of an analysis of one of these women, the repetitious changes in almost outlandish hair styles constantly reflected the wish to be admired and to be noticed by the analyst and others, not only as an individual but as someone who really was an accepted and approved member of a group. She would on occasion ask me what I thought of her latest hairdo. At times her efforts were so extreme that they brought down upon her the derision of others. This repeated the situation in her past when she longed for her mother's approval but obtained derision and ridicule from her efforts to be "modern." The phallic significance of her emphasis upon hair style was, of course, also an important determinant.

Let us now consider the status of the heterosexual development of these women. One has the impression that their heterosexual feelings are not very well developed. Although they do not disclose it as a presenting symptom, these women ultimately reveal that they are sexually frigid. In part, this symptom stems from their pregenital fixations and anxieties referable to their mothers. In part, too, it stems from a lack of relationship with a strong father figure. Less harsh in some respects than the mothers but rendered callous by the exigencies of earning a livelihood during the deprived years (especially during the Depression), he maintained a position somewhat distant from these girls. The father was usually away from home, working long hours. At times these daughters in their fantasy life regarded their fathers as roués, who spent their time away from home in numerous sexual exploits. When he was home, the children saw little of him as he was tired, sleeping, or otherwise occupied. One frequently hears the complaint, "I never really knew my father . . . he was never around . . . my mother ran the household."

The father of these girls thus came to be a somewhat shadowy figure, away a great deal of the time, and someone around whom fantasies were woven. There was often a great deal of friction between the parents in these homes, friction brought about not only because of the intricacies of differences in personality but also augmented by the long, hard hours which each of the marital partners worked and their understandable resentment against the plight in which they found themselves. However, as intense as such feelings may be, the cultural demand almost required a high valuation of the wife and mother by the

husband. Such veneration contributed to her power and his
implied passivity. It was easy enough for the daughters of
such parents to find ample material out of which their Oedipal
and pre-Oedipal fantasies could run rampant. The dominance
of the mother in the household increased the identification with
her and rendered the normal transference of libidinal feelings
toward the father much more tenuous in character. Nonetheless
the expected push toward marriage and a family generally
insured a transition toward heterosexuality. Unfortunately in
these instances, it was frequently of a somewhat questionable
kind insofar as these girls were concerned.

The emphasis by the mothers on being attractive to a man
so that it would be of advantage not only to the girl herself but
would also bring added glory or status to the family, especially
the mother, placed the girl in a position of psychologically
offering herself to the highest bidder. She was exhibiting
herself, with her mother's approval, to gain something for
mother—a man. Thus again, the preferred male became the
person for whom the daughter was sacrificed, and bred further
resentment both toward the mother and toward the future
husband. The implied commercialism of her position, of being
offered to the highest bidder (highest here in the sense of potential social status) tacitly approved prostitution fantasies so
common in girls anyway. From this standpoint, too, the reaction
of being placed in such a position, in contrast to the avowed
high morality inculcated since early times by the parents, led
to inevitable conflicts in their subsequent heterosexual adjustment.

The husbands whom these women ultimately selected and
married bore the stamp of their mothers' approval and, as would
be expected, in many respects were based upon the model which
the parents provided. So frequently the men were not selected
as heterosexual objects but as individuals who continued in the
role of the phallic mothers. But in addition to this, the men
continued the fathers' role, too, as they often tended to be
shadowy and distant. To a certain extent they are idealized by
these women as they are able to provide for them in a material
way much better than their fathers did. However, as these men
are inclined to be rather passive, they tend to give in to these

women's childish demands and whims, especially those of a material nature. They treat the wives as extensions of their own phallus which they adorn. By this behavior the husbands serve to perpetuate the infantile position of their wives. Their "doll-like" behavior then becomes reinforced through the social stimulation of other women like themselves.

The consequences of such an object choice bear out one's anticipations: no adequate sexual adjustment can occur under such circumstances. One patient describes his wife, who is of the character type we are discussing here, as a " 'Jewish nymphomaniac,' she has intercourse once a month." As the avenues toward adequate interpersonal relations, both male and female, are generally blocked, these women have turned more and more toward a narcissistic type of defense so that a superficial description of them invariably emphasizes their vanity.

As with all women, quite naturally, the deeper one penetrates into the unconscious layers of their psychic life, the more one finds the specific determinants of their personality makeup. The familiar basic constellations of Oedipal feelings and penis envy, blaming the mother, etc., are, of course, no different from those of any other women; as are the traumatic experiences of birth of siblings, illness, surgery, primal scene observations, and the conflicts and problems they present. Their unfolding and working through effects an improvement in their personalities and a change in their "living doll" characteristics.

It is most difficult to explain why it is that there are not more Jewish women who act this way, as such mothers as those described above are certainly quite common. We would suspect that ultimately the significant determinants as to what type of characterological defenses develop lie in the quality of the mother-daughter relationship. Moreover, early or adolescent stimulation and facilitation along these lines are very significant. And if these girls then find themselves in a marriage which, because of financial security or their husband's *laissez-faire* attitude, allows the careful fostering of this doll-like appearance, they tend to gravitate toward others with similar characteristics, with a consequent group reinforcement of their mannerisms.

When we see these women in analysis we may feel, too, that this type of narcissistic defense is used by those in whom the need is particularly great to secure the love which they felt was withheld from them and given to their brothers in their childhood.    Furthermore, they were probably the ones who were pretty girls to begin with and for whom the avenue of their physical attractiveness was the only one open to them for gaining any love and attention from their parents.    Other girls, perhaps not quite so pretty and with higher intelligence or special talents, could look for gratification along other lines from friends, teachers, and other mother substitutes, and therefore did not need to develop into this seductive doll-like character.

What is particularly tragic in these instances is that the daughters of these women identify themselves with them.    They are carbon copies of their mothers, manifesting the same shallowness, the same emphasis on money values, the same competitiveness that their mothers have.    Whether they will remain that way or whether contact with others will attenuate this type of identification, only time will tell.

This type of woman is so difficult to treat, particularly for a male therapist, because she brings into the transference an unusual primitive relationship out of her past.    The average analyst, not raised in such a milieu or knowing little about it, cannot empathize with it.    It is frequently difficult for the analyst to recognize his feelings toward the emerging material. The quality of the infantile material brought into the analysis is so primitive as the anlysis progresses that unless he is aware of the significance of this material, he is powerless to help his patient.

Chapter 4

# Premarital Characteristics of the Religiously Intermarried in an Urban Area[1]

JEROLD S. HEISS

$\mathbf{S}$EVERAL investigators have compared the premarital characteristics of people who marry within their faith with those of people who intermarry[2]. In general, these studies have been focused on a single religious group and they have been limited to variables such as religious training, generation, and socio-economic status. The present paper also compares the inter-married with the intramarried, but it differs from the previous research in that its main interest lies in early patterns of inter-action and in that it contains data on respondents from each of the three major religious groups.

It is well-known that almost all religious groups in this country oppose interfaith marriage, and it appears probable, though the data are far from adequate, that a majority of the general population shares this opposition[3]. These facts lie at the source of our interest in the premarital characteristics of the intermarried. From a study of these characteristics we hope to learn how it was possible for them to intermarry despite what seems to be general disapproval of such marriages. We want to know, in effect, how these people surmounted the usual barriers to intermarriage. The problem, then, is one of social control.

Generally, culturally proscribed behavior is prevented by both internal and external controls. The former operate as at-titudes which lead individuals to believe that the proscribed be-havior is wrong. Because of the desire for self-esteem and for the reduction of anxiety, these internal controls, if they exist, can usually prevent undesired behavior. No society, however, depends entirely upon internal controls. Invariably, there are external pressures helping to bring about conformity to social norms, which take a variety of forms from the threat of the loss of esteem to the threat of death[4].

In regard to marriage, both types of mechanisms of social control (referred to below as barriers) are operating to prevent heterogamy. Typically, people have instilled in them attitudes which lead them to oppose interfaith marriage, and these attitudes prevent many such marriages. In addition, external pressures prevent interfaith marriage among people who are not particularly opposed to it. The sanction is usually the possibility that the approval of significant others will be lost.

These controls obviously have not worked in the case of the intermarried; the problem of this research is to determine why. It is assumed that the ultimate source of barriers to interfaith marriage in American society lie in the family of orientation and formal religious organizations. Therefore, if one wishes to discover why the controls were ineffective in certain instances, it seems appropriate to investigate the characteristics of the respondent's parents and the nature of his relationships with his family and religion. If, in the case of an intermarried respondent, it can be shown that these sources did not produce effective barriers to intermarriage, we will consider the marriage to be explained.

## I.   METHOD AND SAMPLE

Within this framework, six general hypotheses were drawn up. Each took the form: people who have characteristic A are more likely to intermarry than are those with the opposing characteristic A'. The rationale for each hypothesis is that possession of the characteristic attributed to the intermarried is thought to be indicative of the probable absence of one or more of the barriers to intermarriage.

The available data did not permit a direct test of the general hypotheses and, therefore, in each case, a series of specific, testable hypotheses was formulated. Support for the specific hypotheses will be taken as evidence of the validity of the general hypotheses.

The data to test the predictions come from interviews of

1,167 people, between the ages of 20 and 59, who lived in the "Midtown" section of Manhattan. This sample was selected from the 1,660 cases studied by the Midtown Mental Health Project. The present sample does not include the 493 respondents in the original sample who had never married nor the 55 whose marriages are not classifiable as interfaith or intrafaith.

The Midtown sample was selected by means of a three stage area-probability sample design. Blocks, houses, and dwellings were the units used, and within each dwelling a single respondent was chosen randomly. Eighty-seven per cent of those so chosen were successfully interviewed; the non-respondents do not seem to differ in relevant respects from those who did cooperate[5]. Comparisons between the sample and census data indicate that the former is representative of the Midtown area. The population of Midtown town is representative of the white population in Manhattan[6].

Respondents were classified according to type of marriage on the basis of the religions in which they and their spouse were reared. A marriage was considered to be an intermarriage when the line between the three principal faiths was crossed.

There are 304 intermarried respondents and 863 intra-married. If categories are combined, Catholics have an inter-marriage rate of 21.4 and Jews a rate of 18.4 per cent. Both of these are considerably below the Protestant rate of 33.9 per cent. It may also be noted that when Christians intermarry they tend to marry other Christians rather than Jews. The incidence of Jewish-Catholic marriages is about equal to that of Jewish-Protestant unions[7].

## II. HYPOTHESES AND FINDINGS

Since we are interested in clues concerning the ways in which barriers to interfaith marriage were removed, it seems appropriate first to consider the religious background of the respondent. One of the main sources of anti-intermarriage attitudes is to be found in the teachings of the various religions. If the parents of the respondent were not religious, he is unlikely to have been effectively exposed to these teachings and, therefore, unlikely to have developed the attitudinal bar to interfaith marriage.

Similarly, one of the important external barriers is the opposition of parents. If the parents were not religious, they would be less likely to oppose the intermarriage of their child. Thus, one of the main sources of anti-intermarriage pressures would be removed. If we further assume that the children of secular parents will probably not be religious, the pressures of the church are also unlikely to be effective bars to intermarriage.

On the basis of this reasoning the first general hypothesis was formulated: *Those whose parents had a weak tie to religion are more likely to intermarry than are those whose parents had a strong tie to religion*[8]. Three specific hypotheses were formulated to test the validity of this first general hypothesis. It was predicted that a significantly higher percentage of the intermarried than of the intramarried will report that: (1) religion had no importance to their parents; (2) their parents never attended church; (3) the respondents themselves did not attend parochial school.

Without religion controlled, all of the specific hypotheses receive support. In general, then, the intermarried are more likely to have had secular parents. In the three religious groups the differences are not always large enough to be statistically significant, although, with one exception, they are in the predicted direction. But this factor explains very little of the intermarriage, for even among the intermarried very few had a secular background.

The intermarriage of some of the respondents nevertheless is explained. They were freed from the barriers to intermarriage by the fact that their parents were not religious. Since the first general hypothesis is supported, we shall remove from further consideration all respondents who reported that religion had no importance to their parents and that their parents never attended church. Thus, the hypotheses which follow refer only to persons who had at least one religious parent. This limitation is necessary because these hypotheses refer to relationships with parents, and for our concerns such relationships have different meaning depending upon whether or not the parents were religious[9].

The second and third general hypotheses refer to the respondents' early relationships with their parents. It is reasoned that respondents who say they had unsatisfactory relationships with their parents are less likely to consider parental wishes when they choose a mate; this would represent the removal of certain external pressures. Moreover, dissatisfaction in a religious home may encourage attitudes favorable to intermarriage or, at least, reduce bias against such marriages. If this is the case, there is also a removal of a barrier at the attitudinal level.

The second general hypothesis follows from this reasoning: *Those who were dissatisfied with their early relationships with their parents are more likely to intermarry than are those who were satisfied.* One specific hypothesis was formulated to test this general hypothesis. A score of early dissatisfaction with parents (D Score) was constructed. It is hypothesized that a significantly higher percentage of the intermarried will receive high scores[10].

For the sample as a whole and for Catholics the hypothesis is supported. In the Protestant and Jewish groups the differences are not large enough to be significant.

The third general hypothesis states: *Those whose early family life was strifeful are more likely to intermarry than are those who came from families in which interaction was relatively harmonious.* The primary test of this hypothesis is based upon the Intrafamilial Conflict (C) Score[11], but additional data, including material from two items used in the C Score, are also presented. It is predicted that a higher percentage of the intermarried will: (1) receive a high score on the C Score; (2) report disagreement with their parents about religion when they were young; (3) report that they often disagreed with their parents when they were teenagers; (4) report that their parents quarreled often; (5) report that there was divorce, separation, or desertion in their family of orientation.

The data show that there was more strife in the families of intermarried Catholics than in those of the intramarried Catholics. A similar relationship, though not as strong, holds for the sample as a whole. The Protestant and Jewish groups, however, do not show many differences on these variables. In fact, there is a significant difference opposing the hypothesis: families of orientation broken by divorce, separation, or desertion were reported more frequently by intramarried Jews than by intermarried Jews.

The fourth and fifth general hypotheses are concerned with the strength of family ties early in life and at the time of marriage. It is assumed that pressures from parents are ineffective when family ties are weak. In such cases parental desires would probably be of little moment when a mate choice is made, and this probably would remove an important external barrier. One of these factors may also be relevant in terms of attitudes. When early family ties are not close, inculcation of anti-intermarriage attitudes is probably less effective than in cases in which the family is tightly knit. This reasoning forms the basis of the fourth and fifth general hypotheses.

The fourth general hypothesis states: *Those who had only tenuous ties to their immediate and extended families when they were young are more likely to intermarry than are those whose early family ties were close.* Data from scores of early family integration, the I Score[12], serve to test this hypothesis. It is predicted (1) that a higher percentage of the intermarried will receive a low score on this index. It is also predicted that a *smaller* percentage of the intermarried will report that: (2) they lived with both their real parents until the age of sixteen; (3) when they were young their grandparents lived with them; and (4) they saw their relatives fairly often.

The I Scores provide strong support for the fourth general hypothesis with reference to all religious groups. Comparison of the marriage types on several of the items which make up this score also support the hypothesis. It may be noted that the presence of relatives in the home is not related to intermarriage rates unless these relatives were grandparents, in which case there is a strong relationship.

The fifth general hypothesis states: *Those who are emancipated from parental influence at time of marriage are more likely to intermarry than are those who are not.* The data contain only two indices of probable emancipation from parents at time of marriage. It is predicted that a significantly higher percentage of the intermarried (1) married for the first time at a late age[13]; and (2) have been married previously.

Both specific hypotheses seem to apply to the Catholic group.

In the other groups there are substantial differences in the predicted direction on the second hypothesis, but the data on Protestants do not show the expected relationship relating to age at marriage.

The relationship between the final general hypothesis and the basic concern of this paper is not too clear-cut. This hypothesis refers to parental problems when the respondent was young because it is thought that a generally difficult home situation may help to weaken the hold of parents upon the child. Thus, the following general hypothesis: *Those whose parents had a "difficult time" are more likely to intermarry than others.* In this case, the specific hypotheses predict that a significantly higher percentage of the intermarried than of the intramarried will report that: (1) their parents were in poor health; (2) their parents had a hard time "making ends meet"; (3) their parents had problems; and (4) their parents were the "worrying type."

This sixth general hypothesis does not receive adequate support from the data concerning any of the groups. Only one of the specific variable produced any significant differences.

The analysis of the six general hypotheses suggested a corollary to the first general hypothesis. If a secular background represents a weakening of barriers to interfaith marriage so too should a family of orientation in which the parents were intermarried[14]. It was predicted, therefore, that the children of intermarried parents have a higher intermarriage rate than those of intramarried parents. The results are consistent with the prediction, yielding a P of .06 for the sample as a whole.

The marriage groups were also compared on a series of miscellaneous variables. The first of these involves consideration of the intermarriage rates of persons occupying different birth order positions. Although the differences are not always large enough to be significant, the findings show considerable consistency. In all of the religious groups those persons who were the youngest in their families have the highest intermarriage rates, only children the next highest, and eldest children the lowest. The "other" birth position group shows no consistent ranking, but the rates of these respondents tend to approximate the group rate.

Three other variables which were considered—father's education, father's socio-economic status, and respondent's education—are all taken as indices of the respondent's socio-economic status. There are significant differences between the marriage types in the Protestant and Catholic groups on all three of these variables. While the data are not completely consistent, the trend is in a different direction in each group. Among the Catholics there is a positive relationship between status and intermarriage rates, but the Protestant group shows an inverse relationship. Data for the Jews indicate no clearcut trends.

A further variable that was studied is educational mobility. Here the only significant difference was found among the Catholics. Upwardly mobile Catholics have a higher intermarriage rate than the group rate. This difference, however, is probably more a reffection of high education than social mobility *per se.*

There appears to be no relationship between rural or urban origin and interfaith marriage rates. Only one significant difference was found—farm-reared Catholics have lower intermarriage rates than other Catholics. This is. probably due to the fact that many of these Catholics are foreign-born.

Except for the low intermarriage rates among first-generation Catholics, the comparison by generations produced no significant differences. The total group show low rates for the first and third generations and high rates for the second and fourth generations, but the differences are not very large.

Differences in nationality background of considerable size were noted. Among the Catholics, the United States group[15], Germans, Russians, and "Others" have high intermarriage rates. All other Catholic nationality groups show rates below the rate for the Catholics as a whole. The Jews are represented, in adequate numbers, by three nationality groupings: Germans, with a high rate of intermarriage, and Hungarians and "Russians, etc.," each with a low rate.

### III.  SUMMARY AND DISCUSSION

The data, as they bear upon the six general hypotheses, are summarized in Table 1.  For the sample as a whole, five of the hypotheses receive what is considered to be adequate support[16].  In general, the intermarried as compared with the intramarried are characterized by: (a) non-religious parents; (b) greater dissatisfaction with parents when young; (c) greater early family strife; (d) less early family integration; and (e) greater emancipation from parents at time of marriage. The Catholic data support these five hypotheses.

TABLE 1.  EVALUATION OF GENERAL HYPOTHESES BY
RESPONDENT'S EARLY RELIGION

| *Hypothesis* | *Catholic* | *Protestant* | *Jewish* | *Total* |
|---|---|---|---|---|
| I. Parents of Intermarried Less Tied to Religion. | * | * | — | ** |
| II. Intermarried More Likely to Report Dissatisfaction with Early Relationships with Parents. | ** | — | — | ** |
| III. Intermarried More Likely to Report Strifeful Family Interaction When Young. | ** | — | — | * |
| IV. Intermarried More Likely to Report Tenuous Ties to Family When Young. | * | * | ** | ** |
| V. Intermarried More Likely to Have Been Emancipated from Parents at Time of Marriage. | ** | — | * | * |
| VI. Intermarried More Likely to Report Parents Had a "Difficult Time." | — | — | — | — |

A dash indicates that the hypothesis is not adequately supported. An asterisk means that the hypothesis receives some support, and two asterisks signifies strong support.

In the Protestant group, though the differences are generally in the predicted direction, in many instances they are not large enough to be significant. Only two of the general hypotheses receive substantial support: intermarried Protestants had relatively weak ties to family and to religion.

Most of the general hypotheses do not seem to apply to the Jewish group. Several of the differences are not in the predicted direction, and few of the specific hypotheses are supported at the .05 level. The data suggest that intermarried Jews differ from intramarried Jews only in the strength of their family ties—while young and at the time of marriage.

One may view these findings in another way. The hypothesis concerning early family integration appears to hold for all groups. The data for two of the three religious groups and for the sample as a whole support the hypotheses concerning emancipation at time of marriage and the parents' religiosity. Only data from the Catholic and "Total" categories support the hypotheses related to dissatisfaction with parents and early family strife. The prediction that the parents of the intermarried had a "more difficult time" is not borne out.

It is clear that not all of the ways in which the barriers to interfaith marriage may be removed have been isolated. This is particularly the case with respect to the Protestant and Jewish groups, where only two of these ways have been found[17]. This shortcoming also holds for the Catholics. Some of the intermarried Catholics have none of the characteristics considered necessary for intermarriage. In all groups certain respondents intermarried despite the apparent presence of the bars to intermarriage discussed in this paper.

The failure to account for all cases of intermarriage has two main sources. First, certain relevant considerations have not been isolated; the data do not show all the ways in which the potential barriers to intermarriage may be removed. Second, since it was necessary to use fallible indices of the factors that were isolated, in some cases the "bars were down," though it was not apparent.

A deviant case analysis is indicated at this point, but no additional data are available for that purpose. It is necessary, therefore, to substitute speculation about other ways in which bars to intermarriage may be removed.

It has been assumed that devotedly religious, intramarried parents oppose the intermarriage of their children. Under certain circumstances this might not be the case. For example, some parents are committed to the idea that choice of a mate should be left entirely to the child; they probably would not apply pressure in opposition to intermarriage. In some cases, one would suppose, the acceptability of the intended spouse as a person would overcome objections on religious grounds. In addition to other possibilities, the conversion of the spouse or, among Catholics, the use of the Church's sanctioning procedure for mixed marriages might make them at least acceptable to the parents. Consideration of such possibilities suggest that the present analysis has somewhat over-emphasized the degree of parental opposition to interfaith marriage. It is believed, however, that in many of the unexplained cases opposition was present, and that we have as yet not explained how it was overcome.

It is very likely that we have isolated only a few of the ways in which a person can be sufficiently emancipated from his parents so that their objections to his intermarriage will not be effective. For one thing, the parents may have been deceased when the marriage took place; our data do not include this factor. A sociologically more significant possibility is that the respondent was strongly convinced that choice of a mate is a personal affair and possessed the psychological maturity to back up his belief.

The paragraphs above suggest some further ways in which respondents may have been freed from *external* pressures opposing intermarriage. What about internal barriers? At the level of attitudes, the following possibilities are illustrative: (1) rejection of religion by the respondent would probably be associated with a rejection of anti-intermarriage attitudes even if the latter were once accepted; (2) commitment to a democratic ideology may be stronger than anti-intermarriage attitudes; (3) unwilling but deep involvement may result in intermarriage despite unfavorable attitudes toward it[18].

The findings from the tests of the general hypotheses have proven of value in the explanation of the differences on the miscellaneous variables discussed above. To give only one example, the high intermarriage rates of college-educated Catholics as compared with Catholics with only elementary schooling could have been predicted because the former more frequently reported secular background, intermarried parents, low family integration, and previous marriage. But in some instances not all the variables provide a basis for prediction, and sometimes the direction of the prediction is not clear for certain factors point one way and others in another. In no case, however, is an incorrect prediction clearly indicated. This may be taken as further evidence that it has been possible to isolate some, but not all, of the factors relevant for understanding interfaith marriage.

Clearly, much additional work remains to be done in this area. It would be valuable if future research could be designed so that it would not have to depend upon reports of attitudes that were held in the dim past. Although such reports in the present analysis seem to be reliable, there is no way to test their validity. Longitudinal studies would be exceedingly difficult, of course, but reports of objective factors relating to childhood rather than attitudinal material probably would enhance such studies.

# References

1. Condensed version of a part of the author's unpublished doctoral thesis, "Interfaith Marriage in an Urban Area," Indiana University, 1958. I should like to express my gratitude to Leo Srole and Thomas S. Langner of the Midtown Mental Health Project for their kindness in making available to me the data upon which this study is based. The Midtown study was conducted by the Department of Psychiatry of the New York Hospital (Payne Psychiatric Clinic)-Cornell University Medical College. The study was instigated and developed by the late Thomas A. C. Rennie; it is currently directed by Alexander H. Leighton as part of the Cornell program in social psychiatry. Thanks are also due Clifford Kirkpatrick and Sheklon Stryker of Indiana University for their many helpful suggestions.

2. Among the studies in this area are Reuben R. Resnick, "Some Sociological Aspects of Intermarriages of Jews and Non-Jews," *Social Forces,* 12 (October, 1933), pp. 94-102; J. S. Slotkin, "Jewish-Gentile Intermarriage in Chicago," *American Sociological Review,* 7 (February, 1942), pp. 34-39; Gerald J. Schnepp, *Leakage from a Catholic Parish,* Washington, D.C.: Catholic University Press, 1942; John L. Thomas, "The Factor of Religion in the Selection of Marriage Mates," *American Sociological Review,* 16 (August, 1951), pp. 487-491; Claris E. Silcox and Galen M. Fisher, *Catholics, Jews, and Protestants,* New York: Harper, 1934; M. C. Elmer, *The Sociology of the Family,* Boston: Ginn, 1945, p. 195; Robert O. Blood, *Anticipating Your Marriage,* Glencoe, Ill.: Free Press, pp. 38-41. An extensive survey of the field, particularly in regard to studies of incidence, appears in Milton L. Barron, *People Who Intermarry,* Syracuse: Syracuse University Press, 1946.

3. There are no data on the attitudes of adults, but several studies report on the attitudes of students. The results of these studies vary greatly. A study of college students in Florida reports that about 90 per cent of them would not be willing to consider a marriage outside their faith. A study of a national sample of high school students, on the other hand, reports that only 20 per cent of the Protestants would not consider marrying a Catholic and 25 per cent of the Catholics would not consider a Protestant as a mate. Other data show opinion to be fairly evenly divided. See, Victor Christopherson and J. Walters, "Concerning Marriage and Family Life," *Sociology and Social Research,* 43 (September-October, 1958), pp. 16-22; Hadley Cantril and Mildred Strunk, *Public Opinion, 1935-1946,* Princeton: Princeton University Press, 1951, p. 431; Judson T. Landis, "Marriages of Mixed and Non-Mixed Religious Faith," *American Sociological Review,* 14 (June, 1949), pp. 401-407; Thomas, *op. cit.*

4. This traditional sociological conception of social sanctions has been recently discussed in Melford E. Spiro, *Children of the Kibbutz*, Cambridge: Harvard University Press, 1958, pp. 299-322.

5. Some demographic data were obtained for the non-respondents. No significant differences appeared when these materials were compared with the obtained sample and with the Midtown population.

6. Further information on the sampling procedure may be found in Thomas A. C. Rennie, Leo Srole, and Thomas S. Langner, *Midtown, Manhattan: The Mental Health Story*, 1964.

7. The range in the incidence of interfaith marriage is very great. The rates found in this study do not seem to be unusual. See Barron, *op. cit.*, pp. 166, 174, 177.

8. Though not stated specifically, the predictions made in all hypotheses are thought to hold for each religious group as well as for the sample as a whole.

9. After removal of these cases the sample numbered 1,118—284 intermarried and 834 intramarried.

10. Since the concerns of this research were not foreseen when the original study was designed, the available materials were insufficient to allow the construction of true scales. In several cases, however, a group of questions seemed to have a common referent, and these were combined into crude indices which may be called "simple scores." These scores indicate the number of apparently related questions that were answered in a given direction. The deficiencies of such scores are, of course, numerous, and they should be taken as first approximations. For the D Score a series of seven statements of criticism of parents was used. The score refers to the number of statements accepted by the respondent as descriptive of his feelings about his parents when he was young. For a list of the questions and a comparison of the marriage types on each question, see Heiss, *op. cit.*, pp. 49-50.

11. Five questions were used in the C Score. The questions dealt with in specific hypotheses (3) and (4) were included with three questions designed to determine the respondent's attitude to family strife. For example: "As a child, how much were you afraid of family quarrels?" *Ibid.*, p. 64.

12. The I Score is composed of the questions dealt with in specific hypotheses (2), (3), and (4) and a fourth question indicative of degree of attachment to the home. *Ibid.*, pp. 71-72.

13. The validity of this item as an index of the general hypothesis is open to question. People who marry late in life may do so because of an over-attachment to parents. Evidence of the latter, however, was found in very few of the cases of late marriage. In these few instances, relatively advanced age at marriage is not considered an adequate explanation of the intermarriage.

14. The reasoning here is as follows: Intermarried parents are not likely to instill in their children anti-intermarriage attitudes unless the marriage is a very unhappy one. Similarly, intermarried parents are not likely to oppose the intermarriage of their children.

15. Persons who are at least fourth-generation Americans were classified in the United States group.

16. The evaluations of the general hypotheses are informal. They are based primarily upon comparisons of the number of significant differences obtained with the number expected by chance alone.

17. A full discussion of why certain of the factors seem to represent the removal of barriers in some religious groups but not in others is not attempted here. This finding, however, does not seem too surprising. These variables, of course, may have different meanings in different religious groups. For example, the barrier to intermarriage among Jews is probably more generally cultural than merely religious. Jews from secular backgrounds may indeed be exposed to anti-intermarriage attitudes and pressures.

18. These matters are considered in more detail in Heiss, *op. cit.*, pp. 118-119.

Chapter 5

# Jews in Contemporary America
## Problems in Identification

KENNETH B. CLARK

**W**ITHIN the past twenty years a number of events in America and throughout the world have focused the attention of the American people on the important problem of racial and religious prejudices. Probably at no other time in the history of America has the problem of race relations been as crucial and as widely discussed as it has been during this period.

The barbaric excesses of the Nazis aroused the conscience of the civilized world and made clear the inhumanity inherent in the myth of racism. It was no longer possible for human beings to accept complacently the former luxury of racial and religious prejudices.

As a result of victory in World War II, America has emerged as one of the most powerful nations the world has ever known. The cold war period, however, has found the power of America in direct conflict with the power of Soviet Russia. In this competition with the Soviet ideology for the minds and loyalties of the peoples of Asia and Africa, America presents itself as the symbol of the powerful force of democracy. America must be successful in convincing these peoples that its democracy is morally superior to the totalitarian materialism which the Russian state offers. Russia's counter-propaganda against American democracy has been most effective in widely publicizing the remaining vestiges of racial injustices which exist in America. The fact that remarkable positive changes in race relations are taking place with incredible rapidity in this country has not been effectively publicized by American propaganda agencies. A single incident of American racism

111

neutralizes many incidents of racial progress in the minds of the millions of Asiatic and African people.

The humanitarian basis for the desire to eliminate the last vestiges of racial and religious prejudices in America is even more important than the international implications of American racism. Even if there were no remaining dramatic and violent manifestations of these prejudices but only day to day rejection, humiliation and dehumanization which human beings are forced to face for arbitrary reasons, these prejudices would still constitute a severe social disease. Like other diseases they require accurate diagnosis and cure, if American society is to function on its highest level of social and political effectiveness.

The tragic waste of human resources which results from institutionalized racial prejudices is expensive in human and economic terms. No nation is ever strong enough to afford the burden of excluding large segments of its population from full participation in its economic and political life. No nation can afford to subject groups of individuals to the psychological crippling and distortion which are the consequences of chronic racism. The damaging consequences of racial and religious prejudices are found not only in the personality distortions which are imposed upon the victims but also in the more insidious psychological damage which infects the members of the so-called dominant or privileged groups. This problem is the legitimate concern of social scientists and social workers of all races and religions who are interested in the problem of developing a more stable society and a morally strong America.

A survey which I prepared for the Mid-Century White House Conference on Children and Youth, the effects of racial and religious prejudices upon personality development presented for the first time a systematic and detailed analysis of this problem. Whenever human beings are relegated to an inferior status in a larger society—whenever they are rejected, humiliated and presecuted, they begin to doubt themselves and question the value and worth of the group to which they belong. Those individuals develop deep feelings of inferiority and a sense of personal humiliation. All human beings desire positive self-esteem and a sense of personal dignity. As the individual learns that he and his group are consistently being stereotyped—

characterized in negative or condescending terms—and that each person is robbed of his essential individuality and personal humanity by these blanket stereotypes, his personal conflicts and confusion deepen. Eventually, they might turn into various and complex forms of self-hatred and a desire to escape an identification with a stigmatized group.

Human beings must find ways to cope with basic personality conflicts or be disintegrated by them. Some individuals caught in this social and personal quandary react by open rebellion, hostility and aggression against their own group, the dominant group or both. Anti-social and delinquent behavior in lower class Negro children may be seen as an example of this type of reaction to racial conflicts and frustrations. Other individuals—generally of the middle and upper middle classes—are likely to seek accommodation to their group frustrations and conflicts by withdrawn and submissive behavior. Or these individuals might react with compensatory and rigid conformity to the prevailing standards of the dominant group. They clutch desperately to the middle class values and standards and express an aggressive determination to succeed in these terms. By this latter pattern of reaction, the minority group person seeks to identify himself with the dominant group—seeks to buy acceptance through the protective coloration of assimilationist devices and conformity in attitudes and standards of behavior. These individuals look upon any distinctive aspects of their primary group identification as negative and as obstacles to personal and group advancement. On the other hand, the compensatory pattern can express itself in an intense group identification which in extreme cases expresses itself in a non-rational form of minority group chauvinism. The minority person who seeks desperately to deny his heritage and his brother who wears his minority status as a severe and inflexible suit of armor have in common the fact that each is seeking in his particular way to save his personality from the full devastating impact of racial or religious rejection.

Members of minority groups are understandably hypersensitive and anxious about their relations with the larger society. They tend to see hostility and rejection even in those areas where these might not actually exist. Repeated negative experiences and the all too frequent realities keep these individuals in a state of constant conscious or unconscious alert.

While the range of individual differences among members of a rejected minority group is as wide as among other peoples, the evidence suggests that all human beings in a racist society are unnecessarily encumbered by racism or other forms of arbitrary limitation of the extent of their participation in the larger society.

The effects of prejudice and discrimination on the personality development and functioning of the so-called majority or privileged group members are somewhat more obscure. This is true in spite of the elaborate and systematic studies of the "Authoritarian Personality" which was conducted by a group of social psychologists at the University of California. These investigators found that the prejudiced individual feels threatened by groups to which he does not belong. If he cannot identify with a group, he must oppose it. This need for an outgroup to oppose and look down upon prevents identification with humanity as a whole. Authoritarian, anti-Semitic and anti-Negro personalities are ambivalent in that, on the one hand, they have a blind belief in authority, they worship power and are willing to submit uncritically to the strong and the powerful; while, on the other hand, they have a deep unconscious hostility to powerful individuals. Since they cannot deal with this hostility directly, they displace it in their open attacks on those whom they consider to be weak and socially acceptable as victims. The existing minority groups become their convenient scapegoats.

Analytic interpretations of the personality patterns of prejudiced individuals may be as misleading as they are clarifying. Many prejudiced people merely learn their prejudices from their society. There are a number of characteristics of the prejudiced individual which are clearly observable. Individuals who learn the prejudices of our society, learn at the same time to gain personal status in unrealistic and non-adaptive ways. When comparing themselves to members of a minority group, they are not required to evaluate themselves in terms of the basic standards of personal ability and achievement. The culture permits and, at times, encourages them to direct their feelings of hostility and aggression against whole groups of people, who are perceived as weaker than themselves. Often, they develop patterns of guilt feelings, rationalizations and other devices with which to protect themselves and make it unnecessary for them to recognize the essential injustice of their unrealistic fears and hatreds of minority groups. The practice of stereotyping minority groups may be seen as an example of one of these devices.

One could engage in a more detailed and intensive analysis of the personality and character of prejudiced individuals. This problem is significant not only from the theoretical but also from the practical social action perspective. This discussion, however, is concerned primarily with the general problem of the effects of various types and manifestations of group rejections upon the overall adjustment and problems of identification of those who are rejected. The limitations of time require us to concern ourselves even more specifically with the problem of the effects of the contemporary American attitudes toward Jews on the patterns of adjustment and degrees of in-group identification found among Jews.

America is a nation of many minorities. In different regions of the country and at different times in American history, different minority groups bore the immediate brunt of hostility, stigma and exclusion. Economic, educational, and political mobility have made it possible for almost all minority groups to be accepted as a part of the fabric of American life. This fact has been described as the Americanization process. As these groups sought to ascend the ladder of acceptability as Americans, it was necessary for them to accept American standards, customs, dress, often at the expense of rejecting their own previous standards and customs. Significantly, also, the Americanization process involved the acceptance of the prevailing American attitudes toward other minority groups. As each minority group competed for status and acceptance as Americans, patterns of hostile feelings toward other minority groups —who are seen as competitors—developed and were intensified. This seemed inevitable in the context of the racism of the larger society and as one of the manifestations of the hectic quest for personal and group security, and material and psychological success.

In America there was a convenient scapegoat group provided by historical circumstances. The presence of the Negro, who has been restricted to a limited caste position in American society, provided a stable base for the upward mobility climb of white immigrant groups. The more complex position of Jews in America made the competitive relationship between them and other white minority groups not quite so clear and direct. Many non-Jewish European immigrants to America might have brought with them residual anti-Semitism or might have acquired the peculiar American form of this social disease as they sought to compete for status within the American social setting.

It is clear, however, that the Negro and Jewish groups have been the chief victims of the most persistent pattern of prejudice and discrimination in America. It would be a mistake to assume from this fact that the pattern of prejudice and discrimination directed against Jews is identical to the pattern directed against Negroes. This mistake has often been made by intelligent and well meaning individuals. While there are some similarities in these two types of American prejudices, there are not only some fundamental differences in the nature of these two types of prejudices but there are also differences in the ways in which each group responds to the type of prejudice which it meets.

There are significant differences in the degree and quality of participation and achievement in the economic, political, educational and social life which are permitted Jews in America and, up to the present, denied to Negroes. Oliver C. Cox in his brilliant study of social, racial and class cleavages in America differentiates between anti-Semitism, on the one hand, as a form of social intolerance in which the dominant group seeks to impose conformity to its values and norms on the minority—and anti-Negro prejudice, on the other hand, in which the dominant group seeks to create, maintain and exploit the assumed differences between whites and Negroes.

While Cox's differentiation may not be a complete analysis of the difference between anti-Semitic and anti-Negro attiitudes in America, it offers a basis upon which differences in the adjustment pattern of Jews and Negroes may be examined. Upon the basis of this analysis, it would seem that the various attempts at assimilation and identification with the dominant society which are found among some Jews would be encouraged by the larger society. There is evidence that this is a questionable assumption. It has, however, been considered by many Jews as an effective way of reducing discrimination against them and preventing potential personality distortions. Assimilationist tendencies among Jews may, therefore, be considered as attempts at practical accommodation to the demands of a prejudiced dominant society.

In view of the fact that America places its greatest emphasis in discriminating against people in terms of the visible factor of skin color, and in view of that the fact the overwhelming number of Jews in this country are white, it should be relatively easy for those Jews, who so desire, to use the method of assimilation in order to escape the overt burdens of prejudice and discrimination. The Negro, however, cannot escape the full brunt of racial prejudice as long as he is visibly different in skin color.

It must be recognized, therefore, that the essence of the difference between the status of Jews and Negroes in American society is the greater opportunity for and attempts at assimilation among Jews in contrast to the barriers against assimilation which are erected by the dominant society in order to exclude Negroes. This does not necessarily mean that Jews in general will accept this approach to freedom from the burdens of minority status—but it does not pose many fundamental, complex and subtle problems of personal identification for individual Jews. Many Jews insist upon maintaining their group identity and sense of belongingness in spite of the pressures which the larger society imposes upon them for so doing. Understandable conflicts, ambivalence, and anxieties seem associated with whatever decision the individual or his family makes in this area.

The basic conflict which the individual Jew must resolve for himself in this relatively unstructured and ambiguous social setting is the conflict between maintaining his identity as a Jew and determining the degree and intensity of his identification or rejecting such identity through assimilation. Individuals may attempt to resolve this conflict by varying degrees and combinations of group identification and assimilation. The particular pattern of adjustment can never be a purely intellectual decision —even though it is often intellectualized and rationalized—but involves varying degrees of motivational and emotional stresses upon the individual. These pressures and strains reflect themselves in some aspects of the personality pattern of individual Jews. Among those Jews who insist upon maintaining their identity as Jews, there are the more overt burdens of defending the ego and protecting their self-esteem in the face of the threat of personal humiliation associated with anti-Semitism.

In addition to those factors already discussed, the problem of Jewish identification involves many other equally complicated considerations. Among such considerations is the question of how does one determine who is Jewish. Mark Zoborowski, of the American Jewish Committee, in his study of the factors which have been used to determine Jewish group belongingness and identification, states that some Jewish educators and scholars have attempted to solve the problem of religious, racial and national heterogeneity among Jews by developing an arbitrary definition of Jewishness in terms of the degree of identification with the Jewish tradition. This definition of Jewishness is determined primarily by the criterion of religious practices. The difficulty involved in this approach, over and above its arbitrariness, is the fact that many people who consider themselves to be Jewish do not identify themselves with the Jewish religion— as this is indicated by synagogue attendance or the observance of other Jewish ceremonies.

Some students have stated that Jewishness is essentially expressed through "a wish that Jews should continue their organized life, by participation in Jewish philanthropies, in opposition to mixed marriages, and in the conviction that they feel better when they live in Jewish neighborhoods."

It would seem on the basis of the available evidence that while the Jewish minority—those who consider themselves Jews and are recognized as such by others—is in some respects different from other Americans, it is not clear the precise way in which they differ. Historical factors play some role in establishing group identity, but this need not be a definitive one. The Jewish group in contemporary America is heterogeneous in terms

of religious orthodoxy and observance, nationality, social, economic and political status.   What gives unity and cohesion to this
otherwise diversified group of individuals are the subjective
factors of the willingness of the individuals in the group to
accept a common heritage, to express a desire for the maintenance of in-group cohesion, and to share a common future
based upon these subjective feelings of belongingness.   Thus the
identity of the Jewish group is established primarily in terms
of the powerful abstraction of the belief in the existence—and
the right to continued existence—of the Jewish group.   It is
reasonable to assume, also, that historically the intensification
of in-group identification among Jews reflected a necessary group
survival pattern in the face of repeated presecutions.   Since Jews
were being oppressed and at times destroyed as if they were a
group, it was inevitable that they react by protecting themselves
as a group.

There is a strong suggestive evidence that anti-Semitism
has shifted from the flagrant attacks of the professional fanatical
anti-Semites to the more insidious attempts at identifying Jews
with disloyalty.   The fact that this is not overtly verbalized as
such makes it no less effective.   Some Jews may seek personal
protection by imitating the super-patriots.   They might believe
that they can save themselves or protect their group by demonstrating that there are some "good" Jews.   By being as
American as the super-Americans, some Jews seek to avoid the
full brunt of anti-Semitism and incidentally prove that not all
Jews are "pro-communist."

It is significant that Jews, themselves, have been most
reluctant to express their mounting anxiety publicly.   There
must be the gnawing fear and anxiety that any public discussion
of the question of anti-Jewish aspects of super-patriotic investigations might release a devastating amount of latent anti-Jewish
feelings in the American people and contribute to the stereotype
belief that Jews are pro-communist.   The resulting evasion and
denial of the reality of this issue, therefore, reflect a serious
strategic struggle for Jews in contemporary America.   This
struggle involves problems of weighing consequences on alternatives, relative stakes and vested interests of different classes of
Jews, assimilationist-group identification conflicts, and probably

group survival itself.

With full recognition of the complexity and delicacy of the Jew's position in contemporary America, one learns from recent European history that the techniques of evasion and denial do not solve a basic social problem or enhance the chances of survival of a minority group. Realistically, the Jewish people in contemporary America face more ambiguous and subtle forms of prejudice than do the Negro people. There are also more subtleties and contradictions in their status and relations with the dominant group. Jews as a whole have a greater materialistic stake in America than do Negroes. They, therefore, have more to lose in an open and direct fight on issues of prejudices and discriminatory treatment. On the one hand, they are sensitive to the forms of prejudice to which they are subjected—they are sensitive to the fact that eminence and outstanding achievement in certain segments of American life do not guarantee them general acceptance, over-all status and privilege in the society at large; on the other hand the strong need for such acceptance demands that they repress their doubts and anxieties and function as if the negative social realities did not exist.

The problem is further complicated by the fact that within the Jewish group itself, Jews of different social and economic classes may have—and often do have—conflicting interests. These conflicts in interest may lead to clashes as to an effective approach to combating anti-Semitism. One of the incidental advantages of the caste rejection of all Negroes by American society is the fact that this has minimized serious conflicts of interests among Negroes. As a more stable upper middle class and upper class Negro group develop and are accepted and accorded special privileges by powerful whites, similar problems of conflicting interests among different classes of Negroes will necessarily develop and complicate the direct struggle of the Negro people for full democracy. As Kurt Lewin has pointed out, "The strength of the conflicting situations increases with the weakness of the boundary between the group concerned."

This basic conflict among Jews in America which appears to have increased in intensity and complexity within recent years manifests itself in many patterns of attempted adjustment and accommodations. Among the more obvious, but less socially important, manifestations of this conflict is the fact that Jewish scholars and social scientists have largely ignored the problem of the effects of anti-Semitism on the personality structure of Jews. Jewish students have studied intensively the problem of the status of the Negro in America and the reaction of Negro to racial prejudices. It is conceivable that this emphasis placed upon the Negro problem by Jewish scholars and agencies reflects their attempts to reconcile the conflict between their assimilationist tendencies—their unconscious identification with the privileged whites—and their latent anxieties about their own minority status. In studying the Negro and his problems, Jewish scholars might not only contribute to improving race relations in America but also avoid coming to grips with the more personally disturbing problems of the effect of anti-Semitism upon Jews. A concern with this problem would bring with it an awareness of the tenuousness of the Jew's position in the larger social setting.

In their struggle against these ambiguous negative forces in the society, Jews necessarily develop patterns of hostility. Sometimes this hostility is directed openly against the rejecting dominant group. This, however, brings with it the risk of retaliation and precludes the possibility of successful full or partial assimilation. At times, therefore, the hostility must be directed either toward another minority group or toward the Jewish group or both.

The channeling of the hostility of Jews toward other Jews may take the subtle forms of self-depreciation, including the acceptance and repetition of Jewish stereotypes as they apply to other obviously "Jewish" individuals or to lower class Jews. The many varieties of self-hatred among Jews must be seen as attempts to resolve the conflict between Jewish identification and assimilation—in the direction of some degree of assimilation. The most extreme illustration of the resolution of this conflict in this direction is found in the practice of name changing and the acceptance of the Christian religion. These individuals break their ties with the Jewish group and attempt to function within the larger society as a non-Jew. Ostensibly these individuals are seeking to protect themselves and their family from the continued social and personal burdens inherent in minority status. Such a decision, however, probably also involves an acceptance of the dominant group's attitudes toward Jews—the individual believes that the Jewish group is inferior and therefore seeks to disassociate himself from it.

For the Jewish individuals who have resolved the basic conflict of identification-assimilation in the direction of accepting their identification as Jews, additional problems for the personality may present themselves when these individuals are required to function in a society which is overtly or latently anti-Semitic. These personality problems require patterns of adjustment which may be viewed as essentially protective against the onslaught of actual or anticipated anti-Semitism. One of the manifestations of this tendency on the part of the individual who is willing to accept himself as a Jew in the face of possible anti-Semitism, is the increase in his sensitivity about Jewishness.

Marion Radke, in her study of children, pointed out a tendency on the part of the Jewish children to be very conscious of their Jewishness at an early age. This early awareness of Jewish identification among Jewish children may be viewed as the first sign of increased sensitivity among Jews who insist upon identifying themselves as Jews. It is self-evident that the children of more assimilationist Jewish parents may not be as conscious of their Jewishness as early as are the children of Jews who are more psychologically identified as Jews. Among Jews who completely reject their Jewishness, if they are successful in this rejection, one would expect that their children would never identify with Jews and therefore would not become sensitive about Jewishness. Indeed there is every reason to believe that among these children anti-Semitic attitudes might develop to the same degree as among children of the gentile population.

Hypersensitivity about Jewishness among Jews may take many forms including the constant concern with racial and religious problems; a seemingly compulsive need to discuss the problems and hardships of the Jewish people even in situations in which these are not relevant; and the tendency to relate almost any social problem or event to the problems of Jews. Another manifestation of protective hypersensitivity seems to be a tendency among some Jews to perpetuate the assumption of the superiority of the Jewish people and to explain the persecutions of Jews throughout history as proof of the resentment and envy which gentiles have of Jewish superiority. This form of hypersensitivity is indistinguishable from the chauvinism of the dominant group. When it is found among gentiles it tends to express itself in the form of anti-Semitism and anti-Negro attitudes. The danger of extreme chauvinistic reactions among oppressed minority groups must be recognized as one of the more insidious consequences of hostility directed against them. The problem becomes more complex by the fact that chauvinism on the part of the minority is used by the prejudiced majority group as justification for their prejudices and therefore tends to reinforce the initial hostilities. It would seem, in the light of this, that this attempt at protection on the part of a minority group, while of some short range ego value for the individual utilizing it, is in the long run self-defeating in that it is essentially an imitation of the patterns of the prejudiced individual and it feeds these prejudices. Finally, it tends to perpetuate a concept of hierarchy and the unreasonable assumption of arbitrary differential status among groups of human beings. The only difference which emerges between the chauvinism of a dominant group and that of a minority group is that chauvinism of the minority group is chauvinism without the power to oppress and to persecute. Furthermore, all forms of chauvinism are irrational and untrue and the most chauvinistic individuals usually contribute little to the alleged virtue of the group from which he is obtaining satisfaction through identification.

Another form of protective reaction to oppression which is found among some Jews is a tendency toward generalized aggressiveness which manifests itself not only in their reactions to members of the dominant group from whom they anticipate hostility but may also express itself in general interpersonal relations. Any individual who has been subjected to chronic humiliation develops a pattern of anticipating humiliation and tends to react in terms of this anticipation. The injustice of the stereotyped concept of Jewish personality being always aggressive is indicated by the fact that obviously not all Jews, nor all Negroes, nor all members of any other minority or majority group react with a single pattern of defense against hostility. While the pattern of generalized aggressiveness is found among some Jews, there is no evidence that it is a characteristic pattern among the majority of Jews. That this stereotype concept is unfounded as a group trait is indicated by the fact that it is rarely defined or specifically interpreted. Even when aggressiveness is found as a pattern among some individuals it is to be seen as a consequence of religious bigotry and hostility rather than as a cause of the prejudices.

Some Jews in their attempts at protecting themselves against the reality of anti-Jewish prejudices may react by patterns of adjustment which are overtly the opposite to aggressiveness. They may adopt a personality pattern characterized by submissiveness and in extreme cases obsequiousness in their relations with non-Jews. The basis of this personality pattern may not only be protective but may also reflect the tendency on the part of these individuals to behave in such a way as to repudiate personally the stereotype of the aggressive Jew. This pattern is similar to that found among upper middle class Negroes who impose upon themselves and their children scrupulous patterns of cleanliness and a rigid adherence to middle class sexual restraint in order to behave as far away as possible from the stereotyped picture of the Negro. The danger inherent in this form of compulsive repudiation of the stereotypes by the individual who seeks to protect himself from racial hostility is that he is likely to become ensnared, inhibited and shackled by this pattern of accommodation. His personality becomes a continuous pattern of self-denial. He denies himself the right to function as an individual with the integrity, equality and dignity which is the natural right of all individuals. His life is a constant conscious or unconscious racial or religious fight. His personality becomes merely an instrument or a weapon in this fight. The energies involved in this continuous struggle are therefore not available for more constructive social activity and personal growth. This burden is added to the usual burdens and complexities which the personality ordinarily must carry. There is a basic confusion in the self-image of the compulsive and submissive minority person whose patterns are determined primarily by his minority status. The individual is never quite sure of whether he can function as an individual or must continue to assume the role of a "good" representative of his group. This pattern may sometimes resolve itself into a caricature of a paragon rather than of a dynamic human being.

Another protective pattern which is commonly assumed to be characteristic of a larger number of Jewish people is the pursuit of intellectual and professional goals. It has been pointed out that a disproportionate number of Jewish young people compete with non-Jewish whites who seek to enter professional and academic schools. The pattern of restricting the number of Jews admitted to professional schools, graduate schools and certain high status undergraduate schools has been explained by the statement that if these quotas were not adhered to these fields would be almost completely dominated by the Jewish people. No one has offered any evidence in support of this statement nor has it been explained why this would be detrimental even if true.

One cannot overlook the possibility that the average lower middle class or middle class Jewish parent may stimulate his child to excel intellectually in order to free himself from the burdens of rejected minority status. The use of academic achievement as a method for social mobility is not restricted to Jews. In the relatively mobile middle class structure found in America this approach to the improvement of social and economic status has been used successfully by many groups and many individuals. The Irish, for the most part, seemed to have used the method of political organization for the attainment of power as their primary technique for enhancing their social and economic status. It appears that in addition to activity in various business pursuits, a frequent method used by many middle class Jews is the method of academic achievement.

The problems which now face America involve the basic fact of survival. If these problems are to be solved successfully, they require the combined efforts of all of the diverse peoples who make up the American nation. America can no longer afford the luxury of racial and religious hatred and persecution. America's minorities now have a clear and immediate responsibility of making the American concept of democracy a strong reality.  This is imperative since it appears that America cannot survive through the strength of its military weapons—these have become too strong to be used for any purpose other than extinction.  America can survive only through the strength and the validity of the democratic idea.  The guardians and the barometer of the effectiveness of this idea are America's minorities.  Each time that they validate this idea in terms of their relationship to the rest of the American people, they contribute a stronger bulwark of democracy for all.  They cannot do this if they continue to be debased, distorted and dehumanized by past injustices.  They cannot fulfill their responsibility to America if they are timid, opportunistic, and afraid and seek personal protection by identification with those who temporarily appear powerful and use their power to bludgeon others into conformity, nor can they help others approach this goal if they adhere rigidly to the protective shelter of intense in-group identifications.  They cannot fulfill this responsibility if they accept the fallacious premise that homogeneity in race, religion, and nationality background is essential to America's strength and is consistent with patriotism and democracy.

In order to make this important contribution to the future of America and to a fundamental democracy throughout the world, America's minorities and others who are clear in their perspective, must hold steadfast in their belief in the rights and the essential dignity of the individual.  They must recognize that only the individual who accepts himself with dignity and without apology has the strength and integrity to make these possible for others.  They must be ready to protect these rights wherever and whenever they are threatened.  They must understand that this fight is an endless fight—not for the rights of any single group as it competes with others in a restricted arena for petty stakes.  This is a tortuous and challenging fight for the dignity which is essential to the humanity of all human beings.  This is a prize which cannot be won by any one group of human beings.  It must be won by all mankind or lost to all.

# II.  THE JEW ON THE COUCH

# INTRODUCTION

The prevalence of mental disease among different ethnic and religious groups in the United States has, for the past five decades, been a subject of sometimes passing and, more recently, engrossing, interest to researchers. This interest extends from the individual's reaction to his religious background to the influence of that religion on his personal adjustment. When Dr. Henry R. Gold writes, "Can We Speak of Jewish Neuroses?" he is reflecting a very specific involvement. In a heterogeneous society like America, where ethnic and religious differences are important determinants of behavior, a proper concern for such relationships is recognized.

Early statistical studies by Drs. A. A. Brill, M. Karpas and G. H. Kirby revealed that the incidence of psychoses among Jews was not disproportionate from what one would expect for the total population. Their findings indicated few Jews in the organic group of mental diseases and virtually none in alcoholic psychosis. On the other hand, it was found that Jews "outnumbered enormously" other groups in the functional psychoses. Twenty years later, in 1928, J. A. Goldberg and B. Malzberg reported that in the absence of basic census data for the Jewish population, it was impossible to state with accuracy whether or not Jews have a higher rate of mental disease than non-Jews, or whether the rates are changing from year to year. However, there was fundamental agreement with the findings of the three earlier studies.

The Goldberg and Malzberg findings were derived from an analysis of data secured at Bellevue Hospital together with similar data compiled from the reports of the New York State Hospital Commission covering the years 1914 to 1926. The study dealt with the comparative distribution by sex of mental diseases among Jews and non-Jews.

More recent studies have moved away from exploring the

ethnic and religious backgrounds of mental hospital patients to the broader canvas of urban populations. A notable one, by Myers and Roberts, is a survey of all patients living in New Haven, Connecticut, who were under psychiatric care on December 1, 1950. These included patients in mental hospitals in that city, in outpatient clinics and in private treatment.

Their findings reveal significant statistical differences among Jews, Catholics, and Protestants in the distribution of total mental illness, the psychoneurotic disorders, alcohol and drug addiction, and the organic illnesses. Jews have a much higher rate of neurosis than the other two major religious groups— two and a half times above expectation. In contrast, no Jews were found among the alcoholic and drug addicts, confirming the data supplied by Kirby's study of 1908 and the subsequent reports of Malzberg in 1930 and 1940.

How is one to account for the extraordinary high incidence of neurosis among Jews? Myers and Roberts feel that this is explained by the Jews' acceptance of psychoanalytic psychiatry, and their willingness to be treated. They write, "There appears to be little conflict between the acceptance of Jewish religious doctrine and psychoanalytic theory . . . Efforts have been made to reconcile the difference between psychoanalysis and religion, as best indicated by Joshua Liebman's *Peace of Mind*. From the Jewish patients' standpoint, there is seldom any direct conflict between his religious values and the therapeutic process . . . In the case of physical illness, Jews usually try to obtain the best available care, regardless of cost or sacrifice for the family. Consequently, in the face of a mental or emotional difficulty, these families are likely to seek the most competent and advanced psychiatric treatment."

This compatibility between Judaism and psychoanalysis is shown, in repeated illustrations, in the article by Meadow and Vetter on Freudian psychotherapy and the Judaic value system. The authors cite the variety of ways by which the functions of Talmudic interpretations run parallel with psychoanalytic interpretations. This is accomplished through the social role of the rabbi and the professional role of the psychoanalyst. The correspondences between Talmudic conceptions and psychoanalytic interpretations are to be found in the areas of truth or ethical goals, in authority relationships, in family patterns, in many sexual attitudes, in rationalism, and in the significance and meaning of words and dreams. The evidence weighs heavily in favor of Jewish cultural values supporting many aspects of the psychotherapeutic process.

## Chapter 6

# Can We Speak of Jewish Neuroses?

HENRY RAPHAEL GOLD, M.D.

𝔉ROM the scientific point of view, there is little to support the idea of a qualitative difference in the mental illnesses of diverse races. There was at one time a much-heralded belief about the basic differences of the intelligence endowments (I.Q.) of various peoples, but that was found to be largely a result of inadequate or inappropriate testing. Kipling's famous saying that "Judy O'Grady and the Colonel's lady are sisters under the skin" applies also in a large measure to the realm of mental disorders.

Yet the outward manifestations of certain neuroses and psychoses and their incidence may vary in different cultures. Freud felt that a community by "mutual identification and common dangers may show symptoms of tension and symbolic mass reaction." It is not difficult to see that each culture or subculture would have its own system of anxiety-begetting symbols which would mobilize the deeper universal individual anxieties. In an article entitled "Observations on Cultural Psychiatry during a World Tour of Mental Hospitals"[1] the author reported on quantitative differences of the incidence of types of mental illness in various cultural regions. To cite one example out of many, there is a relatively large number of postpartum psychoses in India. This contrasts strikingly with a much smaller number of such puerperal psychoses in Thailand (Siam). A tentative explanation was offered that frequent marriages of early adolescents in India are much greater than in neighboring Siam even though geographic surroundings would seem to be quite similar.

As for incidence of mental illness among the Jewish people,

a line of demarcation has to be drawn between psychoses and neuroses. Analytically speaking, "normal," "neurotic," and "psychotic" form a continuum, yet one must agree with Hegel that there are critical points where quantity turns into quality. Thus ice, water and steam have the same chemical formula, $H_2O$, yet they are very different in their physical properties. A distinction must therefore be made between the deeper disorganizations of the personalities termed "psychoses" and the far milder emotional disturbances known as "neuroses." The belief that psychoses are widespread among the Jews belong to a long and dishonorable history of "name calling" in medicine. Thus for a long time neurasthenia was called by Europeans "the American disease." Much credit is due to Dr. Benjamin Malzberg for having helped to explode the myth of great frequency of psychosis among the Jewish people.

However, in the case of neurosis, the story is quite different, especially with regard to the anxiety neuroses and the psychosomatic ailments. Here the historic experience of the Jewish people tended to raise the level of incidence. The following psychodynamic factors influencing that rise are presented here in outline form:

1.   About twenty centuries of intermittent persecution and the ever-readiness to escape from it would tend to produce an infectious state of insecurity in the mass of the people, which in turn would mobilize deeper individual insecurities.

2.   Far more important from the psychological point of view is the inner escapism, the tendency leading to over-identification with the dominant invasive culture. It may express itself in hysterical denials of cultural realities, leading to distortion and minimizing of the spiritual values of one's own people. It may fan deep-seated inferiority feelings, leading to self-hatred and self-demolition.

3.   The Jewish people suffered frequently from unexpressed resentment. Psychosomatic medicine often tries to find the answer to the question, "What becomes of the undelivered punch?" The accumulated hurts of the mistreated minority, which is helpless and stifled in voicing protest, may augment the individual's proneness to psychosomatic disorders.

4.   The over-anxiety for quick cultural adaptation also

exacted a heavy toll. It brought about over-competitiveness among the Jewish people themselves. The inferiority-ridden become further troubled by a success compulsion and a driving need of proving themselves worthy of acceptance. The universal sibling rivalries among children received an extra push from these cultural whips. Great confusion in the minds of the adolescents was also wrought by the enthronement of accidentally successful "marginal Jews" into the role of cultural standard-bearers. In looking for an ideal leader with whom to identify themselves, they were hard-pressed to tell the difference between a "big" Jew and a "great" Jew.

5. The Jewish people also had to endure an unusual degree of isolation, insularity, and consequent loneliness. Here again individual temperaments make a great difference. In the long night of the Arctic, people regress to different levels and get on each other's nerves. It surely produced in the Jewish people as a whole a tendency to over-dependence on the family for comfort and solace. Along with the inspiring virtues of Jewish family life there also developed the less welcome phenomenon of "familianism."

6. Another powerful source of discontent among Jewish people has been a feeling of vocational condemnation. The right occupational choice, which is so important for the maintenance of emotional balance in human beings, has often been thwarted by external social pressures. Centuries of deprivation of ownership and cultivation of land tended to produce a specific Jewish category of the *Luftmensch* (which of course is not to be translated as a "fresh air fiend" but rather as "a person compelled to live by his wits"). The wall-encompassed ghettos of the modern tenement districts tended to limit vocational choice and groove them into ruts. Superimposed on these tendencies there weighed heavily the incubus of political disability and social discrimination in employment.

### I. HOW NORMALCY HAS BEEN PRESERVED

The list of psychodynamic factors presented is by no means exhausted, but enough has been said to raise a challenging question in the mind of the reader as to the "miraculous" preservation of normalcy in most Jewish people. Instead of being surprised at the tendency to a rising incidence of anxiety neuroses and cognate emotional disturbances, one might wonder even more why the neuroses have not assumed epidemic proportions among the Jews. Why have they not spread like the proverbial prairie fire? How do we explain the survival of the firm Jewish family structure and community organization despite all the undermining wrought by those ominous factors of psycho-social erosion?

The answer might be found in three constructive forces which have more than counterbalanced the onslaught of the erosion trends described. These are: (1) a great love of learning; (2) a rare sense of humor; and (3) an inspiring and preoccupying faith.

The love of learning not only saved the Jew from depressive apathy and boredom but sent him on a perpetual voyage of discovery. The primal sense of wonder has been sublimated into scholarly channels. Learning attained to the inspiration of worship. The Talmud was regarded as an ocean, and its great savants were the intrepid admirals.

The Jew was saved from mere bookishness and ivory-tower isolation by his sense of humor evolved originally perhaps as an extra means of defense. It also afforded him a special safeguard of the reality sense by developing greater objectivity. The humor of the Jew was colorful and variegated. It was at times kindly and funloving, at other times stealthy and surprising, and again at times sardonic and annihilating.

Finally, when we speak of the third great saving grace of the Jewish people, the inspiration of the faith, one is not only speaking of the grandeur of theologic credo and the poetry and discipline of ritual. One would like to emphasize the oft-overlooked value of the Jewish ritual program as a great source of occupational therapy. The observing Jew rarely suffered from spiritual unemployment. It was always *Shabbos* or *erev Shabbos*, or it was *Yom Tom* or *erev Yom Tov*. This busy procession of perennial spiritual experiences gave life both added form and content. Its ultimate boon was the growth of waiting power, something which the psychiatrist is working so hard to develop in his impatient patients.

# References

1.  Gold, Henry R., in *American Journal of Psychiatry*, 1951, 108(6).

## Chapter 7

# Mental Health of American Jewish Urbanites:
# A Review of Literature and Predictions

IRWIN D. RINDER

**P**SYCHIATRY has been broadening its interest from an initial exclusive pre-occupation with the disturbed person outward toward the larger social context which produced him. At the same time, the social or behavioral sciences have been focusing down from that larger socio-cultural whole which is their usual level of investigation, to scrutinize the concrete case of the disturbed individual. To the psychiatrist, the type and severity of symptoms presented by the individual seen in the clinic are given psychodynamic depth and breadth when these are related to the family-community-subculture which were the environment of their growth. To the behavioral scientist, the patient population, when classified by categories and computed into rates, becomes an index—symptom, if you like—of social-cultural integration/disintegration.

Research on mental illness can inform us, at least in part, as to how severe are the stresses of life and the resources for meeting these possessed by a given group. A social psychiatric review and analysis of the mental health status of modern American Jews would be one way of learning how the Jewish American fares both in his society and within his body as he leads the unique existence of this social identity at this time and place.

Our analysis will be developed on three distinct levels: (1) *epidemiology*—the incidence or prevalence of mental illness, the distribution of cases among different diagnostic categories, systematic differences or trends taking place in these statistics over time; (2) *socio-cultural* analysis—how and where is this group distributed in society, strengths and vulnerabilities of such distribution, and the functional-dysfunctional potential of particular cultural beliefs, practices, skills, values, aspirations, fears; and (3) *clinical*—results of studies showing individual variations within a group, and differences between groups as measured by scores obtained with standardized instruments applied to individual subjects.

*Epidemiology:* We are fortunate to have at our disposal a piece of work which has systematically assembled most available epidemiological studies[1]. These are brought together under such headings as "Age, Sex and Mental Disorder," "Mental Disorder and Marital Status," "Mental Disorder Among Urban and Rural Populations," "Mental Disorders and Socio-Economic Status," "Mental Disorders Among Negroes," and "Mental Disorders Among Jews." Under this last rubric we find several pages of tables comparing overall rates (hospital populations) of Jews with those of non-Jews; and then comparing rates of Jews and non-Jews on specific disorders, e.g., schizophrenia, paranoia, etc.*

The statistics begin as follows: (rates are crude rates per 100,000 population)

Rates: Jews 44.7, non-Jews 69.2 (1920). Jews 42.3, non-Jews 75.1 (1927). New York civil state hospitals.

Rates: Jews 42.7, non-Jews 81.1—Admissions from New York city to public and private mental hospitals, 1925.

Rates: Jews 31.2, non-Jews 73.6—Massachusetts state mental hospitals, 1926-28.

Rates: Jews 29.6, non-Jews 64.2—Illinois state mental hospitals, 1926-28.

---

* Researchers working with epidemiological rates derived from hospital statistics are alerted to certain possible sources of consistent error or bias. They know that availability of or accessibility to hospital beds may swell some rates, while lack of opportunity diminishes such rates. They also know that religious scruples, cultural biases, ignorance, etc., may dispose some people toward and others away from utilizing psychiatric care facilities. Socio-economic class becomes a factor to be reckoned with if only public hospital populations are studied, and the more affluent members of society uniformly send their mentally ill to private sanataria and clinics. Better research design has developed from knowledge of these potential distortions.

The above and other similar figures consistently show **Jews** averaging about one-half the mental illness of non-Jews **as** revealed by the official statistics of hospital admissions. When we turn to the inspection of rates by diagnostic categories, another interesting fact shows. For the psychoses, which are organized under eight headings and reported through twenty sets of rates, Jews have again consistently lower rates with only one reversal of this pattern and this probably non-significant, since it is a matter of only 0.2. However, when we inspect the category, Psychoneuroses, we find Jews reported as exceeding non-Jews in two of the three sets of comparisons.

The material compiled in the manner just described was almost all gathered in the years 1926-28, with only one **report** from 1938 (N.Y., Bellevue Hospital) and another from 1941 (Boston, Selective Service screening). Are the findings of Jewish under-representation in the psychotic population and over-representation in the neurotic population, even if valid for these earlier decades, still applicable or are they now outmoded?

To determine this, we turn to a recent study of considerable theoretical and methodological sophistication—the study of New Haven by the sociologists Hollingshead and Myers, and the psychiatrists Redlich and the late Bertram Roberts.\* This industrial city of about a quarter of a million population is approximately 60% Roman Catholic, 30% Protestant, and 10% Jewish. The major finding of this project is that social class is the most important correlate of rate and kind of treated mental disorder in New Haven. In all three religious groups, it was found that the upper classes comprise a somewhat smaller proportion of the psychiatric population than they do of the total

---

\* The New Haven study has the deficiency of many epidemiological studies—of taking treated cases rather than true prevalency rates from the community at large. This latter is a desideratum which involves enormous additional difficulties at the present stage of psychiatric diagnostics. However, this research did not restrict itself to hospital figures but sought all treated cases in public or private institutions and clinics, in the care of private practitioners, and those New Havenites who were receiving psychiatric attention in cities and states away from home. In short, their census of treated cases was most thorough and as nearly complete as possible.

community, whereas the lowest class in each case contributes about twice its proportionate share[2].

A somewhat different organization of the New Haven data reveals a number of additional points about both the mental health pattern and social class distribution of Jews[3]. In their social distribution, Jews show greater concentration in the upper and middle classes than is true of other groups. Where they are found toward the lower end of the social spectrum, particularly in classes III (lower middle), and IV (working class), the Jews show a disproportionate rate of psychoneuroses. In these classes Catholics and Protestants are somewhat under-represented and New Haven's Jews have 2-3 times their proportionate share of psychoneurotics.

That Jews as a group show a lower rate of psychosis in New Haven is attributable to their skewedness in social class distribution. If lower class members are more prone to psychosis (or at least contribute more cases proportionately than other social classes), then Jews, having a smaller proportion of their members in this category will accordingly show less psychosis. However, the findings just reviewed suggest that Jews have not only that greater amount of psychoneurosis we might anticipate because of their higher social class achievement, but an additional amount beyond that.

Having discovered such differences in rates, Myers and Roberts, aware that they are utilizing a psychiatric population of "cases in treatment" rather than a true prevalency sample, review the non-illness related biases which might account for these findings. They recognize that important consequences flow from the fact that groups differ in their awareness of psychiatric symptoms, and in their acceptance of psychiatric treatment. Because of Jewish cultural values encouraging intellectuality, Jews are more knowledgeable about mental illness and psychotherapy; more desirous of the best and most modern in medical treatment; more accustomed to the talking out of troubles with a warmly sympathetic listener; hence more likely to become a voluntary treatment statistic in the area of the psychoneuroses. They then conclude, "In summary, we must state that although these explanations for the high rates of psychoneuroses among Jews in terms of the acceptance of modern psychiatry seem plausible, we cannot be certain that the actual occurence of the illness is not substantially higher in this group."

Before leaving the epidemiological approach for another, it is both interesting and highly suggestive, with regard to theory, to examine some differences in the distribution of behavioral disorders among the major ethnic groups of New Haven[4]. The Jewish over-representation of psychoneuroses and under-representation of psychoses (schizophrenia) is especially pronounced when compared to the Irish, Italian and Negro distributions. Noteworthy is the Jewish and Italian absence from the alcohol and drug addiction populations. The Jewish incidence of senile disorders and other organic disorders also appears significantly lower than the rate of others. This raises the hypothesis that the closing off of other behavioral alternatives through the religious-cultural channelling of learned behavior may contribute substantially to the high Jewish rate of psychoneuroses. The traditional Jewish emphasis upon sobriety, the control of hostile aggressive impulses, etc., means that these avenues of behavioral expression, hence symptom formations, are less readily available to one socialized in this cultural community. A detailed investigation of precisely this point, i.e., how different sub-cultures apparently contribute to different patterning of symptoms even within the same disease entity, has been described by M. K. Opler in his work on Italian and Irish American schizophrenics[5].

*Social-Cultural Analysis:* Reference to group differences disposing Jews toward greater awareness and acceptance of psychiatry on the one hand and on the other their location in different illness categories, leads us to the systematic consideration of how different groups create different views of the world for their members. The material we shall summarize here is drawn from an intensive study of the families of Irish, Jewish and Yankee (old family, New England, white, Protestant, Anglo-Saxon) patients in the Boston Psychopathic Hospital[6]. The authors say, "Our goal was to understand the relationship between family social structure and the production of individual stress."

Sons in Irish and Italian families receive less overt affection than those in Jewish and Yankee families. The mother is the dominant figure in the home in all of these except the Italian where the mother's role is buffer between son and patriarchal father. The other maternal roles differ; the Irish mother showing preference toward son but also serving as strict disciplinarian; the Jewish mother being overtly affectionate but over-protective; and the Yankee mother being a moral model. Different types and degrees of stress are felt by sons as a consequence of the varying constellations of relationships just described.

The same is true of role performances expected of these sons. Irish and Italian boys are expected to make financial contributions to the family, while Jewish and Yankee boys are not. For the former, the amount brought in is important; for the latter however, what is important is not how much but the good purposes to which they put their money, e.g., for future advancement. Similarly, Jewish and Yankee boys are expected to be high achievers in school and in their career. In this they have the support of their families, along with the additional expectations that they will develop the social graces and good social contacts. Irish and Italian families expect their sons to obtain regular jobs with regular incomes, and discourage their jeopardizing this immediate good for the sake of uncertain future betterment through education. The families' social expectations are limited to the desire that their sons "stay out of trouble." For the Jewish and Yankee son, stress may result from inadequately meeting the familially acquired aspiration for social mobility. Conversely, the Irish and Italian sons experience stress precisely when they have somehow incubated ambitions which require their continuing education beyond what the family considers the reasonable amount.

Barrabee and Von Mering observe, "Membership in the ethnic group can be a source of stress. This is most frequent with Jewish boys who see their Jewishness as impeding the fulfilment of social or occupational ambitions. Much depends upon the environmental conditions. Indeed, a Jewish boy can select avenues to success that by-pass his Jewishness. However, since this implies a restriction in his freedom of choice, he often cannot shake off a diffuse sense of deprivation about his ethnic membership."

*Clinical Evidence:* Moving from the social and cultural characteristics of the group to the psychological parameters of the individual brings us to the *clinical* level of analysis. How does the individual Jew compare with the non-Jew on selected variables? We are fortunate here, as we were on the epidemiological level, in having convenient access to a study which has systematized and compared the sprinkling of studies which appeared over the years[7]. Sanua gave both an objective and a projective test of personality to a sample of first, second and third generation American Jewish high school students and to a group of non-Jewish students. His findings cast light on both inter-generational differences and Jewish-non-Jewish differences in certain areas of personality.

On the objective test (the Thurstone Neurotic Inventory) he found progressively better scores moving from first to third generation. Scores from the projective test (The Rorschach Multiple Choice Test), however, arranged themselves as a trend the reverse of the first, i.e., the first or immigrant generation had better scores than the second generation which in turn scored better than the third. To reconcile this apparent contradiction in findings, Sanua, following G. Allport's distinction, submits the plausible interpretation that the tests get at different levels or aspects of personality: the Thurstone Test probably measures "social adjustment" (through such questions as "Do you get stage fright?") while the Rorschach measures "inner adjustment." Over successive generations, it would appear, continuous acculturation and assimilation results in the learning of patterns of overt behavior which helps the individual appear adjusted. However, this process is co-related with an increasingly internal malaise, detected by the Rorschach for which there are no conventionally learned "right answers".

By arranging previous studies of Jewish-non-Jewish personality differences in a chronological table, Sanua ingeniously explains previous inconsistencies by showing that from the earliest of such studies in 1929 until 1938, Jewish students obtained scores indicative of poorer adjustment, but that from 1938 until the present students have consistently scored as better adjusted than their Gentile matches. Since these studies employed objective or self-descriptive instruments, both the initially poorer and subsequently better scores may be largely attributable to the progressive acculturation, hence increasing test sophistication of the Jewish subjects.

When Sanua controlled his subjects for generation, he found that the results just described were not attributable to differences in socio-economic status or differences in creed (orthodoxy-reform). The generational variable, acculturation, seems to be the most significant factor accounting for the observed differences in personality. When third generation Jewish boys are compared with non-Jews who are long-established Protestants, i.e., their equals in acculturation, the latter obtain better adjustment scores on the Rorschach than do the Jewish subjects. In fact, every Jewish generation group scored lower in adjustment than the matched Gentile group on obtained Rorschach scores.

The inner maladjustment of American Jews, on the basis of this evidence, seems to be greater than that of their Gentile peers; and the greater the Americanization, the greater the maladjustment. This resembles the "heightened self-consciousness" sociologists have described as characterizing the marginal man. Although some fraction of this malaise may become clinical and warrant later treatment, other portions may become chanellized as social, economic, artistic, aesthetic, etc., drives. The crucial question is whether this maladjustment will overwhelm the individual and become pathology, or whether he can harness and utilize it as his private version of a divine discontent.

Summarizing the diverse materials and different levels of analysis adduced, we offer the following by way of integrative interpretation. Jews probably have a higher rate of neurosis and a lower rate of psychosis than non-Jews in the United States at mid-century. The social and cultural liabilities of members of this group include minority status in a predominantly Christian society; the high level of aspiration which is instilled in youth; the concomitantly high expectations entertained by parents concerning their children; the disabilities of minority status which require one to be an over-achiever in order to gain recognition; the ambiguities of identity for the acculturated who never quite leave an older status nor completely realize a new one (the Jew as marginal man) ; and ironically, success in social mobility, which in itself may be socio-psychologically dysfunctional (numerous studies find the upwardly mobile have higher incidences of neuroses, hostile rejection of parents and family, etc., than the non-mobile).

The social and cultural assets (elements either allaying or supportive against stress) in American Jewish life are also numerous.   There is the degree of security children derive from demonstrated parental affection; there is the patient support of dependency during the long years of education; there is the providing of the young with both a "tradition of success" *and* the skills and values to implement the motivation to succeed. Both of these are very important since in the absence of the latter, failure and frustration are inevitable and the motivation for success becomes a mockery and force for disorganization. Traditional emphasis upon verbal and intellectual skills not only contributes to success and mobility, but is likely related to enhanced skill in self-knowledge, insight, the sustaining of multiple and diversified roles, and the like.

A very modest projection of discernible trends from the past and present into the future would anticipate that if Jewish family patterns persist, if economic stability permits continuing mobility, and if the emphasis upon education and attainment continue to both buttress and challenge the psyche of American Jews, the over-all rate of impairment will continue lower than average.   As upward mobility, acculturation and secularization proceed, the distribution favoring neurosis and away from psychosis could become even more pronounced.   However, should catastrophes such as economic collapse or an ascendance of racial-religious hostility come to the United States the patterns could be reversed, i.e., neurosis would then decrease as psychosis increased.

Regardless of which trend prevails, as the contents of traditional patternings of behavior become attenuated through acculturation, those disorders which do occur will be more "normalized" (statistically speaking) in their distribution. *Shikker iz a Goy* ("drunken is a Gentile") will no longer point to significant group differences and it and similar expressions will

have then become survivals of the folkish social psychiatry of a
bygone day.

# References

1. Rose, Arnold M., & Holger, R.S. Summary of studies on the incidence of mental disorders. In, Rose, A.M. (ed.), *Mental Health and Mental Disorder*. NY: Norton, 1955, Ch. 5.
2. Hollingshead, August B., & Redlich, Fredrick C. *Social Class and Mental Illness. A Community Study*. NY: Wiley, 1958, p. 204 (Table 12).
3. Myers, Jerome K., & Roberts, Bertram H. Some relationships between religion, ethnic origin and mental illness. In Sklare, Marshall (Ed.), *The Jews: Social Patterns of an American Group*. Glencoe, Ill.: Free Press, 1958, p. 554 (Table 2).
4. *Ibid.*, (Table 3).
5. Opler, M.K. Cultural differences in mental disorders: An Italian and Irish contrast in the schizophrencies—U.S.A. In, Opler, M.K. (ed.), *Culture and Mental Health*. NY: Macmillan, 1959, Ch. 19.
6. Barrabee, Paul, & Mering, Otto von. Ethnic variations in mental stress in families with psychotic children. In, Rose, A.M. (ed.), *Mental Health and Mental Disorder*. NY: Norton, 1955, Ch. 9. Any effort to generalize from this study must be cautioned by the following considerations: (a) these families did have psychotic children, although their ethnic characteristics may be generally representative of other families of the same ethnic identity; and (b) the Jewish families tended to be lower class, as opposed to the more typical middle class status of American Jewish families.
7. Sanua, Victor D. Differences in personality adjustment among different generations of American Jews and non-Jews. In Opler, M.K. (ed.), *Culture and Mental Health*. NY: Macmillan, 1959, Ch. 20.

Chapter 8

# Freudian Theory and the Judaic Value System

ARNOLD MEADOW AND HAROLD J. VETTER

### I. THE PROBLEM

**A** THEORY of psychotherapy does not arise in a social vacuum. While the creative seed is produced by the individual scientist, the nutrient soil is provided by the sum total of the scientific, artistic, religious and philosophical ideas of the scientist's era—in short, by his cultural value system.

It is the purpose of this paper to present an analysis of the influence of the Judaic cultural value system on the Freudian theory of psychotherapy. While a few studies of this general type have appeared sporadically in the literature[1, 2, 3, 4], a systematic evaluation of their scientific relevance has not, to our knowledge, been essayed. Hence, it is necessary to devote some preliminary discussion to a few important methodological considerations.

### II. THEORETICAL RATIONALE

The demonstration of the influence of a cultural value system upon a particular theory does not *per se* impugn the validity of that theory. The truth of a scientific theory is determined by its correspondence with those aspects of reality which it is designed to describe. What is, then, the scientific function of a cultural analysis?

One possible function is that of bringing out the more implicit meanings embodied in various theories of psychotherapy by placing them within a broader historical context. For example, in accordance with American culture, one of the goals of the non-directive school of psychotherapy is to help the patient to establish a feeling of equality with the therapist.    Similarly, in accordance with German culture, a major goal of the Rankian school of psychotherapy is to aid the patient in achieving a feeling of superiority over the therapist.    By relating each school of psychotherapy to its respective culture value system, its underlying philosophy is made more explicit.

There is additional significance in the fact that, although the validity of a scientific theory is not tested by its relationship to cultural values, these values may exclude from scientific scrutiny many aspects of the phenomenon under investigation which are of crucial importance.    It is a well-known fact, for instance, that the scientific investigation of man's sexual life was impeded for many years by cultural biases.

Cultural traditions may, of course, promote as well as inhibit the study of otherwise neglected areas of research.    The emphasis placed upon achievement in American culture has undoubtedly greatly influenced the further exploration of mastery needs in the human personality[5].

Psychotherapy is an applied social science; as such, it contains both *existential* propositions, i.e., statements whose truth or falsity may be determined by empirical or experimental methods, and *normative* propositions, i.e., statements which express sentiments about how individuals should or should not behave.    There is often a tendency for an existential statement embodied in a theory of psychotherapy to be accepted as empirically valid on the basis of its correspondence with a normative cultural statement rather than on the basis of the evidence provided by objective data.    Typical is Otto Rank's existential classification of types of man, with the artist representing the highest development of the species, the "neurotic" an intermediate type of development and the "average" man as the lowest on the totem pole.    A conceptualization of this kind may be accepted less critically in Germany than in America for two reasons.    The first is that there is in general a hierarchy in the German culture.    The second is that there is also in that culture a greater social value placed upon the artist.    If by some happenstance a similar idea should occur to an American psychotherapist, surely he would arrange for a team conference or find some other means of effectively repressing the idea.

The most important function which a cultural value analysis can serve is to distinguish between the elements of a theory which are applicable to human beings throughout the world, and those which are only applicable to individuals within a particular culture. Psychotherapists have exhibited a tendency to claim universal validity for theories which have been derived from, and are particularly pertinent to, one culture, or at best only a few cultures. Historically, this type of criticism has been levelled most frequently against Freud. A series of studies now in progress indicates similar biases in the works of most contemporary psychotherapists.

The preceding considerations, with respect to the value of a cultural analysis of a theory of psychotherapy, are applicable to all analyses of this type. Particularly relevant to the present investigation of the relationship between Freudian theory and the Judaic value system is the principle that, in the case of a modern theory of psychotherapy, the cultural determinants often emerge from more than one culture.

Previous studies of the relationship of the Freudian theory of psychotherapy to culture have emphasized, more or less exclusively, the Western European German culture of the 19th century[6, 7]. A more intensive study of the problem suggests that Freudian theory has also been heavily influenced by Jewish culture. Systematic analysis of this influence is presented in the present study.

The data on Jewish culture were obtained by an extensive examination of studies extant in this area. The specific references are listed in the bibliography. We have been particularly indebted to the empirical study of Zborowski[8] which was based on extensive interview material[9]. His description of Jewish culture is restricted to those themes which were universally present in orthodox Jewish culture from the time of the burning of the Temple in A.D. 70 to the present. The data on psychoanalytic theory were derived from an extensive study of the works of Freud.

## III.  FREUD'S IDENTIFICATION WITH JUDAISM

Freud was an assimilated Jew who did not accept many of the theological tenets of orthodox Judaism.  Repudiation of a theological doctrine, however, does not exclude either the implicit or explicit acceptance of the many ways of living associated with it.  Freud's own statements indicate an acute awareness on his part of his Jewish identity.  In his autobiography, Freud[10] wrote:  "My parents were Jews, and I have remained a Jew myself."  Freud's biographer, Puner[11], reports another statement ascribed to Freud:  "It was perhaps no mere chance," Freud was reputed to have said, "that the first psychoanalyst was a Jew."

The study of Freud's quiet struggle with anti-Semitism in his early years as a student has been related by many of Freud's contemporaries, but no one has written of these bitter experiences with more compelling restraint than Freud himself:

> "Above all, I found that I was expected to feel myself inferior and an alien, because I was a Jew.  I refused absolutely to do the first of these things.  I have never been able to see why I should feel ashamed of my descent or, as people were beginning to say, of my race.  I put up, without much regret, with my non-acceptance into the community; for it seemed to me that, in spite of this exclusion, an active fellow-worker could not fail to find some nook or cranny in the framework of humanity."

At the same time, Freud seems to have never fully appreciated the extent to which Jewish culture influenced the structure of his theories.  An elucidation of this influence is undertaken in the subsequent section of the present study.

## IV.  WORLDLINESS AND ATTITUDES TOWARDS
### BODILY PLEASURES

In contrast with Christianity, as well as with many other religions, Judaism maintains that the ultimate goal of human happiness is attainable in the real world.  The positive values of Judaism embrace everything which fosters human happiness in the mundane world; conversely, that which creates unhappiness in the real world is regarded as evil. There is no injunction to sacrifice the human pleasures of this world for the sake of attaining a future state of felicity in the next. The Jewish Messiah is expected to make his visitation in the real world; and the improvement of the lot of mankind is to take place on earth—not in heaven. This emphasis on worldliness establishes the first, and perhaps most basic, parallel between Judaic tradition and Freudian theory.

The play *Professor Bernhardi*, written by the great Viennese contemporary of Freud, Arthur Schnitzler, provides an excellent illustration of the contrast between Jewish worldliness and the other-worldly orientation of the Catholic Viennese society in which Freud lived.

The play tells the story of a young Catholic girl who is a patient in the hospital headed by a Jewish physician of Vienna, Professor Bernhardi. The girl is dying, but in the euphoric mood which sometimes occurs in the mortally ill she thinks that she is perfectly well, and wishes to get up and meet her lover, whom she believes has come to take her home. In the meantime, her Catholic nurse summons a priest to administer the rites of extreme unction. When the priest arrives, Professor Bernhardi refuses to grant him permission to attend the girl, for he is unwilling to destroy her happiness in the few remaining moments of her life. The priest argues with Professor Bernhardi that the last rites will affect the girl's eternal happiness. Dénouement occurs when the Catholic nurse, without Bernhardi's knowledge, informs the girl of the priest's arrival and purpose. With a last cry of horror—"Must I die?"—the girl perishes.

The worldliness of the Judaic ethic finds its counterpart in the worldly ethic of Freudian psychoanalysis. It is the aim of psychoanalysts to enhance the means for attaining happiness in this world. Happiness in any other world is interpreted as an illusion.

Closely related to the worldliness of the Judaic religion is its anti-ascetic character. Consider the following quotation from the writings of the great medieval Jewish philosopher, Maimonides:

"The perfect Torah . . . recommends . . . man's following the path of moderation in accordance with the dictates of Nature; eating, drinking, enjoying legitimate sexual intercourse, all in moderation, and living among people in honesty and uprightness, but not dwelling in the wilderness or in the mountains or clothing himself in hair garments or otherwise afflicting the body."

Similar sentiments are expressed in many of the Talmudic writings. Typical are the Talmudic proverbs "He who has no wife lives without good or help or job or blessing or atonement" and "Where there is no meal there is no law".

The Freudian point of view, which maintains that heterosexual satisfaction is a necessary prerequisite to human happiness, is clearly compatible with this ethic. Equally clear is its incompatibility with the more ascetic philosophy of many of the branches of Christianity. Hence, it is not all surprising that the preponderantly Christian society in which Freud lived should have regarded his doctrine with hostility, derision and not a little horror.

### V.  JUDAIC RATIONALISM AND PSYCHOANALYSIS

While psychoanalytic theory upholds the view that a heterosexual relationship constitutes a *sine qua non* for happiness, it is not assumed that happiness is attained by uncontrolled or promiscuous sexuality. Rather, it is the aim of psychoanalysis to aid the individual in establishing rational control over his sexual drives. In its affirmation of rational control as an ethical ideal, psychoanalytic theory is consistent with a major emphasis in the Jewish cultural pattern.

Zborowski[8] has described the focal significance attributed to rationality within Jewish culture. For many centuries, the learned man occupied a position of pre-eminence in the Jewish community.

One aspect of Judaic learning was traditional, in the sense that it involved the reinterpretation of ancient customs and laws. But even within the context of traditional orthodox Judaism, reason was assigned an important role. The learned man was expected to interpret anew the ancient laws in the light of human reason. In extreme cases, it was considered permissible to modify, through human reason, the strict letter of the law to conform with the spirit of the law. In every case, the spirit of the law was concerned with the preservation of human life and the enhancement of human welfare[12]. The truth, in itself, was regarded as healing, and there was a profound belief that divine will is actuated by intelligence and reasonableness.

A comparison with other modern theories of psychotherapy may serve to clarify the resemblance of Freud's rationalistic ethical philosophy to that of Jewish culture. Influenced by German transcendental philosophy and religion, the Swiss Protestant Jung formulates as the goal of therapy the facilitation of the communication of the patient's conscious mind with his racial unconscious. The American Protestant Carl Rogers, under the influence of the *laissez-faire* philosophy of American democracy, considers the development of the individual's full personality resources the goal of therapy.

It is true that Alfred Adler, who was also a Jew, formulated therapeutic goals which differed from those of Freud. Adler sought to develop the social feeling *(Gemeinschaftsgefühl)* of his patients. But each modern psychotherapist has been influenced by a variety of cultural traditions. Adler's early medical practice brought him into contact with the poorer sections of Vienna. Also, it is known that he was strongly influenced by the humanitarian and Social Democratic movements of his period.

Moreover, "social feeling" as a therapeutic goal is quite compatible with the basic Jewish ethic which has always been socially oriented. Under the influence of the Social Democratic ideology, Adler has merely abstracted for special emphasis one aspect of the basic ethic of humanitarian Judaism.

An even more specific relationship between Jewish culture and psychoanalytic theory may be found in a comparison of Talmudic and psychoanalytic attitudes towards the meaning of words. To the Talmudic scholar, a word is presumed to possess a special hidden significance in addition to its simple and direct meaning. Zborowski[8] cites an instance of the Talmudic treatment of the cryptic significance of words:

> "For example, the Bible says: 'When Sarah died her age was a hundred and twenty and seven years'. According to Rashi, the question must be asked: 'Why the repetition of the 'and'?" The answer is that not only at the time of her death was she a hundred twenty-seven years old, but also at this age she looked as beautiful and young as at

the age of twenty; and that at the age of twenty, she looked as beautiful and young as at the age of seven years."

It is interesting to note, in the example quoted above, an additional similarity between psychoanalytic and Talmudic rationalism.   The Talmudic interpretation of the biblical sentence implied that a small detail of speech may be endowed with considerable significance.   As Zborowski points out, concern with the hidden meaning of words is rationalized by the old Talmudic maxim: "Divrai Hashem lo kedivrai Hawdawn"—"The words of the Lord are not like the words of a person."   In practice, the dictum implies that the slightest detail in the Bible —the repetition of a phrase, a particular choice of words—is fraught with hidden significance.

The Freudian doctrine is remarkably similar.   The determinism of word choice ascribed to God by the Talmudic scholar is attributed by the psychoanalyst to the Unconscious.   For the psychoanalyst, ordinarily unnoticed aspects of speech, a slip of the tongue, the odd use of a phrase—all are pregnant with meaning.   The emphasis placed upon the importance of the omission of a word in the example cited from the Talmud is paralleled in psychoanalytic theory.   Freud devotes an entire chapter to a discussion of a similar phenomenon in *The Psychopathology of Everyday Life*.

### VI.   PSYCHOANALYTIC AND TALMUDIC INTERPRETATION

The use of interpretation provides a further parallel between psychoanalysis and Talmudism.   An example of the nature of Talmudic interpretation is supplied by Zborowski:

"Talmudic interpretation is often called *pilpul*, meaning pepper, and it is as sharp, as spicy, as stimulating as its name implies.   It means comparison of different interpretations, analysis of all possible and impossible aspects of the given problem, and—through an ingenious intellectual combination—the final solution of an almost insoluble problem.   Penetration, scholarship, imagination, memory, logic, wit, subtlety—all are called into play for solving a Talmudic question.   The ideal solution is the *khidush*, a new original synthesis, one that has never before been offered."

Similarly, new and ingenious interpretations are utilized in psychoanalysis as a means for solving the problems of life. Although the content of these interpretations differs greatly, of course, from that of Talmudic interpretations, the method is quite similar.

Corresponding to the parallel functions of interpretations in the Talmudic and psychoanalytic traditions are the social roles of the rabbi and psychoanalyst.   According to Zborowski[8]:

> "The learned man becomes the arbiter in the problem of adjustment which history has made a constant and crucial problem for the Jews.   It is his task to facilitate adjustment for an appropriate interpretation of eternal law in the light of ephemeral conditions.   If the interpretation is clever enough, it can eliminate hardship for all concerned."

In like manner, the psychoanalyst seeks to carry out the role of arbiter in the problem of personal adjustment by rendering appropriate interpretations to or through the patient.

An inspection of the differences among Jewish, Protestant and Catholic conceptions of the relationship of the laity to the clergy may yield additional evidence of the similarity between the rabbi and the psychoanalyst.   Perhaps the best elucidation of these differences can be provided through an analysis of the contrasting Protestant, Catholic and Jewish conceptions of the methods for determining Truth.

The Protestant believes that each individual must find Truth within himself.   The minister or the Protestant church can serve, at best, merely as a catalyst to aid the individual in finding the Truth within himself.   Deviations from the path of righteousness can only be corrected by the individual's searching further for the Truth in his own soul.   We have suggested in a previous study that the theory of psychotherapy which corresponds most closely with this formulation is that of the American non-directive school.

For the Catholic, the Church is the repository of eternal Truth.   Truth is communicated authoritatively to the laity by the Catholic priest who, by virtue of his indoctrination and ordination within the Church, is presumed to know the Truth.   The individual is restored to grace by the confessional and penance when he has strayed from the paths of righteousness.   Hypnotic catharsis and suggestion comprise the psychotherapeutic methods which are, perhaps, the most closely related to Catholic doctrine.

According to the Talmudic conception, Truth is attained most readily by the person who, with the benefit of superior learning, can produce the most rational interpretations of reality. This attitude towards Truth is described more precisely by Zborowski[8]:

> "There is too a reluctance to indulge in easy generalizations. Each problem must be analysed in its own terms and the solution is not necessarily simple. By using innumerable 'ifs,' all possible pros and cons are weighed before a solution is accepted. A statement must not be taken at face value; it may hold a second secret meaning. Accordingly every item has to be discussed and interpreted. In politics or in business, the meeting of co-workers or of partners show considerable resemblance to the discussion of a problem in the *yeshiva*. . . . Truth as perceived by the imperfect human mind is never single and simple; it is never the Truth, and is always subject to interpretation. The only absolute Truth is the Torah, the Divine Law—and that is inaccessible in full to even the most powerful human intellect. This relativistic and provisional approach fosters a tendency to analyse, to probe, to discuss every problem, every phenomenon; to see it not in one aspect but in multiple aspects. There is not a classic opposition between 'yes' and 'no'."

Freud's attitude towards Truth is similar in many ways. Like the Talmudic rabbi, he assumes that a particular phenomenon can be explained by more than a single interpretation. Similarly, the best possible interpretations are often obtained by intricate, sometimes devious, rational interpretation[13].

Riesman[3] has suggested that Freud's preference for the more complex and devious interpretation of a problem can be ascribed to the influence on Freud of the Puritanical "work morality of 19th-century Europe." The "work morality" to which Riesman alludes, however, is more characteristically Northern German with its stress upon the Protestant concept of *Beruf* or "calling." An aspect of personality as basic as attitude towards work is most probably engendered by the mores of the people with whom an individual lives. The population of Vienna at the turn of the century was 87 per cent Catholic, 9 per cent Jewish and only 4 per cent Protestant. On the basis of population statistics alone, it seems improbable that Freud's attitude

towards work is typical of 19th-century European Protestantism.
Moreover, there are specific indications that Freud's attitude towards work is indebted to Jewish culture. The character of Freud's work was essentially intellectual. And it is precisely this type of work which is accorded the highest status in the Jewish hierarchy of values. In Freud's crowded parental home, a room was set aside for him where he was encouraged to study throughout the day and night without interference from either his parents or siblings. Similarly, his wife arranged the household activities to permit him time to pursue his studies with greater concentration. A similar devotion to intellecual work is found among Jews in the garden cities of Babylon or in the crowded ghettos of Eastern Europe, in 19th-century Germany or in 20th-century Brooklyn. The content of the studies which the Jew pursued in these widely separated places and eras differed greatly, of course, but the high social and moral status of the intellectual work remained the same. The Jews always remained "The People of the Book."

## VII. PSYCHOANALYTIC AND JUDAIC CONCEPTS OF AUTHORITY[14]

Authority is involved to a certain extent in interpretation. With their profound distrust of all authority figures, American critics have often assumed that the Freudian analyst was an autocratic type of individual. Refutation for this assumption may be found in a comparison of the kinds of authority represented by the analyst and by the Prussian *pater familias*. The most significant factors which differentiate between the autocratic authoritarianism of the Prussian father and the more benevolent authoritarianism of the analyst reside perhaps in the criteria by which authority is given legitimate institutional sanction in either case.

The authority of the Prussian *pater familias* is absolute and traditional, deriving its justification from ascribed social role. By contrast, the authority of the Freudian psychoanalyst is more relativistic and rational. Cultural approval in this case is based on intellectual achievement.

It is expected that the opinions of the Prussian father will be respected and his commands obeyed, merely because they are those of a father.   Acceptance for the psychoanalyst's opinions, on the other hand, rests on the basis of their superior rationality.

In the Prussian family, a child's resistance to the opinions of his father is met with disapproval.   A patient's resistance to the analyst is accepted in the analytic situation, and is regarded as inevitable.   Resistance to the Prussian father is diminished by the child's feelings of fear and *Ehrfurcht* (i.e., respect) ; or if necessary, father's punishment, usually mediated by the mother.   In psychoanalysis, the patient's resistance is diminished by the analyst's rational interpretation, or by the patient's positive transference towards the analyst.   In the one case, resistance is overcome by respect and fear; in the other case, by reason and love.

These differences clearly suggest that there exists a marked contrast between the Prussian and the orthodox psychoanalytic authority relationships.   If a comparison is made between the analytic and traditional Judaic authority relationships, a much greater degree of similarity is discovered.   While some elements of arbitrariness are present in the Jewish authority relationship, it closely resembles the Freudian analytic relationship between therapist and patient in terms of emphasis upon rationality as the criterion for its legitimation[15].   According to Zborowski[8] :

"A boy who is studying the Talmud is considered almost an adult, especially when he shows special aptitudes.   He may participate in all the debates of adults and his opinion carries equal weight.   A bearded Jew will not be ashamed to bring some difficult Talmudic question to a young boy of 13 or 14 who is known as a future Talmud *Khokhom.* A boy who is known as a genius, *iluy,* will be shown the same deference as a learned adult.   I have witnessed, for example, the respect shown to a child of 8, son of a famous Ukrainian rabbi, because the little boy knew by heart all the prayers and the two complete books of the Pentateuch, together with the accompanying commentary of Raschi. . . . The persistence and antiquity of this pattern is suggested by an episode in the life of Christ, described by the Evangelist Luke (Luke 2:41-52).   The 12-year-old Jesus was found in the Temple discussing the Law and confounding bearded scholars by his scholarly and penetrating questions.   The situation—depicted in well-known paintings by Dürer, Van Dyck, Botticelli and others—bears striking similarity to the treatment and behavior of a young *iluy* in the Eastern European *Shtetl.*"

The Freudian analyst's relationship to his patient is similar; the patient is expected to accept the analyst's interpretation only if it is rationally correct[16]. If the analyst's interpretation is inaccurate, and the patient offers a correct interpretation, Freud believed that the analyst should accept the patient's version. This emphasis upon rationality as a basis for authority in the therapist-patient relationship more closely parallels the authority relationship found in Jewish culture than that which characterizes German culture.

## VIII. THE YIDDISHE MAMA

Of crucial significance to Freudian theory is the series of postulates which centers in the concept of the Oedipus complex. Many writers have displayed an interest in the germinal origins of the Oedipus concept in Freud's thought. Fromm[7] and Erikson[6], for instance, have attempted to relate the Freudian formulation of the Oedipus myth to the patriarchal structure of the German family. While this interpretation undoubtedly possesses some validity, an examination of Jewish family structure indicates that the influence of Jewish culture may be a determining factor of equal importance.

This point might be illustrated by a few excerpts from a recent account of Jewish family life by Landes and Zborowski[17]:

"Indeed, rivalry between father and son is a familiar theme expressed in large and small ways, privately and publicly. It is a commonplace that a man prefers his son-in-law to his son, and a proverb says: 'Every son-in-law has in him something of the father-in-law.' . . . A young son often sleeps with his mother. . . . Although displays of endearment between husband and wife are frowned upon, a great deal of demonstrativeness is allowed between mother and son which mothers encourage. It seems to us that though the marital obligations are fulfilled in the husband, the romance exists with the son. . . . The wife treats the husband as a child. . . . Indeed, we believe that the Jewish man hopes to find a mother again in his wife and is happiest in his marriage when this search has been fulfilled. 'Every daughter-in-law has something of her mother-in-law,[18].'"

An amusing illustration of the Jewish mother-son relationship is given in a current American story:

"A Jewish daughter had arrived home after a date. 'Well,' the mother asked, 'do you like him?' 'I like him, Ma,' the daughter replied, 'but he's kinda neurotic. He's got an Oedipus complex.' 'Oedipus, Schmedipus,' cried the impatient parent, 'as long as he loves his mama, he'll make a good husband!' "

The study of Landes and Zborowski certainly indicates that the Oedipus complex is present in Jewish culture—perhaps in peculiarly intense form. Although it may be contended that the son's affection towards the mother and ambivalence towards the father are also present in German patriarchal culture, there are at least two aspects of Freud's formulation of the Oedipus complex which suggest a specific Jewish cultural influence.

First, there is Freud's contention that the mother-son relationship is more intense and complete than the relationship between husband and wife. "The only thing that bring a mother undiluted satisfaction," wrote Freud[19], "is her relationship to a son; it is quite the most complete relationship between human beings, and the one that is the most free from ambivalence." This conception of the nature of the mother-son relationship parallels quite closely the description by Landes and Zborowski of the Jewish cultural pattern.

Second, there is Freud's[19] assertion that the ideal marital relationship is one in which the wife treats her husband as a child. ". . . A marriage is not firmly assured," writes Freud, "until the woman has succeeded in making her husband into her child and in acting the part of a mother to him." Again we find the unmistakable similarity between the ideal ascribed by Landes and Zborowski to Jewish culture and Freud's concept of the ideal marriage.

With respect to these two points, then, Freudian theory shows a greater resemblance to the typical family pattern of Jewish culture than to German culture.

### CONCLUSION

An attempt has been made to demonstrate a relationship between the Freudian theory of psychotherapy and the Judaic cultural value pattern. A broad similarity in orientation has been suggested with respect to ethical goals, authority relationships, family patterns and attitudes towards art. The parallel formulations on so many points suggest the conclusion that the Jewish cultural value pattern has had at least some influence on the monumental body of theory which marked the contribution of Sigmund Freud to modern thought.

## References

1. Horney, Karen. *New Ways in Psychoanalysis.* NY: Norton, 1939.
2. Riesman, David. Themes of work and play in the structure of Freud's thought. *Psychiatry,* 1950, 13:1-16.
3. Riesman, David. Authority and liberty in the structure of Freud's though. *Psychiatry,* 1950, 13:167-187.
4. Ruesch, J., & Bateson, G. *Communication: The Social Matrix of Psychiatry.* NY: Norton, 1951.
5. McClelland, David C., Atkinsin, John W., Clark, Russell A., & Lowell, Edgar L. *The Achievement Motive.* NY: Appleton-Century-Crofts, 1953.
6. Erikson, Erik H. Ego-development and historical change. In Eissler, R. S., (ed.), *Psychoanalytic Study of the Child.* Vol. 2. NY: International Universities Press, 1946, pp. 359-396.
7. Fromm, Erich. *Escape from Freedom.* NY: Farrar & Rinehart, 1941.
8. Zborowski, M. The place of book learning in traditional Jewish culture. *Harvard Educational Review,* 1949, 19:87-109.
9. Although Zborowski's study is focused specifically on the culture of the Eastern Jewish *shtetl,* many of the cultural themes which he describes form a part of the universal Jewish tradition.
10. Freud, Sigmund. *Autobiography.* NY: Norton, 1935.
11. Puner, Helen. *Freud: His Life and His Mind.* NY: Howell, Soskin, 1947.
12. This type of rationalistic ethic is, of course, not peculiar to Judaism; it was also characteristic of Hellenic culture. Erich Fromm has recently given to it the designation "humanistic."
13. There are differences, of course, as well as similarities between Freudian and Talmudic methodologies. Of these differences, one of the most important is Freud's preference for the method of empirical observation. This preference might be regarded as the natural result of Freud's training in a Western scientific tradition. But even within this tradition, there are marked differences in methodological emphasis which depend, at least in part, on more general cultural factors. Freud's predilection towards an empirical methodology could be considered in terms of its contrast with the experimental methods of other psychologists of his era. Freud never employed the experimental method in his psychological work. Even to the present, many of his followers (e.g., Anna Freud) take a dim view of the fruitfulness of experimental methods in the study of mental processes. Freud's empirical methodology has been explained in relation to his training in clinical methods. While this influence may have been of some importance, it fails to explain why other medically trained psychologists of his period (e.g., Jung) made some use of experimental methods. A more adequate explanation which, to our knowledge, has never been

offered, is that Freud's methodological training was acquired in Vienna, a center of South German culture. Boring, in his *History of Experimental Psychology*, suggests that there was a scientific relationship between the geographical and cultural distribution of empirical and experimental psychology in nineteenth-century Europe. He states:

> "It is interesting to study Austro-German psychology with one's eyes on the map. The tendency has been for experimental psychology to thrive better in the north and for act psychology (which utilized the empirical method) to flourish in the south, although, of course, act and experiment are not necessarily incompatible. For instance, one can arbitrarily draw a line from Metz to Warsaw, leaving Vienna, Graz, Prague, Munich and Würzburg to the south, and Leipzig, Göttingen, Berlin, Frankfurt and Marburg to the north. If one tried to draw a picture of the psychology of each of these artificial groups, one would draw very different pictures, although one would by no means have created a clear dichotomy. . . . In Austria and Southern Germany, the influence of the Catholic Church is great. The psychology of Aristotle adapted to the modern world by Brentano is the appropriate psychology for this region."

Added plausibility for the contention that Freud's preference for an empirical methodology was affected by the cultural influence of southern areas is lent consideration of Freud's training. While a medical student at the University of Vienna, Freud took several elective course in philosophy under Brentano, one of the contemporary great leaders of empirical psychology. Still further support for our hypothesis is given by an examination of Brentano's five basic methodological principles. According to these principles, as expounded by H. O. Eaton in *The Austrian Philosophy of Values*, valid psychological knowledge is obtained from the following sources:

1.  The memory of what an experience was like after the experience itself is past.
2.  The observation of other persons, of their acts and words, at the time the experience occurred, and comparison of these observations with our own acts and their correlative precepts.
3.  Observations of the activities of mental beings of a "lower order"—either infants or animals.
4.  The study of mental diseases.
5.  The study of the psychological, as distinct from the physiological, level of discourse.

Each of these methodological principles was adapted by Freud.

14.  The statements describing German character are based on a summary of studies in this area by Otto Klineberg in "Tensions affect-

ing international studies," *Social Science Research Bulletin*, 1950, No. 2.

15. The deviant Jewish Chassidic movement differed radically from the orthodox Jewish tradition in its attitude towards authority. The Chassidic Jew accepts the statements of his rabbi mainly on the basis of the rabbi's status.

16. In the course of analysis a patient may not accept a correct interpretation consciously. Freud, however, believes that the patient will indicate unconscious acceptance by other behavioral criteria.

17. Landes, Ruth, & Zborowski, M. Hypotheses concerning the Eastern European Jewish family. *Psychiatry*, 1950, 13:447-464.

18. While the authors make specific reference to the Eastern European family, they state that many of their points have equal applicability to the Jewish family throughout the world. Readers familiar with Jewish family life in America will recognize immediately the pertinence of this description to the American Jewish family.

19. Freud, Sigmund. *New Introductory Lectures on Psychoanalysis.* NY: Norton, 1933.

Chapter 9

# The Socio-Cultural Aspects of Schizophrenia: A Comparison of Protestant and Jewish Schizophrenics

## I. INTRODUCTION

𝕿HE purpose of this paper is to present a critical discussion of some of the studies on parent-children relationship in schizophrenia, as well as preliminary findings on characteristics of the home environment of schizophrenic males from two religious groups—Jewish and Protestant, and from two social classes—low and high socio-economic status. The general hypothesis is that early unfavorable home environment affects the psychological adjustment of the individual in an adverse way. One of the basic problems in etiological studies is to relate the kind of home environment to the specific illness or deviance.

One of the recurring findings is that schizophrenic patients had an unwholesome relationship with their mothers. Some mothers were found to be overprotective, rejecting, domineering and aggressive. Fromm-Reichmann[1] coined the descriptive phrase "schizophrenogenic mother." This label has rarely been applied to the father, who was usually reported as a weak and submissive individual. The inconclusiveness of the studies reported in the literature, some of which will be described here, could be attributed to the fact that in most instances the socio-cultural characteristics of the samples under study were neglected variables.

A study by Frazee[2] revealed that the fathers, in her sample of 22 schizophrenic patients, did not have the characteristics described above, namely, weak and submissive. This is what she wrote about them: "Many of the fathers were severely cruel and rejecting. This finding is interesting since it failed to support expectations of the passive, ineffectual father generally assumed in the literature." While there seems to be a contradiction between her study and the earlier efforts, it is believed that one of the reasons for such differences is the fact that most of Frazee's patients came from lower-class families, while the samples in earlier studies included an over-representation of patients belonging to the middle and upper classes.

Another study which throws doubt on the generalization of the "schizophrenogenic mother" was conducted by Hotchkiss *et al.*[3] at the Massachusetts Mental Health Center. Of the 22 mothers who were observed during their regular visits to their schizophrenic sons in the wards only three had the characteristics of the "schizophrenogenic mother." The authors suggested that the characterization by Fromm-Reichmann of the dominant mother, rather than representing a composite picture of the mother of a schizophrenic patient, probably was derived from the conspicuous behavior of a few.

## II.  SOME PROBLEMS OF METHODOLOGY

Various methods have been used to study the home background of the schizophrenic. Most of the earlier studies relied exclusively on hospital records for the source of data. Since information in such files was not collected for research purposes investigators were likely to find an uneven quality in their coverage. The tendency therefore was to select such cases which had sufficient data.

Another set of studies, to be described, pertains to data which have been collected directly from patients or close relatives for the purpose of research. As in the previous instance, however, there was still a selective factor. Only those patients who had mothers who fulfilled certain criteria (such as adequate intelligence, education, residence close to the hospital, etc.) were included. While some investigators limited their contacts to one or two interviews, others obtained their data in the course of protracted therapy with the patients and the parents.

A criticism specific to this type of research is that samples are frequently composed of middle and upper-class patients and lack control groups. Also the number of patients who can be seen by a single therapist is limited mostly to upper-class patients which would tend to slant the data. We would, therefore, obtain only a picture of parent-child relationship in higher social strata.

Investigators in another group of studies had to rely primarily upon data obtained from psychological tests such as the Thematic Apperception Test, California F-Scale, Shoben Attitude Survey Scale, etc. Controls were included in practically all instances. One serious problem, however, is to find an adequate control group. The appropriateness of comparing hospital volunteers with mothers of schizophrenics would raise some questions.

The majority of the studies concentrated on mothers, rather than fathers, of schizophrenics for the simple reason that the mothers were more accessible. This neglect would tend to minimize the father's role in the development of the illness. Only one study, conducted by Lidz *et al.*[4], has appeared in the literature in which the fathers of adult schizophrenics received exclusive attention.

### III. REVIEW OF THE LITERATURE

We shall first refer to three studies whose findings will be contrasted, and later mention a few of the more recent studies and developments.

Gerard and Siegel[5] found that in 64 (91%) of the 70 schizophrenic males they had studied there was exclusive attachment to the mother. In 40 (57%) of the cases the schizophrenic child was considered to be the favorite of the mother. There was extreme overprotectiveness, babying and spoiling.

Tiedze[6], on the basis of interviews with 25 mothers of male and female schizophrenic patients, found that 10 mothers overtly rejected their children, while 15 were more subtle in their rejection.

Thomas[7] limited her study to the mother-daughter relationship of 18 schizophrenics. The mothers could not tolerate any verbal expression of hostility. They were excessively restrictive and punitive after the patients had reached puberty.

While all of the above three studies tried to describe the

type of relationship which existed between the mothers and their schizophrenic children their findings have little in common. There was almost no rejection by parents in the first study; the rejection was mostly covert in the second study; and there was quite open hostility in the third investigation. A closer look at the samples may give a clue to such contradictory findings.

In the Gerard and Siegel study, informants were mostly Jewish and Italians (70%) of lower and lower-middle class. Tiedze's mothers were drawn mostly from Protestant families (64%) in the professional and business class. Thomas' group was made up exclusively of Negro families. It is felt that the data reported by the authors had been colored by a preponderance of specific ethnic and religious groups in the samples. For example, it would be expected that in Jewish and Italian families there would be more babying of children in the lower-classes whereas such practices may not be considered proper in Protestant families of higher classes. Patterns of parent-child relationship in these three groups could have been influenced by the norms of the class and culture to which they belong and this was superimposed on the pathological relationship.

A pioneering work in the study of schizophrenia, across subcultural groups, was conducted in the United States by Opler and Singer[8] with Italian and Irish Catholic schizophrenic veterans. The purpose of the investigators was to present findings on cultural differentiation with respect to both content and etiology of schizophrenic disorder.

Only two of the 10 hypotheses formulated by Opler and Singer will be mentioned here. The first hypothesis was that in the Irish family, the mother instills primary anxiety and the general fear of female figures, while in the Italian families the primary hostility would be particularly felt towards the more dominant father or older sibling. The second hypothesis was that the Irish, lacking firm male identification and experiencing sexual repressions which are fostered by the culture with its high celibacy rates and protracted engagements, would develop in extreme cases latent homosexuality. With the Italians, since there is acceptance of overt expression of sexuality and because of the negative identification caused by hatred against any symbolization of an adult male role, extreme cases would show overt homosexuality. The Irish would be compliant to authority and show no evidence of acting out behavior contrary to the Italian. These hypotheses were confirmed by the data.

The investigation conducted by Lidz *et al.*[4, 9, 10] at the Yale Psychiatric Institute is one of the most extensive studies on families with schizophrenic members. The investigators selected 16 families for intensive interviews during the course of several years and wrote approximately 20 papers. The investigators focused their interest not so much on the mothers, as in previous studies, but on the interaction within the family. The following summarizes their general findings:

> "As the family is the primary teacher of social interaction and emotional reactivity it appears essential to scrutinize it exhaustively. There is considerable evidence that the schizophrenic's family can foster paralogic ideation, untenable emotional needs and frequently offers contradictory models for identification which cannot be integrated" (10, p.241).

All patients seen at the Yale Psychiatric Institute came from upper or upper-middle class families with the exception of two or three families of the lower-middle class. There was some selection in favor of intact homes and ability to support a son or daughter in a private hospital for prolonged periods. With such a selected group of 16 families, with no normal controls, generalizations should be limited in scope.

A recent study on family background of the mentally-ill, including schizophrenics, is the well-known investigation conducted by Myers and Roberts[11] in New Haven. The major purpose of the study was to find out whether social and psychodynamic factors in the development of psychiatric illness were related to a patient's position in the social class structure of American society. The investigators reported that the following conditions were found to occur more frequently in families of Class V than Class III schizophrenics: general disorganization of the home; lack of parental affection, guidance and control; isolation of the father from the family; heavy responsibility of the mother and the responsibility given to siblings in the child-rearing process; harsh but inconsistent punishment.

It should be pointed out, however, that the Class III patients were not comparable to Class V patients. Class III included 73 per cent of patients of North European origin, while Class V included 70 per cent of patients originating from the southern part of Italy. The mother's heavy responsibility and the responsibility imposed on siblings in the child-rearing process may only reflect the cultural mores of the nationality of the families involved in the lower-class. Opler and Singer[8] pointed out that the cultural value system of the Italian sets greater store on paternal and older sibling dominance. The question which might be raised here is whether the findings would be similar if all of Class V patients were white Protestants.

During the past few years a fresh approach has been developing within the general framework of psychotherapy which consists in the study of interaction between patients and parents on a sustained basis. In one instance Bowen[12] studied parents who were living at the hospital with their sick children and who were placed under constant observation. While previous studies have been interested in isolating past factors which could be related to schizophrenia, these investigations were concerned with the existing interactions with the family and particularly with the type of communication among family members. As a result of these investigations such labels as "pseudomutuality,"[13] "symbiotic relationship,"[14] "double-bind,"[15] "three-party interaction,"[16] "overadequate-inadequate reciprocal functioning,"[12] "complementary functioning"[17] have been used in describing intra-family relationships.

This approach, however, considers the family group outside the context of its culture and its community and is limited to cases where both parents are living. None of these studies has presented adequate material on the socio-cultural background of these families. It can be safely assumed, however, that these subjects consisted primarily of middle- and upper-class individuals. Probably because of the special selection of these patients and parents we obtain a general picture of very strong mothers and very weak and ineffectual fathers.

These inquiries do not clarify whether the existence of such distorted family relationships could be considered etiological of schizophrenia. Furthermore, there is little or no discussion of the possible presence of similar distortions in other deviant families since no controls, normal or abnormal, have ever been used. To explain schizophrenia on the basis of distorted communication would make it difficult to explain the occurence of schizophrenia in individuals where, for example, "double-bind" or "symbiotic relationships" do not exist.

This heavy emphasis on the study of patients and parents accessible to psychiatric research centers results in little information on the schizophrenic of Class V—the lowest-income class in which, according to Hollingshead and Redlich[18] 41 per cent of the children under 17 years of age live in homes which have been disrupted by death, desertion, separation or divorce and in which the incidence of schizophrenics is eight times higher than in Class I and Class II combined.

### IV. STUDIES CONDUCTED IN EUROPE

Two investigations conducted in Europe will be mentioned. Delay *et al.*[19] wrote a survey of the literature which included many of the investigations conducted in the United States. One of the first studies undertaken by a European psychiatrist (relating schizophrenia to early home environment) was conducted by a Hungarian psychoanalyst, Hadju-Gimes[20]. This paper, according to Reichard and Tillman[21], represents a landmark since it is the first publication on parent-child relationship representing the patient's point of view. Hadju-Gimes described four female schizophrenic patients whom she psychoanalyzed. She found that the mothers of these patients were cold, rigorous, etc., while the fathers were soft and passive. Furthermore, she found that in all cases the patients had suffered during infancy a period of starvation either because of an insufficient lactation or on account of the mother's cruelty. She hypothesized that neurotics may have parents with similar characteristics as parents of schizophrenics but what may cause schizophrenia is the starvation experience. Since her generalization is based on four cases, further investigation of the pathogenic influences of this triad of conditions (a sadistic mother, a weak father and starvation in infancy) seems necessary.

Alanen Yrjo[22] interviewed mothers, fathers and siblings of schizophrenic males and females who lived in Helsinki as well as in rural areas. He found that the majority of mothers were "stiff and bitter." Very few showed real naturalness and warmth. The majority were inclined to anxiety and uncertainty and had obsessive features. In spite of their marked disturbance most of them had a domineering and aggressive pattern of behavior. He divided his sample into those who had good prognosis and those who had poor prognosis. He found that the mothers of the more disturbed group were more severely affected.

## V. PROCEDURE

In view of the contradictory findings, we conducted the present pilot study to determine whether religion and social class variables, which were neglected in previous studies, could make for different patterns of family relationship in schizophrenic patients, whether differences could be found in the types of social disorganization and whether the role of father and mother and the incidence of mental illness among other members of the family would differentiate the two groups. For this purpose we selected schizophrenic patients—Jewish and Protestant, belonging to two different social classes—lower and middle or upper class.

The following criteria were used in selecting the sample. All patients were between the ages of 18 and 55; older schizophrenics were excluded since it could be expected that they would lack adequate information on parent-child relationships. Some records contained copious information when reports from social workers, family agencies, schools and public welfare agencies were included. Some cases had information on the mother and not on the father and vice-versa, but they were still included in the study. All patients were native-born Americans. The parents of the Jewish schizophrenics were, with very few exceptions, all born abroad, most of them in Russia and Poland. Only "old Americans" were included in the Protestant sample. When the record showed that the parents had some affinity towards the old country the case was not included. Classification according to social class was based on the parents' socioeconomic status. The lower-class group included those parents

who depended on labor—skilled and unskilled—for their livelihood. The middle and upper-classes included white collar
workers, professionals and businessmen. Since all case histories
had sufficient data on education and vocation it was possible to
obtain adequate social class data.

Following several revisions, a special form was devised and
adopted to obtain uniform data from the records. Approximately 150 case records of male schizophrenics, who were
patients or who had recently been discharged from five mental
hospitals in the Boston area, were carefully examined and the
required information was transcribed. All consecutive admissions who fulfilled the criteria were selected for our study. All
references in the records pertaining to the parents' characteristics and to their interaction with their sick sons were recorded.

The categories of parent-child relationship and family disorganization were based on an evaluation of the problems as
presented in the records. Eleven major categories were used in
the sorting of the problems: (1) insanity of the parents—if
either parent was or had been in a mental institution; (2)
extreme irritability, with many inflicting physical punishment on
their sons; (3) alcoholism; (4) dullness; (5) rejection or unfavorable treatment; (6) death; (7) dominance; (8) overprotec-
tion; (9) passivity; (10) normal relationship; and (11) unknown.
Cases lacking information or adequate information for evaluating
a predominant trait were included in the unknown category.

## VI. FINDINGS

The most striking finding is the difference of pathology
existing in parents of schizophrenic patients of Jewish and
Protestant lower-class. Almost half of the Protestant fathers
were or had been insane, alcoholics, or had manifested extreme
irritability, and most of them used excessive physical punishment. The general pattern of a passive and submissive father,
reported in the literature, was missing from our sample, which
confirms Frazee's[2] findings in her Chicago study. Relationship
with the Protestant mothers of the lower socio-economic class
was not ideal since 39 per cent of them were found to be over-
protective and 16 per cent were found to be dominant. However,
the over-protectiveness in many instances might have been

intensified by the father's neglectful or tyrannical attitude towards their sons. This is in agreement with Lane and Singer's study[23] where they found, using a type of Thematic Apperception Test especially devised for this study, that the lower-class schizophrenic sees his mother as overprotective, and contrary to expectations, instead of expressing hostility he would idealize her.

While pathology seems to be more frequent in the Protestant father than in the Protestant mother of lower-class, the trend is reversed with Jewish families of lower-class. Half of the Jewish mothers were categorized as insane, extremely irritable and dull (18%, 15% and 18% respectively). The category of dullness would require some interpretation because of the high frequency found in this group but not in the others. It would be difficult to evaluate the extent to which there was real feeblemindedness among the Jewish mothers, or just an inability to communicate with the psychiatrists who would tend to interpret this deficiency as lack of intelligence. Other dominant traits found in Jewish mothers were overprotectiveness (20%) and dominance (15%). With the Jewish fathers there was no definite pattern, except that in 25 per cent of the cases no pathological trait could be found in the descriptions and we have included these cases under "normal relationship." Little or no data was available on 15 per cent of the Jewish fathers belonging to the lower-class. It seems that if the "schizophrenogenic" label were to be used it could more appropriately be applied to the father in Protestant families and to the mother in Jewish families.

In the middle and upper-classes half of the Jewish mothers were categorized as overprotective. The Jewish father, in two-thirds of the cases of middle and upper-classes, was either rejecting (33%) or dominant (27%) which represents a decided contrast to the Jewish father of schizophrenics belonging to the lower-class. The middle and upper-class Protestant mothers tended to be dominant (26%), extremely irritable (20%), and rejecting (16%). The most frequent trait of the Protestant father of middle and upper-class was rejection or unfavorable treatment of the son (22%). In 20 per cent of the cases Protestant fathers appeared to have had normal relationship with their sons.

## VII.  DISCUSSION

We can see from the sample examined above that there are major differences in the familial characteristics of schizophrenic patients belonging to two religious groups and two different social classes.  It is not surprising that very little agreement could be found among earlier studies which had undertaken the analysis of the most dominant pattern of parent-child relationship in families with schizophrenic patients.  There is no question that the patterns found in these earlier studies were influenced by the norms of the social class and culture to which these patients belonged and that these norms, in turn, may have affected the nature of any pathological relationship that developed.

Generalizations from these reviewed studies should be limited in scope, particularly since there was a wide variation in methodology.  Furthermore, a lack of consistency in these findings is to be attributed to a quasi or total neglect of important sociocultural variables.  While findings in sociology and anthropology in the past few years have given impetus to the development of social psychiatry as a field of investigation, their effect is still minor, particularly in the regular psychiatric literature.  Although the evidence of the importance of family factors in the background of schizophrenics is quite compelling, the patterns of the home environment needs to be more clearly defined and isolated from home patterns which lead to other types of psychoses, neurosis and anti-social behavior.  Furthermore, the non-occurrence of schizophrenia in the other siblings of the family is another area which needs investigation.

## VIII.  SUMMARY

Many studies have shown that mothers of schizophrenics are usually disturbed.  The "schizophrenogenic" mother has been described as rejecting, over-protective, abusive, etc., and the father, as weak, passive and ineffectual.  Approximately 150 case histories of male schizophrenic patients of Jewish and Protestant, lower, and upper-class were examined to determine the major prevalent characteristics in parent-child relationships.

The Jewish mother of lower-class showed more emotional

instability, psychotic breakdowns and dullness than the Protestant mothers. In most of these Jewish families the father was a passive, ineffectual member of the family. In the lower-class Protestant group the pathology was more frequent with the father, with a greater incidence of insanity, alcoholism and excessive bad temper. In general it appears from our findings that Protestant fathers and Jewish mothers of schizophrenics belonging to the lower-social classes are more disturbed than their mates.

# References

1.  Fromm-Reichmann, Freida. Notes on the development of treatment of schizophrenia by psychoanalytic psychotherapy. *Psychiatry*, 1948, 11:263-273.

2.  Frazee, Helen E. Children who later become schizophrenic. *Smith College Studies in Social Work*, 1953, 23:125-149.

3.  Hotchkiss, Georgina D., Carmen, Lida, Ogilby, Anne, & Wiesenfeld, Shirley. Mothers of young male single schizophrenic patients as visitors in a mental hospital. *Journal of Nervous and Mental Diseases*, 1955, 121:452-462.

4.  Lidz, T., Cornelison, Alice, & Parker, B. The role of fathers in the family of schizophrenic patients. *American Journal of Psychiatry*, 1956, 113:126-132.

5.  Gerard, D.L., & Siegel, J. The family background of schizophrenia. *Psychiatric Quarterly*, 1950, 24:47-73.

6.  Tiedze, Trude. A study of mothers of schizophrenics. *Psychiatry*, 1949, 12:55-65.

7.  Thomas, Rose C. *Mother-Daughter Relationship and Social Behavior*. Social Work Series 21. Washington, D.C.: Catholic University of America Press, 1955.

8.  Opler, M.K., & Singer, J.L. Ethnic differences in behavior and psychopathology, Italian and Irish. *International Journal of Social Psychiatry*, 1956, 2:11-22.

9.  Lidz, Cornelison, Alice, Fleck, S., & Terry, Dorothy. The intra-familial environment of the Schizophrenic patient. Part 1: The father. *American Journal of Psychiatry*, 1957a, 20:329-342.

10. —, —, —, —. The intra-familial environment of schizophrenic patients. Part 2: Marital schism and marital skew. *American Journal of Psychiatry*, 1957b, 114:241-248.

11. Myers, J.K., & Roberts, B.H. *Family and Class Dynamics*. NY: Wiley, 1959.

12. Bowen, M. A family concept of schizophrenia. In, Jackson, D.D. (ed.), *The Etiology of Schizophrenia*. NY: Basic Books, 1960, 346-372.

13. Wynne, L.C., Rychoff, I.M., *et al.* Pseudo-mutuality and the family relations of schizophrenics. *Psychiatry*, 1958, 21:205.

14. Limentani, D. Symbiotic identification in schizophrenia. *Psychiatry*, 1956, 19:231-236.

15. Bateson, G., Haley, J., Jackson, D.D., & Weakland, J. Toward a theory of schizophrenia. *Behavioral Science*, 1956, 1:251-264.

16. Weakland, J. 'Double-bind' hypothesis of schizophrenia and three-party interaction. In, Jackson, D.D. (ed.), *The Etiology of Schizophrenia*. NY: Basic Books, 1960, 373-388.

17.   Jackson, D. D. Family interaction, family homeostasis, and some implications for conjoint family psychotherapy. Paper presented at the Academy of Psychoanalysis, San Francisco, May, 1958.

18.   Hollingshead, A.B., & Redlich, F.C. *Social Class and Mental Illness.* NY: Wiley, 1958.

19.   Delay, J., Deniker, P., & Green, A. Le milieu familial du schizophrène. *Encéphale,* 1957, 46:189-323.

20.   Hadju-Gimes, L. Contribution to the etiology of schizophrenia. *Psychoanalytic Review,* 1950, 27:421-438.

21.   Reichard, Suzanne, & Tillman, C. Patterns of parent-child relationships in schizophrenia. *Psychiatry,* 1950, 13:247-257.

22.   Yrjo, Alanen. On the personality of the mother and early mother-child relationships of 100 schizophrenic patients. *Acta Psychiatrica,* 1956, Suppl. 106:227-334.

23.   Lane, R.C., & Singer, J.L. Familial attitudes of paranoid schizophrenics and normal individuals from two socio-economic statuses. *Journal of Abnormal and Social Psychology,* 1959, 59:328-339.

## Chapter 10

# Feelings of Security and of Self-Esteem in Relation to Religious Belief

## NELSON G. HANAWALT

𝕴N reviewing Maslow's (1) *Social Personality Inventory for College Women* (self-esteem), and Maslow's (2) *Security-Insecurity Inventory*, Hanawalt (3, 4) briefly reported some validity studies involving these two tests. The validity of both tests measured up to about the expected level under the conditions of the studies. In connection with Security-Insecurity, Maslow (5, p. 548) makes the interesting statement that "in Jews there is a tendency to be simultaneously high in self-esteem and low in security, while in Catholic women we often find low self-esteem joined with high security." Apparently this statement was based upon a clinical hunch for no experimental data was reported.

The above hypotheses concerning Jewish and Catholic women are reasonable ones in the light of public and professional constructs. The notion that Jews have high self-esteem fits the stereotype of Jews. It is easy to assume that a Jewish prejudice would tend to lower security feeling. In the case of Catholics it is reasoned that the concept of sin lowers the feeling of self-esteem, but that other aspects of the religion serve to increase the feeling of security. The difficulty with this type of thinking is that other combinations of these two variables can be presented with similar rationality. From the professional point of view, it is expected that religion would have an important bearing upon such basic personality variables as self-esteem and security feeling since religious attitudes come to bear upon the child at an early age, and early experience is believed to play an important role in the developing personality.

The purpose of the present study was to test Maslow's

hypotheses using his two inventories as a basis for measuring self-esteem and security feeling. According to his hypothesis for Jewish women, they should score high on self-esteem and low on security. The Catholic women should show similar unsymmetrical distributions but reversed from that of the Jews. The Protestants should presumably show a normal distribution on both tests.

## I.    METHOD

In order to test the hypotheses, a total of 111 college women, equally divided among Catholics, Jews, and Protestants, took Maslow's two tests anonymously. They did not know the purpose of the testing more than that it was an experiment. The original group, Sample A, consisting of 60 Ss, was tested in the spring of 1959.    A replication, Sample B, consisting of 51 Ss, was tested in the spring of 1960.

### 1.   SAMPLE A

A religious attitude rating sheet was distributed to 175 girls between the ages of 17 and 21 years who lived in six dwelling units at Douglass College. On this sheet the Ss wrote their name and address, and checked one of four items: Catholic, Jewish, Protestant, or Other.    In addition they rated themselves on the strength of their religious beliefs:   Very Strong, Strong, Moderate, Slight, or None.   From the returned questionnaires, 60 Ss were selected, 20 from each of the three faiths who had rated themselves either strong or very strong on the religious belief scale.   Maslow's two tests were stapled together and given as a unit.   The tests were handed to the girls individually. They agreed to write only their religion at the top of the first page, and to return the anonymous test to the experimenter in a prepared envelope through the college post office.   All 60 tests were returned.

### 2.   SAMPLE B

In the selection of Sample B a different procedure was used in an attempt to improve the sample.   Active participation in a religious group might, it was reasoned, improve the sample of the three religious faiths. Consequently, the names of active participants in the three religious organizations, Hillel, Newman Club, and Protestant Council, were secured from the officers of the clubs. All of the 150 names secured were sent a booklet consisting of the two tests and a face sheet asking for participation in the experiment. Also, the face sheet asked for answers to the two questions put to Sample A concerning the faith of the respondent and the degree of faith. This information was asked for because it was realized that there are other reasons for activity in a religious club aside from religious belief. Again the *S*s were requested to return the booklets anonymously in prepared envelopes. The sample was selected by numbering the returned booklets of strong and very strong religious belief. Since only 17 Protestants returned booklets in these two categories, the sample was limited to this number from each group. Thus, only the first 17 tests from each religious group, or 51 tests in all, were scored.

## II. RESULTS

Measures of the distributions of scores on the two tests, Social Personality Inventory (self-esteem) and Security-Insecurity are presented in Table 1. It should be remembered that the scores for Self-esteem run from positive to negative,

### TABLE 1
#### Measures of Distribution for the Two Tests

| *S*s | | Self-esteem | | | Security-Insecurity | | |
|---|---|---|---|---|---|---|---|
| | | *Mdn* | *M* | *SD* | *Mdn* | *M* | *SD* |
| Jews | A | — 8 | — 8.15 | 44.59 | 12 | 13.20 | 7.03 |
| | B | —22 | —22.29 | 47.92 | 10 | 16.18 | 12.11 |
| Catholics | A | —10.5 | —19.85 | 48.28 | 20.5 | 21.59 | 11.87 |
| | B | —24 | —28.59 | 44.99 | 12 | 17.47 | 11.73 |
| Protestants | A | —41 | —32.55 | 39.51 | 15 | 14.35 | 9.31 |
| | B | —13 | —52.41 | 36.76 | 16 | 19.59 | 12.39 |

*Note:* There is only one significant difference between the means of the three religious groups for Samples A and B: The difference between the Jews and Protestants in Sample B for Self-esteem ($t = 2.13$, $P < .05$).

with a high positive score indicating high self-esteem and a high negative score indicating low self-esteem. The scores for Security-Insecurity run from zero on a positive scale, with a low positive score indicating security. The medians, as well as the means and *SD*s, are presented since these two tests typically produce skewed distributions.

The first test of the hypotheses was a comparison of the means by use of the *t* test. According to Maslow's Jewish hypothesis, this group should exceed the mean of the Catholic women in self-esteem but be less secure. It will be noted in Table 1 that Jewish women do show more self-esteem than Catholic women for both Samples A and B, but neither difference is significant at the five per cent level of confidence. In fact, Sample A for Catholics ranks a little higher than Sample B for Jews in self-esteem. The second half of the Jewish hypothesis is not supported either since the Jews, in contradiction of the hypothesis, show more security in both Samples A and B than the Catholics, but again the difference is not significant.

Of course the hypothesis for Catholic women was also unsupported, for it is the opposite of the Jewish hypothesis. None of the differences in means between Jewish and Catholic women presented in Table 1 were significant at the five per cent level of confidence. In Sample A, neither the Jews nor the Catholics produced a mean difference significantly different from that of the Protestants. The only significant difference between means in Table 1 was between the Jews and the Protestants on self-esteem in Sample B, but since Sample A did not show a significant difference in this respect, it can best be attributed to chance.

The *t* tests produced no evidence for Maslow's hypotheses, nor did they produce any evidence that differences in religious belief have any effect upon the scores of these two tests, within the limits of the present sample.

Some of the distributions reported in Table 1 were obviously skewed, but probably not to an extent as to invalidate the *t* tests. However, it was decided to test the hypotheses concerning Jewish and Catholic women more directly on the basis of the medians. To do this, new medians were calculated for whole Samples A, B, and A + B. They are reported in Table 2.

## TABLE 2
### Medians for Total Samples A, B, and A + B

| Sample | N | Social personality (Self-esteem) | Security-Insecurity |
|---|---|---|---|
| A | 60 | —20.5 | 15 |
| B | 51 | —28.0 | 13 |
| A + B | 111 | —25.0 | 15 |

First, a median test was made to determine whether or not our two independent Samples A and B differed in central tendency on the two tests. The medians for A + B in Table 2 were used and the test was by means of $X^2$. The null hypothesis that the two samples came from a population with the same median was not disproven for either self-esteem or Security-Insecurity. Apparently the different method of selecting Sample B was without effect.

In order to test the Jewish and Catholic hypotheses, each of the 111 Ss was classified on the basis of his scores on the two test in reference to the median scores. The medians reported in Table 2 were used. The four categories of the classification follow: *(a)* above the median in self-esteem (S-E) and below the median for security (the Jewish Hypothesis); *(b)* below the median for self-esteem and above for security (the Catholic hypothesis); *(c)* median or above in both self-esteem and security; and *(d)* median or below in both self-esteem and security. The median score appearing twice in the headings, caused difficulty in only a very few cases. These cases were handled by allowing the score on the other test to determine the category. There was no S with a median score on both tests. The results of this classification are presented in Table 3.

Since Maslow's two tests are essentially uncorrelated, it is expected that by chance 25 per cent of the Ss would be found in each of the four categories. If the Jewish and Catholic women tend to follow a pattern of scoring high on one test and low on the other, this expectation of 25 per cent in each category should be upset. A $X^2$ test for each distribution of each sample (the lines in Table 3) failed to reject the null hypothesis in a single case. Consequently we must assume that they are chance distributions, and that the Catholic and Jewish women show no special pattern of response on the two tests. They do not differ from

## TABLE 3

Classification of the Ss in Reference to the Medians of the Tests

| Ss | | Above $Mdn$ for S-E and below for Security | Below $Mdn$ for S-E and above for Security | $Mdn$ or above in both | $Mnd$ or below in both | $N$ (111) |
|---|---|---|---|---|---|---|
| | A | 5 | 5 | 7 | 3 | 20 |
| Jews | B | 3 | 3 | 7 | 4 | 17 |
| | A + B | 8 | 9 | 14 | 6 | (37) |
| | A | 8 | 2 | 4 | 6 | 20 |
| Catholics | B | 3 | 3 | 6 | 5 | 17 |
| | A + B | 12 | 5 | 10 | 10 | (37) |
| | A | 3 | 8 | 3 | 6 | 20 |
| Protestants | B | 3 | 3 | 2 | 9 | 17 |
| | A + B | 5 | 11 | 8 | 13 | (37) |

*Note:* Samples A, B, and A + B were each classified on the basis of the Sample medians, consequently the entries in the A + B lines do not always equal the sum of A and B. As tested by $X$": *(a)* none of the nine distributions (lines in the table) shows a significant deviation from chance at the five per cent level of confidence; and *(b)* to be significant at the five per cent level an individual cell entry for Sample A has to be as low as zero or above nine; for Sample B, as low as zero or above eight; and for A + B as low as three or above 14.

the Protestant women in this respect.

Also, using $X^2$ the entries in the individual cells of Table 3 can be tested against frequencies: 25-75 per cent of the Ss. This is a more specific test of Maslow's hypotheses since it is only the first and second columns of Table 3 which concern his hypotheses directly. The null hypothesis should be rejected for Jews in the first column and for Catholics in the second column, but it could be rejected in neither case. In fact, there was only one cell entry in Table 3 for which the null hypothesis had to be rejected, and that was for the Protestants in Sample B under the heading *"Mdn* or Below in Both." Since neither Sample A nor Sample A + B differed from chance expectation for Protestants under this category, the difference in Sample B is best thought of as a chance fluctuation. On the basis of the $X^2$ tests there is no evidence to support Maslow's hypotheses.

The results presented above are all negative as far as Maslow's hypotheses are concerned. This is another example of

## III. DISCUSSION

a clinical hunch which fails to hold when cases are measured objectively and counted. Of course the hypotheses may be true for other segments of the population, but they do not hold in general, and specifically for a population of college women. It is true, as recorded in Table 3, that there are Jewish women who are high in self-esteem and low in security feeling, but this is true of Catholic and Protestant women too.

The results presented in this paper are not to be construed as indicating that religious belief is without effect in determining personality. Neither can it be concluded that religious faith is without effect on security feeling and self-esteem. The results do indicate that religious belief alone, in the three major religions included in the present sample, is not of sufficient strength to show a differentiating effect upon the measures of self-esteem and security used in the study. Religious belief is only one of the threads running through the fabric of security feeling and self-esteem. The pattern of the fabric depends upon the nature of the other threads and their interrelationships.

## IV. SUMMARY

The purpose of the study was to test Maslow's hypotheses that Jewish women tend to be simultaneously high in self-esteem and low in security feeling, and that Catholic women tend to be low in self-esteem and high in security feeling. Two samples of college women of strong or very strong belief, equally divided among Catholics, Jews, and Protestants, were tested on Maslow's inventories which he constructed to measure self-esteem and security feeling. There were no significant differences in the means between the Catholics and the Jews, nor did either of these two groups differ from the Protestant group on these two variables. Based upon the medians, a classification of the 111 Ss according to the Jewish and the Catholic hypotheses failed to show a significant difference from chance for the three religious groups, i.e., a Protestant and a Catholic were just as likely to fulfill the conditions of the Jewish hypothesis as a Jewish woman, and a Jewish or a protestant woman was just as like to fulfill the conditions of the Catholic hypothesis as a Catholic woman.

# References

1.  Maslow, A. H. *Social Personality Inventory for College Women.* Stanford, Cal.: Stanford Univ. Press, 1942.
2.  Maslow, A. H., Birsh, E., Honigmann, I., McGrath, F., Plason, A., & Stein, M. *Security-Insecurity Inventory.* Palo Alto, Cal.: Consulting Psychologists Press, Inc., 1952.
3.  Hanawalt, N. G. Maslow's social personality inventory for college women. In Buros, O. K. (ed.), *The Third Mental Measurements Yearbook.* New Brunswick, N.J.: Rutgers Univ. Press, 1949, 197-198.
4.  —. Maslow's security-insecurity inventory. In Buros, O. K. (ed.), *The Fifth Mental Measurements Yearbooks.* New Brunswick, N.J.: The Gryphon Press, 1959, 189-191.
5.  —. Dynamics of personality organization: II. *Psychological Review* 1943, 50, 541-558.

# III. THE DEVELOPMENTAL PROCESS AND JUDAISM

# INTRODUCTION

Can a dog or a cat be Jewish? How does a child of five develop his ideas of Jewishness? What is the ten-year-old Jewish child's conception of Judaism? How is the Jew defined by a second-grader? The answers to such questions were sought by Dr. David Elkind from 210 Jewish children between the ages of five and eleven. Their responses concerning the nature and origin of Jewishness enabled the author to show three distinct levels of conceptualization. On the first level, children of ages five and six have a general, undifferentiated impression of Jews as being distinct from members of other faiths in hair color and country of origin. Children between the ages of seven and nine distinguish Jews from Protestants and Catholics on the basis of ritual observances and family relationships. On the third level, children of ten and eleven are able to offer abstract conceptions of Jews as a sub-class of people who believe in God and who differ from the other two major faiths only in the content of their belief.

In his article on "The Problems of Jewish Religious Youth," Dr. Boris M. Levinson is primarily concerned with two areas in the lives of 220 Yeshiva College freshmen: (1) their self-concept as religious young people, and (2) the effect of cultural impact on the expressed problems of their religious upbringing. In a much wider study, with a far larger population consisting of 2,000 high school students of all faiths, H. H. Remmers and D. H. Radler discuss the problems of "The American Teenager" in their book of the same name. The figures cited below for Jewish adolescents are extrapolated from their text.

The American Jewish teen-ager is frequently doubly confused because, first of all, he is a teen-ager, and secondly he is Jewish. The problem of identity is central to the problem of adolescent development. Many young Jews find that while coping with the difficulties of becoming adult, they also feel conflict in being Jewish. Why else should 69 per cent of the Jewish teen-agers in the Remmer and Radler study want to know more about religion, whereas 46 per cent of them rarely go to religious services, if at all? Nineteen per cent attend services once or twice a month, 27 per cent once a week, and 8 per cent two or more times weekly. The more that 19 per cent learn about science, the more they doubt their Judaism.

Several inferences can be made for nearly half the students' rare attendance at religious services, although the figures do indicate the youngsters go to synagogue or temple more frequently than their parents. The conflict or discrepancy between their reluctance to attend services and their desire to know more about Judaism apparently stems from deep sources. For 43 per cent of them feel that the Gentile dislikes the Jew; 57 per cent of the Jewish teen-agers want people to like them more; 35 per cent of them are easily hurt; 16 per cent feel they are not wanted; and 12 per cent think their noses are ugly.

It is possible that many or all of these attitudes derive from adolescent adjustive difficulties rather than from society's reaction to their religion. The population for this study was found in the ninth through the twelfth grades of high school; thus the students would range in age from, roughly, twelve to eighteen. These early and middle adolescent years bring with them frequent grave social, physical, physiological, sexual, ethical, vocational, and family adjustment processes. The adolescent is confronted with a Pandora's box of crises, decisions, and behavioral patterns which can make life a challenge or a misery. If he feels himself living in a hostile world, surrounded by hostile people, his religion may become an easy scapegoat or a sublimation for his more aggressive feelings.

Jewish self-hatred is a recognizable individual and group phenomenon. To attribute the antipathetic feelings about Judaism of Jewish high school youth solely to their youth would possibly be too expedient, for these feelings frequently persist through college and later adult life. Lewin has described both periods compellingly in his two papers, "Bringing Up the Jewish Child" and "Self-Hatred Among Jews." These feelings of self-hate are rooted in profound affective disorders.

The Remmers-Radler study indicates that 9 per cent of the

Jewish youngsters have thought of suicide, whereas 6 per cent of the Catholic and 3 percent of the Protestant students have. Fifty-four per cent of the Jewish teen-agers worry about little things (35 per cent of the Protestants and a like percentage of the Catholics form a comparative basis). Sleeping at night is difficult for 11 per cent of the Jewish students; 27 per cent of them feel lonesome; 16 per cent of them feel "blue" much of the time; 7 per cent do not see much of a future for themselves; 23 per cent wonder if they are normal in the way their minds work; 13 per cent worry about their health; 11 per cent think that the world is full of unfriendly people; 12 per cent think they are unlucky; 14 per cent pessimistically believe things are worse than they originally seemed; and 39 per cent want an opportunity to talk about their personal problems. It is significant that every one of these percentages for the Jewish high school youngsters is higher than for the high school students of the other two major religious groups.

So far as Judaism itself is concerned, 16 per cent of the Jewish teen-agers claim that their religion has been a source of unhappiness for them, 45 per cent state it has made them neither happy nor unhappy, 34 per cent feel Judaism has made them happy, and 5 per cent very happy. Thus, less than two-fifths of the sample have a positive orientation toward their Jewishness; nearly half are indifferent and the balance are already self-haters. The ratio of feeling toward Judaism then becomes 39 per cent positive to 61 per cent negative.

If these data are valid and reliable and can be projected to the entire Jewish high school age bracket (even discounting much of the negative feeling as typical of adolescent disjointedness), the prediction for the survival of American Jewry as a religious group would not be very favorable.

One of psychology's cardinal principles is that if the individual is to enjoy good mental health he should feel good about himself and good about others. As long as Jewish youngsters express themselves so negatively about their religion, good mental health is possibly lessened, and so, certainly is the likelihood of their becoming active participants in the life of the Jewish community. Whether their religion contributes a small or great amount to their conflicts during the teen years—and this of course varies with the individual—it is evident from this study that being a Jew very often further complicates the complications of adolescence. Feelings of hostility, aggression, frustration, anxiety, sublimation and depression, and the likely unresolved Oedipal conflict, are directed inwardly toward themselves and sometimes outwardly toward their religion.

Geriatrics is a relatively new science in the study of man, for it has been only within the last few decades that life has been appreciably extended. And as the life-span of Americans increases, the many-faceted problems of geriatrics multiply. The majority of aged Jews in this country today are foreign-born. Because of their religious and cultural heritage they have, perhaps, not only the usual gerontological problems to contend with but also the graver emotional ones. Dr. Maurice E. Linden explores both areas in the chapter on "Emotional Problems in Aging," starting out with the general factors involving the aged and continuing with the specific Jewish attitudes which tend to complicate this period. The Jewish self-concept, the Jewish attitude toward the aged, the "Chosen People" formulation, *Kashruth* and its implications for oral preoccupation, Jewish survival and a readiness to feel persecuted which becomes part of the personality, Jewish scholasticism and ambition, the psychological dominance of the mother in the Jewish family, all play a part in the emotional problems of the aged. Since more recent American Jewish generations have become acculturated with the larger culture, it is probable there will be a diminution of such internal strife as experienced by the immigrant Jews.

Chapter 11

# The Child's Conception of His Religious Denomination: I. The Jewish Child

DAVID ELKIND

## I. INTRODUCTION

*T*HIS is a study dealing with Jewish children's conceptions of their religious denomination. For a starting point the study takes the genetic psychology of the Swiss psychologist, Jean Piaget. Piaget assumes that conceptions develop in discernible stages which follow a regular sequence related to age. In Piaget's view the year levels at which the stages appear may vary with individual, cultural, or training differences but the *sequence* which the stages follow is unmodifiable and necessary. A major purpose of the present study is to discover whether there are discernible stages in the development of the Jewish child's conception of his religious denomination.

The present study differs from related social psychological studies [1,2,3] in its focus on stages of conceptual development rather than on ethnic identification or on awareness of multiple group membership.

## II. METHOD

### 1. *SUBJECTS*

Two hundred and ten Jewish children attending a day camp in Westwood, Massachusetts, were tested. The sample consisted of 30 subjects at each year level from five to eleven randomly selected from a total camp population of over 800 children. The mean age and standard deviation for each year level is given in Table 1.

TABLE 1

Mean Age and Standard Deviation for Seven Year Level Used in Study
N = 30 at Each Year Level

| Year level | Mean age | SD (mo.) |
|---|---|---|
| 5 | 5-7 | 1.33 |
| 6 | 6-4 | 2.77 |
| 7 | 7-6 | 2.65 |
| 8 | 8-5 | 2.66 |
| 9 | 9-4 | 2.96 |
| 10 | 10-6 | 2.87 |
| 11 | 11-4 | 3.44 |

The children came from families differing in religious affiliation (reformed, conservative, or orthodox); in socio-economic status (from lower to upper middle class); and in their emphasis on religious training (from none to having children attend parochial day school). No attempt to control these factors was made. Any uniformities which appeared despite so much uncontrolled variation would have greater significance for a developmental theory than would uniformities appearing in an experientially homogeneous sample. Piaget's view is that experience can stimulate and guide but not dominate the development of conceptions.

## 2. PROCEDURE

Each child was seen individually and asked the following questions: (a) Is your family Jewish? Are you Jewish? Are all boys and girls Jewish? Why? (or why not?); (b) Can a dog or a cat be Jewish? Why? (or why not?); (c) How do you become a Jew? (For young children. What makes you Jewish?); (d) What is a Jew?; (e) How can you tell a person is Jewish?; (f) Can you be Jewish and American at the same time?

The questions were always asked in the above order which produced replies with the least perseveration and repetition. Whenever answers were ambiguous, E asked general questions like "Tell me more about it?" or "How do you mean?" Sometimes E asked pointed questions to test the limits of the child's comprehension or conviction. When children answered "I don't know," *E* encouraged them to guess.

Although children were asked not to discuss the questions among themselves, many youngsters learned of the questions before they were tested. This probably did not contaminate the findings for several reasons: *(a)* there were no right or wrong answers to be transmitted; *(b)* children often got distorted versions and never heard all the questions; *(c)* most children were resistive to the suggestions of their peers and eager to answer for themselves; *(d)* children who did parrot answers were, like all children, poor liars and it was easy for *E* to help the child disregard answers he did not really believe; *(e)* the variety among children's formulations and inner consistency of a particular child's replies could hardly be accounted for by group suggestion. For all these reasons children's responses were regarded as revealing their own conceptions.

### 3. *QUALITATIVE ANALYSIS*

Piaget[6] describes three criteria that must be observed to infer the presence of developmental stages: *(a)* uniformity in ideas at a given year level often extending over several year levels; *(b)* appearance of ideas from an earlier year level as part of, or added to, the more advanced ideas given at a higher year level; *(c)* an increasing correctness (conformance with adult conceptions) of children's ideas with increasing age. All these criteria were met by responses given in the present study. Accordingly these responses were classified by stages.

### III. RESULTS

#### 1. *THE NATURE OF JEWISHNESS*

Answers to questions (a, b, d, f,) were similar and fell into groups which suggested three stages in the development of the child's conception of Jewishness.

*a. What is a Jew?* Children's definitions formed the center of the cluster of ideas which marked each stage.

(1). At the first stage children had only a global, undifferentiated impression of a Jew as a kind of person. If these children spontaneously, or at *E*'s prompting, tried to tell how a

Jew differed from a Catholic or a Protestant, they said that Jews had different hair or skin color or came from a different land, etc.

> Sid (6-3) What is a Jew? ... "A person." How is a Jewish person different from a Catholic? ... " 'Cause some people have black hair and some people have blonde."
>
> Mel (5-9) How is a Jewish person different than a Catholic? ... "He comes from a different country." Which one? ... "Israel."

Errors children made in defining a Jew reflected their failure to correctly categorize religious, racial and national characteristics.

(2). Children at the second stage had a concrete conception of a Jew as a person who behaved in certain ways. A Jew was a person who went to the Synagogue, celebrated Jewish holidays and wore Jewish stars, etc.

> Mar (7-9) What is a Jew? ... "A person who goes to temple and Hebrew School."

Definitions at this stage showed a correct categorization of Jewish characteristics. The definitions were, however, concrete in the sense that they failed to include the non-observable element which the different actions of Catholic, Protestant and Jew had in common. Instead the definitions implied that religious categories, and not merely the members of those categories, were absolutely different from one another. Put differently, children at this stage were in a position to correctly classify a person as Protestant, Catholic, or Jew although they were not yet able to classify the religious groups within a single category.

(3). Third stage children had an abstract conception of a Jew as a person who believed in one God and worshipped in a different way.

> Sid (10-4) What is a Jew? ... "A person who believes in one God and doesn't believe in the New Testament."
>
> Leo (11-10) What is a Jew? ... "A person of a different faith. He believes in one God."

At this stage children correctly included Jewish within the general category of "beliefs." Religious groups were no longer differentiated concretely and absolutely by the behavior of their members but were distinguishd abstractly and relatively by differences in the content of their beliefs. In short, at the third stage differentiation between denominations was not by means of the *religious subject* but rather by means of the *religious object*. Table 2 gives the per cent of children at each stage.

TABLE 2

Per Cent of Children Answering Question, "What is a Jew?" for Three Stages and Seven Year Levels
$N = 30$ at Each Year Level

| Year level | Global a | Stage Concrete b | Abstract c |
|---|---|---|---|
| 5d | 50 | 7 | — |
| 6 | 70 | 30 | — |
| 7 | 23 | 67 | 10 |
| 8 | 27 | 60 | 13 |
| 9 | 3 | 54 | 43 |
| 10 | — | 23 | 77 |
| 11 | — | 27 | 73 |

a "A person with blonde hair, etc."
b "A person who goes to Synagogue, lights the candles on Friday night, etc."
c "A person who believes in one God, etc."
d Forty-three per cent of the five-year-olds gave no classifiable reply.

*b.  Can a dog or a cat be Jewish?*  This question (asked before the previous one) produced answers which served as a check and to amplify the stages described above.

(1).  Children at the first stage had a general impression of Jewishness as a human characteristic, but had no clear idea what it was.  They were satisfied to say that a dog or a cat could not be Jewish because it was a dog or cat, a pet, or went bow-wow.

> Bo (5-9) Can a dog or a cat be a Jew? . . . "No."  Why not? . . . "Because it's a dog."  But why can't it be Jewish? . . . "Because it goes bow-wow."

Replies at this stage suggested that Jewishness was conceived as an absolute quality. When forced to say why a dog could not be a Jew, the child answered as if he were asked why a dog could not be a human being. For these children a dog or a cat could not be a Jew for the same reason that it could not be a horse or a cow.

(2). The second stage child conceived Jewishness concretely both as a group of characteristic actions and as a family quality. These two ideas about the nature of Jewishness led to contradictory answers. When the child thought of Jewishness as ways of behaving he said dogs and cats could not be Jewish because they could not go to the Synagogue, light the candles, etc. But when the child thought of Jewishness as a family quality, he said a dog or cat could be Jewish if it belonged to a Jewish family. Although a child usually gave one or the other answer, its opposite was easily elicited by prompting. Some children spontaneously gave both answers. But at this stage they were not able to resolve the contradiction.

> Sta (8-3) Can a dog or a cat be a Jew? . . . "No." Why not? . . . "They are not human." What difference does that make? . . . "They can't go to the Synagogue or say the prayers . . . but I guess if it belonged to a Jewish family it could be Jewish." Could a lion or a tiger be Jewish? . . . "No, because they are wild. Nobody owns them."

Children's reasons for saying that dogs and cats could not be Jewish were correct but concrete. They implied that dogs and cats could not be Jews only because of bodily limitations (with paws animals could not light candles). For these children being Jewish depended upon the ability to carry out certain actions.

Several hidden aspects of children's thinking were reflected in their reasons for saying that dogs and cats could be Jewish. They were in a sense correct in assuming that Jewishness was a family quality. Their error arose from: (a) an undeveloped conception of a family as all those persons living together, which made a pet dog or cat a member of the family; (b) a primitive idea of participation which gave rise to the idea that belonging to the family caused the pet to possess (to participate in) all the qualities of the family.

(3). At the third stage children conceived Jewishness abstractly as a mental quality. Replies at this stage indicated that animals could not be Jewish because they were "dumb," "had no brains" and "could not understand things like that."

> Sid (11-4) Can a dog or a cat be Jewish? . . . "No." Why not? . . . "Because they are not human and wouldn't understand a religion."
> Tom (11-6) Can a dog or a cat be Jewish? . . . "No." Why? . . . "Cause its mother and father don't have a religion and don't have a human brain."

These answers which associate Jewishness with the brain and mind complemented definitions (given usually at the same time) of a Jew as a person who believed in one God. This provided the necessary check on the children's use of the term "belief." The answers showed clearly that these children understood that belief was a mental quality and that they were not simply parroting an adult verbalization. Table 3 presents the per cent of children at each stage for seven age groups giving answers to the question Can a dog or cat be Jewish?

## TABLE 3

Per Cent of Children Answering Question, "Can a Dog or a Cat be Jewish?"
for Three Stages and Seven Year Levels
N = 30 at Each Year Level

| Year level | Stage | | |
|---|---|---|---|
| | Global a | Concrete b | Abstract c |
| 5d | 60 | 13 | — |
| 6 | 60 | 40 | — |
| 7 | 16 | 77 | 7 |
| 8 | 10 | 77 | 13 |
| 9 | — | 93 | 7 |
| 10 | 3 | 77 | 20 |
| 11 | — | 57 | 43 |

a "Because it a dog, it goes bow-wow."
b "Because it's not human, can't go to Synagogue, light candles, stuff like that."
c "Because it hasn't any mind, wouldn't understand a religion."
d Twenty-four per cent of the five-year-olds gave no classifiable reply.

c. *Are all boys and girls Jewish?* The answers to this question reflected the categorical changes which accompanied the content changes in the child's developing conception of Jewishness.

(1). Children at the first stage had a global impression of Jewish as a kind of category and their first impulse was to say that not all boys and girls were Jewish because some were Catholic.* When, however, they spontaneously, or at *E*'s prompting, attempted to say what else children could be besides Jewish and Catholic, then they added racial and national denominations.

> El (6-2) Are you Jewish? . . . "Yes." And is your family Jewish? . . . "Yes." Are all boys and girls Jewish? . . . "No." Why? . . . "Because some are colored, they speak another language."
>
> Lin (5-10) Are you Jewish? . . . "Yes." And is your family Jewish? . . . "Yes, uh all except my dog, he's a French poodle."

These children, who usually could not correctly categorize national, racial and religious characteristics, were also unable to categorize national, racial and religious denominations.

(2). Children at the second stage conceived Jewish as a distinct category clearly differentiated from other religious and non-religious categories. They said that not all boys and girls were Jewish because some were Catholic and/or Protestant. If they attempted spontaneously, or at *E*'s prompting, to say what else children might be, then they they named only religious denominations.

> Pi (7-3) Are all boys and girls Jewish? . . . "No." Why? . . . "Because some are Catholic and some are Protestant." Can you tell me any more like that? . . . "There is sump'in like Buddhists, but I don't know what the others are."

Though answers at this stage were empirically correct, they were logically incomplete. A logically complete answer would have accounted for *all* possible children who were not Jews. Children at this stage, however, limited themselves only to one

* Most of the children came from the Boston area which is the largest diocese in the country so that the children's school mates and playmates were likely to have been Catholic.

or two non-Jewish denominations with which they were familiar. The incompleteness of their answers lay in their failure to verbalize an inclusive category which contained all possible denominations and so all non-Jewish children.

(3). The conception of Jewish at the third stage was of a sub-category included within the general category of religions. Answers at this stage stated that not all boys and girls were Jewish because "There were other religions."

> Dav (10-6) Are all boys and girls Jewish? . . . "No." Why is that? . . . "God made all different religions."

These answers appeared at the same time, or slightly after the child began saying that Jewishness was a mental quality and a Jew one who believed in one God. Once the child discovered that people of all denominations had in common the belief in a God, he was able to form the general category of religions. The percentage of children at each stage for seven age groups answering the question Are all boys and girls Jewish? is given in Table 4.

TABLE 4

Per Cent of Children Answering Question, "Why All Boys and Girls are Not Jewish?" for Three Stages and Seven Year Levels

N = 30 at Each Year Level

| Year level | Global a | Stage Concrete b | Abstract c |
|---|---|---|---|
| 5d | 67 | 7 | — |
| 6 | 60 | 40 | — |
| 7 | 23 | 67 | 10 |
| 8 | 17 | 63 | 20 |
| 9 | 3 | 74 | 23 |
| 10 | 7 | 17 | 76 |
| 11 | — | 33 | 67 |

a " 'Cause some are Catholic, colored, Irish."
b " 'Cause some are Catholic and Protestant."
c " 'Cause there are different religions."
d Twenty-four per cent of the five-year-old children gave no classifiable response.

d. *Can you be an American and a Jew at the same time?* Answers to this question provided a check on the child's logical ability.    It came last because it was the most direct.

(1).    Children at the first stage conceived being a Jew as an absolute designation which excluded any other designation. Amusingly these children denied they were American if they admitted they were Jewish or vice-versa.

> E. (6-2) Can you be Jewish and American at the same time? . . .
> "No."   Why? . . . Are you an American? . . . "No."   Are you a Jew?
> . . . "Yes."

These answers paralleled similar replies obtained by Piaget[8] when he asked children whether they were Swiss and Genevan.    Several kinds of interpretation are possible.    Psychologically the child took Jew and American as proper names and assumed that like all proper names, there was only one to a person.    Accordingly, if a person was "Jew," he could not be "American" no more than John could be Jim.

Logically the child's difficulty was due to his inability to perform logical multiplication.*    Logical multiplication is the ability to attribute two qualities to one class of objects at the same time; for example, to form the class of brown wooden beads.    In another study Elkind[10] has shown that children at this age cannot at the same time attribute to kindergarten pupils the properties of being both children and boys or girls. In the same way children of the present study thought that being both Jewish and American was an impossibility.

(2).    Children at the second stage conceived of Jewish as a quality compatible with the quality of being American. Typically they answered that "You are born a Jew and live in America."

> Pi (7-8) Can you be an American and a Jew at the same time?
> . . . "Yes."   How is that possible? . . . "Because you can live in
> America and be an American Jew."

These children were clearly able to perform logical multiplication and to conceive that a person could be both Jewish and American.    Explanations for why a person could be both Jewish

---

* The explanation could equally well be made from the point of view of logical addition.    Both types of operation are involved.

and American, however, were empirical: since a person could actually both live in America and be Jewish, he could be both things at once. At this stage being Jewish and American was a fact calling for an explanation by means of other facts.

(3). Third stage children conceived Jewish and American as sub-categories included within two different general categories. They justified their statements that Jews could be Americans by saying in effect that Jewish was a religion and American a nationality, and that they were different things.

> Dav (10-6) Can you be an American and a Jew at the same time? ... "Yes." How is that possible? ... "Because Jewish is a religion and American is a nationality. They are two different things."

Third stage children took being Jewish and American as a logical conclusion which could be deduced from a knowledge of the general categories involved. Table 5 gives the percentage of children at each stage for seven age groups answering the question Can you be a Jew and American at the same time?

TABLE 5

Per Cent of Children Answering Question, "Can You be Jewish and American at the Same Time?" for Three Stages and Seven Year Levels
N = 30 at Each Year Level

| Year level | Global a | Stage Concrete b | Abstract c |
|---|---|---|---|
| 5d | 63 | 17 | — |
| 6 | 74 | 26 | — |
| 7 | 23 | 77 | — |
| 8 | 10 | 87 | 3 |
| 9 | — | 90 | 10 |
| 10 | — | 67 | 33 |
| 11 | — | 60 | 40 |

a "No, can't have two, only if you move."
b "Yes, I'm a Jew and I live in America."
c "Yes, they're different things—Jewish is a religion, American is a nationality."
d Twenty per cent of the five-year-old children gave no classifiable response.

## 2. *THE ORIGIN OF JEWISHNESS*

In Piaget's classic work[5] he found 17 different forms of causality in the child. Piaget dealt, however, primarily with physical causality and not with ethnic phenomena. Some answers obtained in the present study fit into some of the categories mentioned by Piaget but other answers fell into categories not mentioned by him. The categories fell into groups corresponding to three stages.

*a. Artificialism and moral causality.* Piaget describes artificialism as "thinking . . . the things around him take notice of man and are made for man . . . everything is organized for the good of men" (5, p.245). One group of answers was clearly of this type.

> Tom (6-1) How do you become Jewish? . . . "God makes you Jewish."

> San (7-2) How do you become Jewish? . . . "Your mother turns you Jewish."

God at this stage was not a theological conception but a name for a powerful person as San's reply suggests. The use of "makes and turns" justifies classifying these replies as artificialism.

"By means of moral causality the child explains the existence of a given movement or of a given feature by its necessity, but the necessity is purely moral: The clouds 'must' advance in order to make night when men go to sleep" (5, p.261). Some children felt the same way about becoming Jewish.

> Pa (6-5) How do you become a Jew? . . . "Your father is Jewish so you must be Jewish."

To check these interpretations the children were asked if they could change their denomination and become something else. Children at this stage said they could not change because "you have to stay what you are," and besides "you wouldn't want to change." At this stage Jewishness had its origin in desire, intension and moral obligation.

*b. Causality by generation and participation.* Children at

the second stage conceived the origin of Jewishness to lie either in being born of Jewish parents or in the family relationship itself.

Mi (8-1) How do you become Jewish? . . . "You are born Jewish."
Ha (9-4) How do you become Jewish? . . . "Your parents are Jewish so you are Jewish."

Once children gave up the idea of artificialism and moral causality, they attempted to explain the origin of Jewishness by saying one Jew was born out of another. This was the same sequence Piaget found[5]. Children, of course, had no clear notion of birth, and for them it had only the spatial or temporal meaning of coming from something else.

Piaget did not find participations beyond the age of 5-6. But they seemed clearly present in older children of the present study. Answers like the Ha's were quite frequent. They implied (as did the affirmative answers about dogs and cats being Jewish) that because a creature was like others in some respects he was like them in all respects. It may be that participation remains until later ages when the phenomena to be explained are more personal and subjective.

*c. Initiation, practice and ritual.* These forms of casuality were not mentioned by Piaget, but they began to appear in the oldest children of the present study.

Si (10-11) How do you become a Jew? . . . "You are bar mitzvahed. Until you are bar mitzvahed you are not a real Jew."
Pan (11-6) How do you become a Jew? . . . "You go to schul (Synagogue), obey the law sometimes (sic!) and do what a Jew is supposed to do." Once you are a Jew can you change? . . . "Yes, you go to the rabbi. He does something."

As children began to conceive of Jewishness as a mental quality or belief, they gave up participations and generations, and saw Jewishness as an acquired characteristic. The percentage of children at each stage for the seven age groups answering the question "How do you become a Jew?" is shown in Table 6.

## TABLE 6

Per Cent of Children Answering Question, "How do You Become a Jew?"
for Three Stages and Seven Year Levels
N = 30 at Each Year Level

| Year level | Global a | Stage Concrete b | Abstract c |
|---|---|---|---|
| 5ᵈ | 60 | 13 | — |
| 6 | 70 | 30 | — |
| 7 | 33 | 67 | — |
| 8 | 20 | 74 | 6 |
| 9 | — | 83 | 17 |
| 10 | — | 74 | 26 |
| 11 | — | 60 | 40 |

a Artificialism, "God made me."

a Moral Necessity, "You have to be Jewish."

b Participation, "You mother and father are Jewish so you are Jewish."

b Generation, "You are born Jewish."

c Ritual, "Have to be bar mitzvahed."

c Indoctrination, "Have to go to Hebrew School, learn the Torah."

c Practice, "Have to obey the law, sometimes."

d Twenty-seven per cent of the five-year-old children gave no replies to this question.

### 3. THE RECOGNITION OF JEWS

Children's conceptions of Jewishness changed greatly between the ages of five and eleven. The overt signs, however, by which children recognized Jews did not undergo a corresponding development. Though there was a primitive stage at which undifferentiated identifying signs like blondness were used, after this stage children employed the same signs with almost equal frequency at all ages.

There were four types of signs by which children said they could tell that a person was a Jew: (a) undifferentiated signs (US), "They have light skin"; (b) identifying signs (IS), "They wear *Messusahs*, *Yarmelkas*, Jewish Stars, etc."; (c) characteristic actions (CA), "They light the candles on Friday night, celebrate Hannukah, go to the Synagogue," etc.; (d) direct communication (DC), "You can't tell unless you ask them." The percentage of answers given in each category for the seven age groups is presented in Table 7. A comparison of Table 7 with the other tables illustrates how the connotation of a concept may change radically without a corresponding change in its denotation.

TABLE 7

Per Cent of Children Answering Question, "How Can You Tell a Person is a Jew?" for Four Recognition Categories and Seven Year Levels

N = 30 at Each Year Level

| Year level | US a | Recognition category IS b | CA c | DC d |
|---|---|---|---|---|
| 5 | 10 | 3 | 7 | 3 |
| 6 | 40 | 7 | 7 | 7 |
| 7 | 10 | 37 | 30 | 17 |
| 8 | 17 | 43 | 17 | 20 |
| 9 | 7 | 57 | 37 | — |
| 10 | 3 | 60 | 27 | 10 |
| 11 | 10 | 33 | 30 | 27 |

*Note:*—Seventy-seven per cent of the five-year-old; 40 per cent of the six-year-old; 20 per cent of the seven-year-old; and three per cent of the eight-year-old children did not give classifiable responses to this question.

a US—Undifferentiated Sign, "He has dark skin, etc".

b IS—Identifying Sign, "He wears the Star of David, *Yarmelka* (skull cap) etc".

c CA—Characteristic Action such as "He goes to the Synagogue, talks Jewish, etc".

d DC—Direct Communication, "You can't tell only if you ask him, etc".

## 4. HOMOGENEITY OF THE STAGES

Some children answered all questions at one stage only; some answered one question at one stage and four questions at another; some answered two questions at one stage and three at another while by far the smallest number of children answered at least one question at each stage. Table 8 gives the percentage of children giving each pattern of response at each year level.

TABLE 8

Per Cent of Children in Each Response Category for Seven Year Levels

N = 30 at Each Year Level

| Year level | Response category | | | |
|---|---|---|---|---|
| | A | B | C | D |
| 5[a] | 43 | 27 | — | — |
| 6 | 30 | 37 | 33 | — |
| 7 | 30 | 33 | 34 | 3 |
| 8 | 37 | 33 | 27 | 3 |
| 9 | 34 | 40 | 23 | 3 |
| 10 | — | 27 | 63 | 10 |
| 11 | 20 | 40 | 40 | — |

Note.—A = All answers were at the same stage.

B = Four answers were at one stage and the fifth answer was at an adjacent stage.

C = Three answers were at one stage and two answers were at an adjacent stage.

D = Answers were given at all three stages.

[a] Classification for five-year-olds was based on four or more responses. Thirty per cent of these children did not give at least four answers.

The greatest individual variability occurred at age 10. Qualitatively these were children who seemed in the transitional phase between the second and third stages. This group was aware of the inadequacy of their former ideas without being able to replace them with more satisfying notions. Frustration and regression were more likely to have occurred in this group. Regression may, however, also be a necessary part of any conceptual progression. Table 8 shows clearly that the stages should not be regarded as absolutes and that they contain subtle gradations which it was not possible to detail in the present paper.

Not all of the variability in Table 8 was attributable to individual differences. Some of it was due to the unequal difficulty of the questions asked. Table 9 gives the frequency of responses at a given stage for the five questions.

### TABLE 9

Frequency of Observed Replies for Three Stages and Five Questions Stage

| N | Question | Global | Concrete | Abstract | |
|---|---|---|---|---|---|
| 202 | 1[a] | 53 | 90 | 59 | |
| 202 | 2[b] | 45 | 130 | 27 | |
| 202 | 3[c] | 55 | 120 | 27 | |
| 197 | 4[d] | 52 | 80 | 65 | |
| 203 | 5[e] | 50 | 127 | 26 | |
| | $X^2$ | 1.4 | 17.5** | 38.6** | 57.5** |

[a] Are all boys and girls Jewish?
[b] Can a dog or a cat be Jewish?
[c] How do you become Jewish?
[d] What is a Jew?

[e] Can you be an American and a Jew at the same time?
** Significant beyond the .01 level.

Table 9 shows that questions b, c, e, were significantly more difficult than the other two questions. This finding is consistent with those of other genetic studies [4, 7, 9] which have shown that the nature of the materials and questions asked can affect the level of the child's performance quite independently of his level of intellectual development.

The more difficult questions may have been so because they were unfamiliar to the children. Whereas the children might easily have heard or asked "What is a Jew?" or "Why aren't all boys and girls Jewish?", it was unlikely they had ever before been confronted with questions like "Can a dog or a cat be Jewish?" Answers to the more familiar questions were more likely to be influenced by direct instruction and adult verbalizations. Since these influences were likely to increase with age, they may explain why the questions were of equal difficulty at the first stage and of unequal difficulty thereafter.

### IV. DISCUSSION

This paper deals with issues raised by the related social psychological studies: *(a)* Ethnic Identification; *(b)* Ethnic Conceptual Development; *(c)* Compatibility of Multiple Group Membership.

## 1. *ETHNIC IDENTIFICATION*

Several investigators[1,2,3] have found that ethnic identification occurs in the nursery and elementary school years. In the present study the same held true; all of the 210 children readily said that they were Jewish, that their families were Jewish, but that all boys and girls were not Jewish.

## 2. *ETHNIC CONCEPTUALIZATION*

Using questions similar to those employed in the present study Hartley[2] found evidence of development in the conception of "American." Prior to age 6:6 American was used mainly as a symbol (name); between 6:6 and 8:6 the symbol interpretation was abandoned and the child thought of an American as distinguished by an activity; between the age of 8:6 and 10:5 activity definitions continued to appear together with definitions of American as a personal quality "it takes courage, be brave, be smart." These results found with a different sub-cultural and geographical group clearly paralleled the stages described in the present study.

Hartley did not find, however, a developmental sequence in the children's definitions of Jewish! Both Jewish and non-Jewish children defined Jewish primarily in terms of activity. Nonetheless Hartley did find a small proportion of the older children saying that Jewish was a belief, religion, etc. Hartley's failure to find the stages reported in the present study may have been due to his small sample. He used only forty-six Jewish children between the age of 3:5 and 10:6, and only thirty-one of these replied to the question about Jewishness. Also, the conception of American may develop earlier[11] than the conception of Jewish so that Hartley may have seen mainly the second stage of the "Jewish" conceptual development.

## 3. *MULTIPLE GROUP MEMBERSHIP*

Hartley's[2] findings regarding the awareness of multiple group membership were consistent with those of the present study for the younger, but not for the older, age levels. Hartley found that religious and nationality memberships were thought of as incompatible at all the upper age levels in his sample. In contrast the present results suggest that awareness of multiple group membership becomes more differentiated and correct with increasing age. The difference between Hartley's results and those reported here may lie in differences in type of questioning, and in the ethnic composition and size of the samples.

### 4. *THE MEANING OF ETHNIC IDENTIFICATION*

What the present study adds to these social-psychological findings is the meaning of ethnic identification and multiple group membership at different ages. The adult uses the terms "Jew" and "Jewish" in at least three different senses: *(a)* as a proper name to designate a particular person, *The Wandering Jew* or *The Jew of Venice*; *(b)* as a class name to designate a particular group of people, *The German Jew*; *(c)* as a conceptual term to mean a religious belief, *"Protestant, Catholic, Jew all have etc."* While the Jewish adult may identify himself as a Jew in any one, or all, of these senses, the present study suggests that: *(a)* at the first stage children can identify with "Jew" only in the sense of a proper name; *(b)* second stage children can identify with "Jew" both as a proper name and as a class to which they belong; *(c)* children at the third stage can identify themselves as Jews in all three sense of the term as it is employed by the adult. The young child's use of the phrase *I am a Jew* should not be mistaken for an identification with a group or a belief. At the first stage the child uses the verb "to be" only in the attributive sense and not yet in the sense of class inclusion. The meaning of his ethnic identification depends, therefore, upon the child's level of conceptual development.

### V. SUMMARY

Two hundred and ten Jewish children between five and eleven were questioned about the nature and origin of Jewishness. The results were in agreement with Piaget's hypothesis that conceptions develop in a regular, age related sequence of stages. At the first stage (usually 5-6) children had a general undifferentiated impression of Jews as a kind of people differing from Catholics and Protestants in such things as hair color and country of origin. Second stage children (usually 7-9) had a concrete conception of Jews as a class of people distinguished from other religious groups by their ritual observances and family relationships. Children at the third stage (usually 10-11) had an abstract conception of Jews as a sub-class of people who believed in God and who differed from Catholics and Protestants only in the content of their belief.

In their conception of the origin of Jewishness, first stage children attributed being Jewish to artificialism and moral casuality; second stage children attributed being Jewish to generation and participation; while third stage children attributed being Jewish to initiation, ritual, and indoctrination. There was little change with age in the four kinds of overt signs children used to identify Jews. The results were briefly compared with those of social psychological studies and some but not complete agreement was found on issues of *(a)* ethnic identification, *(b)* ethnic conceptualization, and *(c)* awareness of multiple group membership. It was concluded that the meaning of ethnic identification and multiple group membership was dependent upon the child's level of conceptual development.

# References

1. Clark, K. B., & Clark, M.P. Racial identification and preference in Negro children. In, Swanson, G.E., Newcomb, T., & Hartley, E.L. (eds.), *Readings in Social Psychology*. NY: Holt, 1952.
2. Hartley, E. L. Children's use of ethnic frames of reference: An exploratory study of children's conceptualization of multiple ethnic group membership. *Journal of Psychology*, 1948, 26:367-386.
3. Horowitz, R. E. Racial aspects of self-identification in nursery school children. *Journal of Psychology*, 1939, 7:1-9.
4. Piaget, Jean. *The Child's Conception of Numbers*. London: Kegan Paul, 1942.
5. —. *The Child's Conception of Physical Causality*. London: Gegan Paul, 1930.
6. —. *The Child's Conception of the World*. London: Kegan Paul, 1929.
7. —. *Le développement des quantités chez l'enfant—Conservation et atomise*. Neuchâtel et Paris: Délachaux & Niestle, 1941.
8. —. *Judgment and Reasoning in the Child*. London: Kegan Paul, 1928.
9. Elkind, David. The development of quantitiative thinking: Piaget replication study: I. *Journal of Genetic Psychology*, 1961, 98:37-46.
10. —. The additive composition of classes in the child: Piaget replication study: III. *Journal of Genetic Psychology*, 1961, 99:51-57.
11. Weinstein, E. A. Development of the concept of flag and the sense of national identity. *Child Development*, 1957, 28(2).

Chapter 12

# The Problem of Jewish Religious Youth

BORIS M. LEVINSON

## I. PURPOSES AND METHOD

**T**HIS study was undertaken with three purposes in mind:
*(a)* to learn how religiously brought up college freshmen view
themselves, *(b)* to learn the effect of cultural impact on the
expressed problems of traditionally brought up youth, and *(c)*
to provide information to the college guidance staff which could
aid them in assisting the students.

### A. THE CULTURAL SETTING

Our analysis of the problems faced by religious youth must
be viewed in light of the fact that when they enter college they,
in a sense, enter also into a wider world; the incipient cultural
clashes which were germinating in their high school days may
be precipitated at this time. Their statements are, at the same
time, an expression of their disappointments, heartaches, dissatisfaction with present status, training, mode of living, as well
as of their hopes for the future.

These freshmen were reared in families where they had
somewhat similar social attitudes, traits, and learning experiences[1]. They learned, or failed to learn, the social amenities
in the context of the traditional customs of Orthodox Jews.
Similar basic attitudes to sex, to school, to parents, to the
majority culture, indeed their very self-concept, were molded by
these cultural forces.

There were direct and tacit pressures exerted by parents on
these boys to belong to certain groups and to avoid others; to
engage in certain social activities and to shun others. This
brought them into association with lads of similar backgrounds

which tended to reinforce their family teaching.   Moreover, cross currents from the majority culture via radio, TV, movies, etc.[2], have penetrated the closed walls of these homes and served to bring about cultural clashes.   The older the boys were the more it appeared to them that discrepancies existed between their religious beliefs, folkways, and mores, and those of the majority culture.   Any revolt that might have occurred as a result of this struggle between youth and authority would, in this context, not usually be a rejection of the cultural mold, of which most of them were not aware, but of the particular way in which the family exercised control.

It is to be remembered that most of these young men want to make sure that their needs are met within the matrix of values of the traditional Jewish culture.   The conflict of motives thus occurring may become unconscious.   The acknowledged problems of the boys then become the manifest expression of a "not" acknowledged need.

However, the writer in no way means to imply that these boys came from a homogeneous background.   In the very matrix of a traditional culture, there are many variations.   These boys, therefore, differed widely in many psychological variables.   These undoubtedly reflected themselves in the problems troubling the freshmen.

We will thus find in our survey of problems some which are germane to, and possibly exaggerated by, traditional culture, and others which pertain to "every" freshman who is entering college.   Lest the reader think that the traditional culture creates only problems, the writer wishes to stress his belief that it leads toward the development of a positive approach to Judaism and enhanced self-respect and positive self-identification as a Jew[3,4,5,6,7].

We shall now address ourselves to the question—what are the basic problems of this particular Orthodox Jewish group and how did their cultural experiences mold them and how do they view themselves and their world?

### B.   MOONEY PROBLEM CHECK LIST

The Mooney Problem Check List, College Form, was used in

this study.    It contains 330 items which are divided into 11
areas.    One notes, however, these are not mutually exclusive.
As is well known, any classification of problems is somewhat
artificial.    These areas are as follows:

1.  Health and Physical Development.
2.  Finances, Living Conditions, and Employment.
3.  Social and Recreational Activities.
4.  Social-Psychological Relations.
5.  Personal-Psychological Relations.
6.  Courtship, Sex and Marriage.
7.  Home and Family.
8.  Morals and Religion.
9.  Adjustment to College Work.
10.  The Future:  Vocational and Educational.
11.  Curriculum and Teaching Procedure.

Each category consists of 30 items.    The items selected for
the various areas were chosen in such a way that they should
be, *(a)* homogeneous in content whenever possible, *(b)* useful,
inasmuch as they could suggest programs of action that can be
rendered by schools *(c)* representative of the problems in the
area covered and, *(d)* susceptible of statistical computation.

### 1.    THE MOONEY CHECK LIST AND GUIDANCE

The Mooney Problem's "census count" of student problems
is also helpful in guidance for the following reasons, so that:
1.    The faculty may become more sensitive to student needs
and the problems of adjusting to college.
2.    The faculty can plan a curriculum which attempts to
give meaningful answers to freshman problems.
3.    Teachers may help students to overcome the normal
difficulties of adjustment to Yeshiva College.
4.    Through student-teacher understanding of these problems, teachers can help students to know themselves better and
thus lead more satisfying lives.
The Mooney Problem Check List is not a psychological test
in the strict sense of the word.    It is merely a list in which the
student indicates the problems which concern him at the moment.
The student is instructed as follows:  "Read the list slowly,

pause at each item, and if it suggests something which is troubling you, *underline* it. . . . after completing the first step (the underlining), look back over the item you have underlined and *circle the numbers* in front of the items which are of *most concern* to you."

Responses—the underlined and circled problems—are added and this sum is used in evaluating the adjustment of the student respondent.

It is to be noted, however, that in his identification of problems, quite a bit depends upon the young man's ability to interpret situations and realistically to view himself. Since each individual is a law unto himself, he will tend to check somewhat different items from his fellows. What may be of passing significance to one, may be of lasting concern and worry to another. It is easier to unburden oneself about one problem than another. Therefore, the frequency of checking an item or of indicating great concern over it may not, in itself, be a valid indicator of the seriousness of the problem. The summary of scores thus arrived at may be misleading. Furthermore, there is obviously a difference between an underlined problem which may be somewhat disconcerting and a circled one which may be of real consequence to the individual.

### 2. *VALIDITY*

The manual mentions that the test is valid if the following criteria may be considered indicative of validity: *(a)* the students' responsiveness is high, *(b)* their attitude toward the material elicited is constructive, *(c)* there is a wide coverage of problems faced by young people, *(d)* the test has been very widely accepted by educators and psychologists as productive of results in personal evaluation, and finally, *(e)* it was found very useful in research.

There are many studies indicating the usefulness of this technique. Klohr[9], and Gordon[10], found this list to be useful in a college setting; McIntyre[11], found the Check List to be a valid instrument for high school students. Pflieger[12] mentions that a relationship was found between adjustment on the California Test of Personality and the Mooney Problem Check List.

Nevertheless, since we are dealing with an atypical group, we must consider the possibility that this device is not valid for all students. We, therefore, analyzed the answers to the penultimate question of the Check List—"Whether you have or have or have not enjoyed filling out the list, do you think it has been worth doing?"

Responses—Yes 172 (78.18%), No 21 (9.55%), Blank 27 (12.27%).

It is of some interest to note why certain students feel it was worth while, and others feel it was not. Many students thought it was worth while because:

*(a) It provided an opportunity to think through one's problem, and promoted self-understanding.*

"I think this list is very worth while because it gave me an opportunity to think about what bothers me and, in many cases, I saw how trivial these matters really are. It also gave me a chance to write down on paper what I might not speak about for fear of being ridiculed."

"As is usual with these forms, much of what lies in one's unconscious is revealed through the medium of these questions, and these questions certainly have achieved this purpose."

"It gave me an opportunity for self-scrutiny; made me stop and think about facets of my life which would not have itched my interest in the hustle and bustle of life here at Yeshiva."

"I think that the test is marvelously comprehensive, at least as far as I am concerned. It summarizes just about all of my problems. Also, it has helped me to crystallize them in my own mind. Thus, I have come—in a short half hour—to a better understanding of myself and have, I believe, come a long way to a solution of my problems."

"I learned quite a bit about myself. The list helped me to see some of my problems which I had previously either ignored, was unaware of."

*(b) Catharsis.*

"I feel like a person who has just finished crying. The tears mean nothing. They, like this questionnaire, offer an emotional outlet. I now feel very bold and am ready to face the future and my problems with my chin held high."

*(c) Generalization of experience.*

"Some questions I had about myself became crystallized. Also, seeing some of these things on the list made me realize that these problems are not only peculiar to me and 'misery loves company.' "

"It amused me to find that my problems are pinpointed on the list and are not individual."

Other students, while realizing the importance of the questionnaire did not think it was worth while for many reasons.

### (a)   Impossibility of changing one's life's experiences.

"I have enjoyed filling out this list because some of my problems have been put into words here. However, it hasn't been worth doing since I have already realized my problems. I cannot change the circumstances to take my problems away."

"I don't see how this can help me very much since I have been conscious of these problems, have attempted to correct those pertaining to my character, but that I revert to original self very quickly, i.e., I find it hard to remain conscious of the fact that I am attempting to change myself."

### (b)   Distrust of guidance staff.

"Worried whether it will be kept confidential and what those who see it might say."

"Many items are too personal, such as sex."

### (c)   The inappropriateness of the list.

"Dostoyevsky expresses much better than I could my dislike for these tests, or anything which attempts to plot the course of life and assumes that, if the proper questions could be asked, the inspector would have a perspective of life. The human soul is far deeper than those tests assume it to be and it can never be as thoroughly diagnosed as you think possible. These tests may be valuable in that they awaken in one a desire to understand himself and, perhaps, lead towards self-examination and observation."

### (d)   Self-confidence in ability to solve own problem.

"I feel no need in telling myself what I already know. I can solve these problems by myself, given time."

### 3.   RELIABILITY

The test manual indicates that while the test was designed to reflect changes in the individual case, research indicates general stability when used for planning based on survey results. The writer, however, feels that we cannot speak of the reliability of the entire instrument as such but of the reliability of different areas. Culture may repress the expression of problems in one area and encourage the expression of problems in another area. Furthermore, within the same subculture, a student may be more frank in one area than another. As will be subsequently indicated, this affects the responses in various areas and somewhat affects the interpretation of our findings.

Since the questionnaire had to be signed, a possibility exists that some of the students may not have given reliable answers.

Fischer[13], for example, found on the basis of a study of upper class women students, that while the mean number of problems underlined did not vary significantly when the questionnaire was or was not signed, the number of problems circled (serious) tended to be significantly higher when the questionnaire was not signed. On the other hand, it may have, as is true with other structured tests, given us other valid information[14].

Another difficulty to which consideration must be given is the fact that this questionnaire is geared toward an analysis of the problems of the ordinary college boy, and thus may err on areas and problems of concern to Yeshiva boys. The following question, therefore, attempts to tap this area. "Do you feel the items you have marked on the list given you a well-rounded picture of your problems?"—Yes 174 (79.09%), No 31 (14.09%), Blank 17 (6.82%).

The following are the views given by boys who answered in the affirmative:

*(a) Increasing insight.*

"As I filled out the list, I saw many problems that I didn't think of that were bothering me."

"I believe this is the first time in my life that I have seen all my faults at one time. I believe that many of them can be corrected by myself, now that I am more conscious of them."

"I feel that this is the first time that I honestly thought about my problems. Such a thing isn't a bad idea once in a while."

"Evidently this test is based on much experimentation. It manages to cover an amazingly wide range of problems, problems in fact that I considered indigenous to me."

"It just put me face to face with some problems that have been bothering me. I was just surprised to see that you have more problems than you realize."

"It has been worth doing because I see that the same things which I ponder over are possible matters of concern for others. It is good to know that others have the same problems. Psychologically, maybe I want to be like the normal person. Who doesn't?"

*(b)    Additional data for interview.*

"In order to advise me accurately, advisor must have an accurate picture of my problems.  Many of the items here would probably not have come out in an interview with an advisor.  This is an excellent supplement to an interview."

## The reasons for the negative responses were:

*(a)    The problems are not germane to religious youth.*

"The problems in many cases are too general.  In philosophical and religious matters, I feel that I would like to discuss some of my problems with someone."

"Not because of some problems, but if questions were worded differently, I would answer them."

"Some questions are too tenuous and though I might have certain problems similar to them, they are not quite expressed in such a manner that I might answer them in the affirmative."

*(b)    Many important problems are not considered in the questionnaire.*

"There are other things which may be considered problems by myself or others which are not expressed on the question sheet."

*(c)    The test is superfluous.*

"I have no problems at all.  There are some things which I'd like to be changed, but I know that there is no way I could because you can't have your cake and eat it."

"I have given each facet of my thoughts a full investigation so that for me personally this test was a bit superfluous."

*(d)    Problems considered have not, as yet, arisen.*

"No, many of the problems dealt with 'college life' or 'life on the campus' which I have not yet experienced."

"I think that certain questions should have been left out since they don't pertain to college freshmen."

It appears on the basis of these answers that a revision of the Mooney Check List is indicated for these students so as to include problems of importance to religious youth.

### 4.  *PROCEDURE*

In 1955 and 1956, the check list was administered to 220 Yeshiva College freshmen during the freshman orientation period.  The question may be asked as to whether these boys were typical products of the cultural mold exerted by traditional

Jewish culture.

Table 1 shows the high schools attended by the Yeshiva freshmen. Note that 89.54 per cent came either from New York City or out of town Yeshiva high schools. We can thus see that we are dealing with the typical problems of Jewish religious youth.

TABLE 1

High Schools Attended by Yeshiva College Freshmen

| High school | N | % |
|---|---|---|
| New York City Yeshiva High Schools | 172 | 78.18 |
| Out of town Yeshiva High Schools | 25 | 11.36 |
| New York Public High Schools | 8 | 3.64 |
| Out of town Public High Schools | 15 | 6.82 |
| Total | 220 | 100.00 |

II. RESULTS

The average number of items underlined by the freshmen was 42.07. One hundred and thirty-nine problems (out of the 330 items) were underlined by 10 or more per cent of the students.

A. PROBLEM CONSTELLATIONS

A bird's eye view of the main problems of the college freshmen may be gleaned from a study of the problem constellations. Table 2 shows problem constellation of Yeshiva College

TABLE 2

The Problem Constellations*

| Area | N | % | Mean | SD |
|---|---|---|---|---|
| Social and Recreational Activities | 206 | 93.64 | 6.41 | 4.59 |
| Health and Physical Development | 206 | 93.64 | 4.60 | 3.30 |
| Adjustment to School Work | 196 | 89.09 | 6.05 | 4.38 |
| Personal-Psychological Relations | 195 | 88.64 | 5.18 | 3.90 |
| Social-Psychological Relations | 184 | 83.63 | 5.09 | 3.87 |
| The Future: Vocational and Educational | 170 | 77.27 | 4.56 | 2.70 |
| Finances, Living Conditions, Employment | 167 | 75.91 | 4.58 | 4.05 |
| Home and Family | 152 | 69.09 | 4.47 | 2.34 |
| Morals and Religion | 150 | 68.18 | 4.12 | 3.03 |
| Courtship, Sex, and Marriage | 148 | 67.27 | 3.83 | 2.88 |
| Curriculum and Teaching Procedure | 120 | 54.55 | 3.75 | 3.63 |

* It is to be noted that, in all the following tables, the items are arranged in accordance with rank order, the most frequently checked item being at the top and the least frequently checked at the bottom.

freshmen. This indicates the number of students who under-lined one or more problems in any of these areas. We may note that whereas 206 students or 93.64 per cent had one or more problems underlined in the area of *Social and Recreational Activities,* only 120 or 54.55 per cent had one or more problems underlined in the area of *Curriculum and Teaching Procedure.* A further analysis of Table 2 brings out the striking fact that the religious youth have more problems in the *(a)* areas of *Health and Physical Development, Social and Recreational Activities,* and *Adjustment to School Work* than in *(b)* Morals *and Religion, Courtship, Sex, and Marriage,* or *Curriculum and Teaching Procedure.* Possibly it is easier in the context of traditional Jewish culture to accept and acknowledge problems in one area with a relatively little damage to one's self-esteem than in another. Furthermore, cultural imperatives may create more drive and consequently more overt conflict in one area, and repress the culturally unacceptable desires in another.

## 1. *THE ITEMS MOST FREQUENTLY UNDERLINED*

The specific problems of the boys can be pinpointed by examining the items most frequently underlined and most frequently circled.

Table 3 shows items that are most frequently underlined

### TABLE 3
Items Most Frequently Underlined by Yeshiva College Freshmen

| Statement of problem | Frequency | Rank |
|---|---|---|
| Easily distracted from my work | 104 | 1 |
| Wondering if I'll be successful in life | 96 | 2 |
| Not knowing how to study effectively | 77 | 3 |
| Not getting enough outdoor air and sunshine | 76 | 5.5 |
| Worrying about examinations | 75 | 5.5 |
| Worrying how I impress people | 75 | 5.5 |
| Wanting to improve myself culturally | 74 | 7 |
| Feeling tired much of the time | 73 | 8 |
| Not getting enough sleep | 70 | 9.5 |
| Too little social life | 70 | 9.5 |

and, thus of some concern to religious youth. An examination of Table 3 indicates that only these three problems: "Easily distracted from my work," "Not knowing how to study effectively," "Worrying about examinations," may be narrowly construed as pertaining to school. Thus the problems which actually affect the students are not within the narrow definition of collegiate activities, although, undoubtedly, they have an effect on them. It is obvious that helping the student to resolve these problems is as important as helping him to master the more traditional and academic part of the curriculum.

### 2. *ITEMS MOST FREQUENTLY CIRCLED*

Table 4 illustrates the kinds of problems which were considered acute. The largest proportion of these refer to health and social activities.

### TABLE 4

Items Most Frequently Circled by Yeshiva College Freshmen

| Statement of problem | Frequency | Rank |
|---|---|---|
| Wondering if I'll be successful in life | 38 | 1 |
| Not knowing how to study effectively | 33 | 2 |
| Easily distracted from my work | 32 | 3 |
| Not knowing what I really want | 28 | 4 |
| Taking things too seriously | 26 | 5.5 |
| Worrying about examinations | 26 | 5.5 |
| Lacking self-confidence | 25 | 7 |
| Wanting to be more popular | 24 | 8 |
| Having a poor background for some subjects | 23 | 10 |
| Unable to concentrate well | 23 | 10 |
| Vocabulary too limited | 23 | 10 |

It may be noted that four problems: "Wondering if I'll be successful in life," "Not knowing how to study effectively," "Easily distracted from my work," "Worrying about examinations," occur on both lists. Two of these pertaining to school appear on both lists, "Not knowing how to study effectively" and "Worrying about examinations." Apparently these are the most troublesome areas.

### B. HOW DOES THE RELIGIOUS YOUTH VIEW HIS PROBLEM

We noted that some of the college freshmen felt that the Check List did not fully cover the range of their problems. The question arises as to how does he see himself in the context of his expressed needs. The question, "How would you summarize your chief problems in your own words? Write a brief summary," was, therefore, provided to give the student an opportunity for self-expression and to give him a chance to voice his feelings about himself, his heartaches, his troubles, and his misgivings. We are, therefore, citing excerpts expressing the religious youth's sentiments, when discussing the various problem constellations, as we feel that these are the most valuable clues to the understanding of the Yeshiva College freshman.

### 1.  *SOCIAL AND RECREATIONAL ACTIVITIES*

Some of the remarks of the boys in this area are as follows:

#### a.  *Financial difficulties.*

"Lack of funds which prevent me from doing all the things I'd like to or need to, and the impression I make on some people; not being able to fit in with the crowds due to my personality."

#### b.  *Lack of conversational skills.*

"Problems are mostly that I am slow in getting acquainted with others due to lack of common background and knowledge of sports, to keep a conversation going. I am also perplexed about my future and course to pursue."

#### c.  *Not enough time for recreation.*

"My chief problems are not being able to decide on things right, and time for physical exercise and sports due to school work."

#### d.  *Inability to dance.*

"Although I meet girls easily and have as many dates as I want, I often find myself embarrassed because I can't dance. Often it prevents me from meeting someone I'd like to meet. Transportation is a problem only because it is time consuming."

#### e.  *Not enough time.*

"In school too long to get enough exercise, recreational and otherwise, usually leads to late nights in order to get some exercise at all, although I'm very rarely aware of my lack of sleep and tiredness. I become very restless when I do start homework, therefore, I'm easily distracted. I don't have enough time for some other recreation such as my present favorite hobby of classical music. My speech handicap is talking too fast, which leads to stuttering—which I'm slowly curing myself of."

"One of my chief problems is not having enough time. I am speaking of my high school career. I went to school from Sunday until Thursday night. When I got home there was nothing to do on Friday because my friends go to school and on Saturday I can't do anything because of my religion."

Table 5 indicates the dissatisfaction felt by the boys with their lives and their desire to improve themselves culturally and to develop social and recreational skills. Apparently the average Yeshiva boy's life does not lend itself to extensive social participation. Thus, 31.82 per cent complained of "too little

TABLE 5

Social and Recreational Activities*

|  | Underlined | | Circled | |
|---|---|---|---|---|
|  | N | % | N | % |
| Wanting to improve myself culturally | 74 | 33.64 | 19 | 25.68 |
| Too little social life | 70 | 31.82 | 22 | 31.43 |
| Wanting to improve my mind | 68 | 30.91 | 14 | 20.59 |
| Not enough time for recreation | 63 | 28.64 | 22 | 34.92 |
| Wanting to learn how to dance | 63 | 28.64 | 11 | 17.46 |
| Trouble in keeping a conversation going | 52 | 23.64 | 22 | 42.31 |
| Wanting very much to travel | 49 | 22.27 | 8 | 16.33 |
| Wanting more chance for self-expression | 46 | 20.91 | 13 | 28.26 |
| Too little chance to get into sports | 44 | 20.00 | 8 | 18.18 |
| Awkward in meeting people | 37 | 16.82 | 12 | 32.43 |
| Not using my leisure time well | 37 | 16.82 | 5 | 13.51 |
| Too little time to myself | 35 | 15.91 | 13 | 37.14 |
| Lacking skill in sports and games | 35 | 15.91 | 17 | 48.57 |
| Slow in getting acquainted with people | 34 | 15.45 | 11 | 32.35 |
| Wanting more worthwhile discussions with people | 33 | 15.00 | 11 | 33.33 |
| Wanting to improve my manners or etiquette | 30 | 13.64 | 4 | 13.33 |
| Too little chance to read what I like | 30 | 13.64 | 6 | 20.00 |
| Wanted to improve my appearance | 28 | 12.73 | 8 | 28.57 |
| Awkward in making a date | 28 | 12.73 | 6 | 21.43 |
| Boring week ends | 27 | 12.27 | 4 | 14.81 |
| Too little chance to enjoy art or music | 27 | 12.27 | 5 | 18.52 |
| Too little chance to enjoy radio or television | 27 | 12.27 | 1 | 3.70 |
| In too few student activities | 25 | 11.36 | 4 | 16.00 |
| Too little chance to pursue a hobby | 25 | 11.36 | 3 | 12.00 |
| Too little chance to do what I want to do | 25 | 11.36 | 9 | 36.00 |
| Not living a well-rounded life | 25 | 11.36 | 11 | 44.00 |

* In Tables 5 to 15 the problems underlined by 10 per cent or more of the college freshmen are indicated.

social life" and 28.64 per cent of "not enough time for recreation" and "wanting to learn how to dance." Apparently the high school authorities consider social activities as unproductive expenditure of time. Not enough growth in social skills, therefore, appeared during the high school years. This seems to indicate that the school and the home have not made a concerted effort in providing social experience leading toward the development of social poise and social competence.

It appears to this writer that there has to be a reorientation in the educational philosophy of the Yeshiva high schools. A positive approach to mental hygiene must be stressed. Even if scholastic standards suffer (why should they?) the physical and mental well-being of the pupil must be considered first. Just as we need an academic curriculum that meets individual needs, we, likewise, need an individualized social and recreational program. Social skills such as dancing should be taught. These would lead toward greater social acceptability and better heterosexual adjustment.

Boys who are extremely socially handicapped should be guided individually "by hand," if necessary, into desirable social activities. This will lead toward the development of fruitful interpersonal relationships.

### 2. HEALTH AND PHYSICAL DEVELOPMENT

It is to be noted that physical symptoms and complaints in this area may indicate a dissatisfaction with one's physical self, with the way one sees himself as seen by other. One may speculate as to what is the meaning of poor health to the religious youth.

### a. Physical difficulties.

"I am underweight with too little exercise and one allergy. I desire to increase my knowledge with quick reading habits, good concentration. A desire to travel, and get to school in less time, and experience in my field."

"My chief problem is due to the fact that I am unable to hear what people are saying to me at certain times. This, of course, brings about a certain amount of uneasiness. As of yet, it has not affected my life to any acute degree. However, it is quite bothersome."

"I'd like to lose some weight and grow a little taller. I'd like to try and take more interest in sports and activities and like to keep a conversation going."

"My posture is not very bad, but the shape of my spine, which accentuates my head, gives me a fatter appearance and, in turn, makes me appear short. A mark on my face, the result of acne, is not too noticeable, but bothers me a bit. It is covered by my glasses so it isn't so bad."

*b. Quite often also emotional conflicts may express themselves as physical symptoms.*

"I am nervous, careless, and have a handicap with bad eyes and an allergy problem, not being able to read quickly, poor concentration, easily convinced in reference to temptations."

"It is difficult getting to sleep at the dormitory and, as a result, I am always tired, I get nervous very easily, if I can't understand a problem, I must stop work and rest a while."

*c. Lack of time.*

"There is not enough time to do exercise and be in the fresh air. I am also looking for a job to earn extra spending money. I have quite a few colds during the Winter."

We may note that the problems in Table 6 may be roughly broken up into two categories: *(a)* one which would be true in any school or college setting, and *(b)* one which has been exaggerated by the culture of the religious youth. A study, for

TABLE 6

Health and Physical Development

| | Underlined | | Circled | |
|---|---|---|---|---|
| | N | % | N | % |
| Not getting enough outdoor air and sunshine | 76 | 34.55 | 19 | 25.00 |
| Feeling tired much of the time | 73 | 33.18 | 14 | 19.18 |
| Not getting enough sleep | 70 | 31.82 | 5 | 7.14 |
| Not getting enough exercise | 50 | 22.73 | 13 | 26.00 |
| Being overweight | 43 | 19.55 | 16 | 37.21 |
| Allergies (hay fever, asthma, hives, etc.) | 41 | 18.64 | 8 | 19.51 |
| Too short | 37 | 16.82 | 7 | 18.92 |
| Poor complexion or skin skin trouble | 35 | 15.91 | 12 | 34.29 |
| Weak eyes | 34 | 15.45 | 6 | 17.65 |
| Poor posture | 34 | 15.45 | 10 | 29.41 |
| Not as strong and healthy as I should be | 28 | 12.73 | 6 | 21.43 |
| Not very attractive physically | 27 | 12.27 | 10 | 37.04 |
| Frequent colds | 23 | 10.45 | 1 | 4.35 |

example, indicates that many adolescents are disturbed about physical factors[15].

The writer feels that these problems, when one also considers the statement "Not getting enough outdoor air and sunshine," and "Not getting enough exercise," are due to the top-heavy academic load of many Yeshiva high schools. One must know the curriculum of these schools to understand why these problems exist and to realize that the students' statements are based on reality factors. In these high schools, the boys have the following schedules: Hebrew subjects from 9:00 a.m.-1:00 p.m. and secular subjects from 2:00 p.m.-6:00 p.m. They attend school Monday through Thursday; 9:00 a.m.-12 noon on Friday and 9:00 a.m.-1:45 p.m. on Sunday. Very few opportunities are provided for physical recreation. The admittedly long hours, to which must be added the burden of homework, can only bring about the problem of "Not getting enough sleep."

Unfortunately too many Yeshiva boys are unable to complete all the assigned work within reasonable hours and, thus, sometimes work very late in an attempt to catch up. Particularly is this true before examinations (see Table 7).

## TABLE 7
### Adjustment to School Work

|  | Underlined | | Circled | |
|---|---|---|---|---|
|  | N | % | N | % |
| Easily distracted from my work | 104 | 47.27 | 32 | 30.77 |
| Not knowing how to study effectively | 77 | 35.00 | 33 | 42.86 |
| Worrying about examinations | 75 | 34.09 | 26 | 34.67 |
| Not spending enough time in study | 62 | 28.18 | 21 | 33.87 |
| Having a poor background for some subjects | 60 | 27.27 | 23 | 38.33 |
| Unable to concentrate well | 57 | 25.91 | 23 | 40.35 |
| Vocabulary too limited | 54 | 24.55 | 23 | 42.59 |
| Weak in spelling or grammar | 47 | 21.36 | 18 | 38.30 |
| Slow in reading | 45 | 20.45 | 19 | 42.22 |
| Forgetting things I've learned in school | 44 | 20.00 | 11 | 25.00 |
| Slow in mathematics | 43 | 19.55 | 14 | 32.56 |
| Not planning my work ahead | 41 | 18.64 | 8 | 19.51 |
| Afraid to speak up in class discussions | 33 | 15.00 | 12 | 36.36 |
| Having too many outside interests | 30 | 13.64 | 7 | 23.33 |
| Trouble with oral reports | 30 | 13.64 | 6 | 20.00 |
| Unable to express myself well in words | 30 | 13.64 | 9 | 30.00 |
| Trouble in outlining or note taking | 29 | 13.18 | 8 | 27.59 |
| Weak in writing | 27 | 12.27 | 9 | 33.33 |
| Not getting studies done on time | 24 | 10.91 | 4 | 16.66 |
| Getting low grades | 23 | 10.45 | 8 | 34.78 |
| Fearing failure in college | 22 | 10.00 | 8 | 36.36 |

We also find associated miscellaneous physical problems. "Too short." Being too short may indicate that growth has stopped and a question arises in the mind of the young man, "Am I normal? Will I never grow up?"

"Poor complexion or skin trouble" and "Not very attractive physically." The boys who underlined these items most likely felt a discrepancy between their introjected culturally accepted idea of manhood and their deviant physiques. Physical attractiveness is at a premium, even for religious youth, at 17 years of age. It appears almost pointless to add that physical disfigurement may precipitate anxiety attacks and bring about frenzied search for remedies. However, the converse may also hold true. A college freshman, who finds that he is not a social lion, may project his lack of success into not being "attractive physically."

### 3. *ADJUSTMENT TO SCHOOL WORK*

Many boys felt that they have many problems in this area and they wished to have help to resolve them.

a. *Lack of requisite skills for success in school work.*

"My chief problems are as follows: I have not read sufficiently in my younger days and now I feel handicapped by my lack of literary knowledge and limited vocabulary. Now I have to read twice as much to catch up and have little time to do it in. Going to the school I do, my time limits, very strictly, any hobbies I enjoy, such as piano playing."

"My chief problem is my lack of English background. I am in this country five years and somehow I always run across some new item which everyone has known about, but to me, is a new experience."

"I have a very poor Hebrew background. Therefore, I find it difficult to master any language besides English. Too little social life as there are no co-ed clubs around my home. Therefore, I am poor in dancing and social etiquette. Because of my poor athletic ability, I find it hard to enjoy my vacations as others do."

b. *Lack of coördination in work assignments.*

"Nights in which I have very much homework and nights in which there is very little homework. I feel that the teachers should get together and give us a steady stream of homework, rather than overload us one night, and let us off the next."

c. *Tremendous homework burden.*

"Lack of extra time. Too much indoors. Quest to get good marks. The future doesn't seem clear and sure."

"At the present time I think school is the problem. I do, however, feel confident that I can overcome it without much trouble."

d. *Fear of failure symbolic of lack of adjustment.*

"I feel that I'm always nervous and always afraid of failing a course. It seems I worry myself sick about tests and exams."

e. *Poor teachers.*

"I have gained a dislike for certain subjects because of the teachers I have had and have neglected these subjects."

Table 7 indicates that many of the students are concerned with how to make their study effective and worthwhile. They are distracted from their work, worry about examinations, feel poorly prepared for their courses, and don't know how to study effectively.This may also be due to a feeling of insecurity in ordinary social relationships or possibly lack of achievement in other areas.

It is axiomatic that in any school, work would be anxiety provoking. It is particularly true, however, at Yeshiva College. Here the very lives of the boys are wound around their studies and their marks. These expressed problems can, therefore, be considered a symptom of their generalized anxiety, which indicate the pressure and anxiety of the parents. The student must secure high grades at all costs. Everyone at home expects him to attend graduate school. Neither parents nor faculty members, and least of all the students themselves, understand or accept the fact of individual differences. The belief is universal that if you work hard you will graduate *cum laude*. This, in spite of the top-heavy schedule, difficult examinations, and subject matter far removed from everyday life. As a result, almost all the boys are very eager to study so as to achieve high grades. Not to do so means courting social ostracism. High scholastic standing is synonymous with enhanced feeling of worthwhileness and increased respect by classmates. This reflects the cultural stress on learning as being worthwhile in itself.

### 4. *PERSONAL-PSYCHOLOGICAL RELATIONS*

## Some of the remarks make by the students are as follows:

### a. *Insecurity.*

"I am not sure of my capabilities and my aptitudes. Sometimes, because of these 'insecurities' I get sort of moody because I don't know if 'I have it in myself' to make something out of myself. My main problem, I think, is to get to know myself more and to find out exactly where I stand."

### b. *Feelings of inferiority.*

"My chief problems are very simple. I'm a very nervous fellow. Inferiority and conflicts of feeling with my parents."

"I am very serious minded, tense, nervous, inferiority complex— more by desire to accomplish my goal than in helping people—bothered by money matters—get angry easily."

### c. *Lack of self-confidence.*

"I cannot spot the chief problems but rather feel that I lack self-confidence even though continually being praised and very popular. I feel that I am jealous of those people who are smarter than I am. I sit and wonder sometimes why I can't reach those same goals since I've been told I have the capabilities."

"Nervousness, lack of self-confidence at times, thinking too much about sex, worrying about school work and the future."

### d. *Homesickness.*

"I have an adjustment problem. Living away from home, at college, meeting so many different people, has overwhelmed me. I try at times, to make life at college seem unreal, and think about what used to be at home. I rationalized my being here with the thought of getting an education. But why must it be away from home?"

### e. *Personality difficulties.*

"I have difficulty in concentrating on reality."

"I like to read and I also do a little writing on the side but I am generally easily discouraged by negative criticism. I like to think, but this constant thinking has apparently put too much pressure on my mind for I get headaches and fits of depression."

"Being shy—when meeting other people I'm too shy to get acquainted and start to talk to them."

"Overcoming shyness and self-consciousness is my main concern. To become acquainted with a greater majority of people and to make friends easier to ease nervousness. To decide on a vocation that would please myself and my parents as well. To meet a variety of people of both sexes."

"My most important problems are that I have a hard time expressing myself. I always worry about what other people think of me."

"I am primarily perturbed about my home life, nervousness,
temper, being obstinate."

An examination of the problems in Table 8 indicates that
some of the students may have serious emotional disorders. It
is also quite apparent that a few of them may refuse to accept
themselves as they are. This may lead to a constellation of

### TABLE 8
#### Personal-Psychological Relations

|                                         | Underlined | | Circled | |
|-----------------------------------------|:---:|:---:|:---:|:---:|
|                                         | N | % | N | % |
| Taking things too seriously             | 69 | 31.36 | 26 | 37.68 |
| Lacking self-confidence                 | 54 | 24.55 | 25 | 46.30 |
| Losing my temper                        | 46 | 20.91 | 18 | 39.13 |
| Moodiness, "having the blues"           | 44 | 20.00 | 15 | 34.09 |
| Afraid of making mistakes               | 33 | 15.00 | 8 | 24.24 |
| Can't make up my mind about things      | 28 | 12.73 | 12 | 42.86 |

symptoms such as "lacking self-confidence," "moodiness and
having the blues," "feelings of insecurity and the lack of self-
confidence." While it is true that these religious youth are in
their late teens, and therefore, may show intense mood swings,
yet, the students involved should be closely followed up.

### 5. *SOCIAL-PSYCHOLOGICAL RELATIONS*

Some of the boys felt:

*a.   Satisfaction with themselves in spite of acknowledged
problems and poor social adjustment.*

"I am too introverted and self-conscious, yet satisfied with the
introversion."

*b.   Need for social contact.*

"For as far back as I can remember I have not been a good
'mixer.' I was not able to establish close friendships. Perhaps this
gave me a feeling of being inferior. I would like to have more social
contacts."

*c.   Fear of failure in life.*

"At times, I feel that later in life, I may not be successful and
that I may not become a wonderful speaker, an asset necessary in the
Rabbinate. I also feel somewhat inferior and feel that I lack self-

confidence, although I am assured by my parents that all these fears are not well-founded. I also would like to improve myself culturally, although I don't seem to find time or make time for this."

Table 9 shows the problems experienced by the Yeshiva freshmen in the area of *Social-Psychological Relations*.

Note that these problems are somewhat similar to those noted under Personal-Psychological Relations. We may see that the symptoms of "being timid or shy," "feelings too easily hurt," "having feelings of extreme loneliness," may force some of the college freshmen into more satisfactory, for them, world of day dreams. It is obvious that these freshmen feel inferior; are afraid of competition for fear of offending their classmates. These freshmen, unfortunately, are "goody goodies" who never make trouble in school, are considered model students, and their difficulties are never noticed, unless they develop severe problems.

## 6. *FUTURE—VOCATIONAL AND EDUCATIONAL*

In considering this area, we must remember that in the traditional Jewish culture the mother is the main source of affection. The mother will reward the son who achieves culturally approved goals. This further increases the boy's drive for achievement. This practice is somewhat similar to what has been reported by McClelland and Friedman[16, 17].

### TABLE 9
#### Social-Psychological Relations

|  | Underlined | | Circled | |
|---|---|---|---|---|
|  | N | % | N | % |
| Worrying how I impress people | 75 | 34.09 | 15 | 20.00 |
| Wanting to be more popular | 57 | 25.91 | 24 | 42.11 |
| Being timid or shy | 52 | 23.64 | 20 | 38.46 |
| Speaking or acting without thinking | 52 | 23.64 | 14 | 26.92 |
| Sometimes acting childish or immature | 45 | 20.45 | 11 | 24.44 |
| Feelings too easily hurt | 41 | 18.64 | 11 | 26.83 |
| Wanting a more pleasing personality | 40 | 18.18 | 12 | 30.00 |
| Finding it hard to talk about my troubles | 38 | 17.27 | 8 | 21.05 |
| Being too easily embarrassed | 36 | 16.36 | 8 | 22.22 |
| Being ill at ease with other people | 36 | 16.36 | 16 | 44.44 |
| Being left out of things | 32 | 14.55 | 9 | 28.13 |
| Being stubborn or obstinate | 27 | 12.27 | 6 | 22.22 |
| Getting into arguments | 27 | 12.27 | 7 | 25.93 |
| Being too envious or jealous | 25 | 11.36 | 7 | 28.00 |
| Having feelings of extreme lonelines | 25 | 11.36 | 10 | 40.00 |
| Missing someone back home | 24 | 10.91 | 11 | 45.83 |
| Lacking leadership ability | 24 | 10.91 | 8 | 33.33 |

The religious youth has many problems in the area of vocational guidance:

> "My chief problem is the problem of choosing my life's work."
>
> "I am undecided about what I should be in the future."
>
> "I don't know in what special field I can make out well."
>
> "Plan vocation and future being religious and yet worldly."
>
> "I cannot make up my mind entirely on my future vocation. Many people are distracting my intentions with discouragement and have influenced me in my decisions. My life-long ambition was to become a physician but now, hearing well-meant advice concerning the disadvantages of a medical career, I cannot make up my mind whether to continue in that field or branch off into another field of science."
>
> "I don't know exactly what I want to be and can be. I also have a slight problem dealing with the requirements of my chosen vocation. Worried if I will get good grades in the future. A feeling of uncertainty on the next four years which will be the mold for my life."

Jewish religious youth have high achievement needs which, in turn, express themselves in their vocational interests[18]. This area is, thus, very threatening to them. As is well-known, from childhood these boys have been subjected to the kind of pressure which presumed that they would become professionals. These drives have been internalized by the religious youth.

The parents have sent their child to Yeshiva schools; have provided rewards in the form of love, affection, and recognition

TABLE 10

The Future:  Vocational and Educational

| | Underlined | | Circled | |
|---|---|---|---|---|
| | N | % | N | % |
| Wondering if I'll be successful in life | 96 | 43.64 | 38 | 39.58 |
| Doubting wisdom of my vocational choice | 61 | 27.73 | 20 | 32.79 |
| Not knowing what I really want | 58 | 26.36 | 28 | 48.28 |
| Needing to know my vocational abilities | 52 | 23.64 | 18 | 34.62 |
| Need to decide about an occupation | 44 | 20.00 | 22 | 50.00 |
| Needing to plan ahead for the future | 37 | 16.82 | 8 | 21.62 |
| Wanting advice on next steps after college | 35 | 15.91 | 11 | 31.43 |
| Concerned about military service | 34 | 15.45 | 11 | 32.35 |
| Restless in delay at starting life's work | 33 | 15.00 | 8 | 24.24 |
| Wanting part-time experience in my field | 24 | 10.91 | 9 | 37.50 |
| Needing information about occupations | 24 | 10.91 | 9 | 37.50 |
| Choosing best courses to prepare for a job | 23 | 10.45 | 6 | 26.09 |

for scholastic accomplishment. They have implicitly indicated conditions under which the child is acceptable to them and may consider himself vocationally successful and inferentially adequate. The parents set up goals for their child which would bring him a feeling of accomplishment, and vicarious gratification for themselves. They have given regards and punishments to reinforce these drives and provide for the satisfaction of the need for recognition and acceptance.

Need we wonder that 96 students are worrying about success in life and that they have a tremendous concern, and even fear about their future. As a matter of fact, this problem was underlined by more students than any other. It is further obvious that this misgiving of students is based upon reality factors. Success in life depends on success on the job, which means, in turn, having adequate income, a good marriage, occupying a proper place in one's community, meeting the expectations of one's peers and one's parents. As a matter of fact, an insecure freshman may gain prestige among his peers, and in the bosom of his family, by merely stating that he is taking a pre-medical course. After all, the status one acquires in one's eyes in the pursuit of a profession, is a reflection of the prestige this occupation carries in the eyes of the Jewish cultural group from which the adolescent came.

It is to be remembered that the choice of a professional occupation is the *sine qua non* method of moving upward in the Jewish social structure[19]. To confirm this, many interviews with parents indicate, "I don't care what work my son does, as long as he is a professional." Not to do so for a Yeshiva boy means a loss of face for his family and a reflection on his parents. It is through the pursuit of peer approved goals that the adolescent acquires primary status[20, 21]. Of course, this possibly may also reflect the parents' own thwarted vocational ambitions.

One, of course, may wonder—do all these boys have adequate vocational information? Are they all capable of success in the graduate school? And finally, what phantasy activities enter into their expectations?

Since it seems obvious that some of these boys cannot possibly be successful in professional life, other alternatives should be planned with them. It seems most advisable for the guidance department to try, somehow, to counteract parental expectations and downgrade the students' aspirations, by pointing out to them that a job well done is admirable, that Jewish tradition always looked favorably upon work[22] no matter what it was, that the personal qualities brought to the job, the happiness one brings to his associates, are more important than the salary earned, that if one has the proper attitude towards his work, he can always enjoy it and have a constructive sense of achievement.

Generally speaking, there is indication of a need of adequate vocational guidance for the freshmen. The number of occupations in the United States is enormous, and career choice is difficult to make in the absence of knowledge concerning the current status and future prospects of the occupation.

### 7. FINANCES, LIVING CONDITIONS, AND EMPLOYMENT

The concern of the freshmen in this area is well expressed by a few comments selected at random. It is to be remembered that in the traditional Jewish subculture, as well as in the majority culture[23], money symbolizes ability to do what one likes—emancipation from home control. Desire for an income of one's own is nearly universal.

#### a. Conflict because of burden on parents.

"There is little that can be said or done about my financial problems. It is nerve-wracking to have to keep such a close observance of expenditures and I feel terrible that my parents have to minimize their budget and comforts because of the great expense of my college career."

"Financial and health problems in family. Unable to decide on occupation. Traveling home with a heavy schedule."

#### b. Lack of funds for education.

"My chief problems are lack of funds necessary to further my education. I work during my Summer vacation but find it impossible to work during school."

"Due to my financial status, I am worried about my future vocation."

"Financial difficulties—have to support myself and give money to help the family."

#### c. Need for a job.

"Job, up to now I have never had a job and got my money from my parents who I am very close to."

"I would like to get a part-time job in order to see how it feels to earn money by myself."

A perusal of the problems in Table 11 indicates the reality of the freshmen concern. Most of these boys—some 80 per

TABLE 11

Finances, Living Conditions, Employment

|  | Underlined | | Circled | |
|---|---|---|---|---|
|  | N | % | N | % |
| Needing a job during vacations | 42 | 19.09 | 10 | 23.81 |
| Family worried about finances | 38 | 17.27 | 21 | 55.26 |
| Too many financial problems | 37 | 16.82 | 19 | 51.35 |
| Unsure of my future financial support | 32 | 14.55 | 13 | 40.63 |
| Too little money for clothes | 32 | 14.55 | 7 | 21.88 |
| Going through school on too little money | 30 | 13.64 | 14 | 46.67 |
| Disliking financial dependence on others | 30 | 13.64 | 9 | 30.00 |
| Needing a part-time job now | 29 | 13.18 | 12 | 41.38 |
| Tiring of the same meals all the time | 29 | 13.18 | 7 | 24.14 |
| Needing to watch every penny I spend | 28 | 12.73 | 12 | 42.86 |
| Too little money for recreation | 25 | 11.36 | 11 | 44.00 |
| Transportation or commuting difficulties | 23 | 10.45 | 2 | 8.70 |

cent—receive full or part-time scholarship aid. Since this scholarship aid is based upon need, it is understandable that they are concerned over finances.

We must emphasize that these boys wish to be independent, to be on their own, to earn part of their scholarship funds (no question relative to this, unfortunately, is placed in the questionnaire). An opportunity for work experience should be provided. Work experience enables one to learn work habits, teaches one to see the usefulness of school courses. In order to achieve this it will be necessary to modify the academic load.

### 8. *HOME AND FAMILY*

The boys had difficulties because of:

### a. *Overprotection.*

"I feel that I can do many more things than I am allowed to. Recently I received a driver's license, yet parents wouldn't think of letting me drive, especially my mother. This is unfair, as many of my friends whose driving ability doesn't equal mine, drive around at will.   Realizing that they're interested in my welfare does not help—I only lose confidence in myself.   Also, owing to the fact that I have at least eight years to my M.D. degree, I can't possibly tell them I like one girl and I would think of eventually marrying her.   Keeping all my feelings to myself is rather difficult."

"I would like to have more of a free choice in everything I do; go where and when I want to, no matter how small the item.   I do not have a social life at the moment and would like to know if my present status is good or bad for me, and in general, where I stand on everything."

"My mother is very worried about my relations with the army."

"My mother treats me like a baby."

"If I am a few moments late, my mother gets very upset."

### b.   Too great demands by parents.

"I don't like the way I have been treated at home until now; perhaps it will change."

"My chief problems revolve around my relation and attitude towards my parents.   My parents expect as much from me as they get from my brother, and this is impossible."

### c.   Concern about parents.

"Two things are mainly bothering me.   One is letting my mother work very hard so that I may go through college.   I am afraid that I am taking too much from her since she is no youngster any more. I am afraid that I may not be a success after college, thus causing all my mother's work and struggle to go to pot.   I am afraid to go steady because it might endanger my finishing my education.   At the present, I am entangled with a very nice girl and I don't know what to do."

"A main problem or worry of mine is the welfare of my parents with whom I am very close."

Table 12 shows the problems of the Yeshiva boys in the area of *Home and Family*.

### TABLE 12
#### Home and Family

|  | Underlined | | Circled | |
|---|---|---|---|---|
|  | N | % | N | % |
| Parents sacrificing too much for me | 42 | 19.09 | 22 | 52.38 |
| Clash of opinion between me and my parents | 35 | 15.90 | 13 | 37.14 |
| Talking back to my parents | 34 | 15.45 | 13 | 38.24 |
| Being criticized by my parents | 33 | 15.00 | 14 | 42.42 |
| Irritated by habits of a member of my family | 32 | 14.55 | 11 | 34.38 |
| Not telling everything at home | 31 | 14.09 | 8 | 25.81 |
| Unable to discuss certain problems at home | 30 | 13.64 | 10 | 33.33 |
| Worried about a member of my family | 24 | 10.91 | 12 | 50.00 |
| Parents expecting too much of me | 23 | 10.45 | 7 | 30.43 |
| Sickness in the family | 22 | 10.00 | 13 | 59.09 |
| Parents making too many decisions for me | 22 | 10.00 | 4 | 18.18 |
| Wanting more freedom at home | 22 | 10.00 | 10 | 45.45 |

Apparently the religious youth have internalized their home environment and, therefore, the issues they raise are "specific" rather than general. Both father and son usually subscribe to the same values, and place great store on family traditions. This tends to lessen the area of conflict.

However, in spite of the cohesiveness and authoritativeness of traditions, problems still erupt to disturb the surface serenity of the home. There are demands for emancipation from a too warm, too protective, too nurturant, too sacrificing home. However, in their attempt at liberation these boys feel guilty and it is hard for them to express their inner resentment against authoritarian parents. After all, they have been taught from childhood to respect authority. (Their experiences with authority, moreover, have usually been helpful.)

Further, in the traditional Jewish family, as in all other families, emancipation from home depends not only upon the individual family setting but also upon the traditions, values and beliefs which, in a sense, regulate family relationships. To this may also be added the frequent conflict when values formerly held to be unquestioned become doubtful and the painful need arises to reappraise one's family relationships in light of the influences seeping in from other subcultures.

### 9. MORALS AND RELIGION

The religious conflict of the traditionally brought up youth and their agonizing doubts are expressed in their comments:

a. *Conflict between religious belief and the stern necessities of life.*

"If you may call it a problem, it is my sincere and earnest desire to be a religious Jew and raise a family in the spirit of the Torah. I find it difficult to decide on an occupation for each has its limitations. I realize this is not good, for if I do not make a steady income, it will not only be harmful to me but it will be a profanity of the Holy One."

b. *Conflict between traditional practices and life.*

"Traditionally religious in beliefs and action, but find it hard to attach myself to these things conclusively and with sufficient sureness. Especially find these failings if I cannot win someone to my religious point of view."

c. *Religious doubt—this may bring in its strain feelings of extreme guilt.*

"I've read science fiction where there are no limits; and it has shown me how immense the whole question is. Our religion does not answer all the questions in my mind."

"Wonder why the true social order is to be found in Judaism."

"A certain uncertainty with my relationship to religion and how I appear to people."

"Lately, I find myself doubting the very existence of a God. Considering my education it is hard for me to understand what led me to these doubts. However, by talking to others, I am eventually coming to a better understanding of my worries."

### d. Indecision regarding religious beliefs.

"Religious conflicts. Conflicting ideas about religion. Unable to devote enough time to subjects that interest me. Conflicts with parents about religion."

### e. Insecurity expressing itself in desire for security of religious beliefs.

"These stem from a desire for things to be black and white. I feel that I must convince conclusively in order to be in the right."

An examination of Table 13 indicates that relatively few of the religious youth have religious conflicts or doubts. Yet,

### TABLE 13
### Morals and Religion

|  | Underlined | | Circled | |
|---|---|---|---|---|
|  | N | % | N | % |
| Wanting to understand more about the Bible | 37 | 16.82 | 13 | 35.14 |
| Troubled by a lack of religion in others | 34 | 15.45 | 7 | 20.59 |
| Confused in some of my religious beliefs | 31 | 14.09 | 10 | 32.26 |
| Wanting to feel close to God | 30 | 13.64 | 14 | 46.67 |
| Having a certain bad habit | 28 | 12.73 | 8 | 28.57 |
| Needing philosophy of life | 27 | 12.27 | 10 | 37.04 |
| Unable to break a bad habit | 27 | 12.27 | 10 | 37.04 |
| Giving in to temptations | 25 | 11.36 | 8 | 32.00 |
| Can't forget some mistakes I've made | 23 | 10.45 | 6 | 26.09 |
| Sometimes not being as honest as I should be | 21 | 9.55 | 1 | 4.76 |

even though a comparative minority of the freshmen express difficulties in this area, close attention should be paid to it. We must realize that these issues are more critical for the boys whose entire philosophical outlook revolves around religious values[24]. The sudden impact of religious doubt serves to overwhelm them. This is thus much more traumatic for them than for other college freshmen who do not have a religious philosophy.

Furthermore, becoming members of an adult religious and professedly moral community and sometimes finding a yawning chasm between words and deed, professed beliefs and activities, further serves to unnerve them. Indeed some of their adult leaders are themselves confused, and cannot help them regain their former serenity of spirit, emotional security, and feelings of belonging to the "House of Israel."

Did these religious youths find that some of their cherished beliefs no longer correspond to "scientific" reality? Did they feel that there is a conflict between science and religious observance? The freshmen who feel "confused in some of my religious beliefs," "troubled by a lack of religion in others," "wanting to feel close to God," and "needing a philosophy of life," have not apparently been able to transform their childish and immature understanding of Diety to a concept of God as an omniscient power and of reformulating their religious philosophy accordingly.

We must also consider the possibility that these religious doubts are an indirect expression of conflict and rejection of parental values. The writer has also noted many cases of Yeshiva boys who, after severe quarrels with and rejection of their parents, have embraced religious doctrines even more firmly. They looked for much firmer, more enduring and lasting refuge in the face of collapsing moral values, than the ones given them by their parents.

These boys need guidance which would help them transmute immature beliefs into a well-integrated synthesis of religious and moral values.

### 10. COURTSHIP, SEX AND MARRIAGE

Some of the boys' difficulties were:

*a. Not meeting a desirable companion of the opposite sex.*

"Girls, on the whole, are pretty 'giddy' characters. The ones I do meet and like are out of town. This means that I have to be content with letters and, during the Winter, I have no one to go out with. Also, the girls I like are often older than I am."

"I am bothered by my inability to relax and by constant clashes with my parents. I go out on dates but don't really enjoy them because the girl is usually stupid and just wants to neck.  If I had the courage of my convictions, I wouldn't bother with them, but, being 18, I do not have such courage."

"I believe that were I to meet some nice girl or girls that would solve my problems."          (

"I find it very difficult to find a girl among all my acquaintances who I feel I would like to spend an evening with."

"I have not yet found a girl I can honestly say I like and vice versa."

### b.  *Conflict over a girl.*

"I have talked this over with my mother but am still undecided as to whether to continue seeing a girl I like a lot.  But I am afraid of the consequences of going steady with her and attending college at the same time."

"I am in love with a girl and the years of waiting are too long to be sure of.  If I wait, then I may do things not permitted by Talmud. I am sure of my love and so is she.  She is 17."

### c.  *Choice of right mate.*

"My main problem really is how to be a success in the profession I choose.  I am also concerned about choosing the right mate because, eventually, I hope to get married and want the marriage to be a success.  This arouses another problem.  I know I have certain bad habits like my poor appearance; how to meet and date people properly; how to keep a conversation going, and how far to go with the opposite sex."

### d.  *Unrequited affection.*

"I feel annoyed because a girl has suddenly changed her attitude about me among one or two that I ever liked in my life.  Now that I think of this girl, I wonder if there is another who thinks as I do, and I could think as much of."

### e.  *Parent objection to dating.*

"The little problem I am concerned with is my social life.  I have two older sisters who never went out much with boys.  I am somehow different and enjoy the opposite sex very much.  My parents are against my taking girls out.  They do not say it, but I feel it in the way they react."

The area of courtship, sex, and marriage appears to be one of the least troublesome to the freshmen.  One may wonder why. Is it possible that the sex cacophony which comes from the movies, TV, radio, newspaper, billboards, newsstands, etc., failed to penetrate the Yeshiva walls?  Or is it possible that due to religious teaching sex repression has occurred, and the boys are not aware of their sex urges and the consequent problems? Or, is it possible that most of the boys tend to conceal true feelings in this very sensitive area?

All of the foregoing hypotheses may be valid. There is a very strong indication, however, in some of the replies, that sex is a very strong source of conflict, albeit not the only one, nor a major one.

### TABLE 14
#### Courtship, Sex and Marriage

|  | Underlined | | Circled | |
|---|---|---|---|---|
|  | N | % | N | % |
| Too few dates | 51 | 23.18 | 19 | 37.25 |
| Not meeting anyone I like to date | 39 | 17.72 | 18 | 46.15 |
| Wondering if I will ever meet a suitable mate | 35 | 15.91 | 7 | 20.00 |
| Wondering how far to go with the opposite sex | 32 | 14.55 | 7 | 21.88 |
| No suitable places to go on dates | 29 | 13.18 | 7 | 24.14 |
| Sexual needs unsatisfied | 27 | 12.27 | 10 | 37.04 |
| Too easily aroused sexually | 23 | 10.45 | 5 | 21.74 |

The writer, from his experience at Yeshiva University, is aware that in some cases the Yeshiva high schools have failed to further the establishment of heterosexual adjustment. Thus, many a boy graduated from high school without ever having a single date. Furthermore, on the basis of interviews with college freshmen, the writer found that the condition of being "dateless" is rather common in the freshman year. It seems to the writer that the college should attempt to remedy this. More provision should be made for the boys to meet girls and establish proper emotional relationships with them. Furthermore, an earnest effort should be made to teach the ethical values in this connection as consonant with the philosophy of Judaism. The problems of "how far to go with the opposite sex," or what to do about "sexual needs unsatisfied" will then tend to resolve themselves.

The writer is aware of the widespread masturbation among religious youth. This is similar to what is found in other groups[25]. However, due to their traditional upbringing, their fear of physical and psychological damage resulting from their practice is exacerbated. It is important that frank discussion of the boys' fear of masturbation be encouraged and an effort be made to allay their fears. Finally, this point should be reiterated, that one temporary way of meeting one's sexual needs is through masturbation, which is neither harmful physiologically nor psychologically. It is to be remembered that a guidance climate which promotes free discussion on any troublesome or tabooed subject will not only relieve anxieties, but will also be conducive towards the development of very high moral standard[26].

## 11.  CURRICULUM AND TEACHING PROCEDURES

It is to be 2remembered that the homes of these youths favored their continuing with their Hebrew studies. Finding dissatisfaction with the curriculum at this stage might indirectly indicate rejection of parental values.

Some of the remarks of the boys in this area are as follows

a.  *Lack of time for co-curricular activities.*

"I have not enough time to participate in an organization of which I am a member and not enough time to continue body building. I have not enough background in Hebrew and none in Yiddish concerning the Talmud class. I haven't any close friends and no girl friends. I am not liked by most people."

b.  *Failure to become a leader.*

"My chief problems seem to be a lack of leadership in school activities as I cannot seem to be able to become a leader in a class or one of the leaders, also there is the problem of my limited vocabulary and proper way to study. Also how to improve my English. To understand themes of prose and fiction. I have a very poor social life which I should like to improve."

c.  *Dissatisfaction with the required course of study.*

"My chief problem is that I can find no way to do what I want to do. I would like to devote all my time to studying Talmud. I am not able to do this because my parents want me to go to college. Even the time I spend at Talmud is disturbed by many classmates who aren't interested in really studying. The fact that I cannot do what I want in this field causes other problems for me. I now realize when I am wasting time and try to avoid wasting time. This spoils my social life. It also spoils the time time I spend in the classes that I am forced to take."

### TABLE 15
#### Curriculum and Teaching Procedure

| | Underlined | | Circled | |
|---|---|---|---|---|
| | N | % | N | % |
| Hard to study in living quarters | 32 | 14.55 | 8 | 25.00 |
| Forced to take courses I don't like | 31 | 14.09 | 6 | 19.35 |
| Grades unfair as measures of ability | 25 | 11.36 | 2 | 8.00 |

We find that relatively few problems are felt by the students in this area. Since these were entering freshmen who were not acquainted with the course of study, instructors and assignments, they omitted these questions. Furthermore, since for most of them Yeshiva College was the school of choice, they were favorably disposed toward its philosophy, educational policy, and curriculum, and were not ready on admission to visualize possible problems. Another possibility is the fact that since Jewish traditional culture places such a great emphasis upon education a feeling of guilt might develop if the curriculum were attacked. The dissatisfaction with the curriculum is translated into other areas such as too much time sent in school work, etc. Furthermore, since they became inured to the curriculum, they knew how to handle the problems that arose.

### 12. *NEED FOR GUIDANCE*

It seems to the writer that our study carries certain implications as far as guidance of religious youth is concerned. They need warm, understanding, sympathetic, enthusiastic counselors who have a positive approach to traditional Jewish values and who can transmit their philosophy to the students.

It is well established in guidance practice that unless individuals are aware of their problems and are willing to seek assistance to resolve them, nothing constructive can be achieved.

Are the Yeshiva college freshmen aware of their needs? Do they wish this type of counseling? The following question was, therefore, posed to tap the student's attitude toward guidance offered by the college.

"If the opportunity were offered, would you like to talk over any of these problems with someone on the college staff?" Responses: Yes 151 (68.64%), No 28 (12.73%), Blank 41 (18.63%).

It is of some interest to note why certain students felt they would like to discuss their problems with someone and others did not. Many students felt that they would benefit from such a discussion because:

a. *Need for sincere counseling.*

"I hope that maybe I will find some one on whom I can rely for good and sincere help. I have always tried to make friends of older people who I think will be able to help me when the time calls for it and also be an inspiration to me."

"If I were to gain anything, I would like to discuss my problems, in order to improve myself. Except that I would like to talk to a psychiatrist, not just a 'guidance counselor.'"

"My chief problems are religious, philosophical, and some personal defects of my own imagination, I often feel some really need improvement. I would like to request an interview with some one in the guidance department and then I could explain my problems in greater detail."

"I hope that through the answers that I have given on this list, I might be able to obtain from some one, advice on the problems troubling me."

"I haven't had much chance to discuss my problems with a qualified person and I feel this could make a good beginning."

It is obvious that these boys are somewhat disillusioned with the help that their parents give them in the solution of their personal problems, are reluctant to discuss these with them, and look to the college guidance staff for assistance.

It appears, on the other hand, that some of the college freshmen feel insecure and are on guard not only in regard to their parents, but also as far as any help from a guidance counselor is concerned. They wish to be independent of college guidance which they interpret as control. Occasionally these boys may need more help than those who seek it avidly.

b. *No need for guidance.*

"These problems had troubled me for a long time but now, by moving into a new neighborhood, most of these problems are being solved."

"A teacher would be of no use to me, as one can see my troubles are not directly attributed to school. I doubt if I would feel free enough to frankly discuss my worries with a total stranger."

"I don't feel that they are that serious, since I can handle them by myself."

"I feel my problems are personal and I'll solve them myself."

"I cannot answer this question because, though I would like to talk over my problems, it would have to be with some one with certain views on religion and life, and some one whom I trust and respect."

Another important issue is whether the troubled Yeshiva College freshman knows to whom to turn for help. To the question, "Do you know the particular person with whom you would like to have the talks?" 21 or 9.5% said Yes; 103 or 46.82% said No; and 96 or 43.64% left this question blank. These replies are understandable, in view of the fact that the freshmen just entered the college and are not aware of its resources. It is, nevertheless, at this point that the guidance staff should make its presence and functions known to the students.

### III. SUMMARY AND CONCLUSIONS

This monograph reports a study of the problems of Jewish religious youth. It is a part of a comprehensive study of the personality, attitudes, aptitudes, interests, intelligence, adjustment and background of these youths. According to our analysis of Mooney Problem Check Lists completed by 200 Jewish religious college freshmen, these young men experience particular difficulty with problems in the areas of *Social and Recreational Activities, Health and Physical Development,* and *Adjustment to School Work.* A reasonable hypothesis with which to explain these results, it seems to this author, is that the extreme pressure of academic overloading to which many of these students have been exposed has produced not only a tremendous concern for and over-emphasis on academic standing and adjustment to school work but an inevitably compensatory curtailment of social and recreational activities. The traditional Jewish emphasis on verbal learning is undoubtedly an active factor functioning in this situation. Out of 330 items on the Mooney Problem Check Lists, 139 were underlined by 10 or more per cent of the students; the average number of items underlined was 42.07.

# References

1. Eisenberg, A., & Warkow, S. Continuity of higher Hebrew study and Jewish home environment. *Jewish Education*, 1956, 26 (3): 42-50.

2. Duker, A. G. Socio-psychological trends in the American Jewish community since 1900. *Yivo Annual*, 1954, 9:166-178.

3. Golovensky, D. I. Ingroup and out-group attitudes of young people in a Jewish day school compared with an equivalent sample of pupils in public schools. Unpublished Ph.D. dissertation, New York University, 1954.

4. Levinson, B. M. Psychological effects of the all-day school. *Shevilay Hachinuch*, 1955, 15:163-168 (Hebrew).

5. Lewin, K. Bringing up the child. *Menorah Journal*, 1940, 28:29-45.

6. Silverman, S. S. The psychological adjustment of all-day school (Yeshiva) students: A psychological study of 7th and 8th year all-day school students compared with 7th and 8th year students attending public schools. Unpublished Ph.D. dissertation, Yeshiva University, 1953.

7. Sovin, A. Self-acceptance of Jewishness by young Jewish people. *Jewish Education* 1955, 26 (1): 22-31.

8. Mooney, R. L. *Mooney Problem Check List*. New York: Psychol. Corp., 1950.

9. Klohr, M. C. Personal problems of college students. *Journal of Home Economics*, 1948, 40:447-448.

10. Gordon, S. L. Student problems in a teachers college. *Journal of Educational Psychology*, 1948, 39:404-416.

11. McIntyre, C. J. The validity of the Mooney Problem Check List. *Journal Applied Psychology*, 1953, 37:270-273.

12. Pflieger, E. I. Pupil adjustment problems and a study of relationship between scores of the California Test of Personality and the Mooney Problem Check List. *Journal of Educational Research*, 1947, 41:265-278.

13. Fischer, R. P. Signed versus unsigned personal questionnaires. *Journal of Applied Psychology*, 1946, 30:220-225.

14. Meehl, P. E. The dynamics of "structured" personality tests. *Journal of Clinical Psychology*, 1945, 1:296-303.

15. Stoltz, H. R., & Stoltz, L. M. Adolescent problems related to somatic variation. In, *Adolescence*. Forty-third Yearbook of the National Society for the Study of Education, Part I, 81-99. Chicago: Univ. Chicago Press, 1944.

16. McClelland, D. C. *The Achievement Motive*. New York: Appleton-Century-Crofts, 1953.

17. McClelland, D. C., & Friedman, C. A. A cross-cultural study of the relationship between child-rearing practices and achievement motivation appearing in folk tales. In Swanson, G. E., *et al.* (*eds.*),

Readings in Social Psychology, New York: Holt, 1953, 243-248.

18. Norton, J. C. Patterns of vocational interest development and actual job choice. *Journal of Genetic Psychology*, 1953, 83:235-282.

19. Dinerman, M. Some socio-cultural patterns of Jewish teen-agers. *Jewish Social Service Quarterly*, 1955, 31:353-358.

20. Rosen, B. C. Conflicting group membership: A study of parent peer group cross-pressures. *American Sociological Review*, 1955, 29:155-161.

21. Seidler, M. B., & Ravitz, M. J. A Jewish peer group. *American Journal of Sociology*, 1955, 61:11-15.

22. Duckat, W. Jewish attitudes toward work. *Journal Jewish Communal Service*, 1956, 32:243-248.

23. Elias, L. J. *High School Youth Look at Their Problems.* Pullman, Washington: State Coll. Washington, 1947.

24. ———. The adolescent and the synagogue. *Jewish Parent, 1955,* 7:12-13, 19-20.

25. Ross, R. T. Measures of sex behavior in college males compared with Kinsey's results. *Journal of Abnormal & Social Psychology,* 1950, 45:753-755.

26. Kirkendall, L. A. *Sex Education as Human Relations.* New York: Inor Publishing Co., 1950.

Chapter 13

# Emotional Problems in Aging

MAURICE E. LINDEN, M.D.

**G**ROWING old is the most unrewarding aspect of our way of life.

We Americans are a vigorous people who have ever at hand the recent memories of conquests of numberless frontiers, of the thrilling experiences of all forms of emancipation, and of our great feats of strength and production. Conquest has made us bold. Success has given us zeal. Strength makes us eager. Excited by change, naive through good will, ready through freedom, reinforced by abundance, and able through enlightenment, we ardently resist anything that limits, arrests, or harasses. Our culture is a juggernaut of youthful ideals consigning to dust whatever does not move with it. Our values have been the values of youth—vigor, physical beauty, motion, quantitative productivity, and, to some degree, arrogance.

Contrasting and unfamiliar to us are the values of later maturity—reliability, wisdom, stability, quality, and humility. Surrounded by contrary attitudes our aging have little choice but to feel that reaching maturity means realizing social rejection. The half-tolerance, off-hand acceptance, and disinterest toward the aged constitute social exclusion.

And it is this emotional deprivation suffered by millions past sixty that is one of the main forces operating toward making them social dependents, embittered souls and, ultimately, physical and emotional incompetents.

## I. ORIGIN OF REJECTION

Let us consider for a moment the origin of that attitude people in our culture have toward the wrinkled face, grey hair, and less agile bodies.   It seems highly doubtful to me that age alone, or the concomitant changes in the physical self, would be met with such horror and frenzy, if the period in life in which such changes take place commanded a popularity at least equal to that enjoyed by earlier age levels.   Without diminishing the importance of the psychological changes that occur during aging, the postponed neurotic disturbances which can no longer be denied in later years, and the changed goals of living at that time of life, I am nonetheless convinced that a major factor contributing to the fear of age and some of the difficulties that attend it is the cultural attitude toward senescence.

For the sake of our discussion we must at the outset recognize that cultural attitude is not merely the transmission of tradition through education.   A culture develops points of view through needs, both sociologic and psychologic.   When a point of view is perpetuated, it is not only because it is imposed upon oncoming generations, but also because it fits in with the dictates of the deep emotional requirements of those generations.   Thus, for example, some primitive societies sacrifice their elders, who, living with their families at the hem of starvation, regard their own annihilation altruistically as an act of love, while their off-spring simultaneously satisfy in themselves strong lusts for power and supercession.

In our society we are more subtle about such matters.   We neither revere nor crudely discard the aged.   But our passive neglect of them has caused annihilation just as surely as if our mode of action had been more direct.   Witness youth who reject the protective caution of their elders as "conservativism and fuddy-duddyism."   Is not the reactive suffering of the older group, thus hastily by-passed in the stream of life, murderous? Witness industry that arbitrarily regards age 65 as the end of usefulness.   Is not the mandatory retirement thus achieved a ticket to nowhere?   Witness the physician, yes even the psychiatrist, the social worker, the counsellor, who annoyed with problems difficult of solution, says, "Well, what do you expect of older people?   They're rigid, unyielding, unmodifiable, and cantankerous."   Is not the resultant do-nothingness an invitation to indolence, stagnation and regression?

But why this elder-discarding among a people taught to

honor their parents and to love others as themselves?

There are many reasons—general and specific, social and individual. To understand part of this process we must take a brief excursion through earlier periods of personality development. We shall thus see that there is nobody to blame, that the elders bring these difficulties on themselves to a certain extent and that the system of events is self-perpetuating. We shall also see what is necessary to interrupt the cycle.

For the sake of this discussion we may regard the process of growing up as roughly divided into six stages:

Period of—

1. Infantile dependency
2. Childish envy and jealousy
3. Pre-pubertal socialization
4. Pubertal anxiety
5. Adolescent turmoil
6. Adult ambition

While these stages of going forward in human development are characterized by a series of changing orientations toward the social world, they also possess a common denominator—a bivalent attitude toward the elders.

1. The dependent infant, in his efforts to rid himself of dependency, to develop mastery and autonomy, rejects the admonitions of the elders. But he also endows his educators with omnipotence and omniscience due to the sense of smallness and inferiority he feels through being curbed. This exaggerated notion regarding his parents' capabilities is naturally destined for disillusionment.

2. The intense feelings of envy and jealously generated in children as an outgrowth of the romantic emotional interchanges of family life create rivalrous relationships in which the elders are alternately exalted and psychologically excluded.

3. The pre-pubertal child's need to externalize his interests and develop a society built upon sharing of common problem solutions places the elders in the role of problem makers. Inter-factional strife results.

4. To the child puberty means the resurgence of temporarily dormant primary instinctual drives. Archaic prohibi-

tions are revived with renewed intensity with the result that the elders are viewed by the child through guilty and angry feelings as the arch-prohibitors and a privileged group.

5. Mixed feelings of childish inferiority and adult aspirations characterize the adolescent period. Rebellion against the elders becomes the agency through which the adolescent achieves self-direction.

6. The young adult, bent on the development of his family and social achievement, views the elders as the personification of goals as well as the barriers in the way of their realization.

Even so abbreviated a consideration of developmental attitude reveals a host of antagonistic impulses toward the elders. For some people, whose lives are not marred by inadequately solved early life problems, growing up will mean a progressive reconciliation with the elders, with the acquisition of beneficent and essentially altruistic philosophies of life. But for many the early elder-rejecting tendencies remain partially or inadequately worked out and become submerged beneath the welter of traits and characters of personality organized for practicality and necessity.

The next series of events is of paramount importance. Strivings that become psychologically submerged, or repressed as we say, are not lost—they are simply removed from consciousness. The task of maintaining impulses in a state of *repression* requires energy. This side-tracking of mental energy for the purpose of keeping socially undesirable urges out of awareness constitutes the event known as the *development of defenses*. Such defensive mechanisms remain effective so long as nothing occurs to disturb the balance and so long as an adequate quantity of energy remains available. And there's the rub!

Late senescence is marked by events and experiences which succeed both in diminishing the availability of mental energy and in generating psychological turmoil. It is not necessary for the purpose of this paper to belabor the innumerable fortuitous circumstances which beset the aging—such as loss of loved ones, financial set-back, retirement, loss of teeth, etc.; nor need we go deeply into the biophysiological events which produce a progressive waning of physical resources.

The main point here is that as defenses lose their energy

charge they begin to lose their effectiveness. It is as though the lid were off Pandora's box. Out pop the furies, the imps and the vandals. Many hidden impulses virtually swarm into consciousness. Among these are the elder-discarding attitudes.

But, when such hostilities against the elders occur in an elder, they eventuate in self-rejection, or turning of hatred against oneself. And this is the very essence of melancholy. Such a state of mind ushers in the sequence of mental experiences that contribute to a progressive breakdown of personality structure. We are not surprised, then, to see the elder progress again through the stages of growing-up, except that this time it is backwards.

From adult ambitiousness he moves toward adolescent turmoil.

Next comes a puberty-like anxiety complete with all the basic instinctual upheaval.

A period of varying length then follows which is almost exactly analogous to pre-pubertal efforts at socialization.

An ensuing stage is then seen wherein childish envy and jealousy show up as distrust, inappropriate love and hate, and suspicion.

The following several detailed and minute stages of retrogression end up as infancy-like dependency. And that is senility!

## II. MULTIPLICITY OF FACTORS

If we are to treat such people we must understand all the factors that are combined in their makeup—because treatment means furnishing needs. So we cannot let the matter rest with what we have just discussed, because there are at least four more groups of factors that must be dealt with in managing the aged. We have just considered in brief the origin of cultural attitudes that reject the aged, cause them to reject themselves and to regress.

We are obliged also to pay attention to: 1. Life long individual neurotic traits. 2. Psychological recession. 3. Ethnic variations, and 4. Physiological recession.

However, I shall not undertake to develop a group of fully trained gerontologists in a single sitting. It will serve our needs now to pass over three of these topics lightly and spend a little time on the one particularly pertinent to this meeing.

We already know that it is folly to regard all aged people under the banner of a single prototype. Aged people differ as all people differ from one another. Each has his own neurotic patterns superimposed on a basically human substructure. He may be charming or bitter, cantankerous or cooperative, officious or considerate, disdainful or ingratiating, and so forth. Whatever the aged person's main pattern, we can be sure that he got that way through a logical process of accumulating expedient defensive measures throughout his early life. Since these defense patterns are automatic and receive their motive power from areas of mind of which we are not conscious, we regard them by definition as neurotic. Each neurotic system will require its own special method of handling.

Psychological recession found in my list of factors in aging refers to the steps in retrogression which closely parallel the stages of in-folding of body organs in the aging human organism. This is not identical with the almost sudden catastrophic emotional regression I described before which is the older person's way of meeting stress and insults. Recession follows upon regression and amounts to the several minute backward steps in infantile dependency, each being observed as an advance toward helplessness.

The physiological changes found in aging in themselves are an enormous field of study. We have at this time an obligation to note that the aged are a group having particular bodily needs and limitations. Some treatment methods that seem to aim at fancied rejuvenation are injudicious. I believe, further, that it is not only cruel but inappropriate to attempt to curtail drastically lifelong habits of living in the aged even though they may be regarded as unhygienic, unhealthful or injurious. This refers to smoking, drinking, food preferences, forms of exercise and many others.

### III.  SPECIFICALLY JEWISH ATTITUDES

Now let us consider, as succinctly as possible, the factor of ethnic variations[1]. We are concerned today with the Jewish group, although we recognize that each sociologic grouping will have its own pattern of attitudes toward its aged.

Naturally, in this country, the items I have mentioned apply to the Jewish population as well as to any other. However, there are additional factors that are important to the Jew. Permit me to speculate about these factors as they relate to the Jewish aged, for I am ignorant of any extensively controlled studies that could serve as conclusive frames of reference. Anything we may say in this area is subject to argument, many exceptions and items of cultural dilution. Our task is even more complicated by the fact that there are at least three categories of Jews in America: 1. The foreign-born. 2. First generation Jewish-Americans. 3. Subsequent generations.

They differ from one another psychologically to some extent. Complexity is further added to complication when one takes into account the several different cultural areas in foreign lands from which our elders have emigrated.

We shall have to sacrifice accuracy for simplification in our discussion and keep before our mind's eye the constant admonition that we are dealing in bold generalizations. For the present our considerations are further simplified by an obvious fact: that the majority of Jewish aged in this country today are foreign born.

I would classify specific Jewish attitudes into three groups of underlying and motivating dynamisms as follows:

    I. *Religion*
        Ten commandments
        The "chosen people" concept
        Diet
    II. *Heritage*
        The wandering—suffering legend and persecution
        Talmud—scholasticism and intellectualism
        Family relationships and ties
        Sentimentality and grief
    III. *Minority Complex*
        Group solidarity
        Striving for success
        Attitudes of aggression

All of these affect the Jewish self-concept and attitudes held toward the Jewish aged.

So brief a treatise as this one cannot do justice to this delicate, intricate, and challenging subject. Furthermore it is particularly difficult to be objective about it. But I have had the experience not only of observing groups of wholly Jewish aged, but also of seeing them in intimate living arrangements with non-Jewish companions. Some of the following tentative conclusions stem from such observations.

One of the important commandments in the Hebrew testament dictates the attitude that the child must have toward the parents. It may be that a residue of ancient, dutiful reverence for the elders can still be seen in the elaborate provisions and charities we make available to the Jewish aged. Perhaps we should not apply value judgments to such activities. Still, it would seem that a reverential attitude, even if only socially imposed and partly insincere, can help provide for a dignified existence in the sunset of life. We shall see a bit later on that when this factor is added to the many others, however, the combination can give rise to difficulties.

The "chosen people" concept based upon the ancient dogma that the Jew is the Father-God's favorite son is both a psychological asset and a social liability. As a source of dignity and pride it has a sustaining value in the face of hardship, and it may offer a supporting quality to counteract stress. It also serves as a shibboleth for group unification. But it is often seen to present a particularly irritating facade of insidious superiority and snobbery in many of our brethren who, while desiring desperately to be affable, are socially excluded by virtue of their self-isolation and disdain. This is very striking in mixed population institutional settings.

The semi-religious doctrines relative to a kosher diet combined with the Jewish mothers' somewhat exaggerated use of food as an expression of love and a medium of sociability tend to give the Jewish ethnic group an imprint of *oral preoccupation*. As a partial consequence such elements of human interaction as good spirits, friendliness, joy of living, etc. are measured in amounts of food consumed. As a result of this in many Jewish families the normal diminution in appetite that parallels the aging process is viewed with unnecessary alarm. The outcome is that the oldsters are force-fed and fattened, which neither contribute to health nor extend life. Also the heavy emphasis on epicurean culinary perfection, while a cultural delight and an inexhaustible conversation topic, makes group living for the Jewish aged outside of the family circle a frustrating and disappointing experience. It is no surprise, then, to observe that the ministrations to the elders by the dutiful children become orgies of groceries. The kosher diet, like the Catholic, in the great American ethnic merger, tends to accentuate differences rather than similarities and may add to the loneliness that exclusiveness nurtures.

The Jewish historical heritage is a saga of strength, shrewd survival, and magnificence. (It would be a digression to go into its more disagreeable aspects.) Out of a background of violence and torment there has grown the wandering-suffering legend that is so specifically Jewish. The story of persecution at the hands of tormentors has been ever refreshed in the education of the Jewish child, although in this country it is more symbolically than realistically observed. It serves to unite the ethnic group through sharing of a common problem, but it also develops a canniness in the oncoming generations. As a consequence a *readiness to feel persecuted* may become a part of the Jewish child's personality structure, and he may misinterpret his own internal psychological problems with the result that he overlooks his own limitations and blames social factors outside himself. Thus it can be seen clearly, without minimizing real social dangers, that often even in the face of realistic persecutory hazards the Jewish individual adds an element of imagination. In the face of such constant danger, whether real or imagined, there are but a few ways of handling the problem:

1. One may maintain a perpetual vigilance and ready aggressiveness to meet the threat.
2. Another may grow tired of constantly reinforcing defensive measures, devalue himself, and yield to the threat.
3. Still another may decide that the struggle isn't worth the effort and may, so to speak, join the enemy.

As time goes on the first may develop an attitude of being tormented constantly from outside himself. The second may develop a mood in which he feels worthless and is persecuting himself.  The third may develop a progressive sense of internal deceit, and in later efforts at restitution he may grow exaggeratedly contrite and may overdramatically embrace an excessively religious point of view replete with wholly unreal and supernatural beliefs.

The first is an emotional disorder based on a persecution complex.  The second eventuates in melancholia.  The third is a combination of both.  These are seen with startling frequency in the Jewish aged among those individuals having further psychological complications adding impetus to their social attitudes.

The *Talmudic heritage* with its accent on thoughtful consideration, keen scholasticism, and intellectual gymnastics is a saving grace in the Jewish culture.  It fits so harmoniously into the natural accumulation of wisdom that is part of the aging process that it often produces a tranquilizing philosophy to mellow the decline of very late maturity.  But it also creates in Jewish parents a tendency to be ambitious for their children.  In instances where the goals of such ambition are not realized or may in fact really be unrealizable, a mutual hostility may develop between parents and their children which the latter often turn into ardent elder-rejection with the passage of time.

Outstandingly important are the psychological relationships within the Jewish family.  Students of this subject report that mother-son interactions in many Jewish families are intensely emotional.  The Jewish mother may be very overprotective and affectionate.  For the purpose of disciplining her son she often uses the *withdrawal of love* technique.  This may be very distressing to the son who becomes concerned with the fickleness of his mother's love.  He may then develop twofold feelings toward her—seductively affectionate dependency and deeply hidden hatred.  As the mother grows older these disparate feelings in the son may operate simultaneously with the result that he feels a personal deprivation and sadness over her diminishing capabilities and a concurrent uneasy pleasure that his rejection of her is coming to fruition.  Socially this may be seen in the following familiar behavior.  The son stays away from his aged mother as long as he is able, but inquires frequently regarding her health.  He spares no expense for her social and medical care, but refuses to supervise her himself. When his guilty feelings become excessive, he shows up personally amid a great fanfare, showering gifts and affection upon her, only to disappear soon again into a world of busy activity he has contrived for himself. The Jewish daughter is more constantly attached to her mother.

The so-called typical Jewish father does not punish severely. He is more apt to relegate to his wife much of the control over his home life. The Jewish son thus is not likely to have strong hostile feelings toward his father, but he is also not very apt to select his father as a model for his own role in life.

The strong emotions displayed in the Jewish household coupled with the culturally imposed necessity for a social demonstration of grief in connection with the loss and sickness of loved ones account for the high degree of emotionality, sentimentality, and over-reaction the Jewish family shows toward its ailing members. For all of its exaggeration, this is probably a healthy factor in the life of the family, because the show of grief and mourning maintained over a sufficiently long period at the time of the hurtful event may prevent an accumulation of pent-up feelings which would be more disturbing were they delayed to some later date.

It is probably quite unnecessary to consider in any detail the factor of *minority complex* in the Jewish culture. You already know that to every minority an external majority is a threat. Since the threat is a common problem shared by all the minority members, it contributes to group unification and solidarity. The factor of strong emotionality added to that of minority cohesiveness accounts for the strong affectional ties within Jewish groups. Strivings for individual success and independence are outweighed by the element of group need with the result that there is good teamwork in the culture despite a high order of competitiveness among the members. Still it is this very minority element that incites the members to compensatory strivings for success and aggressive competition. It is present both as a sociological factor in the group and a psychological factor in each individual. Efforts at compensation usually lead to overcompensation. This is true also in the Jewish group. As an outgrowth of this, needs to compete become bold aggressiveness and needs to succeed often become expansiveness and megalomania. These factors may show up later in the emotional disturbances of the Jewish aged as over-reactions, as feelings of persecution or depression in the manner that we discussed earlier.

## IV.  THE NEW JEWISH GENERATIONS

Before leaving this portion of our considerations we are obliged to consider certain problems that are specific in the first and subsequent generation Jewish-Americans. An emotional difficulty that must not be overlooked besets the American-born children of the foreign-born parents. While this may not seem pertinent to a study of the field of aging, it will become increasingly significant in the years to come, and it is part of our dedication to the relief of human suffering that we must make logical predictions and prepare ahead. Additionally we shall see that it *is* related to the problem at hand.

One obtains the impression in the intimate relationship of therapy that the foreign-born American immigrant, who has come to this country during late adolescence or following it, is an individual divided between cultures. Whereas his loyalty to America, born of a real appreciation for a democratic way of life and an exhilarated esteem for the independenece and freedom it offers, is as a rule very strong and unchanging, and his efforts to accommodate himself to the new culture are thorough and persevering, the culture of his childhood, from which he migrated, seems to retain a certain tenacity to the deeper strata of his personality. This is revealed in his folkways, speech, and memories. It is also seen as a reversion to type in the regression of senility.

The important point here is the effect this split-culture attitude of the foreign-born parents has on the first generation offspring and the reactive measures employed by the latter. The child in this group from birth to early childhood is exposed to a quasi-American mixed culture that he accepts, since as yet he has no choice. As he moves beyond the circumscribed family confines into the greater outside culture his subsequent efforts to integrate himself into that culture lead him to intensify his normal elder-rejecting impulses. This may induce in him a dual attitude: a need to devalue his own origin in order to assume the pervasive spirit of the outside group, which conflicts with an equally powerful need to protect his origin against the threat of the external majority of which he is also becoming a member. The confused identifications that may result from this conflict often result in personality problems characterized by internal inconsistencies, ambiguous ideals, and excessive defensiveness. Finally, his normal adolescent rebellion will eventuate in strong elder-discarding drives to which he is never wholly reconciled. What this will mean to his aging parent has already been described. It may be a valid prediction, that the years to come will witness a fairly high incidence of penitent and self-derogating depressions among the aging first-generation group as this conflict comes to the fore again in their emotional life.

Subsequent American-Jewish generations probably become fused more readily with the greater culture and may suffer a diminishing quantity of the internal strife to which their forbears fell heir.

## V. VERY LATE MATURITY AND ITS REQUIREMENTS

The cyclic sequences of social and psychological events that produce elder-discarding attitudes in our society eventuate in the lonely and depressed state that progresses systematically into the *senile decline*. A feeling of isolation, friendlessness, uselessness, lowered self-esteem, and reduced self-confidence follows. The anxiety and terror thus generated develop into a passively suicidal frame of mind. Much mental energy is then mobilized by the emotionally disturbed aged for the purpose of attempting to re-establish shattered defenses. The mind thus occupied with repairing itself becomes further isolated from the external environment. At the same time the deep panic within accompanied by frenzied efforts at reconstruction propel the individual to a state of exhaustion. This is seen clinically as torpor, lassitude, waning alertness, memory impairment, confusion, disorientation, and feeble restlessness.

All of the above events are psychological although they are companions to physiological changes. Psychological reactions promise a degree of reversibility. But this does not follow automatically. The question of whether such psychological functions can be reversed depends on:

1. Knowledge of their origin
2. Insight in patient and therapist into their nature
3. An incentive in both to do something about them
4. The amount of irreversible physiological damage also present, and
5. A well-organized setting with a therapeutic atmosphere constituted toward the replenishment of emotional needs.

When it is remembered that the emotionally disturbed aged are suffering from the following main psychological wounds—a rejecting environment, isolation, regression, and the use of sick defensive mental devices—it is comparatively easy to plan a thorough program of treatment no matter what the particular discipline or persuasion of the therapist. I have published in another paper[2] a fairly complete outline of a workable and desirable treatment program. For our purposes today it can be said that all treatment systems designed to alleviate the emotional injuries of the aged must contain the following four essentials:

1. Removal of the patient from a covertly or overtly elder-rejecting environment to one that accepts him. The greater the emotional disturbance, then the more is there a need for institutional care. Institutionalization is not an answer in itself. It must be augmented by trained and indoctrinated personnel and a well conceived plan of therapy. Practice has already demonstrated that substantial results are achieved in this way. For less disturbed aged and those only needing a measure of prevention of psychological senility, the community must organize activity centers.

2. Resocialization. Group living for the aging and aged, even though at first resisted, proves valuable as a counteractant against isolation and to bring about a return of cultural values.

3. Activity. In its many forms this element is indispensable as a bulwark against stagnation. Mental life is never static; if it is not moving forward, it moves backward. Activity combining usefulness with creative participation combats regression.

4. Psychotherapy. There is a broad spectrum of human relationships that have therapeutic value, i.e. furnish needs. The greatest need of the aged is to have the urgency of their sick defenses diminished so that their mental energies can be routed again to wholesome functioning.

While a psychiatrist is not needed in constant attendance for the appropriate care of the aged, the properly constituted treatment program requiries an orientation in medical psychology in order to salvage all that is salvagable. A psychiatrist with gerontological understandings, who is available at least on the periphery of a program, will help avoid therapeutic neglect.

VI. THE SOLUTION TO THE PROBLEM OF CULTURAL REJECTION

For all men who may live to late and very late maturity there is a certain degree of inevitableness that mental and physical functions will decline. But the emotional disturbances of aging appear to be neurotically and culturally induced. The basic emotional inadequacies of childhood, if otherwise deferred from being expressed, are sure to work their way to the surface in later years. Only the best principles of mental hygiene and continued maturation of mankind will, in the long run, have any effect in reducing the deprivations of childhood.

Still, there is an approach to this problem that offers a reason for optimism. As in all wisdom, the promise for the future lies in borrowing from the past. The ancient Oriental, Indian, and Hebrew cultures, which have survived all practical tests through the centuries, contain an element in common that may be their most recommending factor—veneration of the elders. It seems logical to expect that a mode of human existence having rewards near the end of life as well as at its beginnings, will make the mere process of living enjoyable and purposeful for all participants.

It is a matter of good humanity to begin now the long-term project of shaping culture; changing the American temperament in keeping with the changing American scene. The aged have earned their place in the sun. We have a moral obligation as civilized mankind to ease their lot, pay heed to their wisdom, and integrate their skills, experiences and comprehensions into our total way of life. Our acceptance of them and preparations for their welfare can set the cultural stage so that there need be no psychological death before the natural end of human life.

Inherent in modern man's concept of civilization is the obligation to create social institutions dedicated to equality of opportunity for men of all ages.

# References

1. I shall borrow as a definition of the term, ethnic, the following: "We define a member of an ethnic group as a person who regards himself or is regarded by others as distinguished by religion or national origin from the native born white protestant majority." Barrabee and VonMering in *Social Problems*, 1953, 1 (2).

2. Linden, M. E.. *Architecture for Psychogeriatric Installations*. Norristown (Pa.) State Hospital, 1953.

# IV. THE PREOCCUPATION WITH RITUAL

# INTRODUCTION

Psychoanalysts consider rituals generally as steps in the cultural development of mankind, a useful instrument in repressing and controlling the aggressive, impulsive drives of the individual, and of making him conform to the dominant behavior modes of his society. Others feel the value of Jewish ritual as a source of occupational therapy, for its busy procession of perennial spiritual experiences gives life added form and content.

The introductory article by Dr. Sandor S. Feldman points up these ceremonial factors. He illustrates this by citing three ritualistic practices of the Jews: circumcision, dietary laws, and extensive prayer during which the worshipper spits. He goes on to explore the analogy between religious rites and neurotic obsessive-compulsive behavior and concludes with a discussion of the effect of psychoanalytic treatment on the individual's religious beliefs

Few subjects in orthodox Jewish religious law have been treated with such exhaustiveness and precision as the Mosaic prohibition against the simultaneous consumption of milk and meat. Dr. Woolf describes two forces, pertinent to his exposition, that have been important in the history of civilization: first, the derivation of the prohibition from the conflicts between the matrilinear and patrilinear forms of human society and, second, the stratification, the gradual supercession of earlier by later cultural usage, which, in accordance with the interpretations and explanations appropriate to later religious requirements, have gradually become more and more sublimated.

Perhaps an area of Jewish ritual that lends itself most readily to psychoanalytic interpretation are the material accounterments embodied in the phylacteries, the *tsitsith*, the *talith*, and the Star of David. Dr. Montague Eder discusses the ritual observances involved with these ornaments as last remnants of the totem animal once worshipped by the Hebrews, analyzing their symbolism from their primitive origins to their meaning for the Jew today. The use of amulets to ward off evil is a pagan belief, prompted by an internal urge to take steps to protect one's self and to try to divine the future. How the phylacteries, *tsitsith, and talith* evolved and their meaning today, as seen in the fantasies of patients, form the basis for Dr. Eder's presentation.

Dr. Gerda G. Barag's analysis involves still other forms of ritualistic practices: the benediction of the new moon, the observance of the Sabbath, and certain rites celebrated during the Sukkoth festival. As in Eder's article, the primitive origins of these customs are traced, but here within the framework of a Mother Goddess. For instance, Dr. Barag's findings help us recognize in the Sukkoth celebration the remnant of a former orgiastic feast devoted to the mother deity. Although today every orgiastic trait in it has disappeared, a hint is to be found on Simchat Torah, when, as an exception to strict rule, women are allowed to mix with the praying, singing, and dancing men. Evidence for (a) the profound wish to merge the father and mother into one person and thus escape from the conflict of the Oedpius complex, and (b) the identification of the people with the mother divinity are detailed in an attempt to prove that for the religious ideas of the Jews a mother goddess had great importance.

In the next article, Dr. Renato J. Almansi presents a psychoanalytic interpretation of the Menorah, with related comments on the significance of the number seven, the Sabbath, the Second Commandment, and the Golden Calf. He interprets the seven-branched candlestick as a symbolization of a fiery sacrificial idol within whose blazing interior human victims were immolated to propitiate the deity. According to this analysis, the seven branches of the Menorah correspond to the seven orifices of the idol's face.

This interpretation is seen continuously in history and mythology and falls into the general framework of the primal-horde hypothesis formulated by Freud in *Totem and Taboo.* Here, according to the available historical evidence, the original sacrifice was that of the first-born son, which was widely practiced in antiquity and particularly in the Semitic world. The victim of this sacrifice was devoured by the fire inside a metal idol (Baal, Moloch, or Kronos) whose flaming facial orifices were later symbolized by the Menorah. Therefore, in Dr. Almansi's view, the Menorah and the idol for which it stands corresponds to a sadistic, castrating father. The ritual sacrifice represents a condensation of two elements—the castration of the son and the act for which he is punished, viz., entering the mother's body.

The symbolism of the Menorah, which is typically Oedipal in character, is also reflected in the subject matter of the last article in this section, the blessing of the Kohenites. In this act, as described by Dr. Feldman, Jews of the priestly class offer a benediction while standing shoeless before the Holy Ark, with their prayer-shawls over the head, their hands stretched out, with the fingers arranged to form five empty spaces.

The removal of the shoes, Dr. Feldman demonstrates, is a symbol of submission, in this case meaning castration, which in turn signifies giving up the hostile attitude toward the father. Through the peculiar lattice-like divison of the fingers in the blessing, which is a striking and essential feature of the rite, God (via the Kohenite) looks at the people. Thus the priests are identical with God, and the congregation both with God and the priests. One who sees the rite, observes Dr. Feldman, gets the impression that it is a recapitulation of the scene at Mount Sinai. "The worshippers engage themselves out of fear in fervent and devout prayers, they huddle together, cover their faces, don't dare look up, they prostrate themselves before Yahweh." This scene is, in essence, the repression of the urge to hate the father and to kill him. Thus, Dr. Feldman sees in the rite a Freudian phylogenetic pattern that symbolically reflects several stages in the sexual development of man and in the unfolding of the superego.

## Chapter 14

# Notes on Some
# Religious Rites and Ceremonies

SANDOR S. FELDMAN, M.D.

**R**ITES, rituals, and observed manners of their performances (called ceremonies) were handed down mostly from the dim past. They were divine orders given to the people by exalted personalities or by traditional mouth-to-mouth channels.

Most of the ideas presented as "notes" in this paper were stimulated by Freud's fundamental writings on this subject[1]. Then came Freud's *Totem and Taboo* and *Moses and Monotheism*. In the course of time a considerable number of psychoanalytic scholars made further investigations, and have shown (what Freud already had) that the rites were mighty steps in the cultural development of mankind; that they were taming the everstrong anti-social, sexual, and egoistic drivers of the individuals and of the group. On this occasion, Sandor Lorand's paper, "The Anathema of the Dead Mother"[2], should be mentioned first. The most outstanding in scientific weight and in numbers are the contributions of Reik, Róheim, and Jones.

The deep meaning of the rituals gradually was covered up and even distorted by superficial interpretations and by popular rationalizations. Nevertheless, the analysis of many such individuals who observed some of the rituals revealed that their meanings were known to them. Repressed drives appear through their derivatives; analysis reverses the process and traces them back to their beginnings. This is then backed up by the anthropological studies which relate ontogeny and phylogeny.

Let us take as an example the rite of circumcision. The Bible demands it and it is a covenant between the Lord and his

279

people; nc explanation is given. The popular view buries its deep significance by attributing a sanitary advantage to the circumcised over the uncircumcised. But analysis of both discloses that circumcision, on the basis of *pars pro toto*, is a settlement between two parties; instead of being killed or totally castrated by the father, only part of the body, the foreskin, is removed. We know that circumcision has other deep meanings, but discussing them would go beyond the scope of this paper and my abilities.

In countries where circumcision became a routine "sanitary" procedure, circumcision, with some exceptions, had lost its meaning. There were instead other religious rituals and ceremonies which originated from the same sources and had identical psychogenesis.

The same rationalization has taken place in the Jewish dietary laws; they are minutely observed by the pious. Their meaning was lost in the consciousness of the individual observers; instead a sanitary significance was again attached to them. Most religious leaders reluctantly lend support to this rationalization, and seem to be satisfied so long as the people exercise them.

There were persons who observed certain rituals, dropped them in the course of time and later took them up again; there were others who, for a length of time, observed the rituals in a calm religious way, but later changed them into a compulsive-neurotic performance.

This clinical observation will enable us to point the difference between the compulsiveness of the neurotic and of the religious persons. (In this paper, "compulsive" and "obsessive" are used alternately.)

A Jewish woman related in her analysis that in their home the family rigorously observed the dietary laws. When she was five years of age, the family abandoned the observance of this law with all its ceremonies, and so did the patient. But at the age of about ten she demanded that the family resume the old custom, but they refused; whereupon she forced her mother to cook only for her in the dietary way or she would refuse to eat. We learned in her analysis that at that age, for some reason, and for a short period of time, she shared the bedroom of her parents and observed her parents in intercourse. She was in an anguishing dilemma; if she made it known that she was awake, they would be angry at her for disturbing them; if she didn't, she would be guilty of observing the forbidden.

Among others, there are two main demands in the dietary laws; one which forbids the eating of the flesh of certain animals, the other the isolating of certain foods in such a way so as to prevent them getting mixed in the stomach. Our patient perceived the *latter part* of the meaning of the dietary laws, and by observing them she tried to convince her conscience that she did not desire the forbidden, to commit incest.

The other patient was a pious Jewish woman who religiously observed all the elaborate prescribed rites and ceremonies. There is hardly any activity or step one takes, from the moment one awakens and opens his eyes until he closes them again, which is not connected with at least a specific prayer or ceremony.

At one time the observance of the rites which before had given her profound gratification now turned into a compulsiveness that paralyzed her actions. She was never sure that she performed the rituals correctly, and had to repeat them. She was in a permanent anxiety state, and only complete physical exhaustion could end the repetitious and obsessive continuance of her ceremonial actions. The change came when she set up her own household which imposed upon her new activities and responsibilities.

In my opinion, this is the difference between the compulsiveness of the neurotic and of the religious. The religious person observes the rituals as prescribed, and with this his *duty* ends: he is pleased and feels good about it. Not so the neurotic who is always in doubt; therefore for him the rituals constitute a torture because they never end. The patient was always close to a panicky state because she never was sure and could not foresee when she would end the ceremonial actions. Her blasphemic, aggressive and coprophilic drives were so strong that she could not convince herself, through the rituals, of her innocence.

In order to shed further light on the psychogenesis of religious ceremonies, I will discuss four of them. They are performed only by those Jews who rigorously observe the ceremonies of the daily services.    These Jews are given to extensive prayer.

In the course of praying, there is a part in which the man prostrates himself, in words and in bodily motions, before the Lord.    When he resumes his erect position, he turns aside and either spits or only indicates the spitting.

In the second ritualistic feature, there is a prayer at the conclusion of the service.    When the last sentences are recited, the man takes three steps backwards, in the course of which he spits aside (or only indicates it), then he goes forward to resume his original position.

Spitting has different meanings.    It can have a magic fertilizing effect, e.g., when some persons receive money, they spit into the palms of their hands, rub them together and recite a sort of magic formula, expressing the wish that the money multiply and they become rich.    On the other hand, spitting can be an indication of despising (moreover, "one doesn't ever spit at another").    Spitting also can be a magic gesture to indicate getting rid of an evil impulse or thought; to show that one does not identify himself with the wish expressed in the impulse or the thought; e.g., a female patient with sadistic and necrophilic tendencies had to spit whenever she saw a funeral procession pass by.

My investigations have convinced me that in the abovementioned ceremonies, spitting was a compulsive action due to doubts in the Lord and to blasphemic tendencies against Him. At the point when devotion is intended to be at its height, or, in the second case, when the long service finally ends, the thought breaks through, "How glad I am that the burdensome duty has ended."    The stepping back is necessary because—for blasphemic reasons—the man might pass winds and the Lord would punish him for this grave form of blasphemy.    In order to demonstrate to himself and the Lord that this is not his intention, he steps back.

The third one to be mentioned here is a defense mechanism frequently observed in compulsive neurotics.    In the daily service there is a prayer which ends with "I am the Lord, your God" and is followed by another which begins with the word "Truth" (true).    The man who says the prayer watches anxiously so as not to pause between the two parts.   He says the words "Lord" and "Truth" (true) in one breath lest a blasphemic thought, e.g., it is *not* his God and the Lord is *not* the Truth, should force itself between the two words.

The fourth is again a compulsive action which is done at the end of the well-known prayer, "Hearken Israel, The Lord is our God, the Lord is One."   (The "One" is expressed in Hebrew with "Echad.")   Many religious persons anxiously watch that the letter "d" in "Echad" should be distinctly spoken and to be sure, they carry the "d" to a certain length.   We know this from patients who suffer from compulsive doubts and who have to emphasize or repeat certain words intending to eliminate the doubt.

Freud found a striking analogy between the religious rituals, ceremonies, prescriptions, etc., and the obsessive-compulsive neurotics.   Moreover, deep analysis proves that their psychogenesis is identical and also that there are essential differences between them.

The religious ritual serves the *collective* interest, while the rites of the neurotic serve only the specific interest of *one* person. The religious person in a group observes the rituals in order to live *together* with others, while the neurotic through his rituals *isolates* himself.

It never happens that ten or even two neurotics would congregate into an organized group for the sake of performing together the rituals such as for example, washing, counting, or other ceremonials.   The rites and ceremonials of a group are almost performed demonstratively; pious persons are not ashamed to gather and display their faith through rituals.   A member of such a group is keenly aware that he belongs to the group, and if alone, by chance, he would with dignity and no embarrassment pray, kneel, prostrate himself, make the sign of the cross, put on his phylacteries, whether seen or not; while the neurotic does it secretly or only in the presence of a trusted or needed person.   The neurotic invents his own rituals, while the religious one accepts what is prescribed by religious authorities and traditions.   He observes them because the group, into which he was born or which he chose, honors them.   The religious person admits his "sins" publicly; the neurotic hides them from others and himself. As a member of a group, the religious one atones and he is forgiven; the neurotic never settles the conflict between his sexual and aggressive drives and his conscience.

In Freud's papers, there is a certain sentence which reads "This [compulsive] neurosis can be regarded as a private religious system, and religion as a universal neurosis." This was bitterly contested by many writers, disregarding the fact that a previous sentence had read: "An obsessional neurosis furnishes a *tragic-comic travesty* of a private religion," and is furthermore "A pathological counterpart to the formation of religion" ([1], my italics).

The neurotic does not sublimate his instinctual drives, while the religious one does, as shown by Lorand[2], and in my papers [3, 4, 5].

At this point we might be in a position to discuss a question which is frequently raised: Does psychoanalytic treatment interfere with or "destroy" the patient's religious faith? This is the concern of some patients before treatment, and also the concern of the Church. The religious faith of those persons who believe in a Creator as a source of ethical and spiritual guidance remains intact.

Psychoanalysis being a process in which all values are reevaluated, those persons who exercise only the rituals and have no belief in God must and also desire to come to a decision. There are those who abandon the rituals and turn to God, others who abandon them without doing so. Religious faith and rituals are not necessarily an inseparable unit. Some patients have given up (some before, others after their analyses) several or all rituals; others left their Church and joined one which did not observe all rituals but only some.

Psychoanalytic treatment does not turn an atheist into a religious person, nor does it make a religious person an atheist. Some intellectual believers were deeply impressed by the psychoanalytic interpretations of rituals; they found more reason to observe them. As far as the essential tenets of religion are concerned, psychoanalysis has proven that a high-level superego development is necessary to achieve and maintain a healthy emotional, mental, and even a physical balance. Ideals cannot be completely achieved; our instinctual drives and social aims are in a constant and bitter struggle. Therefore those who attack psychoanalysis from this point of view defeat their own avowed aims. They are rather inclined to sacrifice ethical values for the benefit of the organization which handles them. There are some religious thinkers who value the baby more than the water which cleanses it.

# References

1.  Freud, Sigmund. Obsessive acts and religious ceremonies. In, *Collected Papers*. Vol. 2. NY: Basic Books, 1955, p. 28.
2.  Lorand, Sandor. The anathema of the dead mother. In *Psychoanalysis and the Social Sciences*. Vol. 1. NY: International Universities Press, 1947, 235-244.
3.  Feldman, Sandor S. The blessing of the Kohenites. *American Imago*, 1941, 2:296-322.
4.  ————. Notes on the "primal horde." In *Psychoanalysis and the Social Sciences*. Vol. 1: NY: International Universities Press, 1947, 171-194.
5.  ————. The sin of Reuben, first-born son of Jacob. In *Psychoanalysis and the Social Sciences*. Vol. 4. NY: International Universities Press, 1955, 282-287.

## Chapter 15

# Prohibitions Against the Simultaneous Consumption of Milk and Flesh in Orthodox Jewish Law

M. WOOLF, M.D.

𝔉EW subjects in orthodox Jewish religious law have been treated with such exhaustiveness and precision as the keeping apart of milk and flesh in eating. Milk and foods derived from it may not be consumed sooner than six hours after the consumption of meat, though meat may be eaten two hours after milk. Separate vessels, crockery and table implements must be used for foods made with meat and milk; milk and meat must not even be cooked simultaneously and so on.

These ramifying and complex regulations are said to be derived from an extension and elaboration of a single prohibition in the Bible, which in itself has a somewhat mysterious sound: "Thou shalt not seethe a kid in his mother's milk." The numerous rules and injunctions which have become attached to this single prohibition are explained as avoidances and safety measures to ensure that there shall be no involuntary, unconscious or accidental breach of this important law. It might happen, for instance, that some milk bought at a particular place might come from the same goat as a kid offered for sale at another place at the same time. The person who purchased and made use of the two foods might then, without being aware of it, break the law. It is true that such a possibility might not be excluded with absolute certainty in the case of a lamb or kid; but it is impossible to imagine why it should be that the rules applying to the flesh of lambs, kids or calves should also be extended to fowls. This fact alone shows how illusory is the usual explanation of these many regulations as avoidances and safety measures or, as the Talmud puts it, *syngim* (hedges) around the primary law. The inadequacy of the explanation is finally brought home to us when we read in Frazer[1] that similar and even stricter laws and customs in regard to the separation of milk and flesh exist among many peoples and may even perhaps have once been a universal phenomenon in primitive cultures.

In any case there has been no lack of attempts at explaining the biblical law against seething a kid in his mother's milk. And amongst them there has been one upon psycho-analytical lines by Frieda Fromm-Reichmann, on which I must make a few comments.

"Thus," Fromm-Reichmann ([2] p. 242) argues, "by simultaneously consuming a male goat (= totem animal = father) and the milk of its mother, a man is committing the primal crime of incest. We may therefore assume that the ban upon the simultaneous consumption of flesh and milk is to be regarded in the first place quite generally as an unconscious defence against an incestuous wish."

In case this evidence should not entirely convince, Fromm-Reichmann seeks confirmation of it in two other biblical texts: viz. the prohibition against removing the mother-bird from the nest at the same time as her young, a veto which contains the promise of a reward for obedience to it. "Here again," Fromm-Reichmann[2] maintains, "the removal of the creatures clearly signifies an identification with the mother-bird and with her young, and their simultaneous removal signifies incest, which this prohibition therefore aims at preventing in the same way as does the prohibition of seething a kid in his mother's milk. Similarly, according to Radó, the commandment to "honour thy father and thy mother" is the only one of the Ten Commandments to contain a promise of reward, because in its unconscious meaning it too serves to prevent incest."

As regards the commandment to "honour thy father and thy mother," I would cite Ferenczi, who observes that the commandment does not enjoin love for the father and mother, but only honour, and in that sense may really be understood as an indirect prohibition of incest. But when we read that the mere removal of the mother-bird and her young "clearly signifies an identification" with these creatures and that "their simultaneous removal signifies incest," we are tempted to ask what human action would not signify such identification and what prohibition would not forbid incest. To ascribe every prohibition to a veto on incest is surely an over-simplification of the matter. Why ever, if the law-giver wished to prohibit incest, should be have recourse to such ingenious subtleties as forbidding the seething of a kid in his mother's milk, or taking the mother-bird from the nest at the same time as her young? He could—and did—issue this prohibition directly and openly in another passage, and associated it, not with a reward for abstinence, but with the threat of capital punishment in the event of its transgression.

Fromm-Reichmann ([2.] p. 243) then extends her interpretation to cover pre-genital impuses and declares: " 'Seethe not the kid in his mother's milk,' in the language of the unconscious, at the oral stage (also called by Freud the cannibalistic stage) means: Thou shalt not seethe (cook) the son in the milk of his mother (= thy wife), i.e., thou shalt not cook, and therefore not eat, thy son,' etc." Fromm-Reichmann—it is interesting to note—further says that "the killing of children in particular is expressly forbidden to the ancient Hebrews in the Bible—quite apart from the general prohibition to kill." Why then, we cannot help asking, these disguised allusions in such a strange and obscure form (in a legal code, too), when the law-giver does not hesitate to prohibit the killing of children by a direct and clear pronouncement? I must confess frankly that I do not see how Fromm-Reichmann's statements help to explain all these incomprehensible and strange-sounding prohibitions.

Let us first look closely at the original Bible text, namely, the prohibition: "Thou shalt not seethe a kid in his mother's milk." The verse occurs three times in the Bible, twice in Exodus (xxiii, 19 and xxxiv, 26), and the third time in Deuteronomy (xiv, 21), which is four centuries later in date and only repeats what was said before, but this time in association with other ritual eating prohibitions. In Exodus, on the other hand, which is generally held to be one of the oldest parts of the Bible, this prohibition is linked with other events, commandments and vetoes which are of great value and importance to our study. The most noticeable thing about this text is that it does not really contain an eating prohibition at all, but only a prohibition against *cooking*. The old commentators, and also, as we have seen, those of quite recent times, appear to have taken it for granted that whoever cooks a food must also eat it. To me this is by no means self-evident. But the prohibition to cook in the mother's milk consists of two different elements: (1) the prohibition against cooking, and (2) the prohibition against cooking in the mother's milk. The next thing that strikes us is that this prohibition, in both these passages from Exodus, does not even constitute a separate and independent verse, but is only the second half of a verse, of which the first part says: "The first of the firstfruits of thy land thou shalt bring into the house of the Lord thy God"—which in fact suggests that this prohibition is related to the sacrificing of the firstborn. It is this reference, for example, which led Bialik and others to associate this prohibition with certain specific customs and usages of the Jews at the Feast of *Shebuoth*, the festival of the firstborn (also called the Feast of Weeks—the Christian Pentecost—occurring seven weeks after the Passover). Bialik ([3,] p. 20) speaks of this "meal of a sacrificed kid" as "the symbol of prosperity and fecundity .... And," he goes on, "wonderful to relate, it is to this day a Jewish custom—and one which has puzzled all the investigators—to eat a milk meal on the Feast of Weeks, somewhat unusually close after meat; and those who are very particular eat meat cooked in the milk of almonds."

Bialik sees in this custom a survival of a former custom—afterwards prohibited—of eating lamb cooked in its mother's milk. That may be so, but I see no justification for associating this prohibition with *Shebuoth*, for the verse which precedes this prohibition and which stands in direct and reiterated connection with it, says: "Thou shalt not offer the blood of my sacrifice with leavened bread; neither shall the fat of my sacrifice remain until the morning" (Exodus xxiii, 18); and the second Exodus passage (xxxiv, 25) expressly mentions the *Pesah* (Passover, Easter) sacrifice: "Neither shall the sacrifice of the Feast of the Passover be left unto the morning. The first of the firstfruits of thy land thou shalt bring into the house of the Lord thy God. Thou shalt not seethe a kid in his mother's milk." That is a quite unmistakable reference to the Passover sacrifice.

The verse about the bringing of the first of the firstfruits does not conflict with acceptance of the Easter sacrifice, since the second day of the Passover is the real *beginning* of the sacrificing of firstfruits, of the first sheaf (*Omer*). This explains also the words at the beginning of the verse—"the first of the firstfruits."

However, the association of the prohibition with the Easter sacrifice throws fresh and very important light upon our question. Turning now to Chapter xii of Exodus, we read (1) that the Passover is brought into connection with the killing of the firstborn in Egypt. With the blood of the lamb a mark was to be made on the door of the house—as evidence that in that house the sacrifice had been made, and God, who would see the sign, would pass over that house—hence the word *"Pesah"* (meaning "pass over"). (2) The flesh of the sacrifice must only be *roasted,* it is forbidden to *boil* it. None of the flesh must be left over to the next day; it must be eaten in haste and what remains over *must be burned during the night.* In other words, the prohibition offers a choice, not between eating or not eating, but between *roasting in the fire or boiling in water* (or milk?). And here light is thrown upon another question: the bread, too, must not be leavened, but dried upon stones heated by the sun —like the kid roasted in the fire. The meal must be neither boiled nor baked in the oven, but prepared either directly in the sun or before the fire. Now *Pesah* is a festival of spring, and spring festivals are everywhere and among all peoples festivals of sun and fire. The ancient Semites, as we know, were sun- and fire-worshippers, and the customs and usages here described are of very old origin, much older than monotheism and the exodus from Egypt.

Habits and customs are very stable social structures, which long outlive the actual situations and circumstances which brought them into existence. The living conditions which caused a custom or usage to be instituted will have entirely changed and their real meaning may long have vanished from the consciousness of the community—yet these usages and customs will be strictly observed and even become hallowed by time. They then usually become nationalized, imbued with fresh meaning and content, more or less adapted to the new realities; the old bottle are filled with new wine. Although a particular people may adopt a new religion or assimilate a new way of living, many customs and practices pertaining to the old religion continue to be observed; they are merely re-interpreted and are brought into association with events or conditions pertaining to the new faith.

The most familiar example of this kind is the Christian feast of Christmas Eve—the festival of the newborn Sun-God on December 24—which has been re-interpreted as the festival of the birth of Christ.  But the custom of lighting a fire has remained, and in Russian villages the ancient heathen customs of the *Kolyades* survived until the Bolshevik revolution, and may even persist to this day.  Boys and girls went from house to house carrying six- or eight-sided revolving paper discs representing the sun and sang hymns in honor of the ancient Slav Sun-God Yarilo.

A second beautiful example, taken from Jewish ritual, is related by the well-known biblical scholar, Georg Beer ([4,] p. 90). Even in pre-Mosaic times the Sabbath was observed by the Israelites as a day of rest, both in civilized parts and in the desert.  The choice of the seventh day may be connected with the four phases of the moon.  The term *"Shabath"* is akin to the Babylonian *"shabattum,"* the name given to the *nefasti* or evil days.  These were the 1st, 7th, 14th, 21st and 28th days of the month, which again are associated with the phases of the moon. On those days no work was done, because no blessing went with it.  The old custom of not working on the seventh day was later adopted by monotheism, but re-interpreted and afterwards codified as honoring the holy day.  What was once the un-hallowed and unblest day was converted by monotheism into the holy day.  Here we see the Ucs. mechanism at work, which corresponds to what Freud has called "the anti-thetic meaning of primal words."  That is to say, a term is affectively transformed into its opposite: that which is sinister, accursed and impure becomes something blessed and holy.

There is no doubt that something of the kind took place among the early Israelites in regard to the spring Feast of *Pesah*.  The old heathen festival of sun and fire with all its usages and customs underwent a new interpretation and was brought into association with the important historic event of the exodus from Egypt and the national liberation from slavery. The original customs were those of the great spring festival in honor of the old fire- and sun-god of the Israelites. Quite recently, thanks to the important discoveries made from 1929 onwards in the ancient township of Ugarit in Syria, now called Ras Shamra, we have been made acquainted with the whole pantheon of early antiquity in the Syria and Palestine of pre-historic times. The chief deity was the Sun-God and Fire-God known as El[5]. This was the principal deity of the nomadic tribes of Israel, who wandered with their herds and flocks in the land of Canaan and the surrounding deserts. Frazer says: "We can hardly doubt that the rules and the commandment in question do belong together as parts of a common inheritance transmitted to the Jews from a time when their forefathers were nomadic herdsmen ([1,] p. 154)."

During the spring festival in honour of El, the Sun-God, the firstborn of the flocks were solemnly sacrificed, while human sacrifices were also offered to the god—the firstborn sons. Thus Beer[4] writes: "At *Pesah* the Israelites sacrificed their first-born, a human sacrifice made at the beginning of the harvest season in April; *Pesah* also falls at this time. These human sacrifices of the firstborn were afterwards redeemed and replaced by the Passover lamb. Under Christianity this practice is made, as it were, retroactive, and the son, now the Son of God, has in his turn replaced the Passover lambs as the "Redeemer.' "

These facts throw new light on the picture of the Passover night as described in Exodus xii. Various points are now seen in a different and clearer aspect. I will reproduce the passage: "In the tenth day of this month they shall take to them every man a lamb, according to the house of their fathers, a lamb for an house. And if the household be too little for the lamb, let him and his neighbor next unto his house take it according to the number of the souls, every man according to his eating shall make your count for the lamb. Your lamb shall be without blemish, a male of the first year: ye shall take it out from the sheep, or from the goats. And ye shall keep it up until the fourteenth day of the same month: and the whole assembly of the congregation of Israel shall kill it in the evening. And they shall take of the blood, and strike it on the two side posts and on the upper door post of the houses, wherein they shall eat it. And they shall eat the flesh in that night, roast with fire, and unleavened bread; and with bitter herbs they shall eat it. Eat not. of it raw, nor sodden at all with water, but roast with fire; his head with his legs and with the purtenance thereof. And ye shall let nothing of it remain until the morning; and that which remaineth of it until the morning ye shall burn with fire. And thus shall ye eat it; with your loins girded, your shoes on your feet, and your staff in your hand; and ye shall eat it in haste: it is the Lord's passover. For I will pass through the land of Egypt this night, and will smite all the firstborn in the land of Egypt, both man and beast; . . . And the blood shall be to you for a token upon the houses where you are: and when I see the blood, I will pass over you . . . And none of you shall go out at the door of his house until the morning . . . " And another passage adds: "In one house shall it be eaten; thou shalt not carry forth ought of the flesh abroad out of the house; neither shall ye break a bone thereof . . . And when a stranger shall sojourn with thee, and will keep the passover to the Lord, let all his males be circumcised, and then let him come near and keep it; and he shall be as one that is born in the land: for no uncircumcised person shall eat thereof."

There is something dark and mysterious about this whole description; it is like an echo from some primæval mystery of blood. The darkness and incomprehensibility hint at occurrences the meaning and content of which escape our understanding.

I trust that in this purely scientific and objective enquiry it may not be out of place to insert a constructive hypothesis, particularly if it helps to shed light upon dark places. With that preface I venture to put forward a suggestion which, although it may seem very bold, may possibly make the whole picture more intelligible. It is, at the same time, entirely consonant with the psychology of primitive man.

The idea of deceiving the gods, if need be, of outwitting or tricking them, was very common among primitive people. We have excellent examples of it even in the Bible. For instance, when God asked Cain, after the latter had killed his brother: "Where is Abel thy brother?" Cain, assuming an air of complete innocence, answered in the familiar words: "Am I my brother's keeper?" The mythology of other peoples is far richer in such examples. To mention only one, I may briefly recapitulate the story of Tantalus, which is moreover directly related to our theme. Tantalus, a son of Zeus, was admitted, by reason of his noble origin, to close friendship with the gods, although himself numbered among mortals. He was even permitted to eat at the table of Zeus. But he abused this trust, betrayed to mortals the secrets of divinity, stole nectar and ambrosia from their board and divided the spoil among his human companions. He hid the precious golden hound, stolen by another from the temple of Zeus in Crete, and, when asked by the latter to return it, denied on oath having received it. Finally, in his arrogance he invited the gods again to his table and, in order to test their omniscience, had his own son Pelops slaughtered and served up to his guests. Only Demeter, lost in sad abstraction at the rape of her daughter Persephone, partook of a shoulderblade from this grisly dish; the other gods perceived the deception.

In this legend men attributed to the gods their own detestation of the sacrifice of their children and fixed the guilt upon the evil designs of men who doubt the divine benevolence. This eased their consciences and lessened their fear of punishment for unwillingness to make the sacrifice. They employed in this the mechanism of unconscious thought so familiar to us in dream-interpretation—the mechanism of reversal into the opposite: unbelieving men practised a deception and made sacrifice of their children, which in the eyes of the gods was an abomination. That clearly corresponded to a wish of their own. But, as happens so often in dreams, the same mechanism recurs in the same story, but this time for the purpose of concealing a disagreeable repressed thought. The real deception, which historic man doubtless committed, consisted precisely in the fact that they replaced the children, whom they were supposed to sacrifice to the gods, by animal victims.

That, too, is the substance of the suggestion I have mentioned and which I advance in explanation of the grim and mystically dramatic account of the Passover sacrifice.

It is night-time. On the fourteenth evening of the lunar

month, the night of the Passover, the moon shines brightly in the sky, but the sun, the solar deity, is far away. (The Egyptians, for instance, believed that during the night the Sun-God dwells far away in the underworld, where he has to wage a mortal struggle against powerful demons before he can fight his way back into the sky.) Pity for their own children, aroused in the ancient Hebrews, no doubt impelled them to profit by the god's absence and, by a small deception, to save their children's lives. Towards nightfall, when the sun had disappeared below the horizon, a lamb was slaughtered at the entrance to the house; the door-posts were smeared with blood, the animal was then roasted whole, "his head with his legs and with the purtenances thereof," exactly, no doubt, as the child was burnt in the fire. Trembling with fear and expecting the deceived and angry god to appear at any moment, they ate in haste with their loins girded, shoes on their feet, staff in the hand, ready at any minute to flee from the house to escape punishment by the angry El. Whatever could not be quickly consumed, was burnt in the fire that same night before dawn, without leaving traces and without "breaking a bone thereof," in order that the god, when he reappeared in the morning sky, might see only the blood of the sacrifice on the threshold and discover no parts of the victim from which the deceit could be detected.

The strange details of the Passover sacrifice, in themselves so incomprehensible, speak strongly for this interpretation, which furnishes a complete explanation of them.

In the houses on the door-posts of which no blood was found, the firstborn were slain by God himself. In Exodus xiii the law of the redemption of the firstborn is discussed in detail and linked directly with the flight from Egypt and the slaying of the firstborn of the Egyptians: "And every firstling of an ass thou shalt redeem with a lamb; and if thou wilt not redeem it, then thou shalt break his neck, and all the firstborn of man among thy children shalt thou redeem," that is, just as at the sacrifice of *Pesah*.

But why should it have been precisely the night of *Pesah?* In his book on the Ugarit finds, Ginsberg[6] points out that in Palestine goats and sheep bring forth their young in the rainy season of winter, which means that in the spring, at the time of *Pesah*, the firstlings are just a year old and, as regards humans, I have already quoted Beer's opinion that the ancient Israelites were wont to make their human sacrifices at that season. The separation of the *Pesah* offering from the redemption of the firstborn came much later and is referred to in the much later book of Deuteronomy (xvi), where the lamb is referred by an offering of money.

We may therefore assume, I think, that the night of *Pesah* celebrated three different events belonging to different stages or strata of history:

(1) The lowest stratum—the spring festival of El, the Sun-God, with large offerings of the firstborn of men and beasts, a feast dating from the very beginnings of the Nomadic Age.

(2) The festival of the mercy of God, who has renounced the sacrifice of children and allowed their redemption by the lamb.

(3) The liberation of the people and their release from slavery, the return to national freedom and independence (with a re-interpretation of rites and customs) and the resumption of former national habits and customs, and of the old national religion.

We have strayed a long way from our strict task, which was to explain the remarkable prohibition against seething the kid in his mother's milk. From the purely historical standpoint the explanation seems today to present no very great difficulty.

Bialik ([3,] p. 20) declares that the cooking of the kid in its mother's milk was part of the cult of Astarte, worshipped by the Canaanite Phœnicians as the goddess of fertility and love. He refers to an oral statement by Mendele Mocher Sepharim (S. Y. Abramovich), but without giving the exact sources from which the latter derived his opinion. However, the discoveries at Ugarit have fully confirmed Bialik's view. Among the finds was a large tablet covered with cuneiform inscriptions, which, along with other rites of Astarte worship, contained the injunction to kill a kid and cook it in its mother's milk.

This prohibition is therefore purely religious in character: a struggle of monotheism against heathenism, of the national

Jewish faith against the religions of heathen neighbors. But this explanation is not altogether satisfactory. We have already mentioned Frazer's view that this veto, like the other milk and flesh laws, is of much older origin than monotheism and belongs to the prehistoric age of nomadism and pastoralism. In that case the prohibition receives a further meaning and content. The worship of Astarte itself, however, belongs to another, namely, an agricultural civilization, which, at the time when the ancient Israelites were still nomads, flourished in these parts among the neighboring peoples. We must see in this veto, therefore, the expression of an old prehistoric struggle, one which runs like a red thread of cultural development through many passages of the Bible: the struggle between nomadism and the beginnings of the age of agricultural civilization. We see evidence of this struggle in the very pages of the Bible, in the story of Cain and Abel. It raged not only among the Israelites, nor exclusively among Semitic peoples; it is a universal struggle of mankind for civilization. Customs and usages forbidding the simultaneous consumption of milk and meat, with all the accompanying details, exist, Frazer tells us, not only among Jews, but also among many African tribes, which, although Moslems by religion, stand fairly low in the scale of culture. And among these peoples, too, these customs exhibit the same unmistakable tendency. Frazer ([1.] p. 156) writes: "Pastoral peoples who believe that the eating of vegetable food may imperil the prime source of their subsistence by diminishing or stopping the supply of milk are not likely to encourage the practice of agriculture; accordingly it is not surprising to learn that in Bunyoro cultivation is avoided by the pastoral people: it is said to be harmful for the wife of a man belonging to a pastoral clan to till the land, as, by doing so, she may injure the cattle. Among the pastoral clans of that country women do no work beyond churning and washing milk-pots. Manual work has always been regarded as degrading and cultivation of the ground as positively injurious to their cattle. Even among the Baganda, who, while they keep cattle, are diligent tillers of the soil, a woman might not cultivate her garden during the first four days after one of her husband's cows had been delivered of a calf; and, though the reason of the prohibition is not mentioned, we may, in the light of the foregoing evidence, surmise that the motive for this compulsory abstinence from agricultural labour was a fear lest, by engaging in it at such a time, the woman should endanger the health or even the life of the new-born calf and its dam."

The same is true of many other pastoral tribes in Africa, which are "solicitous not to suffer milk to be contaminated by vegetables; hence they abstain from drinking milk and eating vegetables at the same time" ([1.] p. 154).

Jewish legislation contains no such separation of milk and vegetables as articles of diet. But we do find in Jewish laws clear signs of this "cultural struggle" between nomadism and an agricultural civilization, especially in the prohibition of *shainez*, of weaving flax and wool into one garment. Bialik ([3.] p. 20) appropriately remarks: "The raiment of the ancient Hebrews, with the religious rites associated with it, is (as an early *midrash* [interpretation] amazingly hints) the complete and sensible embodiment of—what do you think? Of the story of Cain and Abel." It is, he adds, "a reminiscence of the ancient feud between the pastoral tribes, whose clothing was of wool, and the agricultural tribes, who wore flax."

Although the historical bearing of the prohibition against seething a kid in his mother's milk may have been brought nearer to our comprehension by what we have said, the deeper meaning of the act itself still remains hidden from us. What is really the inner meaning of this unintelligible act or, rather, why and how does it acquire its particular and almost mysterious significance?

Frazer explains it by the process of what he calls "sympathetic magic." According to this, the meaning of the prohibition lies in the fact that, in the belief of early man, the boiling of the kid in its mother's milk is harmful to the mother-goat. Frazer cites many similar prohibitions among African peoples and claims that, when questioned, these people themselves put forward that reason.

It is impossible, however, to accept Frazer's explanation. The term "sympathetic magic" really means no more than being "drawn into sympathy by magical and irrational ways and means." Nor can the statements of primitive peoples be accepted as evidence; these habits and customs are of very ancient origin, they are quite unintelligible to those who practise them to-day and are retained because they are hallowed by tradition. Such statements are no more than typical rationalizations of unconscious mental tendencies and impulses. The meaning cf magic has been sufficiently explained by Freud himself (7. p. 84ff.). Its essence consists, according to Freud, in the fact that a psychological law of association of ideas—of similarity or contiguity—is accepted as having a real existence; the internal psychological process of human thought is transformed into reality. As when, for example, a man who desires to avenge himself upon another is content to perform the hostile act upon an effigy of the other man or even upon waste products from his body: the resemblance between the effigy and the original is a substitute for the identity of the act. Magic, according to Freud, is the technique of animistic thinking.

But this way of thinking is familiar to us; it is the same as our own unconscious thinking or, to use an exact term, the primary process. This makes it easy for us to understand the meaning of the prohibition: "Thou shalt not seethe a kid in his mother's milk." In unconscious thought, in dreams, cooking or boiling symbolizes the residence and maturing of the fruit in the mother's womb. By alchemy the homunculus is slowly cooked, adapted "to the natural conditions of delivery." The addition of the words "in his mother's milk" must be regarded as clear confirmation. Nothing is more natural to primitive, as to unconscious, thinking than to believe, when a child comes into the world and simultaneously his mother's breast yields milk (which the child needs for his sustenance), that the child was already nourished by that liquid while in the mother's womb, which is the same thing again as though it lived in that liquid. It is for this reason that seething the kid in his mother's milk became the symbol of fertility in the worship of Astarte. In other words, seething the kid in his mother's milk means placing the child back in its mother's belly, giving it into the full and undivided possession of the mother. "The son belongs to the mother." Thus, in the springtime festivals and mysteries of Western religions, as indeed throughout the cultural world around the Mediterranean, the chief part was played, not by the father, but by the son; the latter was adored by his mother, killed by his father and rose again in the spring under such names as Tammuz, Adonis and Dionysus.

This matriarchal right the Bible veto apparently seeks to destroy. The son belongs not to the Astarte mother, the goddess of fertility and love, of the earth and its crops, but to the paternal, omnipotent Sun-God, El. The latter may even roast or burn the son in his fire, in the fierce beams of his light.

In association with this, we can also understand the meaning of the unleavened bread *(Massoth)*. As I have already said, the Bible explanation of the custom of baking bread of unleavened dough and eating the *Pesah*—namely, that the Jews had to leave Egypt in such haste that their dough had no time to grow sour and rise—is unsatisfactory: (1) because the preparations for the feast, which was held on the 14th of the month, began already on the 10th, (2) because the unleavened bread was eaten at the Passover feast of the sacrificial lamb: it had been prepared and eaten before the exodus took place. In a word, the meaning and importance of the bread must have been different, but the Bible text says nothing of that. We are therefore left with no alternative but that of a symbolic interpretation, as in the case of our flesh and milk prohibition.

It is of further interest to learn that the symbolic importance of the baking of unleavened bread, as the Bible describes it, on a stone heated by the sun, is the same as the seething of the kid in his mother's milk. Thus Freud ([8,] p. 135ff.) writes: "That an oven stands for a woman or the mother's womb is an interpretation confirmed by the Greek story of Periander of Corinth and his wife Melissa. According to the version of Herodotus, the tyrant adjured the shade of his wife, whom he had loved passionately but had murdered out of jealousy, to tell him something about herself, whereupon the dead woman identified herself by reminding him that he, Periander, 'had put his bread into a cold oven,' thus expressing in a disguised form a circumstance of which everyone else was ignorant. In the *Anthropophyteia*, edited by F. S. Krauss, . . . we read that in a certain part of Germany people say of a woman who is delivered of a child that 'her oven has fallen to pieces.'" In short, the oven is a symbol of the femal genitals, and bread baked in an oven symbolizes the delivery of a child. That rising dough can be an appropriate symbol of female pregnancy needs little proving to those acquainted with the language of symbolism.

It is evident that the preparing of the bread on a hot stone and not in the oven, and with unleavened dough, was an old custom of the Israelite wanderers in the desert, and formed an important part of the ritual at the feast of the Sun-God[9]. It is also evident that the baking of leavened bread in the oven— an essentially female symbol—was forbidden at this festival, like the seething of a kid in his mother's milk.

According to the primitive, animistic mentality, a process, once set in motion, cannot remain what it was originally; it has to undergo extension. And so we find a displacement from below to above, from the uterus to the stomach. That which may not be "seethed" in the womb, may also not be "seethed" in the stomach. This, moreover, fully accords with the primitive infantile theory of oral impregnation. And, as the result, a kid may also not be cooked along with milk in the stomachs of men, i.e., may not be digested with it. To this day the word "kochen" (to cook, boil, seethe) is still used in Germany with the meaning 'to digest.'

In connection, precisely, with magic, Freud ([7.] p. 88ff.) speaks of the primitive fear of touching. It is the essence of what is known as "contagious magic": two mutually hostile or dangerous elements must not be brought into contact. If the kid may not be cooked in its mother's milk, or eaten at the same time as milk, neither may it be brought into contact with milk.

For the rest, the process develops in obedience to exactly the same laws as the fear of contact among obsessional neurotics, namely along the associative path by the process of displacement. The prohibition is displaced from the kid to flesh of every kind, from milk to any milk product, and from the stomach and uterus to all vessels and containers. One may then object in vain that it would be absolutely impossible for a young gander or capon to be cooked at all in its mother's milk. Such objections are wholly irrelevant, for prohibitions do not obey the laws of logic and reality, but the laws of the unconscious thinking of the primary process.

Thus the different flesh and milk laws among various peoples

in Asia, Africa and, as Frazer says, in Europe too (he instances
Bulgaria and Estonia), undoubtedly came about independently
of one another.  This need not surprise us, for all peoples had
at one time to undergo the same processes of cultural development, to pass through the same stages, and mental development
took the same course with all of them.  The animistic way of
thought was characteristic of them all, as it still is of so many
of them.  These habits and customs are only a precipitate of
this process of cultural development.

Here are a few examples.  The simultaneous consumption
of meat and milk or milk products is forbidden to the Jews by
law.  Now Frazer ([1,] p. 50) tells us:  "Tne Masai | in Africa |
are at the utmost pains to keep milk from touching flesh. . . .
They will not suffer milk to be kept in a pot in which flesh has
been cooked, nor flesh to be put in a vessel which has contained
milk, and consequently they have two different sets of pots set
apart for the two purposes.  The belief and practice of the
Bahima are similar. . . . But it is not merely in a pot that milk
and flesh may not come into contact with each other; they may
not meet in a man's stomach. . . . Hence pastoral tribes who
subsist on the flesh of their cattle are careful not to eat beef
and milk at the same time; they allow a considerable interval
to elapse between a meal of beef and a meal of milk, and they
sometimes even employ an emetic or purgative in order to clear
their stomach entirely of the one food before it receives the
other.  For example, the food of the Masai consists exclusively
of meat and milk; for the warriors cow's milk, while goat's milk
is drunk by the women.  It is considered a great offence to partake of milk . . . and meat at the same time, so that for ten
days the Masai lives exclusively on milk, and then for ten days
solely on meat.  To much an extent is this aversion to bringing these two things into contact entertained that, before
a change is made from the one kind of food to the other, a
Masai takes an emetic."  This purgative consists of blood mixed
with milk "and is said to produce vomiting as well as purging,
in order to make sure that no vestige of the previous food remains in their stomachs. . . . Similarly the Washamba of German
East Africa never drink milk and eat meat at the same meal."
So, too, the Bshima and the Banyoro "abstain from drinking

milk for about twelve hours after a meal of meat and beer. . . .
Among the Nandi of British East Africa meat and milk may not
be taken together.  If milk is drunk, no meat may be eaten for
twenty-four hours. . . . When meat has been eaten no milk may
be drunk for twelve hours, and then only after some salt and
water has been swallowed.  If no salt . . . is near at hand, blood
may be drunk instead . . . Among the pastoral Suk of British
East Africa it is forbidden to partake of milk and meat on the
same day ([1,] p. 153)."

These commandments are even stricter than among the
Jews, though of the same kind.  The Jews later reached the
religious stage of development and codified these habits and
customs.  It is true that Mohammedanism was imposed by force
upon the semi-savages of Africa, but, generally speaking, they
remained in the animistic stage of development and retained the
old heathen customs in contrast to their religion.

Merely for the sake of completeness, I will mention three
further usages of different African tribes.  These do not refer
to the problem of flesh and milk and are therefore not directly
connected with our topic, though Frazer mentions them in this
same connection.  Nor do we find among the Jews any similar
or parallel laws:  (1) Certain African tribes are forbidden to
cleanse the milk-vessels out of which they drink or eat.  (2)
Milk must not be kept in metal vessels, only in wooden bowls,
gourds or earthen pots.  (3) Milk must not be boiled and, particularly, must not boil over into the fire ([1,] pp. 125, 127, 118).
Unfortunately Frazer only cites the facts, without furnishing
any evidence which might throw light on these habits and
customs, and help to explain them to us.  This being so, any
analysis would have to rely on somewhat superficial data, and
for this reason I prefer to leave the question for further study.

Lastly, I should like to mention one more very important
and illuminating idea of Bialik's[3], which is that all Jewish
legislation on these matters is only a *codification* of old habits
and customs dating from the earliest, deepest and perennial
sources of the sacred myths and legends, that is, in our view,
from the period when primitive, animistic thought held sway.
It is therefore impossible to attribute to these customs any
practical and socio-ethical purpose within the meaning of

modern state legislation.

The results of our enquiry may now be summed up as follows:

The prohibition "Thou shalt not seethe a kid in his mother's milk" in its psychological structure closely resembles an obsessional symptom or rather a compulsive prohibition. Like an obsessional symptom, it has a long history, developing in many strata corresponding to separate ages or epochs. (1) In the uppermost stratum it represents a juristic precipitate of the religious and national struggle between Jewish monotheism and heathenism. (2) At a lower level it is an echo of the historical struggle of the peoples of the earth, including the Semites and, especially, the Israelites in the days of their wanderings, against the superior, but hostile, agricultural civilization of their neighbors. (3) Plunging deeper still into history, back to the age of magic and animistic thinking, this prohibition reflects the conflict between the matriarchal and patriarchal forms of society. The magical and animistic mentality of that period is further reflected in the symbolical terms in which the prohibition is couched.

# References

1. Frazer, J. G. *Folk-Lore in the Old Testament*. Vol. III. London: Macmillan, 1918.
2. Fromm-Reichman, Frieda. Das judische Speiseritual. *Imago*, 1927, 13:235-245.
3. Bialik, Haim N. *Halachah and Aggadah*. London: Zionist Federation, 1944.
4. Beer, G. *Exodus*. Tubingen: Mohr, 1939.
5. Compare also the wonderful nineteenth Psalm: "The Heavens declare the glory of God," which, according to Dubnov, is a song of praise to the Sun-God El. (English readers will find an excellent account of the discoveries at Ras Shamra in S. H. Hooke's short volume, *The Origins of Early Semitic Ritual*, London: Humphrey Milford, 1938.)
6. Ginsberg, H. L. *The Ugarit Texts*, 1936.
7. Freud, Sigmund. *Totem and Taboo*. NY: Penguin Books, 1938.
8. —————. *Introductory Lectures on Psycho-Analysis*. NY: Garden City Publishing Co., 1929.
9. It may be mentioned that in the story of Sodom and Gomorrah Lot gave the angels *matzoth* (unleavened bread) to eat. (Genesis, xix, 3.)

Chapter 16

# The Jewish Phylacteries and Other Jewish Ritual Observances

MONTAGUE D. EDER, M.D.

$\mathbf{A}$BOUT two years ago, clinical material directed my attention to the study of Jewish ritual observances, particularly the phylacteries, praying shawl and door-post symbol. About the same time papers were published in the *Imago* (1930, Nos. 3/4) by Reik on "The Praying Shawl and Phylacteries of the Jews" and by Langer on "The Jewish Phylacteries." This paper will deal with clinical material, with a summary of psycho-analytical views and with a reference to other literature in the following order:

A.  A descriptive account of the form and usages of:
    (i)  The Phylacteries (Hebrew—*tefillin*).
    (ii)  The small, four-cornered garment (Hebrew—*tsitsith*, tassels, fringe, or *arba'kanfoth*, four corners).
    (iii)  The large, four-cornered praying shawl (*talith*, scarf).
    (iv)  The door-post scroll (Hebrew—*mezuzah*, door-post).
B.  General Jewish religious opinion on the use and meaning of these ornaments.
C.  The views of some modern scholars which may be classified into (1) the Amulet, (2) the Phallic theory.
D.  Some clinical observations.
E.  Psycho-analytic theories—Abraham, Frieda Fromm-Reichmann, Marie Bonaparte, Georg Langer and Th. Reik.
F.  Conclusions.

Glover[1] in a recent lecture to the Royal Institute of Anthropology pointed out several ways in which anthropologists might work together for the advancement of knowledge, the analyst bringing his clinical material garnered from individual study and the anthropologist his field data that might or might not confirm the former. I believe that a study of Jewish ritual observances offers a field of research in this respect of exceptional value, because we can often combine the clinical evidence with the study of primitive customs in the same individuals. I do not suggest, of course, that Jews are primitives in the technical connotation of the term, but the ritualistic observances which they still practise are of remote origin and largely unchanged, and Jews offer, of course, plenty of clinical material for the analyst.

A. (i). The Jewish *Phylacteries* (from the Greek *phylassein*, to guard), are known to the Jews as the *tefillin* or ornaments, a word whose origin is obscure and will be considered later; the phylacteries are leather straps or thongs, to which are attached leather cases which contain *four* paragraphs from the *Torah* or Law, written on parchment. The paragraphs are: Exodus xiii. 1-10; Exodus xiii. 11-16; Deuteronomy iv. 4-9 and xi. 13-21. The traditional way of carrying out the precepts is still observed:

The four paragraphs are written twice on parchment, once on one piece, and once on four pieces, each piece containing one paragraph. The two sets are put into two leather cases (*bayith*), each of which is divided into four compartments for the four separate strips of parchment and marked outside by the letter *shin* = the Almighty. Two sides of the case have the *shin* impressed on them, the right and the left; on the right, the letter has three strokes . . . (usual), on the left it has four strokes in order, it is said, to ensure the right order of the four paragraphs which the case (*bayith*) contains, from left to right. Through a loop attached to each case a leather thong is passed, the two parts of which are tied together in such a manner as to hold the case or *bayith* on the arm or on the head. On the arm that case is placed that contains the four paragraphs written on one piece, on the head, that which contains them written on four pieces. The former is called *tefillah shel yad*, 'tefillin of the hand,' the latter *tefillah shel rosh*, 'the tefillin of the head.'

The tefillin are put on in the following way:—(1) Head tefillin, *Tefillah shel rosh*. The case is placed in front, just over the forehead in the middle, and the knot of the thongs on the back of the head over the middle of the neck; the rest of the two thongs hang down in front, one on each side. (2) Hand phylacteries, *Tefillah shel yad.* The case containing the parchment is placed on the inner side of the left upper arm, near the elbow; the knot is kept near it, and the thong is twisted seven times round the arm and three times round the middle finger. The thongs must be laid on the bare flesh and the leather must be black on this side; red is expressly forbidden.

*Tefillah shel yad,* of the hand, is put on first, being mentioned first in the Bible. The reverse order is observed in taking off the tefillin. In modern times the tefillin are worn only during the morning prayer. In the evening it is said to be but natural that the small shawl and the tefillin should be laid aside, as the greater part of the night is devoted to sleep; the rule was therefore generally adopted: "The night is not the proper time for laying tefillin." The opposite principle, however: "The night is likewise a suitable time for laying tefillin" had also its advocates among Rabbinical authorities.

The commandment of tefillin applies to all *male* persons from their thirteenth birthday; women are forbidden to use tefillin. With the completion of the thirteenth year a boy becomes of age as regards the fulfilment of all religious duties.

The tefillin are not worn on the Sabbath or on festivals. The very days of rest are thus reminders of the truths of which the tefillin are 'a sign.'

It was formerly customary to wear the tefillin all day, only taking them off before eating, sleeping or performing the execretory functions. It is forbidden to take the tefillin to a lavatory or to the bathroom and coitus must not be performed whilst tefillin are exposed; should this take place, the hands must be washed before putting on tefillin. Tefillin are not worn so long as a dead body is in the house, nor is one permitted to approach a corpse or visit a cemetery whilst wearing the tefillin. The tefillin must be made of leather from a 'pure' skin, passed as such by the ecclesiastical authorities; the inscriptions are exactly defined both as to text and position; should a mistake be made in the writing a new parchment must be taken.

A. (ii). Besides the tefillin, the orthdox Jew uses two other ritual garments: the small *tsitsith* and the large praying shawl.

The *tsitsith* or fringes are enjoined by Deuteronomy xxii. 12.   In obedience to this commandment, there are two kinds of four-cornered garments provided with 'fringes.'   The one is small, and is worn under the garments the whole day; it is called *arba'kanfoth*, 'four corners,' or *talith katan*, 'small scarf.'   The other and larger one is worn over the *garments* during prayers at morning and evening service.   It is called simply *talith*, scarf, or *talith gadol*, 'large scarf.'

The *tsitsith* or fringe, which is appended to each of the four corners, consists of four long threads drawn through a small hole about an inch from the corner; the two parts of the threads are bound together by a double knot; the largest thread—called *shammash*, 'the servant'—is then wound seven, eight, eleven and thirteen times round the other seven halves of the four threads, and after each set of windings a double knot is made.   If one of the four fringes is imperfect, e.g. two of the threads being torn off, the tsitsith is called *pasul*, 'disqualified' and must not be worn until that fringe is replaced by a new one.

There is, however, "an important element in this Divine commandment, which is now altogether neglected," says Friedlander[(2)], viz.:   "And they shall put upon the fringe of the corner a thread of purple blue wool" (Numbers xv. 38).   Tradition determined the exact shade of the purple blue indicated by the term *techeleth* in the Talmud where the various ways of its preparation are given.   But the colour seems to have been rare, and Jews are warned against using imitations of techleth.   Regulations were also made providing for the cases where *techeleth* could not be obtained.   The natural white colour was then substituted and no other colour was allowed.   After the period which saw the Talmud concluded, doubts seem to have arisen as regards the exact shade of the purple blue demanded and thus the use of the thread of purple blue wool gradually ceased to form part of the tsitsith.

A. (iii).   The praying shawl or *talith* is only worn during morning prayers.   It is a large, square shawl worn over the head with its freer ends hanging loose from the shoulders.

A. (iv).   The last of these ornaments to be mentioned here is the door-post scroll or *mezuzah*, a piece of parchment on which the two first paragraphs of Shema (Deuteronomy vi. 4-9,

xi. 13-20) are written. The parchment is rolled together, put into a small case and fixed on the right-hand door-post of the house and of each room. A small opening is left in the case, where the word 'God' written on the back of the scroll is visible.

B. There are, besides, says Friedlander[3], on the back of the scroll, just behind the names of God in the first line, three words of a mystic character consisting of the letters following in the alphabet the letters of these divine names. The words have in themselves no meaning, and it may be that their object is simply to indicate from outside where the names of God are written, and to prevent a nail being driven through that part in fixing the mezuzah to the door-post. I return later to this.

The object of the mezuzah as commanded in Deuteronomy vi. 9 and xi. 20 is to remind the Jews of the Presence of God, of His Unity, Providence and Omnipotence, both on entering the home and on leaving it; of the all-seeing eye that watches us and of the Almighty who will one day call us to account for our deeds, words and thoughts[4]. On entering the house or room, the mezuzah is touched and kissed.

According to Maimonides[5] the duties connected with tefillin and mezuzah are to remind us continually of God. "The performance of all these precepts inculcates into our heart useful lessons. All this is clear and further explanation is superfluous."

Strebel[6] contends that the tefillin were not used till after the Babylonian captivity; the phylacteries referred to in Matthew xxiii. 5 are the tsitsith or fringed garment.

Modern enlightened orthodox opinion maintains that it is improbable that the commands as to tefillin were to be taken literally, but it is admitted that the phylacteries were very early used as protection against evil, although there was no foundation for this superstitious use in the Biblical texts. The same view is taken by some non-Jewish commentators: "The command of writing and binding the law as a sign upon the hands . . . ought doubtless to be understood metaphorically"[7]. Though enlightened Jewish opinion admits that the use of these ornaments goes back to heathen times, the view that the Biblical injunctions were based upon other than God's commandments is not accepted.

C. The opinion generally held by scholars is that these ornaments are amulets which the Jewish people, like other primitive peoples, adopted "as the result of an internal urge which made him take steps to protect himself and to try to divine the future.   There is no doubt that the *Tetaphoth* (phylacteries), Mezuzah and the Sisith were amulets, and that the use of them goes back into prehistoric times.   Originally the tefillin were precious stones which invariably possessed the power of driving away evil spirits and therefore had no need of inscriptions"[6].

Wallis Budge considers that the Hebrews used amulets in Biblical times and "it is tolerably certain that the pagan belief in the efficacy was tacitly and unofficially adopted by them."   He considers the Kabbalah, the book of Jewish mysticism, supplies ample evidence that all these inscribed amulets were magical charms; the inscriptions were also intended to cure sickness. In Budge's book[8] the evidence will be found for the view that the various ornaments were derived from Egyptian, Persian, Sumerian and Babylonian origins.   He gives a good account of the amulets used by these peoples, as well as the importance that was ascribed to their colour, shape and form.   Ridgway has pointed out that the use of jewellery owes its origin to magic; they were amulets, and to enhance the natural powers of the stones various devices were cut on them[9].

The leather for the thongs of the phylacteries is a matter of careful selection—not any piece of leather may be used; the leather thongs, like the fringes of the shawls, point to their being part of a whole coat or dress; the Lord God, it is recorded in Genesis iii. 21, made coats of skin for Adam and his wife. Dress is, Robertson Smith[10] points out, a fixed part of social religion and is, itself, a charm and a means of divine protection. It is common practice, says Frazer[11], to sacrifice an animal and to cut the skin into straps and place the straps round the wrists or on the fingers of persons, to benefit them.

The phylactery worn upon the head has again the same meaning as the horns of honour—the horns as seen today in the bishop's mitre—"as protective amulets," symbolical of the highest of the gods.   The single horn—as represented in the head phylactery—is probably derived from the single horn which is intended to represent in human beings the pair of horns.   The horns of Moss in the Michelangelo statue are horns worn by Moses according to Exodus xxxiv. 29—"Moses wist not that the skin of his face sent forth horns"[12].

T. R. Campbell Thomson[13] has pointed out that to wear amulets on the person has always appealed to the savage mind and the word phylactery exactly expresses their use. From the blue beads plaited into horses' manes and tails and sewn into children's skull caps, up to the elaborate skin purses containing long charms written out by the bazaar scribe, they remain as much a perpetual charm to the Semites as the cross is to the Christian.

Leaving the phylacteries, there is evidence in Budge and other authorities that the praying shawls (large or small) were not only magical, but were part of the sacrificial life. Robertson Smith compares the fringes or tassels of the small or praying shawls with the thongs of goat-skin which were worn by the Libyan women. It is also the dress of sacrificial life, describing a man's religion and his sacred kindred[14]. When this dress ceased to be worn in ordinary life it was still retained in holy functions.

The sexual nature—male and female—of these Jewish amulets is suggested by Elworthy[15] and other writers and fully described by Hannay[16]. According to Dr. Max Joseph[17] the coloured fringes served to distinguish the male from the other-wise very similar female dress.

In the priest's blessing, given on the Day of Atonement, the priests, standing before the Ark or receptacle in which the Law is kept, envelop themselves completely in the praying shawl (talith) entirely covering their heads; the hands are raised in prayer and while they are uplifted the fourth and fifth fingers must be separated from the other fingers and kept in this strained position during the ceremony. Elworthy[18] explains that this position of the hand with the fourth and fifth separate fingers points to the close connection between it and the all-powerful horns of the sexual women goddesses—Ishtar, Isis, Hera, Diana, etc., whose help was supposed to be ready to protect their suppliants and whose horns the hands thus posed readily signify. Hannay, who is a very unreliable philologist, derives the word *phylactery* from *phallus*.

The mezuzah (door-post scroll) is a Babylonian word with the meaning of 'God's place.' Hastings[19] gives the evidence for its widespread usage—among the Phoenicians it was often provided with a phallus. A similar custom is found to this day in Moslem countries. "On the Mohammedan New Year every family—especially those of the towns—hangs a green branch on the door of the house." This custom is also practised throughout Palestine upon the first entry of the bride into the house of the bridegroom, as well as during the erection of the wooden frame of a tiled roof and sometimes on completing an arch. In the case of the roof, an olive branch preferably is fastened to the top of the wooden frame. These customs are meant symbolically, the green branch of a living tree being the sign of prosperity and peace. It is for this same reason that a woman, a house or a mare, which is supposed to have brought good luck, is described as having 'green' foot or hand —*idjirha hadrà, idha hadra*[20].

Langer[21] describes, with references, similar ornaments (door-post) in use in ancient and modern times: Babylonian, Graeco-Roman (phallus). It is found among the African Negroes, the Melanesians, the South American Indians. A primitive form of the mezuzah is the stone pillar which Jacob erected and made into a living God by pouring oil upon it.

In the mezuzah, as I have pointed out, three words are written on the back of the scroll just behind the one word God —that is, four words are visible, an indication again that, like the four-pronged *skin*, there is a union of the male and female, as is clear again from the position of the mezuzah, placed at the entrance of the door—the female symbol. The same redundancy and emphasis is seen in the horse-shoe, frequently hung up for luck, over the front door, often found on the door of the church, to indicate, Hannay says[22] the female nature of the church. He adds that the female symbol had to be very sexual in the Hebrew practice, as the female was taboo in their religion.

D. Passing from the description of the ornaments, the religious explanations and the interpretations of scholars, I come to some clinical observations taken from Jewish patients.

### I.  PHYLACTERIES

On several occasions, when a patient—aged 34—was in

some special hostile mood towards me, sadistic fantasies would occupy most of the session. These frequently took the form of injuring or mutilating the phylacteries he fantasied himself as wearing. "I am biting the case open and chewing up the contents—I don't mind the pain it gives me—I am not afraid of a little belly ache. I have got rid of it now—Your beautiful penis is gone; I now split it up (the case was meant as penis) from the entrance and dig a long needle into your inside—I am going to tear the straps into ribands—Yes, I am going to flay you alive. What have you done to me? Yesterday I went to the telephone to answer R. who had phoned me up; I had a pollution. I spit upon your tefillin—give me your hands and I will cut them off."

The patient came to me for complete impotency. He had had many girl friends, but had never had sexual intercourse with women or men, although he had slept with women and experienced all varieties of fore-pleasure. Evidence of latent homosexuality—generally of a reactive character—came up in analysis. He had never masturbated to his knowledge, but had experienced noctural and diurnal pollutions since puberty. I had recommended him to practise masturbation and these phylacteric fantasies were produced after he had one night followed my suggestion. It was not uncommon for him to have an emission on leaving the room of a male friend—especially if the friend had not been seen.

He came from a small town abroad; his mother was the dominant figure—ran the business and the house; his father was a mild, inoffensive man, suffering from chronic indigestion. The family was orthodox and my patient, who had gone to the usual cheder or Jewish school and learnt the Talmud, began to put on the tefillin at the usual age of 13. He had later abandoned all religious beliefs and observances.

The fantasies express sufficiently clearly the patient's desire to castrate me by tearing or biting the tefillin which I was supposedly wearing.

He recalled childish memories of feelings of rage when he saw his father and brother (six years older) saying their prayers with the tefillin. Between the ages of 6-8 he was very envious of his elder brother being able to perform the tefillin laying which was not yet allowed him.  On more than one occasion he had dropped the tefillin when sent to bring them to his father. The tefillin became a source of envy when his brother reached 13 and the special significance of the phylacteries to him as penis symbols dated from that time.

Similar fantasies have been expressed on many occasions by other patients.  Sometimes the tefillin were wound round my penis; on other occasions it was myself who was dragging the straps away from the patient; in one instance I had wound the straps round the patient's penis and I had put the headpiece in my mouth and was thus strangling his organ; sometimes it was wound round his neck.  In another fantasy, the patient was suffering great pain from the tightness with which the straps were wound round his arm.  He recalled having as a boy heard his father complain of the pain in his arm from having actually applied the phylacteries too tightly.

Ideas have been expressed by other patients that by not using the phylacteries I shall be punished either by death or by the deaths of my wife and children.  I add that none of these patients themselves used the ritual ornaments, although all had been brought up in their usage.  Sometimes it was the patient's illness which was the result of his non-religious practices, but here it was not only the abandonment of the phylacteries and tsitsith that was in question, although this would come into the category of bad deeds.

In a dream fragment, the patient was chained to me by the arm upon which the phylactery was bound and the strap had to be cut before he could be free.  This strap was here very suggestive of the umbilical cord.  I was often a mother figure to this patient, but doubtfully so in this dream.  I call your attention to the dream and its possible significance in connection with psycho-analytical views—mentioned later on—that the arm tefillin, the smaller case, signifies the female organ, while the head case, the larger, stands for the phallus originally and later perhaps for both phallus and female organ.

On another occasion when the thongs of the tefillin I was hallucinated as wearing were beating the patient's back and gluteal regions it seemed to him that my tefillined self was a dark or black god (Satan—the enemy), and he appealed to me the white God, to save him from the black God—the Satan. Black represented the darkness and the ill deeds seen and done during the nights; the thongs of the black god's phylacteries led to the popular pictures of the devil with tail. The patient at the next session quoted from Job: "So went Satan forth from the presence of the Lord and smote Job with sore boils from the sole of his foot unto his crown." 'The doubling' so well recognized in myth and folklore is displayed in this fantasy when the phylacteried analyst is Satan, the bad or hostile father, with the emblems of the Black God or Satan, while the friendly "good" father is the protecting God prohibiting the patient from his own projected aggressive or sadistic impulses.

## II. THE TSITSITH OR SMALL GARMENT

The tsitsith is, as I have said, the small four-cornered fringed garment worn constantly under the coat by all males. Unlike the other ritual garments it is used from childhood. Of course, only male children are allowed the privilege; to leave off the garment is a sin. I do not know what penalties are imposed in the Talmud if the individual has forgotten it in his dressing, but the fantasies of my patients led to severe punishments for this omission. It is perhaps from childhood's association with the mother in dressing that led to frequent association between the tsitsith and woman, mother, sister and wife. So far as I know there is nothing wrong in the exposure of the tsitsith under the dress, but it was regarded by the patients as a matter of shame if any of the fringes hung down beneath the coat, very much as a boy might be ashamed if his shirt was hanging out and from the same motive: desire to expose the male organ and fear at the discovery of the desire, giving rise to the shame. But there is an additional motive in the shame which I was able to analyse in one case. A patient's early anger was relived as he recalled on one occasion his sister laughing at him because the corners of his tsitsith were hanging out back and front. He got into a rage, hit his sister and said he would make her wear the garment—it wasn't a man's dress at all, and when he was grown up he would put on tefillin. For him it was a girl's dress, because the head went between the two narrow bands. It wasn't a man's attire because it didn't show. This, to him, was an indication that the organ was a female symbol. The two ends, he said, were outside the head like the two legs of a woman were outside the male in coitus and again the tsitsith was concealed as were the female genitals, not exposed like the tefillin and talith—male organs. It was small because he was only a boy and yet he was proud that his sister could not wear it—she had no penis.

Unlike the tsitsith, the talith or large praying shawl is worn only at prayers and again only by the male—its use does not begin till after confirmation at 13. The following 'talith dream' touches upon some other ritual practices.

### III. TALITH DREAM

"I dreamt I was going to the Club, the locality of which seemed in my native town. I saw Mr. A., an old friend, outside and as he is not a member I wanted to take him with me. To my surprise, he walked straight in. I was rather annoyed. The inside of the club seemed to me like the Beth-Hamidrash in my native town. I noticed that Mr. A. didn't have on his hat and then I saw that none had their hats on. I kept mine on. Presently it was the synagogue in my native town (the Beth-Hamidrash was part of the same building). Mr. A. and Mr. D. —both elderly men—were there and others, praying. I now saw they wore their hats and talithim. Mr. A. came up and said I should put on a talith. This made me furious and I tore off the talith both from Mr. A. and Mr. B. and knocked their hats off, which I kicked into a corner. There was a general hubbub."

The Beth-Hamidrash is the house of study adjoining the synagogue, used by adults for the study of the Bible, Talmud, etc. All males over 13 use it as a place of meeting, of theological discussion and study. The wearing of the hat is obligatory among orthodox Jews when reading any of the sacred books. Mr. A. and Mr. D. are friends of the dreamer who represent different aspects of his father. In the synagogue during prayers the hat is worn as also the talith. The aggressive act was one of impiety and sacrilege; here there was no difficulty in discovering the symbolic meaning: castration of father (and of God).

I may add that many homosexual fantasies are connected by the patient, who was a man of 45 years, with the Beth-Hamidrash. He had been brought up in the orthodox fashion in a small village in Russia and came for treatment on account of complete impotency, among other troubles. At the age of 20 he married, to escape enlistment, the first girl available. She was the daughter of the local butcher; he was potent with her for the two years their marriage lasted, although he hated and despised his wife from the first night. To make this particular hatred understandable, I must enter a little into other Jewish observances. Those animals which are allowed to be eaten by Jews must be killed in a particular way. This ritual killing—known as *Shechita*—is entrusted only to male persons possessing a knowledge of the rules and who are skilled and trustworthy. The chief rabbi or the ecclesiastical authority examines and licences the individual to become a ritual slaughterer—known as the *shochet*. The *shochet* has also to decide before and after killing whether the animal is fit for consumption; he must examine the lungs and so on to see that it was not diseased before death. In many small communities the *shochet*—who, it will be seen, must be a person of some attainments, veterinary and ritual knowledge—acts as minister and teacher. A sharp distinction is drawn between the *shochet* (ritual slaughterer) and the butcher, whose business it is to cut up and sell the slaughtered beast. The *shochet* is a person of some importance in the community, while the butcher, who may be quite unlettered, a mere tradesman, is often regarded with contempt, the lowest of the tradesmen.

It may seem a little surprising that a slaughterer should ever administer or teach. It would certainly be astonishing if the local vicar were to act in this double capacity. But the *shochet* is engaged in a *ritual* slaughter, and I have no doubt he is the direct descendant of the priest who 'shall lay his hand upon the bullock's head and kill the bullock before the Lord.' The meaning of that sanctified killing I need not enter upon here. The *shochet* has, I have little doubt, greater claims to priestly recognition according to Jewish tradition than the Chief Rabbi and the ministers who appoint the shochet.

The dreamer's wife was the daughter of the most despised

tradesman in the village—the butcher—and carried this contempt with her person.   The dreamer had married much beneath
him, but, with her, hating and despising her, he could have sexual
relations.   He left his wife after the second year and had since
lived in many parts of the world and had served in the war.   He
had been impotent ever since he left his wife, although he had
attempted intercourse with Jewesses and non-Jewesses in many
countries, often living for months or years with a woman whom
he liked.

To return from this digression to the main point—that is,
the talith as representing the father, and, in particular, the
father's penis.   The symbol of the hat is well known.   The
orthodox never discard some head-covering—cap or hat—the
reason advanced being that some of the words of the Holy
Language might inadvertently be used.   The explanation will be
found in the symbolic meaning of the hat—no castrated male
must appear before his fellows—or his fathers—or his God.
Indeed, none with any physical blemish might become a priest.

In other dreams the dreamer becomes greatly distressed at
his inability to find his talith, or he is afraid that he has not
taken it with him and that he will be asked questions about it.
These dreams have, in general, the idea that without a talith he
is not a complete man; his friends will discover that his peculiari-
ties are due to his being impotent.

A fantasy from the same patient:

"I want to come and sit on your knees; I want to kiss you
and have your arms round me.   I dare not come because you
are saying your prayers with the tefillin."

Earlier memories justified such fears; his father was very
pious in the fulfilment of his ritual duties and would allow no
one, not the beloved children, said the patient, to disturb him
at those times, unlike so many even quite orthodox Jews who,
perhaps feeling more at home, can carry on a pleasant gesture
conversation whilst praying.   Any advance on the part of the
little child would be checked by his mother or frowned upon by
his father who seemed a very stern and forbidding figure with
the tefillin or when clothed in the talith.   Analysis has shown
that early childhood is much impressed by changes in the adult's
dress as well as by changes in the furniture or being taken to a

different room. Thus to my patient the stern, aggressive father became associated from earliest babyhood (as suckling) with the tefillin and the kindly easy-going father with the absence of tefillin or praying shawl; this father was again associated with the mother who never appeared in such a garb. When my patient desires close sexual relationship with me—sitting on my lap—examining my penis—intercourse with his mother and father—his super-ego rejects it in the name, so to say, of the tefillined father, the forbidding father, and thus he projects the tefillin on to my head and arms. I am at once mother and indulgent father, and at the same time, the aggressive, frustrating and castrating father.

The last ritual ornament for which I will offer clinical material is referred to in the following.

## IV. MEZUZAH DREAM

"It was a large house, perhaps an Italian hotel, surrounded by beautiful gardens. In the grounds a procession of women going up a deep valley with trees all round; the brook came tumbling down the valley. They wore light-coloured dresses—perhaps nightdresses. The women were in a big courtyard. Many men were there—they had black beards. They were taking down the Mezuzoth and carrying them; I supposed they were leaving the house. The men were dancing with the mezuzoth in their hands—I said, 'Oh chassidim'! The men and women were mixed up. Perhaps they were dancing together or were they all mad? I woke with a nasty feeling."

The dreamer, an English-born Jew of 24, who had discarded all religious observances but was very superstitious, had seen the previous evening *La Boutique Fantasque* in the company of his fiancée and his mother and sister. His father was dead, but there was a portrait of him about the house, as a youngish man with a beard. After his death, the family had moved to a new house. There were no mezuzoth in the new house; probably there were in the former house. The bearded men represent the patient's father, who was of chassidic descent, with his penis (mezuzoth) in his hand, a masturbation permission. The women were those with the dreamer at the ballet, and others.

The dream recalled his many fleeting love affairs.   He knew that the engagement would not go through—he wearied of every girl after the first embrace or the first kiss.   Further associations led to the dreamer's memories of the primal scene; he slept in a room adjacent to the parents' with the doors open. The chassid father took all the women—mother, sister, fiancées —the dreamer could not get one.

A full analysis of the dream would reveal the dreamer's life troubles—I only bring it here on account of the mezuzoth figuring as the father's male genital in the primal scene, where the case and its contents symbolize the female genital organs and its shape the male; another instance of that condensation in religious ritual ornaments to which Langer calls attention.

These hallucinations, fantasies, dreams, are a representative excerpt from clinical material gathered mainly during the last eight years, in course of analysis from male patients, who, whether born in Eastern Europe or elsewhere, were brought up in households where Jewish traditions obtained.   In some cases the analysis was conducted in Yiddish or a mixture of Yiddish and German.

I have not included anything from Jewish women, because it would introduce further difficulties into the issues this paper is hoped to illustrate.   Some of the patients had abandoned the practice of the traditional observances, some remained strictly observant, but all the former, as of course the latter, retained something that pertained to their religious upbringing.   In some cases this something expressed itself merely in such an apparent triviality as a distaste for other than Jewish cookery, perhaps accompanied by fierce denunciations of Jewish belief and ritual 'superstitions.'   The retention of orthodox belief and practice or their abandonment certainly influenced the personality and had a bearing on the individual's choice of neurosis and on symptomatology but proved not relevant here.

By a condensation to which we are accustomed, the phylacteries represent the aggressive and/or castrating father, the frustrating mother and parental intercourse; while the analyst is either part of the phylacteries or may figure as the helpful and kindly father, mother defending the patient (son) against the evil parents in the phylacteries.   When the patient desires to kiss the phylacteries, talith or mezuzah there are ambivalent motivations.

The meaning of kissing the ritual ornaments so far as I have been able to work it out between the patients and myself (hallucinated as wearing the phylacteries or talith) represent different stages in development, varying with the analytic situation. The kiss is a love offering of himself to the phylactery (father imago); it may sometimes be accompanied by erotic sensations and even erection. The kiss is propitiatory, it is an attempt to allay anxiety arising out of the primal scene. It is here a surrender of himself to the phylacteries, representing the parental imagos. The analyst is often separated from the phylacteries and acts as intermediary between these ornaments (imagos) and the parents. The analyst is a benevolent father and oftentimes has the attributes and functions of the priest. The kiss may disguise an aggressive assault upon the phylacteries: the oral-sadistic stage which is usually indistinguishable, in practice, from the cannibalistic desires. In the patients cited, the aggression was attributed to the (father imago) phylacteries where the analyst was identified with the ego of the patient or to the tefillined analyst (analyst and tefillin being one). It is quite usual for the patient to consider he is defending himself against the aggressive or sadistic father (phylacteries).

It may seem that the analytic situation where the analyst may figure as wearing the phylacteries and by them endowed with loving or hostile attributes, while at the same time the analyst may be divorced from the phylacteried analyst, makes the position much more complicated than it is in, say, the case of the Jew carrying out the religious ritual. But such evidence as I have—it is not conclusive—leads me to believe that the ritual ceremony may be fraught with equal complication; the evidence is from the reminiscences of patients—some have been given—observing their fathers or brothers at prayer and from memories of anxiety and panic in repeating their prayers. In general, of course, the anxiety is displaced and rationalized on to incidents of daily life.

E. Having now given the general description and interpretative accounts of these Jewish ritual observances with some clinical observations, I shall put before you certain psychoanalytic theories.

In a commentary on Reik's *Ritual: Psychoanalytic Studies*, Abraham[23] calls attention to the significance of the priestly gesture which I mentioned and to the complete cloaking of the priests with the talith.  He regards the position of the hand as standing for the cloven hoofed animal, one of the rare four-footed beasts whose flesh is allowed to be eaten (Leviticus xi. 26), that is, the ram.

After showing that the ox and the ram are totem animals, Abraham comments on the remarkable fact that just those animals are permitted to be eaten which are also indicated as the only sacrificial four-footed animals.  "If we remind ourselves," he continues, "that in many cults, the most solemn festivals consist in the priests' covering themselves with the skin of the totem and imitating the posture of the totem, the following deduction is pretty obvious: in the priestly benediction, the priests (cohenim) imitate by their gesture of the separated fingers the cloven hoof of the totem (ram)."  The praying shawl of white wool is a substitute for the ram's fell.  The priests are, in the ceremony, equivalent with the totem and thus with God.*

Frieda Fromm-Reichmann[23a] considers that the opinion that a horned animal was the original Jewish totem animal is confirmed by the usage of the phylacteries.  The leather straps, she contends, represent the animal's fell, in which the person praying is covered; the case in the middle of the forehead stands for the one horn of the beast, and, by a simple displacement, the second case, that is, the second horn, is moved from the forehead to the upper arm.  She considers that "the complete identification with the animal by means of covering oneself with hide and horns can only reasonably refer to the totem animal, confirming the hypothesis that horned beasts were the original totem animals of the Jews."

* The thread of coloured wool, in Hebrew, *techeleth*, ordered upon the fringes is translated as 'purple blue.'  The exact shade of the original colour is said to be unknown and the coloured fringe has been abandoned for what looks like a pseudo-rational ground.  The snail from which the purple was obtained became rare and the colour too expensive.  Purple is in the unconscious a substitute for red—the colour of blood, i.e. of the blood of the sacrificial animal (totem).

Marie Bonaparte[24], in her essay on the symbolism of head trophies, has shown that the horn is a symbol of the castrated male organ.

Reik, starting off from the reproach to the Pharisees about the breadth of their phylacteries, concludes, after a very detailed examination of the literature, that the praying shawl is a substitute for the ram's skin, and that the phylacteries offer complete identification with the totem animal through its hide and horns.

## V.  ABSTRACT OF TH. REIK'S PAPER 'GEBETMANTEL UND GEBETRIEMEN DER JUDEN'

### (*Imago*, 1930, 16:388-434)

Beginning with a description of the use of the tefillin and talith in ancient and modern times, Reik proceeds to their religious significance.  Religious literature gives a baffling wealth of proscriptions portraying the magical character of the tefillin. The explanations offered by authorities are often very suggestive, but usually insufficient.

Klein[25] considers that the tefillin or totaphot of the Old Testament was regarded as a physical mutilation, a branding on the forehead of the first-born son who was offered to God at the original Passover feast.  This was entirely forgotten later and the texts were read as referring to amulets.  Reik thinks that although there is a modicum of truth in this theory, Klein has gone astray.  It is probable that the totaphot had originally another meaning, and that it was later regarded as an amulet, but there must be some connection between the primary and later meanings; it is insufficient to conclude that the original meaning was altogether lost.  Physical mutilation does not fit in either with the form or nature of the tefillin.

Strade[26] pursues the same path; he attempts to establish a connection between the mark set upon Cain—a primitive tattooing—and the use of tefillin; in so far as this theory emphasizes the character of tefillin as a ritual mark, it is more satisfactory than Klein's, but it does not explain how tattooing became a system of cases and straps and does nothing to clear up the peculiar significance or the special ritual of tefillin.

Baentsch[27] likewise regards the totaphot as an amulet; an ancient tattooing cult sign—an amulet developed into the tefillin. Holzinger[28] likewise regards it as a tattooed Jahwe sign. Wellhausen[29] also regards the totaphot as amulets on the frontal straps. Robertson Smith[30] considers that "the phylacteries are survivals of old superstition and their use in prayer may be taken as what the superstition was. They are appurtenances to make prayer more powerful." In favour of the amulet theory are Grünbaum[31], Blau[32], Bousset[33], Schürer[34], and many other authorities.

It seems ever clearer, says Reik, "that the Higher Criticism believes it has solved the problem when it concludes that the tefillin are amulets, mascots, and so on. Criticisms of this theory are listened to impatiently by the learned." M. Friedländer[35], for example, regards the tefillin not as a genuine Jewish creation, but as a gnostic sign of the serpent. Gnostic signs pierced the Jewish masses, and, since they could not be suppressed, received sanction; Reik considers amidst much error there is a spark of truth in this view.

Hirsch[36], Mack[37], and Kennedy[38] consider that the Biblical commands are to be taken metaphorically.

Although the Talmud maintains that Moses was taught to lay tefillin by God on Mt. Sinai there has been much discussion in recent years as to the period of its introduction. Wünsche[39] considers it to be pre-Christian; Klein[40] thinks it of Persian origin; Kennedy[41], by verbal comparisons, dates its introduction to about 300 B.C. Josephus[42] and his contemporaries regarded it as an old institution. Although it is uncertain when the Jews began to lay tefillin, the Mishna furnishes abundant information at the period after Christ's birth. In the eighth and tenth centuries A.D. the tefillin received scant respect[43]. The wearing of the fringed garments (tsitsith) has been generally recognized as a very ancient custom. Similar ornaments were in use among the other Asiatic peoples—Persians, Babylonians. Kennedy[44] regards the fringes as originally amulets. The fringes, like the phylacteries, originally signified phylacteries or amulets. Robertson Smith's[45] hypothesis that the fell of certain animals was holy to ancient Semites, to which attention has already been directed, is, in Dr. Reik's estimation, of much greater value than the views of the archaeologists and other critics. "His hint is of decided importance, but the explanations which he was able to give are too general to solve the riddle of the tsitsith."

The Biblical command—Exodus xiii. 9—"And it shall be for a sign unto thee," etc., follows, without apparent connection, passages referring to the feast of Mazzoth and the dedication of the first-born. It is difficult to see what is the connecting link. Many commentators agree with Kennedy[46] that "the feast of Mazzoth and the dedication of the first born shall alike serve as perpetual reminders of the Egyptian deliverance and of Jahwe's resulting claims upon them" and comes to the conclusion, already mentioned, that the tefillin is a metaphorical reminder of these claims. After an exegetical and philological critique, Reik concludes that the dedication of the first-born has something to do with a mysterious sign, a sign designated in three places by the word TOTAPHOT. The meaning of this word is obscure; its root undoubtedly means originally *to get about, to run about*.

Reik finds the position peculiar. On the one hand, religious tradition claims that the tefillin are to be used as reminders, that they were commands given by God to Moses on Mt. Sinai and are of the utmost religious significance. It is not known of what they are reminders, it is not believed that God actually did so command Moses and it is not understood what can be the significance in a combination of leather cases and leather thongs. Against tradition, commentators on the Old Testament maintain that it was a late discovery that had nothing to do with the original religion of Israel. A Biblical text which is to be understood purely metaphorically was many centuries later given a verbal rendering and so misunderstood. The tefillin are amulets to keep away evil spirits. The traditional view seems absurd while the theories of the commentators, though not free from contradictions, seem reasonable and logical. Rationally, the choice would not be difficult to make. But there is hindrance to the acceptance of these rationalistic arguments, namely, the remarkable contradictions which are not removed by the rational considerations.

Reik proposes a new way—psychoanalysis—to solve these several riddles, but it is to be used as an heuristic method only,

not making use of any psychoanalytic suppositions derived from
the psycho-pathology of the neuroses.

His new point of departure for his analytic investigation is
a book by Lund[47], published in 1701, on *Old Jewish Relics*, which
gives an accurate description of the Jewish ritual and contains
a section on tefillin. The parchment rolls, the author noticed,
containing the Biblical verses, are bound by the hairs of a cow
or calf, taken from the tail, which have been well grown and
cleansed, 'purified'. The hairs are not tied together but are
twisted together by the fingers, leaving a hair outside so that
it can be seen from without. Lund noticed that in a certain
Rabbi's tefillin a red hair about one and a half fingers' length
hung out. He discovered that it was in memory of the red cow;
they prayed to God that as the red cow bore their sins and
purified them from uncleanliness, God would also purify them
from their sins—it reminded the devout of the golden calf to
which they prayed in the Wilderness.

It is not a very far jump from this cow's hair to conclude
that the head tefillin had to do with a piece of clothing. Reik's
hypothesis is that the head tefillin is the survival of a dress
which the Israelites wore on certain occasions. The hand tefillin
and the leather thongs, the tsitsith and the talith likewise represent similar primitive practices. The hand tefillin stand for the
hoof of the animal and the leather thongs for its skin. The
four fringes are references to the four legs of the animal, the
knots in the threads of the tassels standing for its joints.
Originally the fringes hung down to the ground; a further point
in proof of its resemblance to the animal's legs.

Anthropological research has shown us that most primitive
people use such clothing for magical purposes. References are
made to the works of Frazer[48], Lewis and Clark[49], Robertson
Smith[50], Spencer and Gillin[51]. Robertson Smith has shown
that amongst the Semites, the skin of the sacrificial animal had
a particularly sacred character. It was the draping of the idol
or sacred stone and likewise the dress of the worshippers. God,
his worshippers and the sacrificial victim were akin. Smith adds
that the thongs correspond to the fringes of the tsitsith. The
Assyrian Dagon worshipper offered his sacrifice to the Fish-god
draped in a fish-skin; the Cyprian wore a sheep-skin when

sacrificing a sheep to the sheep-goddess. Like other peoples, the Hebrews clothed themselves in the skin of their totem animal, whether bull or ram, and so identified themselves with the sacred animal. Originally the whole skin was used, but gradually, as the totem religion lost its importance, and under the influence of other elements, the great changes to the later tefillin took place. What was originally the most important element—the totem animal—was subsequently reduced to the minimum and just hinted at in the hair left without.

The change is gradual; only some parts of the skin are used to indicate identification with the totem animal. What was most important is now reduced to the minimum; what was formerly most important is now only hinted at. In the place of the natural parts of the animal, say, the horns of the ox, there are artificial substitutes. Their relationship with the old sign is only shown by similarity of material and of form. Their sacred character and their usage in ritual and in cult are demonstrated inasmuch as their former function remains.

If the tefillin had later the character of an amulet or charm it was because it originally represented the living God himself —through its substitute the totem animal. Though it may have but a metaphorical value in the intellectual Judaism of the day, analytical investigation shows that the pious Jew is nearer to the feelings and thoughts of his ancestors than the pseudo-scientific investigators, the Higher Critics, have ever understood.

Reik considers certain objections that may be made to his hypothesis. He has assumed, for instance, that the talith represents the rest of a sacred ram's skin. The tsitsith indicated the four legs of the animal. The fringes and knots hint at the muscles and limbs of the same animal. The objection that the threads cannot, on account of their position, be likened to the feet of an animal is met by the reminder that the shortness of the talith belongs to a later phase of development; originally it was a long garment; Lund says that the fringes of the rabbis reached to the ground.

The tefillin, originally a piece of the God himself, became an amulet; that is to say, whoever wears such a portion of the God stands under His special protection. This value is, of course, derived from the idea that the wearer of the tefillin

originally became God himself and the gods need no amulets
The original import is again recognisable when, for instance
religious tradition maintains that the inter-twining of the thongs
of the head tefillin form the letters of the name of God.   Is not
the original nature of the tsitsith shown in the mystical explana
tion of the value of the numbers—the total giving at once
JAHWE alone and at the same time the number of the religious
commands?   Identification of the believer with his God whose
garment he wears is really primitive religion, the essential command.   The Lord himself wore tefillin—as seen when we consider
the original significance of the horn which ornamented the sacred
animal.   The explanation the Talmud gives of the prophecy that
the peoples of the earth would be afeared before Israel is that
the nations would be in fear of the head tefillin, surely an
allusion to its original meaning, the national totem on the head

Returning to his starting-point, Reik points out that the
Pharisees, in wearing such broad phylacteries and enlarging their
borders, were demonstrating the signs of the living God.

The objection that the talith is made of wool and represents
the ram or sheep and not the ox is readily met by the reminder
that in many tribes one totem animal was substituted for another
and frequently the two animals remained for a long time the
objects of worship.

Religious usage justifies the direction that has been taken.
The command to kiss the tefillin reminds us that the ancient
Semites covered their religious symbols and idols with kisses.
These holy stones, trees, etc., were originally the gods themselves.   The Israelite kissing his tsitsith is carrying out the
same reverential act as the Arab who kisses the Kaaba, or the
pious Catholic who used to kiss the Pope's toe.   It may be
postulated that the talith is to be regarded as the original of
that sacred piece of clothing which serves the Catholic in his
repentance—the scapular.   The wearing of the scapular is bound
up with as many rites as the use of the talith.   Klein's view that
related the commands about tefillin with other ordinances now
finds its place, Reik considers, in his own hypothesis.

It cannot be a matter of indifference that the ritual is
mentioned in connection with the extremely ancient Passover
festival and that the father informs his questioning son that the

tefillin are a sign or a memory. The archaic nature of the festival is well substantiated; the command to eat the paschal lamb raw indicates an earlier custom—the consumption of the bleeding and still quivering flesh. Equally primitive is the sprinkling of the door-posts with blood, the ancient nomadic fashion, the warning to leave something of the sacrificial animal for use next day. There is no doubt that the slaughtered animal was originally the sacrificed God himself. Now we understand why the command about tefillin, which is derived from the skin of an animal, is linked with the great totem repast. The apparently irrelevant 'It' of Exodus xiii. 9 referred originally to that divine fell and not to the command which belongs to a later stage.

### I. ABSTRACT OF GEORG LANGER'S PAPER: 'DIE JÜDISCHEN GEBETRIEMEN'

#### (*Imago*, 1930, 16:435-485)

Langer begins his paper with a very detailed description of the tefillin (thongs and cases) and of their ritual usages; most of this has been already given, but I abstract from Langer some further descriptive material.

Both the cases are cubic; these are rather small among Western and much bigger among Eastern Jews. They must be made from the skin of any 'clean' animal. Any bag used to carry the tefillin must not be used for ordinary purposes. In former times—and occasionally even today—the pious and the learned wore tefillin all day, removing them only before sleep, at meals or for bodily needs. This constant usage caused in many cases a severe paralysis of the arm. A left-handed person lays the tefillin on the right hand as the torah commands that it shall be on the weaker limb. If a member of the family dies, the male relatives must not lay tefillin. They are laid again after the funeral. A bridegroom and his wedding asssociates are freed from tefillin through fear of an unbecoming light-heartedness. Should a woman wish to lay tefillin, she must be prevented. Yet tradition relates of some especially pious 'thorough' women who in Biblical times were allowed to use tefillin. The command about laying tefillin is so important that it is regarded as equal in itself to all the other 613 laws of the Torah.    After usage the thongs are to be carefully rolled up and placed in a bag.    Should anyone let the tefillin fall to the ground before being placed in the bag, he must fast.    The cases are kissed at laying and laying off the tefillin.    God wears tefillin according to the Talmud.

The two parts of the phylacteries, the cases with their parchment text and the leather thongs, require separate consideration.    The binding of these thongs reminds us at first sight of a fettering, of a self-fettering in the full sense of the word.    Such a view is in complete contradiction with the principles of Jewish religion, which demands a healthy state of all the bodily organs.    The origin of such a fettering must be sought in some repressed wish to injure something other than the harmless left upper limb.    Psycho-analysis recognizes fettering as a symbol of castration, in this case, of self-castration.    This corresponds with the purpose of the tefillin, which, according to Jewish tradition, is to warn mankind against sin.    Castration is the best protection against sin.    The thongs have also in general a positive erotic meaning.    For instance, in the old Roman Lupercalia feast, the Luperci, clad in goat-skins, beat the women present with thongs of goat-skin, that they might become pregnant[52].    In myth and saga, leather is symbolic of a death or castration wish[53], but has also an erotic meaning; the latter, partly motivated, probably, by the fact that fresh leather exercises a sexual effect upon the sense of smell[54], a sensation which would be experienced by the Jewish boy at puberty who joyously gets up at dawn to lay the tefillin, which are usually new, with the sharp smell of fresh leather.

In ancient China, two skins were part of the regulation wedding present[55].    In the ecstatic tearing or sacrifice of the Dionysian animals, in the orgiastic bacchic Maenadic festivals, the clothing finishes with skins[56].    The sacrificial father-animal is castrated, and the mystic, clearly by identification with the former, clothes himself in his skin.    In the Dionysian festival, in the central part of the Satyr drama the players were clad in aprons of goat-skin and phallus[57].    These ancient customs must have, as is especially clear from this last example, a content similar to those described by Zulliger[58] in the goat-skin masks of the 'Roichtschäggeten' in the Lötschen-Tal.

Fromm-Reichmann's[59] explanation that the tefillin are a ceremonial identification with the father totem animal is confirmed by our material, but the complex tefillin problem must not be regarded as fully explained by this hypothesis. This material suggests two important considerations which have received scant attention; the tefillin fettering as a castration-substitute (self-castration and father castration) and the tefillin in its ambivalent Janus face of Life and Death.

Schuster[60], dealing with the wearing of long gloves and of cords around the head carried out by male algolagnics, concludes that gloves are to a certain extent fetters in which the hands are enveloped. The hand thongs of the phylacteries fulfil a similar function to the gloves of the algolagnics and the thongs of the head phylacteries correspond with these head-cords. Fettering as a castration symbol satisfies the masochistic component of instinctual life where God as sexual object is regarded as having sadistic tendencies.

The central point of the problem lies, however, not in the thongs, but rather in the cases. Cases (sometimes of an obviously phallic nature) strikingly similar to the head totaphot are found among African Negroes, especially in their masks. At the same spot as the Jew places the case on the head, that is, in the middle of the hair above the forehead—following Jewish tradition as against the Pentateuch—the Negro mask has a cubical, empty body without any written content[61]. Indian godheads wear a small horn on the forehead, clearly of the same origin. Bieber[62] gives illustrations of the head phallus of Abyssinian Negroes. Among Negroes, the head phallus is often replaced by a frontal tattooing. There are circular as well as modified square tattooings. Such tattoo markings correspond with the Biblical verse which enjoins that the cases shall be placed above the nose, that is, between the eyes. There are Negro masks dating from the Biblical period which are ornamented with the characteristic circular drawings.

This kind of tattooing partly recalls the Israelitic *korhah* mentioned in Deuteronomy xiv. 1. Reik[63] recognizes the connection between the *korhah* and the Jewish head tefillin. The Talmud seems to have suspected the connection of the tefillin with Africa.

Egyptian kings[64] wore the magic serpent hair ornaments at the same places where the Jews placed their head tefillin and the Negroes their head phalli.   The Romans replaced the phallus by a symbolic horn[65].   In earlier Talmudic times the totaphoth were either cubical or cylindrical.   The cylindrical form was only later fully replaced by the cubical.   The Talmud describes the 'round' form of totaphoth as a danger.   Obviously the danger was to belief rather than to anything physical.   In other places in the Talmud, the cubical shape of the head case is the only proper shape; it was so verbally given to Moses on Mt. Sinai.   But verbal commands by God do not require any explanation.   The 'danger' which the Mishnah feared was only present in one instance—namely, when the round totaphoth was nut-shaped.   The nut often found in ancient graves was dedicated to the moon[66]; its cultural usage can be followed right up to modern times.   The nut has an intimate connection with wedding and birth feasts.   It is more especially a symbol of the maternal womb.

The replacement of the original cylindrical shape of the totaphoth by its cubical 'house' shape (similarly among the Negroes) has a deeper meaning.   The house is a female genital symbol.   There is plainly a process of concealment in the symbol formation, the striking appearance of the too obvious phallic shape is softened by connecting it with a female symbol, which at the same time symbolizes coitus.   In an article on the function of the Jewish doorpost scrolls[67], Langer gave some examples of the change of male into female attire and connected this with the change in the social system from gynocracy to patriarchy.   Malinowski recognizes the problem when he states, "What is the nature of the influence of the nuclear complex on the formation of myth, legend and fairy tale; on certain types of savage and barbarous customs, forms of social organization and achievements of material culture?   This problem has been clearly recognized by the psycho-analytic writers who have been applying their principles to the study of myth, religion and culture.   But the theory of how the social mechanism influences culture and society through the forces of the nuclear complex, has not been worked out correctly.   Most of the views bearing on this second problem need a thorough revision from the socio-logical point of view." Langer accepts this with certain reservations.

This change of attire plays an important rôle in the phylac-teric emblems, and Langer records a number of such instances among Egyptians, Jews[69] and Moslems[70], Nandi and other Hamitic races[71], Indian girls in S.W. North America[72] from the travels of Frobenius[73]. From these observations confirming his own work Langer concludes that the tendency to transvestism in religious symbol formation betrays a permanent wish of the unconscious. The painful representation of the father figure is softened by the addition of the symbolic mother attributes and at the same time coitus is displayed.

While the totaphoth were obviously worn on the forehead for display, their original phallic shape became modified in favour of a cubical shape, a very concealed female symbol; the case of the hand tefillin, at least among Oriental Jews, main-tained almost fully its phallic shape.

Originally the hand and head cases, like the amulets of many other cults[74], represented the phalli. It was only in Talmudic times that the phallic form of the head box gave place to the female cubical "house" form; the European Jews then repressed the phallic shape of the head box by covering it with a cloth.

Referring to the bird-like shape of the head tefillin in legend and usage and to the well-known meaning of the bird in folk-lore, Langer points out that the head tefillin has an obvious resem-blance to the male organs; the testicles represented by the loose ends of the thongs, the scrotum by the thongs drawn through the base of the case and the prominent case itself would correspond to the penis *in statu erectionis*. The tefillin bag must be likewise equated to a scrotum; after use the two tefillin rolled together must be placed in the bag, not one on top of the other, but next to one another, recalling the position of the testicles in the scrotum. In fact, the Eastern Jews call the scrotum, in vulgar parlance, the tefillin bag.

The Pentateuch recommends that the words of the Torah should be borne *between the eyes*, which was carried out by writing them on the head cases. Traditionally, the cases were placed above the forehead at the juncture of the hair and exactly in the middle. With the two eyes this forms a triangle—an erotic symbol; among the Greeks it was known as a female symbol and in the Hindu religion the triangle is a symbol of God. Other sources are referred to by Langer, showing that the triangle as well as the eye can be either a male or female symbol. The eye in the centre of a triangle, common in the mystic symbolism of the church, was originally a symbol of the union of male and female. The Shield of David was a symbol of both creative principles, known as such also to the Babylonians, Etruscans, and South American Indians. The Shield of David is by preference sketched or drawn on the bag for the tefillin, and Spiez[75] has proved the phallic meaning of the triangle. Langer gives various sources for the phallic meaning of three in connection with the bindings of the hand thongs thrice round the middle, i.e. on the third and longest finger. The hand tefillin are wound seven times round the upper arm; this number, found in religion, myth and folk-lore, is closely connected on one side with death motives, and on the other with libidinal and creative desires. The hand in mythology represents the phallus, confirming the view that the hand tefillin are related both with castration and with increased phallic power.

The prohibitions against coitus, etc., in the presence of the phylacteries, are to lessen anxiety in the presence of the totem-father-phallus. The phylacteries are an apotrophaic defence against demons who select just such places as the closet.

The thongs have an ambivalent Janus face, as have, in general, ritual clothing, masks and especially the skin. In the horned phylacteries which have been shown to be a kind of mask, the ambivalent content of the skin, the mask and the thongs are condensed.

These phylacteries condense in themselves the elements of eros, death (or castration), bound together with the displacement of a male symbol to a castrated, disguised male-female emblem forming a classical example of the kind of combinations common in 'concealed' religious symbols.

The connection eros-death seems here to be an extension of the Œdipus complex where Eros seems to take the place of the Mother imago and death (castration; self-castration) the introjected father in the ego or the subsequent unconscious feelings of guilt. In this enormous work of condensation there is, as ever, the tendency of the unconscious to bring together in one single expression a great variety of contradictory ideas, together with the tendency of the resistance to make the real meaning unrecognizable.

Langer has three appendices: (1) The relationship of the tefillin with African culture; (2) fire; (3) the serpent, dealing especially with the phallic nature of the serpent and adding a further meaning to the snake-like thongs of the phylacteries.

## II.  CONCLUSION

The Jewish and Christian orthodox view of these ritual ornaments and practices is that they are God's ordinances given to Moses on Mt. Sinai. Enlightened opinion, which attempts to rationalize whatever it finds obscure, asserts that the Biblical texts are meant metaphorically only.

An examination of the practices shows the meticulous precision devoted to every detail of the practice—both in the making of the article and in its ceremonial usage.

The researches of scholars—like Budge, Kennedy and others—have understood that the ornaments are magical charms or amulets in use the world over; but their investigation has in general stopped at that point.

Only one or two researches have gone a step farther: Robertson Smith has seen the connection of the phylacteries and the shawls with sacrificial animals; Elworthy in the gestures and horns. Hannay recognized the full import of the sexual symbolism of all these ornaments (as well as of all ritual usages).

Material derived from Jewish male patients exemplify the sexual symbolic nature of the ornaments and practices— fantasies, dreams of which I have only given an excerpt, demonstrate that the ornaments in question are not regarded merely as phallic or cunnic but are connected closely with the father and mother imago, with castration ideas, with the primal scene, with the content of the Œdipus situation in its fullest sense.

It will be recalled that the phylacteries and talith are to be worn by every male from the thirteenth year, when he becomes a son of the covenant (Barmitzvah). In remote times, among the Hebrews, circumcision took place at puberty[76]; in the fifteenth century A.D. a curious rite was performed at the ceremony connected with cutting the barmitzvah boy's hair[77]. The symbolic meaning of hair-cutting as castration is well known and needs no elaboration here.

The patients tend to separate the wearer of the phylacteries or talith from the ornaments themselves. The phylacteries, etc., become identified with the stern, cruel and aggressive father and mother, while the wearer is the indulgent or kind father-mother imago. The phylacteries thus become projections of the introjected 'bad' father and mother imagos and the patient (or wearer) propitiates his own aggressive desires or archaic fantasied deeds by acts of propitiation: great care in the usage of the phylacteries, reverence shown to the ornaments, kissing them, which may have many different meanings, dependent not on the patient's situation but on object cathexes that correspond to emotional attitudes extending chronologically from the suckling to the adolescent.

The tefillin and talith are found to be representative of the aggressive father who is ready to castrate and devour the son and against whom the son invokes the protection of the untefillined father, usually by not accepting this fantasy of the devouring father, or the son seeks to propitiate the 'bad' father by offering himself (kiss; reverent gesture) and/or by prayer.

The understanding of the material I have adduced is, however, carried much further, by the investigations of psycho-analysts—Abraham, Marie Bonaparte, Reik, Langer. The ornaments are last remnants of the totem animal once worshipped by the Hebrews and containing traces of an earlier cult.

The analysis of my patients points to the psychological if not to the historical truth of the law forbidding the Jews to let their seed pass through to Moloch. The mezuzah dreams and fantasies show the psychological truth of the blood spilling that the elders of Israel were commanded to strike upon the lintels and the left side posts of their houses. In Exodus xxii. and xxiii. the blood colour is derived from a bunch of hyssop and is a protection against the slaughter of the Hebrews' first-born, while the first-born of the enemy—the Egyptians—are to be sacrificed.   Purple so frequently stands for blood in the unconscious that one cannot help suspecting that techeleth, the thread of purple blue wool, is a reference to the slaughtered totem animal; Abraham and others have shown that the woollen praying shawl is a substitute for the ram's fell.

We now see that the motives for the sadistic fantasies of my patients are primeval.   In attacking the father in the tefillin they are attacking the totem animal—the whole ritual of sacrifice detailed in Leviticus is a study of the murder and eating of the *Urvater,* the primeval great father

> whose mortal taste
> Brought gods into the world and all our woe.

Having traced back the phylacteries, praying shawl and door-post symbol to their primitive origin, it remains to discover the historical sequence from primal Father to primal God and the substituted totem animal; how the totem animal gradually lost almost all its recognizable qualities, so that finally, as Reik says, we have but a single hair left whereby to discover the totem animal in the phyclacteries.   These changes are the historical records of thousands of generations and the records are too imperfect to enable us at present to trace the sequence step by step.   However, our study of contemporary minds such as those of the persons whose analysis, so far as it is germane to the problem, I have set out here, enables us to throw light on the functions of the phylacteries and other ornaments, and thus enables us to understand what purpose was served by the modifications.

When the analyst is hallucinated as wearing the tefillin and when the analyst's person is doubled, the patient has made something that may be compared with the analysis of a complicated chemical compound; he has resolved, partially or wholly, his parental imago into its primary elements.   In this case the elements are the aggressive or sadistic parents and the indulgent, loving parents.   The parent who has been hallucinatively introjected (the sacrificial totem animal in history, the living father in the individual) has become a source of pain, of discomfort and is ejected and projected in the form of the phylacteries, talith, mezuzah.

Under the ordinary conditions of the religious Jew the projected imago becomes an object of reverence, of worship. The father (penis or whole father) has not been castrated or annihilated—here he is, daily to be seen, touched and kissed; to be treated with an extravagant and exaggerated respect or love to prove how false was the individual's unconscious sense of guilt in regard to the father (mother) imago.

The function of the phylacteries is to resolve the need of punishment by setting up an image of the living god. True the Hebrews are warned, "Thou shalt not make unto thee any graven image, nor any likeness of anything that is in heaven above or that is in the earth," but the phylacteries appear to the conscious self as little to transgress this commandment as do the paintings of the cubists and vorticists. The function of the phylacteries and ritual ornaments is to preserve the balance between id impulses and superego demands in the Œdipus situation allowing the ego to act more or less harmoniously.

The ritual procedure works in this way so long as the nature of the objects or ritual worship, though unconscious, are recognized, so long, that is to say, as the unconscious idea that the phylacteries have a symbolic nature is appreciated though the exact meaning of the symbols remain unconscious. It is under these conditions, as anthropologists are now attempting to make colonial and home governments aware, by the understanding and application of the 'contact of cultures', that cultural 'problems' will be solved. "It is no use trying to substitute one culture for another by an act of compulsion," writes Driberg[78].

There are many forms of compulsion, and sociologists have recently drawn attention to the results in their studies of racial minorities in immigrating to new environments—in their studies of the 'sacred-stranger'. The 'sacred-stranger', under the pressure of an alien environment, tends to lose his traditions; the ego becomes heterogeneous; when this takes place there is such repression of the unconscious ideas expressed in the phylacteries and talith that these lose all symbolic meaning—lose, if you like, their magic virtue and are no longer superstitiously reverenced; but the phylacteries, no longer felt to be symbols in any way of the living god or of father-imago, have entirely lost their function and the superego has no way of tension-release except by guilt, desire of punishment and so on—the neurotic way. The symbols have become metaphors and Biblical commentators correctly recognize the ornaments as mere metaphors—that is, no longer subserving any need of the individual; no longer related to the individual unconscious.

But this path from symbol to metaphor, from appeasement of the unconscious feeling of guilt by a symbolic representation to the attempt to appease it by rationalization (metaphor) approaches no nearer to reality; an outer compulsion has led to these steps and therewith to the disappearance of the original virtue without substituting anything acceptable to the ego. Religion has lost its content and is replaced by rationalization and dogma.

# References

1. Glover, Edward. Common problems in psycho-analysis and anthropology. *British Journal of Medical Psychology*, 1922, 12:109.
2. Friedlander, M. *The Jewish Religion*. London, 1891, p. 333 *sq*.
3. *Idem*, p. 337.
4. *Idem*, p. 340.
5. Maimonides, Moses. *Guide for the Perplexed*. London: Routledge, 1925, p. 332.
6. Strebel, G. S. *De Antiques Judaeorum: Ritibus et Moribus*, 1664, p. 8.
7. Jennings, David. *Jewish Antiquities*. 1825, p. 217.
8. Wallis Budge, E. A. *Amulets and Superstitions*. 1930, p. 217 *sq*.
9. Ridway, W. Jewellery and magic. *B.A.A.S. Report*, 1903, p. 815.
10. Robertson Smith, W. *Religion of the Semites*. 1923, p. 437 *sq*.
11. Frazer, J. G. *Folk-Lore in the Old Testament*. Vol. II, p. 4.
12. Elworthy, F. T. *Horns of Honour*. 1900, p. ix.
13. Campbell Thompson, *Semitic Magic*. 1905, p. ix.
14. Robertson Smith, *Op. cit.*, p. 439 *sq*.
15. Elworthy, F. T. *The Evil Eye*. 1895, pp. 198-199.
16. Hannay, J. B. *Sex Symbolism in Religion*. Vol. I, pp. 212-222.
17. Joseph, Max. Art. 'Tefillin.' *Judisches Lexicon*, 1930.
18. Elworthy, F. T. *Horns of Honour*, pp. 75-79.
19. Hastings. Art. Charms and amulets. *Encyclopedia of Religion and Ethics*.
20. Canaan, T. Plant-life in Palestinian superstition. *Journal of the Palestinian Oriental Society*, 8 (3):159.
21. Langer, Georg. Zur Function der jüdischen Türpfostenrolle. *Imago*, 1928, 14:457 *sq*.
22. Hannay, *Op. cit.*, p. 221.
23. Abraham, K. Der Versöhnungstag. *Imago*, 1920, 6:88 *sq*.
23a. Fromm-Reichmann, Frieda. Das jüdische Speiseritual. *Imago*, 1927, 13:240.
24. Bonaparte, Marie. Du symbolisme des trophées de tête. *Revue française de Psychanalyse*, 1:677.
25. Klein, Gottlieb. Die Totaphot nach Bibel und Tradition. *Jahrbuch für protestantische Theologie*, 1881, 7:661 *sq*.
26. Stade, Bernhard. Das Kainszeichen. *Zentralblatt für alttestament Wissenschaft*, 1894, 14.
27. Baentsch. *Handkommentar zum alten Testament. Herausgegeben von Nowak. Exodus—Leviticus—Numeri*, 1903, p. 113.
28. Holzinger. *Kurzer Handkommentar zum alten Testament*. Tübingen, 1900.
29. Wellhausen. *Reste arabischen Heidentums*. P. 165.
30. Robertson Smith, W. Divination and magic in Deuteronomy xviii, 10, 11. *Journal of Philology*, 1885, 13:286.
31. Grünbaum, Max. *Gesamte Aufsätze zur Sprach—und Sagenkunde*.

Berlin, 1901, p. 208 *sq.*

32. Blau, Ludwig. *Das altjüdische Zauberwesen.* Strassburg, 1898, p. 87 *sq.*

33. Bousset, William. *Die Religion des Judentums im späthellenische Zeitalter.* 1926, p. 179.

34. Schürer, Emil. *Geschichte des jüdischen Volkes im Zeitalter Jesu Christi.* Vol. II, p. 568.

35. Friedländer, M. *Der Antichrist in den vorchristlichen Quellen.* Göttingen, 1901, p. 161 *sq.*

36. Hirsch, Emil G. Art. Phylacteries. In *Jewish Encyclopedia,* Vol. X, p. 26.

37. Mack, Edward. Phylacteries. In *International Standard Bible Encyclopaedia,* Vol. IV, p. 2392.

38. Kennedy, A. R. S. Phylacteries. In Hastings, James (ed.), *A Dictionary of the Bible.* Vol. III, p. 871.

39. Wünsche. Art. Tephillin. In Herzog, (ed.), *Realenzyklopädie für protestantische Theologie.* 1907, Vol. XIX, p. 512.

40. Klein, Gottlieb. *Die Totaphot,* p. 678.

41. Kennedy, *Op. cit.,* p. 872.

42. Josephus. *Antiquities.* Vol. IV, viii, 13.

43. Rodkinsohn, M. *Ursprung und Entwicklung des Phylacterienritus bei den Juden.* 1883.

44. Kennedy, *Op. cit.,* p. 871.

45. Robertson Smith, *Op. cit.,* p. 437, footnote 2.

46. Kennedy, *Op. cit.,* p. 871.

47. Lund, Johannes. *Die alten jüdischen Heiligtümer.* Hamburg, 1701.

48. Frazer, J. G. *Totemism and Exogamy.* 1910, Vol. I, p. 26 *sq.*

49. Lewis and Clark. *Travels through the Source of the Missouri River.* Vol. I, p. 123.

50. Robertson Smith, *Op. cit.,* p. 435 *sq.*

51. Spencer and Gillin. *The Native Tribes of Central Australia.* 1899, p. 343.

52. Wissowa. *Religion und Kultur der Römer.* P. 209.

53. Jereimahs, Alf. *Altes Testament.* P. 658.

54. Elster, Alexander. Kleidung und Mode. In Marcuse, *Handlexicon.*

55. Wilhelm, Richard. *Chinesische Volksmärchen.* Jena, 1921, p. 51.

56. Thrämer, E. In *Roscher,* p. 1038.

57. Mannhardt. *Baum und Feldkulte.* Vol. II, p. 138 *sq.*

58. Zulliger, Hans. Die Roichtschaggeten. *Imago,* 1928, 14:447 *sq.*

59. Fromm-Reichmann, *Op. cit.,* p. 240.

60. Schuster, J. *Schmerz und Geschlechtsrieb.* Leipzig, 1923, p. 8, *sq.*

61. Einstein, Carl. *Negerplastik. Münich,* 1920, Illus. 105 and 51.

62. Bieber, J. *Antropophyteia.* Vol. V, Tables 1, 3, 4, 8.

63. Reik, Theodor. Kainzeichen. *Imago,* 1919, 5:33.

64. Röder, Günther. *Altägyptische Erzählungen.* Jena, 1927, p. 240 *sq.*

65. Scheftelowitz, J. Das Hörnermotiv in den Religionen. *Archiv für*

*Religiones-Wissenschaft*, 15:451 *sq.*

66. Bachofen, J. J. *Urreligion.* Vol. 1, p. 494.

67. Langer, *Op. cit., Imago,* 1924, 10:464.

68. Malinowski, B. Psychoanalysis and anthropology. *Psyche,* 4.

69. Samter. *Geburt, Hochbeit und Tod.* 1911, p. 91 *sq.*

70. Jeremiahs, *Op. cit.,* p. 407.

71. Fehlinger, H. Geschlectsleben der Naturvolker. In Hirsch, Max, *Monographien.* No. 1. Leipzig, 1921, p. 78 *sq.*

72. Hrdlicka, Ales. *Physiological and Medicinal Observations among the Indians.* 1908, p. 125 *sq.*

73. Frobenius, Leo. *Erlebte Erteile.* 1928, Vol. V, p. 440 *sq.*

74. Bonaparte, *Op. cit.,* p. 677.

75. Spiez. Zwei Kapitel über kulturelle Entwicklumg. *Imago,* 1924, 10:330.

76. Kirschner, & Rosenfeld, M. Art. Barmizvah. *Jüdische Lexikon.*

77. Abrahams, Israel. *Jewish Life in the Middle Ages.* London: Goldston, 1922, p. 160, footnote.

78. Driberg, J. H. *At Home with the Savage.* 1933, p. 32.

## Chapter 17

# The Mother in the Religious Concepts of Judaism

GERDA G. BARAG, M.D.

𝕵N his investigation on the psychology of religion, Reik[1] emphasizes that "the Israelites like all other Semitic nations had (at least in pre-Jehovistic times) a goddess of love and motherhood, analogous to Istar, Kybele and Astarte. This supposed mother-goddess of the Israelite tribes must have belonged to a period of which no book or epic poem tells[2]."

However, psychoanalysis is a science which, as a sort of archeology of the Psyche, teaches us how to dig up what has been deemed buried in oblivion or to find at least small but instructive traces. The progress of our science has proved repeatedly that by sufficiently deep soundings the archeological proofs for many earlier psychic realities can be established. Therefore it seems justified not to be content with Reik's supposition nor with Jones'[3] statement "that a nebulous mother image floats in the background of Hebrew Theology," but rather to throw some more light on this nebulous form by finding out the actual remnants and to cite the sources. The first attempt in this direction was made by Fromm[4]. The main point of his disquisition is the emphasis laid on the prohibition of work by the Sabbath-laws which he justly recognizes as an expression of the prohibition of incest, an opinion which however had been already presented by Róheim[5]. To those traits which belong to the "joy of Sabbath" Fromm paid much less attention, considering them as a later preponderance of positive tendencies in the sense of the "return of the repressed[6]."

As far as I know no more spade-work has been done on this

theme to date. The attempt will be made here to present the material, gathered from all Jewish religious writings, in the best possible order without claiming to have achieved completeness. Whoever knows the wealth and intricacy of Jewish literature and the difficulty of penetrating its thoughts, not to mention the literature in other languages, will appreciate the great difficulties of such an enterprise.

The present disquisitions are used as sources: the books of the Bible, the Babylonian and Jerusalemitic Talmud, the Tosefta, the various Midraschim and Kabbalistic as well as Chassidic writings. With full intention the Apocrypha and what is known about the Judaic-Christian sects has been excluded since these represent syncretistic formations which contain in a measure that cannot be exactly ascertained Hellenistic, Persian and perhaps old-Egyptian (Gnostic?) ideas so that using these sources would give support to the objection about "foreign influences" which is to be expected anyway.

At the earliest, superficial survey of the material, gathered in this manner, certain difficulties of arranging it became already visible. At first sight the simplest arrangement seems to be according to the age of the sources,—that is putting the books of the Bible first, then the Talmuds and Midraschim (but these latter in which order?) and finally the kabbalistic and chassidic writings; this would be analogous to the tracing of the mother-fixation of an individual through the different epochs of age. Such an arrangement would have certain advantages, but it can be used only in parts. The attempt to begin by getting a picture of the historic development soon must fail, mainly because the oldest sources by no means are those which contain the earliest, primeval material. For instance, the water-sacrifice celebration, which will be discussed at some length, is not mentioned in any one of the Biblical books; what has come to our knowledge is derived from Talmudic or paratalmudic sources. At best we find a laconic note about a water-libation before God as an evidently generally known custom, as in the book Samuel I (7, 6). The benediction of the new moon which has remained customary to this day is not even mentioned anywhere in the Bible. That is due to the strict censorship to which the sacred texts have been subjected when, in the time of Ezra and Nehemia, they were put into their present form. They were "canonized" (definitely so at a much later date); that is, their content was adapted to the existing theological laws and dogmas and everything that contradicted them got eliminated. At this time the supposition of a mother-goddess was strictly proscribed, if not by the people, then certainly by those scholars who did the work of editing and censoring. That her cult in spite of it could remain alive for centuries, even within the framework of the official religious service, although perhaps not longer clearly recognized as such—this sounds improbable, but it will be proved in the course of the present disquisition.

We return from this excursion to the consideration of the discrepancy between the primeval character of the material and the age of the literary source. As mentioned, especially some talmudic items contain a rich mine of material; the Talmud has not been considered sacrosanct in the same degree as the Bible and therefore was not censored, or rather mutilated in the same inexorable way. (We may here disregard the medieval censorship caused by the Christian authorities.) Moreover, it contains opinions, deliberations, tales and parables which at first were not considered as binding for everyone, since they were issued by men who, although highly honored by tradition as sages, were not regarded as moved by the spirit of God, like the prophets, beginning with Moses. Perhaps the editing or rather the compilation of both Talmuds was done at times of grave political disturbances when it was necessary to salvage as much as possible of the traditions without paying too much regard to theological discriminations.

Without deflecting the attention altogether from the historical development, it seems more to the purpose to arrange the factual material under another viewpoint, namely according to the kind of attitude maintained toward the Mother-Goddess. Three aspects appear by which the disparate fragments can be classified.

1) The direct relation of the Goddess Mother. (Adoration. Symbolic possession by cult-acts or in a hoped-for future.)
2) Identification with the Mother.
3) The merger of her with the Father-God, by furnishing

him with feminine—or motherly traits.

Of all these only fragmentary details and remnants can be demonstrated which, although they permit us to conclude with certainty that a "Mother-image, floating in the background, must have existed," are not sufficient for the reconstruction of a definite and perfectly unified picture. Not even the name of the Mother-Goddess can be traced, certainly not the original one; those designations which we are going to discuss are without exception of a later date. We set aside here the Astarte (Ashera) who is often mentioned in the Bible since the name makes it doubtful how far something "foreign" was adopted. The readiness for such an adoption, however, demonstrates the longing for a cult of the Mother, as every "seduction" represents in last analysis a giving in to one's own desires. What information has been preserved by tradition concerning these "own desires" and their gratification surpassing the simple imitation of other nations?

We will begin with the "festival of drawing water" mentioned above. On the first day of Sukkot (the feast of leafy bowers) as the Babylonian and Jerusalemitian Talmud and Tosefta report it almost identically, water, which had been drawn the preceding day from the Schiloach (a stream outside the walls of Jerusalem) with solemn ceremonies of which the details only partly have come down to us, was offered at the great altar of the temple as a libation or as offering. The exceptional and meaningful character of this act is accentuated by the fact that all the rest of the year no other fluids than wine and oil were used for sacrificial purpose. The Talmud itself testifies that this was a cult of the highest antiquity, sanctified by immemorial custom[7], by designating it not only as a commandment given to Moses on the Sinai but even as existing from the days of the creation of the world[8]. Every detail of the festival was given so much importance that the gate by which the priests returned with the water from the stream Schiloach was called the "Watergate"[9]. This for an act which was performed but once a year!

In an endeavor to explain the meaning and the purpose of the water-sacrifice on the altar it was interpreted as a symbolical illustration of the demand for abundant rain[10], but even through this, probably later, interpretation of an archaic cult as an act of imitative magic still transpires the original meaning. The rain is conceived as a fertilizing process by which the earth becomes pregnant; it is spoken of as the meeting of bride and bridegroom[11]. This sexual character of the feast is accentuated by the participation of a newly wed or eventually sham married couple[12]. The newest investigations make it highly probable that as in the Mesopotamian and Canaanite so also in the oldest Jewish ritual the ceremony of a sacred sexual intercourse must have played an important part[13].

The full original meaning of the water-sacrifice becomes manifest when we learn that channels for the outflow of the water were placed under the altar and that various legends and mythic explanations were woven around these channels. Two facts were said to be their characteristics: they ("Schittin") belonged to the things made in the first days of creation[14] and they lead to the deepest depths of the earth, the primeval abyss, the "T'hom"[15]. That the sacrifice was spilled in a thin ray from the perforated spout of a special vessel[16] makes the meaning of the symbolic act which was performed with the Mother Earth even more manifest[17].

The permanent connection between the cult of the Mother-Goddess and orgiastic popular festivals is well known. This must have been the case in Jerusalem too since the Talmud among other things reports with great detail that a part of the preparations, made on the evening before the festival, was the raising of barriers by which the male and female onlookers were strictly separated "because it had been a customary occasion for frivolous behavior." This was considered as a necessary precaution for it was believed that during this festival the instincts of evil held a special domination over the mass of people[18]. This interpretation of the water-sacrifice makes us understand why so much praise was bestowed on Rabbi Shim'on ben Gamliel of which it was said that nobody had ever been known to bow on this occasion before God as well as he did; he used to bore his big toes into the earth and bowing down kiss the earth *i.e.*, without throwing himself on it with his entire body[19]. At the time of the feast Jerusalem was illuminated so magnificently that a woman was said to have been able to sort lentils at night[20]. A torch-procession formed a part of the celebration and a great and pious man, the aforementioned Rabbi Shim'on ben Gamliel, excelled on this occasion also by his special zeal and skill for he used, for the greater glory of God, to juggle with not less than 8 torches[21].

When we put this torchlight parade beside the prescription to shake the frond of palms (Lulaw) at the Sukkot-festival, which has to be performed while certain formulas of blessings are uttered, it becomes understandable why the pagan author Plutarch[22], probably having in mind the Thyrsos-staves, declared this water-sacrifice festival to be identical with the feast of Dionysos. The "Lulaw," held high by every believer while he carried it up the temple-hill, would have to be taken as the symbol of his own phallos (Ethrog-testicles?) and the "Sukkah" which has to be inhabited for 8 days must mean the mother's womb[23]. And indeed many centuries after the destruction of the temple and consequently after the abandon of every sort of sacrificial service, the founder of a new trend in Chassidism, Rabbi Nachman of Brazlaw, has intuitively found out this symbolic sense of the Sukkah and pronounced it[24]. Such a magnificent festival, devoted to the mother deity in which even the symbolic incest was present, must of necessity contain also traces of the defiant rebellion against the father. Certain hymns seem to point this way, but also a remark of the Talmud, according to which the priests marched in front of the east wall of the temple and defecated there with their backs turned toward the rising sun[25]. We can, however, look at that as the archaic gift of the child; another passage in the Talmud which says that the adoration of the Ba'al P'or was performed in the same peculiar manner[26] allows both interpretations. To my regret no other information has come to my knowledge by which the conscious intention of the Jewish priests of that period is made definite.

In connection with the interpretations of this festival which was devoted to a Mother Goddess, I want to add some remarks on the "Holiest of Holies" in the temple. Actually we know very little about it and have to imagine a small and perhaps window-less room in which the ark of the covenant stood. If the narrow cell and the holy chest symbolize the womb, then it is of special interest to learn that on the days of the Effuinox an eastern gate which was closed all year, was opened so that the rays of the rising sun fell in through all intermediate spaces accurately and directly[27]. A hardly less interesting contribution to this concept is given by a remark of the Babylonian Talmud. It says that the holiest of holies was separated from the other rooms by a curtain through which the carrying poles of the ark of covenant pierced or at least showed their outlines, and the Talmud uses here the thoroughly appropriate comparison with the breasts of a woman which show their outlines through her shirt[28].

In conclusion we can recognize in the Sukkot-festival the remnant of a former orgiastic feast devoted to the mother-diety. At the time of the temple the intoxicating joy must have been beyond description; we are told several times by tradition "who has not seen this feast has not seen a feast in all his life[29]." Prominent men of the time report that they didn't find time to sleep for three consecutive nights and indulged at best in a short nap, leaning on each other[30]. The feast is celebrated to this day although without water-libations and under repression of its original meaning. Every orgiastic trait has disappeared but in the "Simchat Torah" (the joy of the Torah; on the feminine-mother role of the latter some more will be said presently) just a hint of it has survived; on this occasion, by a characteristic exception to the usual custom, women are allowed to mix with the praying, singing and dancing men. And again it was one of the masterminds of Chassidism, Rabbi Shneôr Salman from Lody, who understood intuitively the deeper meaning of the libation-sacrifice and found for it a clear expression[31].

Another ritual which has to be discussed within the framework of this investigation exists—maybe in unchanged form—till this day as a law and an absolute duty for every believer: it is the blessing or verbally the consecration of the full moon. Here it proves specially important not to consider the books of the Bible at first hand as the source which as the oldest must have conserved the oldest material. They don't contain any information about this rite. Only slight hints permit a conclusion that the beginning of the month ("Rosh Chodesh") was celebrated, among other things, also by the special sacrifice of

an animal.  On the other hand, the ceremony which is still performed today is transmitted in an old Brajta of the Babylonian
Talmud[32], which says that it is prescribed to say, facing the full
moon in holiday vestments and perfumed and standing with feet
close together and a finger stretched toward the moon:   "As I
dance (jump) toward you and don't touch you, so others may
dance toward me (jump against me) without touching me.   Her
(*i.e.*, the moon's, which is here conceived as feminine) terror and
fear may fall from the outset on them (the foes of the praying
person)."   After that he must offer to the present companions
in prayer (the minimum of two is prescribed) "Peace" (Shalom)
and and go home with a glad heart.   It has to be added to these
remarks of the Talmud that the moon in Hebrew is a bi-sexual
word[33].   In the formula; quoted above, male and female forms
are used alternately; in the designation of the ceremony as an
entity, however, the female form is made use of, "Kiddush
L'wanah".

When we consider the content of the prayer-formula mentioned above more accurately, we find that the wish to touch the
moon is represented by pantomime (jumping toward it with outstretched fingers) and at the same time the resignation (admission of the impossibility of doing it) is expressed together with
the hope of a reward, namely not being harrassed by one's
enemies.   It is easy to find out who the supposed enemy is; why
should everyone who recites the prayer offer expressly three
times "peace" to his companions who like him had tried in vain
to touch the moon?   It seems to me not too hazardous an
excursion into the realm of phantasy to maintain the opinion
that here in a concentrated form (as we are accustomed to find
it in obsessional acts) not only the wish to get hold of the
mother, the subjection under the prohibition and the renunciation are expressed, but also rejection of the war among the
brothers as a result of the all round surrender of the possession
of the mother.   Finally it might be mentioned that on the
occasion of the water-sacrifice festival which in Syria as well
as in Egypt was celebrated with even more of orgiastic liberty,
a "gay war" used to take place with people throwing things and
splashing water on each other, etc., exactly as today at the
European carnival[34].

The chassidic Rabbi Nachman from Brazlaw, who has been quoted above, discovered centuries later the hidden meaning and identified the "Kiddush-ha-Chodesh" (consecration of the moon-month) with the wedding formula by which a Jewish man marries a woman[35].

That the benediction of the new moon pertains to the cult of the Mother-Goddess becomes manifest by other details too, for instance by a mention of "womb-pregnants" which stands in no logical connection with the framework of the entire prayer. We know that in other religions, *e.g.*, in the Babylonian, the moongoddess is the protectress of pregnancy[36]. In the usage of the Talmud the fullness of the moon which had to be declared by an ecclesiastical court is designated as "i'bur ha-Chodash" respectively as "i'bur ha L'wanah". "I'bur" signifies verbally impregnation and in one passage the consequence is drawn by comparing the full moon with a pregnant woman[37]. This impregnation of the moon is effected by the worshippers, that is of the mother by her sons. That the incest is directly commanded by the father is a distortion of the facts of which all religions made use[38].

A third institution which by its importance for the religious life of the Jews overshadows everything else is the Shabbat. I continue here the work of Fromm, who recognizes in the prohibition to work on this sacred day the incest-prohibition and submitted his arguments at full length. The question whether the connubial intercourse on the Sabbath has to be considered as prohibited or permitted or as an act specially pleasing to God arises at various times in the history of Jewish religion and has become a controversial point of an importance that has been widely under-rated. It was prohibited by the Saduccees and recommended by the Pharisees[39], denied later by the Karaits and other, probably related, sects[40] in the middle ages. These changes connect with the variations of the patriarchial versus matriarchial attitude to certain problems at different times which will have to be discussed and investigated on another occasion.

We return to the general consideration of the Shabbat. It has been emphasized before that Fromm doesn't bestow sufficient consideration on the character of wish-fulfilment in the joy of the Sabbath; it may remain undecided if and how far the Sabbath might have had sorrow and penance as its original content and if the wish-fulfillment represents really a return of the repressed.  In any case it would deserve a closer study. The fact that the Sabbath in the Hebrew language has the feminine gender is worth noticing.  Now, the Talmud tells us that Rabbi Janai on Friday evenings used to celebrate the arrival of the Sabbath with the words:  "Come O Bride"[41].  The poet Jehuda Ha-Levy made this formula the theme of his famous song and so accentuated still stronger the significance of the Bride as the "crown of her husband."  Furthermore, it has been made expressly an obligation to honor the Sabbath by a cheerful mood, holiday dresses and, most of all, holiday food[42].

The Talmud, as well as the other authentic sources, underline the importance of oral pleasure and the use of big fishes (penis-symbol) is mentioned with praise[43].  Fishes were consecrated to the old Syrian Goddess Atargatis and bred by her priests in special ponds.  It was considered as sacrilegious to lay hands on these fishes but at certain festivals they were eaten with solemn rites by the worshippers of the Goddess[44].  On the other hand fishes are recommended by the Talmud as aphrodisiaca[45].  When a Roman emperor expressed his astonishment that the Shabbat-food of the Jews had such a specially good smell, Rabbi Jehoschua ben Chananje assured him that the Jews used a peculiar condiment, called Shabbat[46].  Drunkenness is said to have occurred frequently on the Shabbat[47]. Three meals are commanded on the Shabbat; fasting is absolutely prohibited.  This has been emphasized by later authorities too, as Rabbi Josef Karo who sees in eating and drinking an essential element of the Sabbatical joy[48].  This is made still more clear by innumerable sayings of eminent chassidim, as Rabbi Dow Baer from Meseric and many others.  One of them, Rabbi Levi Jizchak from Berdytschew, has hit the nail on the head by stating that "on the Shabbat man returns to his root." Indeed the periodical return to the mother can hardly be better designated!  The popular belief has overemphasized still more this oral significance of the Shabbat by insisting that "who eats his fill on the Shabbat, will not suffer from hunger all week[49]." Returning to the mother and taking possession of her is linked with a special emphasis to oral gratification. There the just, sitting around a long table, are united to an endless meal, the "S'udat Zadikim." Quite in accordance with the given interpretation, the Talmud calls the Shabbat a foretaste (the sixtieth part) of the eternal bliss. The golden age, expected to begin with the appearance of the Messiah (and in which the possession of the mother played an important part) is designated as "a day that is entirely Shabbat"[50].

In an unpublished article, I have tried to prove that this age of beatitude embodies the father's renouncement of the mother in favor of the son. This can be demonstrated for the Shabbat. It represents, according to a Talmudic statement, a precious gift which was conferred by God on Moses for the use of the people of Israel. The Shabbat is called here a bride, of which the people of Israel is the groom[51]. This idea must have been current long ago in Biblical times, since the prophet Jesaja (62. 4. 5) sees the return of the exiled people to its country as the taking possession of the virgin by her lover. This becomes still more obvious when we lend an ear to the mystic writers. In the book, Sohar, it is said that the really just, *i.e.* those who know the secrets of the Kabbalah, ought to reserve the marital intercourse for Friday night. This is declared expressly as a duty for the night of the beginning of the Shabbat and it is emphasized that just at this time in the heavenly spheres the sexual union takes place of the just ("Zadik") with the Sch'china (the divine feminine principle) and also of the God-father ("Abba") with the divine Mother ("Ima"). We can track this thought nearly unchanged or embroidered with some additions (as the interpretation of the K'dusha prayer, etc.) through all the Kabbalistic and Chassidic literature which followed the Sohar. Thus we recognize constantly in the Shabbat the periodically returning mother, of whom the sons take possession not only orally, but also like a man of his wife. Heinrich Heine understood emotionally this profound truth when he lets the Jew, after enduring all week the misery of a doglike outcast, feel like a king on the Shabbat. On the other hand we can discern the cause of the sad, let-down mood at the end of the Shabbat which has been so often described by East-Jewish poets and storytellers.

The contemplation of these three religious institutions will be sufficient for the present; without doubt some others, consecrated to the cult of a mother-goddess in the past and present, could be discovered by a diligent search. On the basis of the literary material with which I became acquainted, it is impossible to say anything more precise about this primeval Mother-Goddess of the tribes of Israel; not even her name can be ascertained with sufficient probability. Furthermore, the question whether every one of the tribes may not have worshipped a separate Goddess cannot be fully investigated since that would lead us to the wider problem of matriarchy in Old Israel[52] and the after-effects of its secular conflicts with the finally victorious patriarchy.

If, however, we adopt the hypothesis accepted by Freud in his book about Moses of the existence of so called Lea- and Rachel-tribes, we could pronounce the following although unproven opinion: these could have well been the names of the supposed Mother-Goddesses! The later tendency of the prophets and the popular tradition to mention only Rachel as the tribal mother would then make it probable that the priests and scholars who edited the canonical books belonged to the Rachel-tribes and therefore gave added importance to the mother-goddess of their own tribe and suppressed the one of the others. (In the Kabbalistic literature of a much later time, beginning around the 14th or 15th century, hints are to be found of dim speculations about Lea and Rachel as lower forms of the divine mother e.g., in the writings of Chaim Vital[53] and others.)

To the more accurate observation are revealed several mythological-theologic ideas which served as screen—or substitute—figures behind which for centuries the never abandoned hope for a divine mother could be hidden. The hypothesis of a modern biblical scholar has to be mentioned here[54], who declares the names "Sheol" (i.e., the place of the departed souls) and "Thom" (the primeval abyss at the creation of the world) which both are repeatedly mentioned in the Bible to be simply names of the feminine divinities of Israel. Certainly, the ritual law, discussed above, declares that the water splashed on the altar on the occasion of the water sacrifice-festival gets, by flowing through the channels ("Shitin"), already mentioned, down to the deepest depth of the earth, to the "T'hom." Even more unquestionable as a symbol of the mothers' womb is the "Sheol," the place to which according to the Biblical concept the dead, the spirits of the dead descend, similar to the Greek Orkus. The Talmud[55] compares the Sheol expressly with the womb, yet no proof can be deduced from that whether the primeval goddess had this or another name.

Of more importance for our investigation are two other theological concepts which, however, are of later date so that for this and other linguistic reasons it is out of question that they ever could have borne the name of the mother-goddess. At the same time they point, by favor of the material at our disposition, with greater clarity to the existence of such a mother-goddess. These two are the "Torah" and the "Sh'chinah."

The Torah is, of course, first and foremost the teaching revealed by God, and especially the divine laws pronounced in the five books of Moses; it is notorious that the most important duty of the Jew consists in devoting himself to their assiduous and minute study. Yet, side by side with this somewhat dry and sober conception, we find in the Talmud and in the Midrashim another allegorical aspect of the Torah as a female being, closely related to God. The Talmud says laconically: "Everywhere where the Torah is mentioned she has a feminine gender"[56]. This is linguistically so manifest that it would be unnecessary to mention it, but for something else hidden behind it. Probably only one part of the popular traditions concerning this point has been preserved. This femininity is illustrated by sundry parabolical stories, such as that God considers the Torah as his beloved daughter whom he has given as wife to the people of Israel and, like a loving father, he lets her depart from him with a heavy heart[57]. However, he consoles himself with the thought that in this way the bond with his people is confirmed, if not created. The bestowing of the divine teachings (Torah) on Mount Sinai is celebrated to this day on the last day of Sukkot as a feast of rejoicing ("Simchat Torah"). Those who are called up on this day for the Torah-benediction are designated with the honorific title of "Bridegroom of the Torah" (Chatan Torah), even the boys who are in the religious sense still minors, *i.e.* under thirteen. According to the local rite of Saloniki a single individual of the community gets elected and glorified as *the* bridegroom of the Torah.

The Torah, who functioned as an adviser of God at the creation of the world, is by this endowed with the dignity and the equal rights of a co-regent and wife and appears occasionally as the accuser against the sons of Israel, as when one of them has the impudence to profane verses of the Song of Songs by singing them while drinking in the tavern and thus giving to the sacred book a profane-sexual meaning. The expression, "Your sons have made me a fiddle[58]," makes it clear that the prohibition is set to hinder, even in thought, any connection between the mother and sexuality.

It is difficult to distinguish between the Sh'china to which we turn now and the linguistically bi-sexual, yet mostly used as feminine, "Ruach-ha-Kodesh" (Holy Ghost)[59]. On the other hand the Sh'china is exclusively feminine and signified verbally something like the presence or the habitation of God, on a certain place, or as the German Protestant theologians call it: "Einwohnung." She is likened to Miriam, the sister of Moses, as she stood on the banks of the Nile and observed the fate of her little brother. In the interpretation of some verses from the Song of Songs (III, 4, "I bring him into the house of his mother" and V. 2 "The crown with which his mother crowned him") the Sh'china is taken to be the mother; finally she is the one who procures food for the inhabitants of the earth at every hour[60].

Here too we have every reason to suppose that many more of these more or less obscure hints must have existed[61], for in the book Sohar which made its appearance first in the middle of the thirteenth century, the Sh'china is mentioned innumerable times expressly and without the least possible doubt as the Divine Mother. First in the Sohar, and then for centuries in the entire Kabbalistic literature, we see seated on the throne of heaven a divine Ima side by side with a divine Abba, the first-named being identified constantly with the Sh'china. We see her as a true mother taking care of her people, especially of its food, but she also stands together with the children before the highest throne to praise God[62]; she defends her children, prays for mercy for them and prefers to go with them into exile rather than abandon them. This is taken from the Talmud where it is said repeatedly that the Sh'china has accompanied the people into exile[63]. Usually she represents Mercy and Compassion before the divine tribunal whereas the severe father stands for Justice. On almost every page of the Sohar these are used as mystic-speculative synonyms for father and mother. However, the attitude of the sons, even in the mystic sense toward the divine mother, is not entirely free from ambivalence; not only that it happens that now and then the roles are reversed, *i.e.* that the mother presents the severity and the father the mildness, but to the mystic-theological concepts of the Sohar also belong the "left side" and "right side" as synonyms for the mother and father. The left motherside, also called the "other one," is identified with "Samael" (also called S.M.) who produces everything that is bad and evil. We cannot enter here into the huge mass of various speculations of the most complicated kind concerning the "highest" and "low" mother who is, however, differentiated from the physiological mother of the single individual, nor into the classification of the divine emanations ("Sfirot") as feminine and masculine, and their interrelations.

The role played by the Sch'china is not limited to being a mother to her children; she is also the wife (sometimes designated as bride) to her divine husband; she adorns and embellishes herself for him, expects him on her royal couch and unites herself to him sexually in boundless bliss and with the jubilation of the divine hosts in the manner of husband and wife. Not only the heavenly hosts and the stars glorify this union, the truly pious and those who are initiated into the mysteries of the Kabbala do it by their prayers, their praises and the fulfillment of the prescriptions of the law. This is based transparently on a reaction-formation: the son has not only renunciated the possession of the mother, but helps to unite her with the father. The Kabbalistic-Chassidic mysticism enjoins that the prayer should be connected with a direction toward a certain aim in the heavenly spheres (Kawanot). The highest principle of the divers mystic "Kawanot" is the following basic formula which in some prayerbooks is set on front in big letters: *"So that the holy one, blessed be his name, may unite himself with the Sch'china."* While the pious and the just effect this through their prayers and their mystic concentration on it, the sin and wickedness of the iniquitous consists in their hindering this union, conveying further disorder into heavenly spheres, so the repressed content is represented by attributing to man the power to help or hinder the union of father and mother.

This restriction of the paternal power by the sons, partly also by the mother, in various forms, is an outstanding trait of Jewish theological speculation which exists already in the Talmud and in the Midrashim, but can not be fully treated here. However, the surrender of the mother is not entire or definitive; this is indicated again by the Sohar's speaking also of the union of the pious with the Sch'china. As in the discussion of the Sabbath and of the Torah, we find here too this motive play an essential role: the father out of his kindness cedes the mother to the sons. Moreover, the father of all men, Adam, had also abstained from marrying his own daughter for no other reason than because he wanted to give her in marriage to his son Cain[64]. This incest between brother and sister, which was approved by the father, plays a part later on in the speculations of some Kabbalists who let masculine and feminine "Sfirot" marry each other so that some extremely complicated relationships resulted between them[65].

We may ask with some surprise how it happened that a book like the Sohar, which pronounces openly such thoughts, was not banned by the legitimate authorities. Certainly, polemics were aroused but in spite of all that the Sohar remained victorious and became one of the three books (with the Bible and the Talmud) which permeated and dominated the entire Jewish life. A great number of eminent rabbis didn't disdain to study the Sohar and other Kabbalistic books, to add commentaries to them and write in a similar vein. This tolerant attitude shows that such speculations were not alien to them; it is true that the Sohar and later Kabbalistic writings as well emphasize that the "mating" of the divine father-mother pair was "meant to be a merely spiritual one" and that both persons were fundamentally only two aspects of the same being[66], and this statement took the ground away from the accusation of heresy concerning the dogma of the absolute oneness of God. However, it would be erroneous to see in this nothing more than an excuse; rather it ought to be understood as an expression of the profound wish to merge father and mother into one person and thus to escape from the conflict of the Oedipus complex. Of that we will treat presently in more detail.

## II

The second aspect under which a part of the material can be arranged is the identity of the people with the mother-divinity and its passive-homosexual relation to the father. The traditions which speak in this sense will be presented now; how they originated and developed historically cannot be fitted within the framework of the present investigation.

The prophets Hosea (2, 3), Jesaia (50, 1), Jeremia (50, 12), Ezechiel (19, 12) mention a "mother of the people" who in the name of God is regarded as his wife and addressed alternately with warnings and with sweet words. Who is this mother? Although a contemporary authentic comment is lacking, the meaning of the text is clear enough; the later commentaries[67] beginning with the partly paraphrasing-commenting "Targum Jonatan" (an Aramaic translation for the simple people who didn't know Hebrew) identify this mother with the "Knesset Israel" (the community of Israel). This concept is already in the Midrashim and later in the Sohar elaborated as the trans-cendental representative of the people. (Foreign people too are conceived as feminine by Jesaia 23, 10, 15; 47, 1, and Jeremia 46, 11, 19, 24, 49, 2, 50, 42, 51, 33.) The Jewish people appears in the writings of the prophets and in other books of the Bible and consequently also in the Midrashim[68] embodied in another female figure too: the daughter of Zion, also called "Zion" for short. To her are sometimes given predictions of future greatness and sometimes remonstrances. When the people everywhere had to suffer, she appears accordingly in the later Midrashic literature as a mourning woman, clad in black. The prophet Jesaia (66, 5) salutes the people, coming home from exile, as a "bride" and, as a consequence, the prophets reproached the people for every lapse in their faith as "whoredom," *i.e.* as adultery. The Talmud adheres to this concept in designating God as father[69] and the "Knesset Israel" as mother. The people, living in suffering and under pressure, felt itself abandoned by its God, but didn't give up its hope for a better future; so the "Knesset Israel" was not considered as a widow or as one who was definitely driven out by her husband, but as being separated from him temporarily. The Sohar calls this central female figure sometimes Sch'china and sometimes "Knesset Israel." The promise of a better future relies on the certainty that the temporarily abandoned spouse will one day return to her divine husband.

The homosexual fixation to the divine father is by no means the result of a fantastic psychoanalytic interpretation: it can be proven beyond contradiction by the Talmudic tradition. According to it there existed in the holiest of holies of the temple (certainly in those of the two earlier ones) two figures of angels in the closest embrace. Once a year the people was shown these double figures and was told: "Look, such is the love of God for you as the love of man and woman[70]." The rest of the remarks of the Talmud and Rashi's commentary to this passage leave no doubt of the sexual meaning of the embrace. It is said that on the occasion of the destruction and plundering of the temple (the second?) this caused the conquerors to make censorious remarks about the Jews[71].

## III

This brings us to the third aspect under which again a great part of our material can be grouped. There is a tendency to merge father and mother into a single personality, for instance by furnishing God the father with motherly-feminine traits. The attempt to arrive at a solution of the Oedipus complex in this way has been made by non-semitic nations also[72]. It has played an especially important part for the concept of the Deity evolved by Amenhop-Echnation[73] and could therefore possibly have been taken over from him if we accept Freud's ideas of the Egyptian origin of the Jewish monotheism. However, this consonance cannot be simply accepted as a proof of the origin, since the tendency to unite virility and femininity in the same Deity seems to have been held in common by many and maybe by all Semitic religions[74].

It is notorious that the priests of the jealous Father-God

fought with the utmost vehemence and with—at least super-ficially—final success against the worship of other divinities and especially against the female "Asherot"[75]. This absolute deflection toward the father and away from the mother may have happened parallel with the change from a matriarchal society to a patriarchal one. This went so far that to the woman was ascribed only a secondary importance for the creation of the child, as the depository for the man's semen[76]. (A simple ignorance of the physiological processes is out of the question since in other places the existence of a "feminine semen" is fully recognized.)[77] Such an extreme repression of the mother could be effected only by merging her with the father so that the resulting one person was given some feminine traits. Already the prophet Jesaia (66.13) sees God comforting his children "as a mother does." As Mordechai is said to have suckled his niece Esther[78], so the heavenly Father had long ago sent to the Jewish children, who were exposed on the fields of Egypt, His angels who put two stones in their little hands which they suckled like their mothers' breasts[79]. With the help of skillful play with words, God gets even compared with a pregnant woman[80]. After all, the feminine character of the Sch'china has been sufficiently demonstrated and could be proven by numberless other quotations and the Sch'china is not only con-sidered as an emanation of God, but identical with Him[81].

In my opinion the fundamental idea and veritable content of monotheism consists generally in the merging of father and mother into one person. (The son ought to be added which gives the trinity; but in this we cannot enter here.) Before this merger of the two parents into one divinity succeeded, some controversies must have arisen, even in theological circles and at a relatively late epoch of which, however, only a vague echo has reached us[82]. The Sohar sees father and mother clearly as two distinct figures, and proclaiming at the same time the absolute unity of God, tries to produce it by merging them[83]. This is exactly the meaning and aim of the mystic fundamental formula by which peace and happiness in the upper and lower regions was to be produced. This explains the profoundest meaning of the "Sh'ma Israel" (Listen, oh Israel, our God is the sole and one God), this fundamental profession of faith which is destined to accompany the pious Jew through all his life until his last breath[84]. Again the book Sohar is shown as a source of inestimable value since this concept of the profession of faith is formulated by it clearly and expressly[85].

This exhausts the essential material at my disposal, but I believe it proves that for the religious ideas of the Jews a mother goddess had great importance, and not only in the dim past since her repression until our time succeeded only incompletely. On this basis it becomes questionable if to speak about a "father-religion," especially in relation to the Jewish one, is justifiable, yet the intensely significant question remains unanswered why and when the tendency started to repress the mother-goddess from the consciousness of the Jewish people. To show that this attempt didn't succeed entirely was the aim of this exposition, but detailed study of the attitude toward this conflict at different times would eventually throw a new light on the history of the Jewish people. We are as yet unable to find out whether the struggle between matriarchy and patriarchy was its cause or if this conflict, as well as the religious struggle, were the expression of the same profound Oedipus-conflict present within the single individual as well as in the "mass-psyche." It would be worth while for science to study historical developments as an interplay between repressed and repressing forces, as Róheim[86] proposed. It is certainly true as far as the history of the Jewish religion is concerned. Freud's theory of monotheism from Egypt may not be absolutely satisfactory since nobody can acquire a spiritual gift which he does not possess in a profound sense, for which he is not somehow "matured." In the meantime the conflict goes on everlastingly for even when the change back to a polytheistic faith seems to have become nonsensical[87] the unity of God is proclaimed by many thousands in the "Shma' Israel" so that father and mother may become unified and peace may reign in heaven and in the hearts of the believers.

# References

1. Reik, Theodor. Der eigene und der fremde Gott. International Psychoanalytischer Verlag, 1933, p. 63.

2. *Cf.* E. Pilz. Die weiblichen Gottheiten Kanaan's, *Ztschr. d. deutschen Palaestina Vereins,* 1924, 47:33.

3. Jones, Ernest. Psychoanalysis of the Christian religion. In *Essays on Applied Psychoanalysis.* London: Hogarth Press, 1923, p. 118.

4. Fromm, Erich. Der Sabbath. *Imago,* 1927, 13:223-234.

5. Roheim, Geza. Die wilde Jagd. *Imago,* 1926, 12.

6. Anan, the founder of the sect of Karaites, derived his prohibition of sexual intercourse on the Sabbath from Exodus, 34, 2, by equating it with ploughing of the earth (mother); he refers also to Jud. 14, 8.

7. Bab. Sukkah 34 a. 50 a. Ta'anait 3 a.

8. Bab. Sukkah 50 a.

9. Tosefta Sukkah Chapt. 3.

10. *Ib.*

11. Bab. Brachot 59.

12. M. Grunwald Zur Vorgeschichte des Sukkot-rituals, *Jhb. für jüdische Volkskunde,* 1923, 25:442.

13. S. H. Hook. *The Origin of Early Semitic Ritual.* London, 1938, 54-55.

14. Bab. Sukkah 48 b. Tosefta *loc. cit.*

15. *Ibid.*

16. Bab. Sukkah 48 a.

17. *Cf.* my earlier article, "Zur Psychoanalyse der Prostitution," *IMAGO,* 1937, No. 3—The "day of atonement" too seems to have had in the earliest time an orgiastic character as suggested by the reading of the laws which forbid the marriage within certain degrees of relationship. L. Finkelstein. *The Pharisees.* Philadelphia, 1938, Vol. 2, p. 659, Note 30.

18. Bab. Sukkah 51 b. 52 a. Jer. Sukkah Chapt. 5 (beginning) Tosefta Sukkah Chapt. 4.

19. Bab. Sukkah 53 a.

20. *Ibid.*

21. *Ibid.* and 51.

22. De symposica, Lib, IV. Quaest VI.

23. M. Grunwald. Zur Vorgeschichte des Sukkotrituals I. B.

24. Ma Haran: Likutey Halachot. 40, 13.

25. Bab. Sukkah 53 a.

26. Bab. Sanhedria 64 a.

27. Jul. Morgenstern. The gates of righteousness. *Hebrew Union College Annual* 1929, 6:31-32.

28. Bab. Joma 54 a.

29. Bab. Sukkah 51 a; Jer. Sukkah 1 b 6.

30. Bab. Sukkah 53 a.

31. Likutey Torah, D'warim. Drushin l'Sukkot p. 159.

32. Bab. Sofrim Kap. 20.

33. Talmud and Midrashim often look at the moon as the female counter-part to the sun that is considered male.

34. D. Feuchtwanger. Das Wasseropfer und die damit verbudenen Zeremonien. *Monatschrift d. Ges. f. d. Wiss. d. Jdt.* 54, 1910, 11.

35. Likutey Ma Ha Ran 40, 22.

36. G. Róheim. Mondreligion and Mondmythos. *IMAGO.*

37. Bab. Sanhedrin 42 a.

38. A patient phantasied that his home town was taken by soldiers who compelled him to have sexual intercourse with his sister.

39. Rudolf Leszynski. *Die Sadduzaer.* Berlin 1912, pp. 135, 202.

40. Leon Nemoy. Al-Qirquisanis' account of the Jewish Sects. *Hebrew Union College Annal,* 1930, 12:326.

41. Bab. Shabbat 119 a.

42. Tana Debej Elijahu, 20, 6.

43. Fr. Cumant. *Les religions orientales dans le paganisme roman.* Paris, 1929, p. 108-9.

44. So Bab. Brachot 40 a., Jebamot 103 a., Joma 18 a. conf. Preuss: Bible-Talmud Medizin, p. 538.

45. Bab. Shabbath 118, Bejza 16, M'chilta Jitro Sh'iltot d' Rabbi Hai Gaon. Sh'ilta 1.

46. Bab. Shabbot 119 a. Berreschit Rabba Chpt. II.

47. Bab. Erubin 61. Plutarch: De Symposiaca Liber IV. Quaest. VI.

48. Maggid Mejscharim.

49. Ignaz Bernstein. *Juedische Sprichwoerter,* p. 236.

50. Bab. Shabbat 10 b.

51. "Bereshit Rabba Chpt. II Jalkut Schlm' oni. Recanatis Commentar "Torah schlemah."

52. Hrch. Holzinger. *Ehe und Frau im vordeuteronomischen Israel. Wellhausen—Festschrift.* Glessen  17/5  1914.—V. Aptowitzer. Spuren des Matriarchats im juedischen Schrifttum. *Hebrew Union College Annual,* 1927 Jul. Morgenstern. Beena Marriage (Matriarchat) in Ancient Israel and its historical implications. *Ztschr. f. alt-test. Wissenschaft,* 1929.

53. R. Chaim Vital. *Sefer Likutey Torah.* Wilna 1879.

54. George Beer. *Welches war die aelteste Religion Israels?*  Giessen 1927.

55. Bab. Brachot 15.

56. Bab. Kiduschi 2.

57. Bab. Jewamot 63. Sanhedrin 72 a. Sh'mot rabba Chpt. 33 Wajikra rabba Chapt.  20 Tanchuma Sh'mot, Ejle Pikudey 4.

58. Bab. Sanhedrin 101 a. Kallah Chapt. I. Jer. Sanhedrin 20.  Wajikra Rabba Chapt. 19. Shir-ha-Shirim rabba 5, I.

59. *Cf.* Jones. Psychoanalysis of the Christian religion.

60. Bab. Sota, 9. II a 13 Shmot Rabba 52. Shir-ha Shirim Rabba 3, 2, and 21.
61. For instance, in Bab. Chagiga II.
62. "The mother also owes adoration to the father," says Midrash Bereshit rabba. Chapter 2.
63. For instance, Bab. Megilah 29.
64. Bab. Sanhedrin 58.
65. R. Moscheh Korodovérs. *Shéur Komah,* Warschau, 1884, p. 66.
66. *Ibid.*
67. As Raschi, Ibn Esra, Kimchi, etc.
68. Psikta rabbabti, Psikta de Raw Kahana.
69. Bab. Brachot 35 b.
70. Bab. Joma 54 a.
71. *Ibid.* 54 b.
72. E. Balint. Der Familienvater. *IMAGO* 1926, 12.
73. K. Abraham. Amenhotep Echnaton. *IMAGO* 1914, 1.
74. W. W. Baudissin, *Adonis and Esmun.* Leipzig, 1911, p. 264. Detlef Nielsen: Gemeinsemitische Goetter. *Oriental, Lit. Ztg.,* 1913, 16.
75. This trait, characteristic for monotheism, is perhaps most sharply accentuated by the Islam. The Koran designates especially the pre-Islamitic goddesses as "devils" (Sure IV. "The women" V. 6) and emphasizes expressly that "God has no female companion and absolutely no partners" (Sure VI "The beasts" V. 101).
76. Wajira Rabba 14.
77. Bereshit Rabba 18. A. Jellinek. *Bet 'ha-Midrash.* Leipzig 1853, p. 155.
78. Bereshit rab. 30.
79. Sh'mot rabba 23.
80. Bab. Brachot 29 b.
81. Especially clear Bab. P'ssachim 87.
82. So *e.g.* Bab. Brachot 6 P'assachim 50 Chagiga 11.
83. *Cf.* D. Nielsen. *Der Dreieinige Gott in religionshistorischer Belenchtung.* Kopenhagen, 1922, p. 385.—R. Israel Baal-Schem-Tow declared that God, Torah and Israel form a unity. Keter Schem Tow (Slawita) II, p. 29.
84. Bab. Brachot 10, 13, 15, 57, 61.
85. Sohar Bamidbar 162 a.
86. G. Róheim. Die Völkerpsychologie und die Psychologie der Völker. *IMAGO,* 1926, 12:279.
87. So in the Talmud: Bab. Gittin 57 b.

Chapter 18

# A Psychoanalytic Interpretation of The Menorah

WITH RELATED COMMENTS ON THE SIGNIFICANCE OF THE
NUMBER SEVEN, THE SABBATH, THE SECOND
COMMANDMENT AND THE EPISODE OF THE GOLDEN CALF

RENATO J. ALMANSI, M.D.

𝕿HE seven-branched Hebrew candlestick, the Menorah, has not yet—to the best of my knowledge—invited psychoanalytic interpretation, probably by very virtue of the fact that it is an object with which we are thoroughly familiar, and because its use as a lamp or candlestick overshadows the fact that it is a ritual object connected with the very beginnings of the Hebrew religion.

As will be shown, the Menorah can be interpreted on a psychoanalytic level. Its oversight merely confirms the truth we know so well, that the objects we take for granted, which are most familiar, and which seem to need no further explanation because of their very simplicity, are those which often conceal the deepest meanings. If this hypothesis is correct and the Menorah admits of psychoanalytic interpretation, then we would be led to suspect from the strength of the repression that the secret it conceals is a very important one indeed.

My interest in the interpretation of the Menorah was aroused by several facts:

The Menorah is a very ancient object, the first mention of which is found in the book of Exodus[1] wherein God himself instructed Moses in great detail how the Menorah should be made:

and the Lord spoke unto Moses saying. . . . "thou shalt make a candlestick of pure gold, of beaten work shall the candlestick be made, even its base and its shaft, its cups, its knops and its flowers shall be of one piece with it.    And there shall be six branches going out of the sides thereof; three branches of the candlestick out of the one side thereof; and three branches of the candlestick out of the other side thereof; three cups made like almond blossoms in one branch, a knop and a flower, and three cups made like almond blossoms in the other branch, a knop and a flower; so for the six branches going out of the candlestick.    And in the candlestick four cups made like almond blossoms, the knops thereof and the flowers thereof.    And a knop under two branches of one piece with it, and a knop under two branches of one piece with it, and a knop under two branches of one piece with it, for the six branches going out of the candlestick.    Their knops and their branches shall be of one piece with it; the whole of it one beaten work of pure gold.    And thou shalt make the lamps thereof, seven; and they shall light the lamps thereof, to give light over against it.    And the tongs thereof, and the snuff dishes thereof shall be of pure gold.    Of a talent of pure gold shall it be made, with all these vessels.    And see that thou make them after their pattern, which is being shown thee in the Mount."

We note that in this passage no mention is made of the central stem of the Menorah.    The only reference is to the lateral branches, although it is obvious that since the Menorah had seven lamps the central stem be considered equivalent to the other branches.    Moreover, great emphasis is placed here upon the fact that the Menorah was to be made in one piece and therefore to be considered as a unit.    That the Menorah was to be made of gold also has a significance which will be clarified.

Another element of interest is the bizarre and puzzling general shape of the Menorah which, with minor variations, has persisted traditionally throughout the ages.    In the *Jewish Encyclopedia*[2] one may see pictorial representations of Menorahs which date far back to antiquity but are essentially similar to those used today[3].

I was also struck by the close association of the Menorah with the Tables of the Law, as in the biblical narrative the Menorah is placed in a position of great prominence—in the Tent of Meeting[4].    Not only did the original Mosaic candlestick have a fixed place in the Tent of Meeting, but it had to be oriented in a specific way.    According to some commentators, its sides were to be in a north-south position, according to others in an east-west position. According to Talmudic tradition, Moses' candlestick stood 72 inches tall[5].

The mystic character of the seven-branched candlestick is heightened not only by the fact that since ancient times it has been a symbol of Judaism—and even more conspicuously in the present day—but also by the fact that the Menorah is found in numerous representations of the past which are related to magic, such as amulets, magic papers, etc[6].

Some interesting legends flourished in later Judaism about the origin of the Menorah. Ginzberg[7] mentions the legend wherein Moses twice found, upon coming down from heaven, that he could not remember how to construct the candlestick.

> "When he betook himself to God a third time, God took a candlestick of fire and plainly showed him every single detail of it, that he might now be able to reconstruct the candlestick for the tabernacle. When he found it still hard to form a clear conception of the nature of the candlestick, God quieted him with these words, "Go to Bezalel, he will do it aright." Then when Bezalel did it instantly, Moses told him "Truly dost thou deserve thy name Bezalel 'in the shadow of God' for thou dost act as though thou hadst been in the 'shadow of God' while he was showing me the candlestick."

This legendary difficulty of Moses' in remembering the exact shape of the candlestick is an indication in itself that the shape of the Menorah was a mysterious matter that could not easily be comprehended by the human mind, which in turn is an indication that an interpretation of the Menorah must take into account its particular shape.

Interesting as these legends[8] and their interpretations may be, they cannot satisfy the analytically minded. We must have an interpretation which makes sense psychologically and at the same time takes into account every detail presented by the object we are examining.

With these facts in mind I started investigating more closely the problem of the Menorah. The first detail on which I fixed my attention was that the candlestick God ordered Moses to make consisted of seven lamps, which was its most outstanding characteristic. It is well known that the number 7 has always held an extremely important position in Hebrew lore. According to the *Jewish Encyclopedia*[9] seven was for the Jews the most sacred number. Its sanctity was found by some in its factors 3 and 4; by others in conjunction with the number of the planets, and was enhanced by the institution of the week and of the Sabbath. In fact, the *Jewish Encyclopedia*[10] states that the Menorah represents the creation of the universe in seven days, the center light being the Sabbath.

This number appears in the seven days of creation, the institution of the seventh year of release, the forty-nine years between the Jubilees, the seven lamps, the *sprinkling of the blood seven times*. It has been considered of some significance that the Day of Atonement is the tenth day of the seventh month[11]. Also, the number 7 was found quite frequently in the apocryphical literature, in the Talmud and the Midrash. L. Ginzberg lists the seven-fold division of the earth, the seven things that were created first, seven words, seven heavens, seven divisions of Paradise and of Hell, seven great miracles, the seven pious men, the seven evils, the seven benedictions, the seven female demons, the seven names of Jethro, the seven oxen, the seven rams, the seven attributes of God, the seventy names of God, Israel and Jerusalem. In Philo we read that seven limitations determine everything physical; there are seven kinds of boils; the trumpet had seven sounds; seven voices were heard on Sinai. Mention is also made of seven stones, seven pillars, and of the seven-fold punishment. And it is said that God prefers the number 7.

In the Hebrew religion the seven-branched candlestick has always had a symbolic meaning, although the interpretations vary. The seven lights are said to represent the seven planets[12] which, regarded as the eyes of God, behold everything, the light in the center signifying the Sun. The idea was also advanced that the Menorah embodied the mystic concept of a celestial tree with leaves reaching to the sky, bearing fruit typifying the planets. This symbolism is assumed to be due to foreign influence, probably Babylonian, as in that religion the seven planets were the chief deities[13].

This preliminary review of the literature on the subject (which is by no means complete) leaves no doubt that while the number 7 had a particularly important and sacred character for the Jews, the real and positive reason for its sanctity is not understood and cannot be understood psychologically on such grounds. Abandoning, therefore, all the traditional and mystical interpretations, I set about thinking of something which is fundamental and basic in nature, and is one and seven at the same time.

As I reflected on this problem, thinking of all the possible things that are seven, I made the association that there are seven orifices in the human face—two eyes, two ears, two nostrils and the mouth. Even when this point was focused the unconscious resistance was so strong that it took me considerable time to visualize the direct connection between the facial orifices and the Menorah. Yet, obviously the middle branch of the Menorah represents the mouth which is the only facial orifice that is single and on the midline. If we trace three concentric semicircles on the human face, each of a larger radius than the preceding one, we can then connect the two nostrils with the innermost semicircle, the two eyes with the next, and the two ears with the last, thus completing a figure similar to the Menorah. Also, the external semicircle with its rounded shape would follow fairly accurately the contour of the lower part of the face.

As to the rest of the Menorah, the stem and its base, in several ancient schematic drawings the vertical stem is shown as ending in a transverse line which, in turn, is supported by three and sometimes four vertical legs. The stem and the base of the Menorah could, therefore, be interpreted as a schematic representation of the neck and upper extremities or, more likely, the trunk and legs.

This interpretation appears to account satisfactorily for the legends relating to the fixed orientation of the Menorah. In most religions, especially in antiquity, the worshiper oriented himself toward a specific point of the compass during prayer. This direction, for the Jews, has traditionally been the east. In fact, they call east, west, north and south "before," "behind," "left" and "right" respectively, indicating that the east is their point of orientation[14]. This interpretation also accounts for the legendary height of the Menorah (72 inches) which corresponds to the height of a tall man[15].

If these premises are correct, the Menorah as a whole is a symbolic schematic representation of the human body in which the cephalic portion is tremendously emphasized while the genital organs are apparently repressed. This repression, however, is merely apparent. Each branch of the Menorah was decorated with three cups made like almond blossoms, a knop and a flower. According to Hannay[16] "knop means bud, especially lotus bud, and lotus buds are a universally used symbol of the phallus, while we know the connection of Luz in the form of an almond, so that here we have the Indian Lingam-Yoni altar, or the doubled sexed symbol of reproduction. A purely phallic combination in the very core and sanctum of the Hebrew religion." In turn, Luz[17] is the name for the coccyx, the "nut" of the spinal column. In ancient times there was a belief that being indestructible, the coccyx would form the nucleus for the resurrection of the body. In the Talmud it is narrated that the Emperor Hadrian was told that the revival of the body at the resurrection would begin with the "almond" or "nut" of the spinal column. During the Middle Ages the coccyx was called the *Juden Knöchlein*. Brugsch[18] believed that possibly this legend may have had its origin in Egypt, where the spinal column of Osiris was buried at the close of the days of mouring for him, after which his resurrection was celebrated. The obvious identification of the almond blossom with the vertebrae is of no small interest in the interpretation given herein. Finally, according to L. Ginzberg, the tabernacle itself was interpreted as a symbolic representation of the human body[19].

At this point, the reader must be as dissatisfied and puzzled as I was, once this conclusion was reached. While the interpretation of the Menorah as a symbolization of the human face is in itself satisfactory in several ways, suggestive as it may be it still falls short of answering certain basic questions, such as: What is the significance of this face? Why was it so important? Why did such a representation have to be repressed? These questions are a sure indication that the interpretation is still incomplete. Evidently some important element is still missing. Upon careful reflection we conclude that the only important consideration left, the only important detail still unaccounted for, is the function of the Menorah itself, i.e., that the Menorah was a lamp, each of whose seven cups bore a flame.

If, with this in mind, we go back to the representation of the human face, and place the flames where they properly belong, where the branches of the Menorah originate—at the mouth, the nostrils, the eyes and the ears—then the actual significance of the Menorah begins to be clear. It is a symbolization of a hollow idol's head (actually a whole idol) *illuminated from within.*

Were there such idols in antiquity? Most certainly so. And in this connection our minds immediately go to the sacrificial idols, the hollow idols within whose interiors burned sacrificial fires, particularly for human sacrifices.

The literature on this subject is so extensive that only a few corroborating facts need be mentioned. The Moabites had an idol simulating Baal, called Chemosh, which was their national god and on critical occasions human sacrifices were used to propitiate him[20]. In Samaria, under the Assyrian regime, a god of Sepharadim was worshipped whose name was Anammelech, to whom children were sacrificed. In the same city a similar god called Adrammelech also enjoyed such sacrifices. The practice of sacrificing human victims was resorted to in Carthage, in times of stress[21] or to avert a national disaster[22]. The god that demanded such victims was apparently Milk, the Molech or Moloch of the Old Testament. Baal-Ammon, or Moloch[23] was represented as an old man with rams' horns on his forehead and a scythe in his hand. In his temple there was a colossal statue of bronze in whose arms were placed the children to be sacrificed so that they slipped from the arms into the furnace burning within the idol. In Greece human sacrifices were encouraged by the Delphic oracle, but the custom had become repellent to conscience by the sixth century although it was not entirely extinct in the Greek world by the time of Porphyry. A great many legends have been preserved about the Minotaur, the mythical offspring of Pasiphae and a bull, to whom *seven boys and seven girls* were immolated every eight years by being roasted alive in a bronze bull image. Cook[24] states that the Minotaur was originally a Cretan king posing as a sky god and his semibovine form is related to the fact that in Crete the sun was conceived of as a bull. The periodic sacrifice of human victims indicates that the divine powers of the Sun King needed renewal at the end of each eight-year period.  This identification of the Minotaur with the King Minos and with the sun leaves no doubt that it is a cruel father-figure.  Parallel to this is the Saturn myth—that he had by a nymph a male child whom he named Jeoud, "one and only."  At the onset of a war which brought the country into imminent danger, Saturn erected an altar, brought to it his son clothed in royal garments and sacrificed him[25].  A similar situation is the one in Indian mythology which is attributed to King Hariscandra, who promised Varuna his son if he would *give* him one.  In Rome, at the Saturnalia human victims were still slain until the fourth century A.D.[26].  In ancient Egypt a young girl of noble family, dressed as for a wedding, was thrown into the Nile to consecrate a canal.  The court and high officials were immolated at the king's death at the time of the first dynasty[27] and slaves were sacrificed at the funerals of their masters, as their souls were supposed to accompany and serve the deceased. This custom was later substituted by that of placing in the tomb statues of the slaves, bearing their names[28].

Sumner and Keller[29] discuss in detail human sacrifice in all parts of the world.  According to them this custom still exists at the present time in certain parts of the world.  The reader interested in more details on this subject is referred also to the chapter "Human Sacrifice" in Hasting's *Encyclopedia of Religion and Ethics*.

There is no doubt that human sacrifice was practiced by ancient peoples, the most famous center of such practices having been Phoenicia and her colonies, where child sacrifice by burning was a prominent feature of the worship of Malik-Baal-Cronos.

Every evidence from the Bible points determinedly to the fact that not only were the Jews acquainted with the rite from ancient times but that they practiced it even up to a relatively late date.  Its great antiquity is shown by the story of Abraham's sacrifice.  In Leviticus xviii, 21, the Israelite was forbidden to sacrifice any of his children to Molech; and similarly, in Leviticus xx, 2-5, it was enacted that a man who sacrificed his seed to Molech should surely be put to death.  Curiously enough, then, it was provided that he should be cut off from the congregation.

Such a difference in the punishment is in itself an evidence of the ambivalence of feeling regarding this practice. In I Kings, xi, 7, it is said that Solomon built a high place for Chemosh and for Molech in the mountains before Jerusalem. In 2 Kings, xxiii, 10, it is stated that one of the practices which Josiah stopped was that of sacrificing children to Molech. As to the nature of the cult itself, it is clear from Isaiah LVII, 5, and Jeremiah XIX, 5, that the children were killed and burned. The phrase employed for these sacrifice is "to make one's children pass through the fire to Molech[30]." Critical scholars agree that in the last days of the Kingdom sacrifices were still offered to Jahveh as king or counselor of the nation, and that the prophets were strongly opposed to this practice because it was a heathen cult and because of its cruelty. These sacrifices were motivated by the worshippers' feeling, in the midst of the disasters which beset the nation, that even such a price would not be too high to regain the favor of Jahveh[31]. The ritual was so closely associated with Jahveh worship (Ezekiel xxiii, 39) that Jeremiah protested that it was not of Jahveh's institution (vii, 31, xix, 5). Also Micah (vi) rejected the idea of sacrificing the first-born to Jahveh.

The perusal of the work of biblical scholars leaves no doubt that there was a tendency to identify Jahveh with Baal, and for this reason[32] Molech and Baal are repeatedly designated in the Scriptures as false gods, different from Jahveh. An expression of the reaction of the Hebrews against such identification can also be found in the fact that while the name Moloch derives from the Hebrew word *Melech*, i.e., King, which was an appellation of the Semitic Supreme Deity, this name, in later times, was altered by giving it the vowels of *Bosheth Shem* (the Shameful thing), which was the contemptuous name for Baal[33].

One of the most interesting facts, from our point of view, is that human sacrifice undoubtedly started as an offering of the first-born. Later the custom was transformed into the sacrifice of other humon beings—slaves, enemies and criminals —and finally it was transformed into the offering of the firstlings of cattle and products of the earth, the ransoming of the first-born[34] and circumcision[35]. The latest form of redemption resulted in the hierodule or sacred slave, whereby the first-born took up duties in the temple[36]. Despite this, instances of sacrifice of a first-born son are recorded in the cases of King Mesha[37], King Ahaz[38], and Manasseh[39].

It is stated in the *Encyclopedia of Religion and Ethics* that the custom of sacrificing the first-born son was a common one among the Semites, as demonstrated by the fact that many jars with the bones of children have been found in Palestine in places where sacrifice would naturally be performed, such as under the corners and thresholds of houses and under the floors in the high places[40]. Similarly, Frazer traces the origins of the Hebrew Passover directly to the sacrifice of the first-born infant which, in his opinion, was an article of the ancient Semitic religion; he bases his argument on Exodus xiii, 2,15; Micah vi:7 and Numbers xviii:15. Similar customs regarding the first-born son, either in the form of sacrifice or of redemption have also been found in widely scattered parts of the world—in Uganda, among the Hindus, in Syria and among the heathen Russians[41].

Another point of interest is that sacrifices of this sort were usually performed by burning the victims inside a hollow metal idol. This, as we have seen, was the case with the Minotaur and probably is alluded to in the legend of Talos, a bronze giant, made by his father, Hephaistos, god of fire, who clutched the victims to his breast and leaped with them into the fire so that they were roasted alive[42]. In the tradition of Phalaris, tyrant of Agrigentum, and his brazen bull there may be an echo of similar rites in Sicily.

That the Semites employed the same ritual was stated by Rabbi Simon who, in speaking of the statue of Moloch standing outside Jerusalem, said:

> "It was a statue with the head of an ox, and the hand outstretched as a man's, who opens his hands to secure something from another. It was hollow within. The child was placed before the idol and a fire made underneath until it became red hot. Then the priest took the child and put it into the glowing hands of Moloch. . . ."[43]

The Carthaginians used for the same purpose a calf-headed image of bronze and the children were made to slide from the hands of the monster into its hollow heated body[44]. Similar rites were practiced in Mexico and in Peru by the Incas. Such rites were, in fact, universal. A great hollow statue of metal was found on the island of Carolina in the Gulf of Mexico, which is a monument to a cannibalistic god, within which still lay the fragments of burned human beings[45]. It is possible that on an unconscious level similar motives may underlie the fact that on the island of Bali, sarcophagi made of hollowed-out tree trunks in the shape of cows[46] are used for cremating corpses of the nobility. Frazer also quotes numerous examples of ceremonies performed in many parts of Europe, particularly in Belgium, where effigies and osier giants were burned at the Mid-summer Festivals, which he believes dates back to ancient Celtic and Druidic customs, whereby criminals and men accused of witch-craft were burned inside of osier columns and effigies to pro-pitiate the gods for the crops and to free the population from wizardry.

It is significant, also, that the fire itself which was used in the sacrifices embodied an identification with the sun and incor-porated the idea of purity with its power to burn up and destroy all sins and harmful influences.

The final results of fire—the ashes—have preserved in mythology and folklore signs of the emotions of our ancestors in relation to sacrifice. From the most ancient times, ashes (especially ashes strewn over the head) have been used as a symbol of repentance and penance. Ash Wednesday is still the beginning of a period of abstinence and penance. Ashes were used in amulets, in divination, in exorcism of demons, and for purification. In ancient Egypt, in Bechuanaland and in Bengal, ashes of human victims were scattered over the fields in fertility rites[47]. Such ceremonies are doubtless parallel in significance to the periodic sacrifice to the Minotaur in order to renew his powers at the end of each eighth year, and indicate the primitive belief in the necessity of the death of the son to preserve and renew the potency and generative powers of the father.

That the sacrificial idols are essentially sadistic father figures certainly needs no emphasis from a psychoanalytic stand-point. As we have previously seen, fire (which is in itself a masculine symbol) was equated to the sun, which has been universally identified with the masculine powers. Baal, as the procreative and productive power, was worshipped under the form of the phallus, Baal-Peor[48] and during his services gross licentiousness and unlimited sexuality were encouraged and practiced[49]. Jahvah himself is very often referred to in the scriptures as "fire"[50]. The bull, in whose shape the metal sacrificial statues were often made is also a universally accepted symbol of the phallus. It is of interest to note that in the Aegean religion the bull often was represented as crowned with the sacred axe[51]. The vast antiquity of bull worship, its double identification with the father and the victorious son who has slain him, and its highly sadistic components, are dramatically shown in a pyramid text of the fifth dynasty (3600 B.C.), but certainly predynastic in origin, which describes the sky bull Unas who was more powerful than the father who fashioned him:

> "Unas . . . . a god who lives upon his fathers and feeds upon his mothers! . . . Unas is a lord of wisdom whose name his own mother knows not. . . . Unas is the bull of the sky, with heart keen to trust, that lives upon the being of every god, that eats their entrails. . . . The dwellers of the sky serve him and the cooking pots are wiped out for him with the thighs of their women. . . . He is crowned as lord of the horizon. He has smashed the vertebrae and the spinal marrows, he has carried off the hearts of the gods. . . . He punishes, and their magic is in his belly, his dignities are not taken from him. He has swallowed the understanding of every god"[52].

The masculine character of the sun and of the sacrificial idols, as well as the many characteristic legends attached to them, leave no doubt that the human sacrifice as originally performed in the person of the first-born son finds its deep roots in the struggle between fathers and sons, which has been postulated by Atkinson and Robertson Smith and accepted by Freud as having taken place in the primal horde.

As is well known, Freud evolved the theory that in the primal horde which was dominated by the cruel despotic father who sexually used all the women of the clan, a memorable struggle arose in times beyond the memory of men. This struggle between the father and sons sometimes ended in the death of the father; on other occasions it may have ended in his victory which was followed by the slaughter or the castration of the sons. This hypothesis has been strongly confirmed by all that we know of the origins of religious rituals as well as by everyday experience which shows the presence of such a basic situation even in the mind of man today. The position of the first-born in this struggle is obvious. He had been the first to pass through his mother's genitals, thus committing a symbolic incest. He was the strongest and therefore the one who logically aspired to succeed to his father's power. Therefore, he must have been the ringleader, the one who had the greatest responsibility in the overthrow of the father and he was, therefore, the one on whom the guilt and the retribution fell most heavily.

The mark left by that primitive struggle on the unconscious of generations to come, the guilt that followed the deed and the recurrent temptation to renew it, explain why the custom of human sacrifice—which had to be repressed—could not be abolished, at least in a symbolic form. This explains why the motif of the father devouring his sons could not be completely relinquished and had to be idealized and transformed into a light-giving object while still retaining some of the characteristics pertaining to its deepest origin. Obviously, in the re-establishment of the father's authority which took place in the Hebrew religion, a reshaping of the figure of the father occurred in which the sadistic castrating components of the father figure were repressed and the benevolent and ethical features emphasized. This finds its parallel in the prominence accorded the cephalic part of the body in the Menorah.

The fact that this process could not be complete is, of course, consistent with the origins, ambivalence and strength of the emotions involved. The father, therefore, was split—partially at least—into two different personalities: the benevolent, spiritual, ethical God on one side and the phallic, instinct-ridden sadistic figure of the Idol-Devil on the other. Traces of this are easily found in ancient literature[53]. The same motif reappears in early Christian literature, wherein St. Paul says: (I Cor. viii:4) "We know that no idol is anything in the world, and there is no God but one," and in another passage shortly after (X. 19:20) "But I say that the things which the Gentiles sacrifice, they sacrifice to devils, and not to God; and I would not that ye should have communion with devils."

This contrast has, of course, been greatly emphasized in Christian literature, up to the present time.

If we now try to go beyond the significance of the Menorah which has been outlined, we will find that on a deeper level of interpretation the conclusion reached thus far are further confirmed.  If we look at the Menorah from a purely geometrical angle we are immediately struck by the fact that actually this object embodies, indissolubly fused, the two basic symbols that continually recur in the productions of the unconscious—the straight line and the curved line—the symbols of the masculine and the feminine, united in copulation.

Continuing along these lines of thought, the triple repetition of the curved line may well indicate the female genitals in their entirety, as the external semicircle may indicate the labia majora, the middle the labia minora and the internal one the uterine cervix; while the middle stem of the Menorah would indicate the phallus.   This, in turn, is confirmed by the fact that, as we have previously seen, the middle stem of the Menorah corresponds to the mouth, and therefore, to the phallic tongue.

If this interpretation is correct, of necessity one would have to align the Menorah with the other numerous double-sexed symbols found in other religions, such as the pestle and mortar, the lingramyoni of the Indians and the ankh of the Egyptians. The Jews, too, revered similar symbols in an extremely repressed form.

The interpretation given now is, therefore, consistent, and further clarifies the interpretation discussed before, as, going beyond the pure and simple symbolization of a sacrificial idol in an extremely condensed and yet unmistakable form it indicates the motives and the conflicts of emotions which led to the institution of the sacrificial rite.

In the rest of the article we propose to follow some problems which are related to the significance of the number *seven* and the Sabbath, the second Commandment and the episode of the Golden Calf, as a study of these subjects has revealed an intimate connection with the interpretation of the Menorah.

## I.  THE SIGNIFICANCE OF THE NUMBER "SEVEN" AND OF THE SABBATH

If the premise that the seven lamps of the Menorah may be

interpreted as a symbolization of the glowing facial orifices of a cruel sacrificial idol is correct, we would reasonably expect that the number *seven* may have played some role in history and mythology consistent with this interpretation. The evidence found in this connection leaves no doubt that originally this number represented the very incarnation of evil and was, therefore, the most unlucky number.

In Babylonian mythology the number *seven* had a most important religious and mystic significance. The seven chief deities were simply called "The Seven" and were originally deified weapons of war[54], the seven pronged weapon of Ninib. They were one and seven-fold, they were addressed in the singular as one deity and yet they were distinct. They were identified with the fire-god, with Sibitti[55], and especially with Labartu, the frightful female demon who had seven names, who preyed especially on children and was referred to as "the seven wicked Labartu." (This deity obviously represents a devouring mother figure.) "The Seven" were depicted as frightful animals and were the helpers of Nergal, the implacable judge of souls and the slaughterer of mankind[56]. The belief in such evil one- and sevenfold deities was not confined to the Babylonians but was common also in Assyria[57], in Syria[58] and among other nations. For example, in Chaldean mythology the seven evil deities were known as "shedim," storm demons who were represented in ox-like form[59]. To such demons the ancient Hebrews also offered sacrifices[60]. To counterbalance the evil influence of "The Seven" the Babylonian imagination created a sevenfold benevolent deity to protect them against the "wicked seven." This deity was identified with the sun, the moon and the five planets or with the Pleiades, and its name was used to indicate the universal divinity which was mentioned in the texts as a unit.

An interesting symbolization of the Babylonian sevenfold deity is found in some cylinder seals where the deity is represented as a hand with seven fingers surrounded by worshippers.

Consistent with the dual character of "The Seven" the number itself had two entirely separate significances. On one side it indicated totality and completeness, and in Babylonian cosmology it stood for the seven stages of the universe. The expression "seven and seven" was used to express the fullness of the sacrifice to the deity and respect to the king. A common salutation in messages to the king was: "To the feet of the King, my lord, I fall seven and seven times[61]." The number seven had the same sacred character for the Hebrews. On the other hand, seven was the number of bad luck and wickedness. Arallu, the frightful Babylonian Hell, had seven gates. Musmahhu, the horrible serpent, had seven heads. Many rituals, particularly those connected with sacrifice, had to be repeated seven times. This number appeared very often in exorcisms and magics. The character of wickedness attached to this number remained for long centuries. In the New Testament there are repeated references to the seven bad spirits and the seven devils[62], and the later Christian theology created the concept of the seven deadly sins[63]. In the gnostic concept of the universe, seven world-creating powers are considered hostile and half devilish[64].

The connection between the number seven and deities, fire and danger, is found not only in Semitic religions. One of the chief Indian gods is Agni, the red god of fire, born of the lotus, representation of the sun and of the lightning. This redhaired, three-headed god is traditionally depicted with seven arms which are interpreted as the seven rays of light. A definite association between him and the number seven is also shown by the fact that according to certain descriptions he had seven tongues, or as it is sometimes expressed, "out of his mouth come the seven rays of light[65]." Another Indian deity, Tara the compassionate and succoring, born of a tear of the all-compassionate Avalokitesvara, is on occasion depicted with seven eyes on her forehead (White Tara of the seven eyes). That this deity has many shapes of terror (Bhrikuti Tara "with frowning brow" and Ekajata who brandishes the sword, the arrow, the bow and the skull) shows the same duality that we have found in the Babylonian "Seven" and equates this deity with the evil mother of the unconscious. According to Frazer[66], in the backwoods of Cambodia lived two mysterious mystic kings, known as the King of Fire and the King of the Water. Their kingship lasted for seven years, during which period they inhabited seven towers perched upon seven mountains, passing from one to the other each year.   In Tibet, the god of the fireplace is Nang-Lha, who changes his abode seven times a year.

For the Hebrews the number seven was an extremely sacred number which recurs innumerable times in the Bible and in Hebrew ritual.   Stalnaker[67], who has made an extensive study of the subject, believes that the number seven in the Bible is the symbol of perfection in many things at times diametrically opposed to each other, such as forgiveness and vengeance, plenty and famine, servitude and freedom, reward and punishment, grace and abomination.   It was also the symbol of perfection in such things as conquest, strength, destruction, cleansing, purification, sacrifice, and wisdom.   In sacrifice, the recurrence of the number seven was quite frequent.   The "clean" animals were taken into the Ark by sevens, because from them the offerings for sacrifice were to be chosen.   Animals were not considered good for food nor worthy of sacrifice until seven days after birth.   In Balak's sacrifices, seven altars[68] were used in each of the three sacrifices.   In the first, seven oxen and seven rams were offered.   In each of the second and third, seven bullocks and seven rams, and in the sin offering the blood was sprinkled seven times.   In connection with the Feasts of the Lord, the number seven appeared innumerable times also and was particularly associated with the offerings by fire[69].   The feast of Passover emphasizes particularly the importance of the number seven, which is especially interesting because of the intimate relationship between this feast and the redemption of the first-born son. Finally, any object which was cleansed seven times was considered as entirely purified.

The belief in the special properties of number seven is found not only among the Semites.   Among the Malanau, a Sarawak tribe, seven is very prominent in rites of exorcism[70], and among the Wachega of East Africa the seventh month of the year is the most unlucky[71].   The Akikuyu attach extremely unlucky significance to the seventh day[72].   The number seven is also the most unlucky number for the Nandi[73].

The origin of the word "seven" itself bears the stigmata of its significance.   According to the very learned monograph of J. Hehn, the Babylonians translated the number seven of the Sumerian texts with the word *kissatu* which means seven and also *fullness* and *completeness*.  This word derives from a common root with the verb *sebu* which means to satiate and *to be satiated either in a physical or moral sense* (to be full of happiness and joy).  We therefore seem to be witnessing a process of sublimation exactly parallel to the change that occurred in the character of the seven Babylonian deities and to the transition from a sacrificial idol to the Menorah.  This change in significance with partial or total conservation of the repressed object represents a substitution which follows obsessive patterns and confirms the intensity and depth of the sadistic impulses to be repressed.  An exactly similar transition took place in the character and significance of the Sabbath.

As is well known[74], the weekly day of rest and worship that the Hebrews celebrate on the last day of the week represents a social and religious phenomenon common to many people of antiquity and to almost all people today—even some of the most primitive.  Originally, in very primitive societies, such periods of rest were not regular but were called in critical epochs such as times of danger and stress, periods of change or transition, or when untoward events were expected.  It is believed that the primitive mentality imposed a taboo on such days and that the rest and cessation from all activities in such tabooed periods (often including abstention from sexual practices) was basically a precautionary measure to ward off the threatened danger by abstaining from any action and by propitiating the deity with prayers.  The study of primitive societies reveals that such taboos spread to include special periods of every kind, such as the beginning of fishing and planting, market days, housebuilding, sickness and death; storms, earthquakes, tornadoes, floods, fires, eclipses and the appearance of comets, also called for such taboo.  Some of these taboos, particularly that which imposes abstention from work after a death, have persisted to the present time, and many others have been incorporated into religious and other festivals.  It is noteworthy that a particularly strong taboo was imposed after a death or on sacrificial days.  The strength of the Sabbath taboo among the Hebrews is well known.  The transgressor was threatened with death[75].  On the Sabbath, a goat laden with the sins of the people was sent forth into the wilderness where it was sacrificed to Azalel, a bad angel or demon. The Day of Atonement was probably a primitive ceremony of sin riddance, of long antiquity, which was much later incorporated into the ritual[76].

Irrespective of the transformation that the original tabooed days later assumed, they were originally unlucky days and their joyous and festive character appeared only much later.

Whether the Hebrew Sabbath is a derivation of the Babylonian Sabbath (which is most probable) or whether they originated independently through their common Semitic ancestry has not yet been ascertained. However, no doubt exists about the close relationship between the Babylonian and the Hebrew Sabbath. The Hebrew word "Sabbath" itself is derived from the Assyrian *Sapattu* or *sabattu* which, in turn, originated from the Sumerian *sa-bat* (*sag* meaning "Heart" and *bat* "to reach the end or to die"). It was paraphrased by the Babylonian with *ûm nuh libbi* ("day of rest of the heart of the angered gods")[77]. This word was used to indicate the 15th day of the month and therefore coincided with the period of the full moon. In an Assyrian calendar which appears to be a transcript of a much older one probably going back to the age of Hammurabi, all days are called favorable except the 7th, 14th, 21st and 28th day of the lunar month which were called *ûmu limun* ("evil days") and were marked by offerings and sacrifices made by the king to the deities. On these days "the shepherd of great peoples shall not eat flesh cooked upon the coals or bread of the oven." The 19th day of the month was the "week of weeks" as it ended the seventh week from the beginning of the previous month and was called *ûm ibbû* ("day of anger"). The restrictions on ordinary life that were imposed on such days were applied almost exclusively to the holy orders, the king, high priest, seers and physicians, and the sacrificial ceremonies were the most prominent features of such unlucky days. This holds true for the Hebrew Sabbath which also was originally a day of sacrifice[78]. To the Jews, however, the Sabbath also became eventually a day of prayer and study, a sign of their communion with God and of their covenant with Him[80], and as such its infringement was punishable with death. It is noteworthy that the lighting of a fire on such days was a particularly serious sign of disrespect to the deity[81].

The historical and philological considerations outlined above seem to tie the number seven indissolubly with the idea of fire, sacrifice, fear, danger and death. The one and sevenfold deity of the Babylonians parallels the Menorah which, as we have seen, is one and sevenfold itself and both are equated to a human body, the one head of which has seven orifices.

If we try to reconstruct, at least tentatively, the sequence of events that led to the institution of the Sabbath we may start from the hypothesis that sacrifice had a double connotation for the Semites. It symbolized to them both the murder of the primal father and also the sacrifice of the first-born son who, once the father's authority had been re-established, became the scapegoat for the collective crime of the sons. Such sacrifices, therefore, served not only the unconscious purpose of re-enacting the murder to the primal father but were also a threatening reminder of what could happen to any one who would repeat it. The sacrifice of the first-born son was then instituted, but even this soon became inadequate as no man can sacrifice more than one first-born son in the course of his life, while the need for repressing incestuous impulses is continuous. At the same time, the progress of ethics made the sacrifice of the first-born son more and more repugnant. The solution evidently lay in the substitution of animals for human sacrifice. At the same time, to avoid a dangerous weakening of the incest taboo, the sacrificial rite had to be made into a regularly and frequently repeated act, as a permanent reminder for millenia to come that the barrier against incest was not to be transgressed.

The choice of each seventh day for such rites, I venture to suggest, may have been prompted by two separate and yet coinciding motives. As noted in the first chapter, seven is the number of God, a god whose anthropomorphism is still thinly concealed and who is still nearer to the earthly, powerful, despotic, devouring father than it later became. The choice of the number seven seems, therefore, to be the most fitting to remind humanity of his ever-present authority[82]. On the other hand, the institution of the week and sacrifice are intimately connected with the moon whose phases take place every seventh day. The moon, which was an object of worship to the ancient Semites[83], has been identified as a female deity by many people of antiquity[84]. Its feminine character is strongly reinforced by the connection of the lunar month with the menstrual cycle. The association of the sacrifice with the phases of the moon, therefore, introduces in the sacrificial rite the third element needed to complete the triangle—the woman for whom the memorable struggle between fathers and sons was waged.

## II. AN INTERPRETATION OF THE SECOND COMMANDMENT

In the light of what we have seen, the prohibition against images contained in the second commandment, which so early in Hebrew history became one of the chief tenets of the Hebrew religion, suddenly becomes clear. So strong a taboo was attached to images that in very ancient times a very pious rabbi became famous because he prided himself on never having laid his eyes on an image, not even that engraved upon coins! In ancient Judaism, idols were stigmatized as "non-gods," "things of naught, of vanity, of iniquity, wind and confusion"; as "the dead" and as "carcasses." Baal-Zebub was called "Beel-Zebul," which is equivalent to "dominus stercoris." The mere destruction of an image was not sufficient—it had to be pulverized and sunk in the Dead Sea. Idolatry was the first in the list of the three cardinal sins for which death was the penalty. In order to prevent idolatry, association with Gentiles was made difficult and elaborate precautions were taken to avoid the possibility of the infiltration of idol worship.

In this connection, it is of interest to quote literally the second commandment[85]: "Thou shalt not make unto thee a graven image, nor any manner of likeness of any thing that is in the heaven above or that is in the earth beneath, or that is in the water under the earth; thou shalt not bow down unto them nor serve them."

Another most interesting passage is found in *Deut.* iv, 15-24: "Take ye therefore good heed unto yourselves—for ye saw no manner of form on the day that the Lord spoke unto you in Horeb *out of the midst of fire*—lest ye deal corruptly, and make you a graven image, even in the form of any figures, the likeness of male or female, the likeness of any beast that is on the earth, the likeness of any winged fowl that flieth in the heaven, the likeness of any thing that creepeth on the ground, the likeness of any fish that is in the water under the earth. . . . *But you hath the Lord taken and brought forth out of the iron furnace, out of Egypt,* to be unto him a people of inheritance, as ye are this day. . . . Take heed upon yourselves, lest ye forget the Covenant of the Lord your God, which he made with you and make you a graven image, even the likeness of any thing which the Lord thy God hath forbidden thee—*For the Lord thy God is a devouring fire,* a jealous God."

The psychologist will certainly fail to see clearly the reason for the stress placed upon idolatry and the ban against images. In fact, one might well argue that the veneration of an image is not definitely inconsistent with a high type of religious worship, so long as it is clear that the image itself is not the representation but merely a symbol of the deity. Such an arrangement was conveniently adopted by the Catholic, as well as many other religions.

This prohibition is so much more surprising if we consider that at the time it was first promulgated the veneration of images and idols was universal and the custom so deeply rooted that it persisted among the Hebrews for many centuries after the Exodus. Moreover, the need for some material object of worship could not be avoided even in the Jewish religion which shows that even a spiritual cult, when it must cope with practical reality, cannot altogether dispense with objects invested with a magical character. No sufficient reason for this extremely strong taboo can be found on a conscious level; so, as always in such cases, one must admit the presence of very strong unconscious motives underlying such probitions.

On the basis of what has been presented, I dare to venture that one reason for the prohibition of images was the need to repress the image of the sadistic parental figures and that it later spread to all other types of plastic representation. This hypothesis seems strongly confirmed by the following:

(1)  The second commandment says nothing about the folly of treating an inanimate object as though it were alive. It speaks only of "making a similitude, the likeness of any form that is in Heaven above or that is in the earth beneath or that is in the water under the earth."

Bevan[86] understandably asks what it was that the commandment actually prohibited; whether it was only the *worship* of an image or whether it was forbidden to *make* representations of certain objects, whether for worship or not.

(2) Apparently some confusion existed as to the exact subject of the taboo, whether it applied to images of living creatures and living creatures only, or to any object at all, without distinction. Josephus[87], in describing the embroideries of the Tabernacle, interprets that any animal forms were to be avoided in their designs, whereas the Rabbinic tradition which began to be written about a hundred years after Josephus, made no such distinction and prohibited all images indiscriminately. It is evident that here, too, we witness the usual phenomenon of the progressive spreading of a taboo.

(3) Even more significant is the fact that originally a distinction was made between a picture in the flat and an image in the round. This is brought out, for example, by the prescription in the Talmud about signet rings: In *Abodah Zarah* 5, 2, it is stated that if one possesses a signet ring with a projecting image he may not wear it but may make impressions with it because they will appear concave. However, if the image on the ring were concave, he could wear it but could not use it for making impressions because the image would appear in the round. Also, Rabbi Abbaye (A.D. 273-339) justifies the objection taken by Rabbi Samuel to an image, by saying that the representation was a projecting figure and not a flat picture, implying that had it been a picture there would not have been much harm in it[88].

Another demonstration is that pictures, in the flat, of animals and even prophets were found in the excavation of Jewish cemeteries and synagogues (such as at Vigna Randanini, in some Jewish catacombs in Rome, in Jewish tombs in Tunisia, in the synagogues at Capernaum, at Hamman-Lif and particularly at Dura Europos, where frescoes of the Old Testament and of the prophets were found).

The same idea of the greater wickedness of images in the round than pictures in the flat seems to be embodied in the writings of St. Epiphanius, a Greek writer of the fourth century[89] who states that at first idolatry started only by means of colored paintings and pictures, but a *deeper step into evil* was made when man started molding statues. Also, since medieval times, the Greek Orthodox Church has felt that an image in the round was more objectionable than a picture in the flat.

Therefore, there seems to be little doubt that images in the round were considered more wicked than concave images or flat pictures, and according to the previous interpretation, this may well be connected with the fact that an image in the round is the nearest thing to a statue and so embodied the idea of the dreaded sacrificial idol.

(4)   Not only were statues much more objectionable than pictures, but repeated references to metallic statues apparently indicate that the fact of being made of metal was important in itself and unconsciously carried an element of particular wickedness.   In *Exod.* xxi, 20, we read:   "Ye shall not make with Me— gods of silver or gods of gold—ye shall not make unto you." The same idea is repeated in *Psalms* CXXXV, 15, 16:   "The idols of the nations are silver and gold, the work of men's hands.   They have mouths, but they speak not; eyes have they, but they see not; they have ears, but they hear not; neither is there any breath in their mouths."   The Epistles of Jeremy:   "Gods of silver and of gold and of wood, borne upon shoulders, *which cause the nations to fear.* . . . Their tongue is polished by the workman, and they themselves are overlaid with gold and with silver; yet are they but false and cannot speak[(90)]."   Also *Hos.* xiii, 1-2.   "When Ephraim spoke, there was trembling, he exalted himself in Israel! but when he became guilty through Baal he died.   And now they sin more and more, and have made their ᵐolten images of their silver, according to their own understanding, even idols . . . . of them they say:   *They that sacrifice men kiss calves."*   The latter part of this quotation is particularly significant, as will be demonstrated.

The same idea is found in the second commandment itself, which primarily refers to molten and graven images.   The significance of these facts is obvious if one thinks that sacrificial idols had, of necessity, to be made of metal.

(5)   In the *Book of Exodus,* XXXIII, 20-23, another interesting aspect of the taboo on images of God is laid down, which shows that the face of God was felt to be much more

strongly tabooed and holier than his back. When Moses asked to see God, the answer was *"Thou canst not see My face, for man shall not see Me and live."* And the Lord said: "Behold, there is a place by Me and thou shalt stand upon the rock. And it shall come to pass, while my glory passeth by, that I will put thee in a cleft of the rock and *will cover thee with My hand until I have passed by. And I will take away My hand and thou shalt see my back; but My face shall not be seen."*

If our previous premise is correct, the reason for this very fascinating and puzzling passage is not difficult to understand. The face of God is much more dangerous than the back, inasmuch as the human victims were immolated in front of the sacrificial idols, and for this reason the face was more strongly tabooed than the back of God, which Moses was permitted to see.

The dangers connected with the sight of the face of God are clearly shown in North American mythology, by the myths which have been found in every part of America of Great Heads, a sort of bodiless man-eating monster which pursues men in order to devour or destroy them. These Great Heads have tentatively been identified by some mythologists with the sun and the moon, which were conceived of as traveling heads or masks. In some variations of the same myth, traveling rocks are substituted for the head[91].

The same taboo on the face of God which we have noted above in the XXXIII chapter of *Exodus* is found also in the narrative of the XXXIV chapter where Moses, coming down from Mt. Sinai, radiating divine light, had to cover his face with a veil.

That such taboos were not limited to the Jews is shown by an ivory statuette from Carthago, showing a headless Punic goddess with hands raised in an attitude of prayer.

Residuals of the same taboo in relatively recent times have been found by Frazer in Africa, where numerous Sultans concealed their faces as a sign of authority[92].

An interesting parallel regarding this taboo has been made by Tarachow who has very adroitly suggested that the taboo on looking at the face of God may be closely related to the taboo on looking at the genitals of one's father. This seems so much more plausible if one thinks of the common identification of the head with the male genital organs, and of the multiple identifications with both the male and female organs which we find so often clinically in relation to parts of the face such as the nose, the eyes, the mouth and the ears. The castration threat attached to such a taboo finds its highest expression, therefore, in the mortal danger attached to the sacrificial idol.

### III.  THE EPISODE OF THE GOLDEN CALF

One of he most interesting and well-known scenes in the Bible is that in which Moses broke the Tables of the Law upon discovering that the Jews had reverted to the veneration of the Golden Calf.   This episode has been studied analytically in detail by Theodor Reik in his work on *Ritual* and we add an interpretation which stems directly from the considerations thus far outlined.

The story is well known—the Jews were greatly distressed by the absence of Moses who had been on the sacred mountain for forty days and forty nights.   They felt abandoned and in their distress they made a Golden Calf to propitiate the deity in their crucial predicament, and offered sacrifices to it.   When Moses descended from the mountain and saw this, he broke the Tables of the Law in anger; he then gathered the sons of Levi and ordered them to mete out punishment upon the idolaters. *Exod.* xxxii, 27, 28: . . . . "Put ye every man his sword upon his thigh and go to and fro from gate to gate throughout the camp and slay every man his brother, and every man his companion, and every man his neighbor.   And the sons of Levi did according to the word of Moses; and there fell of the people that day about three thousand men."

The reading of this episode naturally evokes speculation as to what prompted Moses to break the Tables of the Law.   It is rightly assumed that this was the result of anger—yet a dispassionate reflection of the circumstances falls short of explaining the reasons for such dire wrath.   One must remember that idolatry had been a very common custom of the Jews and was practiced not only during the time of Moses but for several centuries after him[93].   How can Moses' anger be explained to make psychological sense? In accordance with the general principle that every reaction must be caused by a reason which is proportionate to its primary causes, only an extremely heinous sin could explain Moses' ire. But, if we bear in mind that the object of his wrath was a metallic calf to which the Jews had sacrificed (incidentally the Bible does not state the nature of the sacrifice), it becomes probable that what actually constituted the capital sin committed by the Jews on that occasion was a reversion to human sacrifice!

Aside from the fact that the calf venerated on that occasion was made of metal, other hints can be found in the Bible along the same lines. A sacrifice was made; it was a sacrifice which constituted the greatest possible crime in Moses' eyes. When punishment was meted out for such a crime, not only did Moses order a mass killing, but it was specified that each man kill someone near to him[94]. Whereas this passage could easily be interpreted to mean that none of the sons of Levi should have the slightest compunction because of friendly or family ties, we see here an instance of punishment according to the lex talionis —a crime that had consisted in sacrificing the sons to an idol could be expiated only by a holocaust of related people.

A biblical narrative which has some interesting points of contact with the story of the Golden Calf is found in the third chapter of Daniel. Nebuchadnezzar set up in the plain of Dura an enormous statue of gold and ordered all the people of his kingdom to worship it under threat that those who refused would be cast into "the midst of a burning fiery furnace." It was related to the king that three Jews—Shadrach, Meshach and Abednego—did not worship the golden image. The king called them to task and upon their continued refusal sentenced them to the designated punishment. Filled with fury, the king "commanded that they should heat the furnace seven times more than it was wont to be heated." When they were thrown in, however, not even one of their hairs was singed and the king, approaching the furnace, saw four men walking in the furnace. Whereupon he was convinced and made a decree imposing very severe punishments against anyone spoke against the God of the three Jews.

In this story we find an interesting association of the motif of a golden image set up for veneration and of a burning furnace used for sacrifice of humans, thinly disguished as punishment. The situation of competition between the God of the Jews and the pagan gods parallels exactly that found in the episode of the Golden Calf.

Returning to the episode of the Golden Calf, we have noted that it occurred during a time of great national stress. It was exactly at such times—and when great dangers were imminent—that human sacrifice was resorted to. On such occasions even the king could be sacrificed, as the highest price at which divine favor could be purchased. This was not only a custom of the early Semites. In the history of the Nordic countries, for example, it is found that the first king of Vermaland was burned in honor of Odin, to stop a great drought; Earl Haakon of Norway offered his son in sacrifice to Odin to obtain a victory. The peasants of many parts of Europe were wont, from time immemorial, to resort to a ritual of fire in seasons of distress and calamity, particularly when their cattle were attacked by epidemic diseases. These fires were called by the Teutonic people "Need Fire," sometimes "Wild Fire." This custom was occasionally practiced down to the first half of the nineteenth century in various parts of Germany, England, Scotland and Ireland, and among Slavonic people it lingered even longer[95].

Halloween is a residual of a Druidic feast of the greatest antiquity, which marked the end of the harvest and the beginning of winter. It was also the festival of Samhain, the lord of the dead, and on that night Samhain was supposed to assemble the souls of all who had died the previous year. Because of their sins, these souls had been confined in the bodies of lower animals, and the first of November (Celtic New Year's Day) Samhain released them from their ordeal. Horses and human victims were sacrificed. The human sacrifices were traditionally burned inside wicker cages shaped in the form of giants or large animals. This custom continued in medieval times in the form of burning black cats alive inside wicker cages, the cats being associated in the popular mentality with witches. Even today, in Ireland, in the Halloween parades it is traditional for the leader to wear a horse mask. Bonfires are lit in Ireland and in Scotland on Halloween night in our times. The jack-olantern with the flaming candle still bears witness today to the universality and timelessness of a cruel ancient motif which, in its ritual form, finds its typical expression in the Menorah.

# References

1.  *Exodus XXV*:31-4.
2.  *Jewish Encyclopedia.* N.Y.: Funk & Wagnalls Co., 1903. Chapter "Candlestick."
3.  E.g., lamps found at khirbath Sammaka near Carmel, in the ruins of Carthage, in a rock-cut tomb near Jaffa, in the Jewish catacombs at Venosa, at the entrance of a tomb at Wadi-al-Nahal, etc.
4.  *Exodus XL*:24.
5.  *Jewish Encyclopedia.* Chapter "Menorah."
6.  *Ibid.* Chapter "Amulet."
7.  Ginzberg, L. *Legends of the Jews, 3.* Philadelphia: The Jewish Publication Society of America, 1911, pp. 160-161.
8.  *Ibid.* p. 219. Still another legend is that God took white fire, red fire, green fire and black fire, and out of these four kinds of fire fashioned a candlestick with the prescribed decorations; even then Moses was not able to copy the candlestick, whereupon God drew its design upon Moses' palm, saying "Look at this and imitate the design I have drawn upon thy palm." But even this did not enable Moses to execute the commission, whereupon God bade him cast a talent of gold into the fire and the candlestick shaped itself out of the fire.
9.  Chapter "Numbers and Numerals."
10.  Chapter "Menorah."
11.  Gräme Rhind. W., 1859.
12.  *Jewish Encyclopedia.* Chapter "Candlestick."
13.  *Ibid.*
14.  Hastings, J. *Encyclopedia of Religion and Ethics, 10.* N.Y.: Scribner's, 1919, pp. 73-88.
13.  The identification of pieces of furniture and other inanimate objects with the human form, as commonly expressed in dreams, is too trite to bear stressing. For the sake of completeness, however, we will note that the association of the human and animal figure with lamps and candelabra can be traced back to the most ancient times. From Chaldea, Assyria, Etruria (Lehmann-Haupt, C. F., *Der Vorarmenisch-Chaldäische Bronze-Kandelaber des Hamburgischen Museums für Kunst u. Gewerbe,* 1929) and India (Robins, F. W., *The Story of the Lamp.* London: Oxford University Press, 1939, p. 82) we have numerous examples of lamps in which the stem is a human figure supported by legs ending in animal paws. Such zoomorphic features are, incidentally, found commonly even today in pieces of furniture and stoves. Roman lamps were often shaped as a human hand, usually representing Seilenos or a Negro, the latter having a sacrificial significance (Bartoli, P. S., *Le antiche lucerne sepolcradi figurate.* Rome,

1704). These particular forms were common among Romano-Egyptian lamps; the heads and faces especially seem to have emanated from Alexandria (Robins, *op. cit.*, pp. 58-59). Homer (Odyssey, vii, 100-103), in his description of the Palace of Alcinous, speaks of gold-sculptured candlesticks representing youths standing upon altars and holding flaming torches in their hands. Numerous similarities have been found between the Menorah and ceremonial lamps used in other religions. A very common type of Indian lamp represents the flower of the lotus set on a cup (Robins, *op. cit.*, p. 85). Indian temple lamps of the multiple reservoir type with seven or eight bowls are closely reminiscent of the Jewish Menorah and of the Hanukah lamp (*ibid.*, pp. 8, 82).

16. Hannay, J. B. *Sex Symbolism in Religion*. London: Religious Evolution Research Society, 1922, pp. 527-528.

17. *Jewish Encyclopedia*, Chapter "Luz."

18. Brugsch, H. K. *Religion und Mythologie der alten Aegypter*. Leipzig: J. C. Heinrichs, 1888.

19. Shu'aib, Terumah 36b-36c. Shibbale ha-Leket 3.

20. *Jewish Encyclopedia*. Chapter "Chemosh."

21. *Encyclopedia Britannica*. Chapter "Phoenicia." See also *Diodorus XX*:13.

22. Porphyry, De Abstin. ii, 56.

23. *Encyclopedia Britannica*. Chapter "Carthago."

24. *The Classical Review*. November, 1903.

25. Doane, T. U. *Bible Myths*. N.Y.: J. W. Bouton, 1883, p. 39.

26. *Encyclopedia Brittanica*. Chapter "Sacrifice."

27. Petrie, W. *Religious Life in Ancient Egypt*. London: Constable & Co., Ltd., 1924, pp. 35-36.

28. Groff, W. *On the Religious Significance of Sculptures and Paintings Among the Ancient Egyptians*. Cincinnati Art Museum, No. 899.

29. Sumner, W. G. and Keller, A. G. *The Science of Society*, II. New Haven: Yale University Press, 1928, pp. 1251-1289.

30. *2 Kings xxiii*:10.

31. *Jewish Encyclopedia*. Chapter "Moloch."

32. *Jeremiah xix:51, Leviticus xvii*:21 and *xx*:2-5.

33. *Encyclopedia Britannica*. Chapter "Moloch."

34. *Exodus XIII*:1-7, *XXXIV*:19-20.

35. A most interesting study on the subject is Sandor S. Feldman's "Notes on the primal horde." *Psychoanalysis and the Social Sciences*, I. N.Y.: International Universities Press, 1947, pp. 171-193.

36. *Numbers iii*:39-46.

37. *2 Kings iii*:27.

38. *2 Kings xiii*:3.

39. *2 Kings xxi*:6.

40. Hastings, J., *op. cit.*, 3. Chapter "Canaanites," p. 187.

41. *Ibid.*, 6. Chapter "First Born," p. 32.

42. Frazer, J. *The Golden Bough.* N.Y.: Macmillan, 1942, pp. 280-281.

43. Burder, S. *Oriental Customs.* London: Longman, Hurst, Rees, Orme, & Brown, 1822, p. 134.

44. Frazer, *op. cit.*, pp. 280-281.

45. Georg, E. *The Adventure of Mankind.* N.Y.: Dutton, 1931, p. 202.

46. Covarrubias, M. *Island of Bali.* N.Y.: Knopf, 1937, pp. 373.

47. *Funk and Wagnall's Standard Dictionary of Folklore, Mythology, and Legend.* N.Y..: Funk & Wagnall's, 1950. Chapter "Ashes."

48. Inman, T. *Ancient Pagan and Modern Christian Symbolism.* N.Y.: Peter Eckler Publishing Co., 1922, pp. 118-119.

49. *Jewish Encyclopedia.* Chapter "Baal and Baal Worship."

50. Ghillanij, F. W. *Die Menschenopfer der alten Hebräer.* Nürnberg: J. L. Schrag, 1842.

51. Hastings, J., *op. cit.*, I. Chapter "Aegean Religion," p. 145.

52. Shorter, A. W. *A Handbook of Egyptian Gods.* London: K. Paul, Trench, Trubner & Co., Ltd., 1937, pp. 96-98.

53. *Deuteronomy XXXII:17*, "They sacrificed to devils and not to God." *Psalms CVI:37*, "They sacrificed their sons and daughters to devils." *Leviticus XVII:7*, "They shall no more offer their sacrifices to S'irim" (hairy creatures).

54. *Mythology of All Races,* Vol.: Semitic; pp. 146-147.

55. Hastings, J. *Encyc. of Religions and Ethics,* Chapter: Canaanites. N.Y., 1911, p. 184.

56. Thompson, R. C. *The Devils and Evil Spirits of Babylonia.* London, 1903, p. xxxvi. The following poem gives a description of the idea the Babylonians had of "The Seven" (p. xlii):
> "Of the 7 (the first) is the South Wind,
> The second is a demon with mouth agape that none can
>   withstand,
> The third is a grim leopard that carrieth off children.
> The fourth is a terrible serpent,
> The fifth is a furious heat . . . .
> The sixth is a rampant . . . . which against god and king
> The seventh is an evil windstorm.
> These seven are the messengers of Anu, the king,
> Bearing gloom from city to city,
> Tempests that furiously scour the heavens
> Dense clouds that over the sky bring gloom. . . . "

57. *Ibid.*, pp. xlv-xlvi.
Assyrian poem on the seven spirits:
> "They scour from land to land,
> Driving the maid from her chamber,
> And the man from his house.

And the son from his father's house,
Knowing no mercy, they range against mankind.
They spill their blood like rain
Devouring their flesh and sucking their veins."

58. Thompson, *l.c.*, p. xliv. "A Syriac Charm":
"Seven accursed brothers, accursed sons, destructive ones, son of men of destruction!—We go on our hands so that we may eat flesh and we crawl along upon our hands so that we may drink blood. . . . Why do you creep along on your knees and move upon your hands?"

59. *Jewish Encyc.*, Chapter: Demonology.

60. Belial, another name for Satan, "had seven spirits of reception" at his service. *Reuben*, 2.

61. Hehn, J. *Siebenzahl und Sabbat bei den Babyloniern und im Alten Testament.* Leipzig, 1907.

62. *Matthew 12*, 45; *Luke, 11*, 26; *Mark, 16*, 9; *Luke, 8*, 2.

63. *Encyc. Britannica*, Vol. p. 77-.

64. *Ibid.*, Vol. 10, p. 453. Chapter Gnosticism.
This significance of the number seven seems confirmed by the many references we find in different mythologies, including the Semitic, to seven-headed monsters, dragons, serpents, hydras and witches. To quote only one, in Greek mythology Cerberus was at times pictured with seven heads. (Roscher, W. H., Sieben-u. Neunzahl im Kultus u. Mythus der Griechen. *Abh. d.k.Säch. Ges. d. Wiss.* Bd. xxiv, I. pp. 51 and 120.)

65. Keith, A. Berrisdale, *Mythology of all Races*, Vol. VI: Indian and Iranian.

66. Frazer, James G. *The Golden Bough*, abr. ed., pp. 108-109.

67. Stalnaker, Leo. *Mystic Symbolism in Bible Numerals.* Philadelphia: Dorance & Co., 1952.

68. *Num.* 23; 14, 29, 30.

69. *Lev.* 23; 8.

70. Webster, H. *Rest Days.* New York: Macmillan, 1916, p. 208.

71. *Ibid.*, p. 209.

72. *Ibid.*, pp. 209-210.

73. *Ibid.*, p. 210.

74. Hastings, J., *Encyc. of Religions and Ethics.* Vol. X: The Sabbath, N.Y., 1919; also Webster, *op. cit.*

75. *Lev.* xvi, 31 and xxiii, 26-32.

76. Webster, *op. cit.*, pp. 81-82.

77. According to Zimmerman, the word "Sabbath" is derived from the verb *shabátu*; i.e., to discontinue, to desist (the day on which the wrath of God subsides).

78. *Num.* xxxvii, 9-10. *Isa.* i, 8. Hos. ii:11.

80. *Ezek.* xx; 12 and 20. *Exod.* xxxi; 13-17.

81. *Exod.* xxxv; 3. *Num.* xv; 32-35.

82. Philo, in *De Decalogo*, 20 (ii. 197) wrote: "Seven is the image of God!"

Abraham, K., Der Versöhnungstag, 1920:   At the end of the day, after closing prayer and responses follows a seven-time repetition of "Jahveh is the only God."

83.  According to the *Jewish Encyc.*, Chapter: Moon, the moon was regarded by all Oriental nations as a divinity whose worship was forbidden to the Israelites (*Deut.* xvii. 3).

84.  The Jews practiced the cult of the "Queen of Heaven," making sacrifices to her, for a long time (*Jer.* iii, 18, xliv, 17; *Jewish Encyc.*, Chapter: Moon).

85.  *Exod.* xx; 4.

86.  *Holy Images.* London, 1940, p. 45.

87.  *Arch.* iii, *Par.* 113, 126.

88.  *Rosh as Shanah*, 246.

89.  Reported by Bevan, *l.c.*, pp. 51-52.

90.  *Baruch* vi, 4.

91.  *Mythology of All Races.*   Chapter: North American Mythology, pp. 290-291.

92.  *Op. cit.*, pp. 199-200.

93.  The persistence of calf worship long after Moses is evidenced by Jeroboam's placing in the sanctuaries of Beth-El and Dan images of Jahveh in calf form.   Similar images were found in the temple of Micah and perhaps were present in the temple of Gilgal.   In the temple of Solomon, twelve oxen on which rested the great laver showed a residual of bull worship among the Jews.

94.  *Exod.* xxxii; 25-28.

95.  Frazer, *op. cit.*, pp. 638-639.

## Chapter 19

# The Blessing of the Kohenites

SANDOR S. FELDMAN, M.D.

𝕱REUD, in his "The Case History of an Infantile Neurosis," says that "We bring with us phylogenetic patterns that, like some philosophical 'categories,' receive the life-impressions. . . . They are deposits from the civilized history of humanity. The Oedipus Complex that contains the child's relationships to his parents belongs to them. . . . If the impressions don't fit into the hereditary patterns, phantasy does them over again. . . . Just such cases prove the independent existence of the patterns. We can observe that pattern wins over experience."

Needless to say, not only the Oedipus Complex belongs to the patterns mentioned by Freud. As I see it, these phylogenetic patterns play a great part in group psychology, and without them we can hardly get on in the psychology of a people. In the life of the individual, as Freud says, the life-impressions don't occur according to pattern. My investigations resulted in the recognition that the individual, when in the group, returns to the phylogenetic patterns. In this lies the strengh of the customs, rites, and ceremonies. Path-finding analysts, Freud, and after him especially Reik, Roheim, and others, have given us the methods with which to work profitably in the hard and delicate field of folk-psychology. We must rest content that the investigation here is not so sure as in the analysis of an individual. But if we do it with due caution, the probability of the correctness of our findings may be accepted.

I applied the following method. (A) I thoroughly searched the whole history of the object of my investigation. I examined what it is today and what it was at the beginning. (B) I endeavored to find out the mental attitude towards the rite of those who have preserved and practiced it throughout the ages, and (C) what effect the rite had on those who believed in it. (D) I sought parallels to the rite in other ethnological fields. In A, B, and D, the investigations brought satisfactory results; not so in C. This has a reason of its own, and it is this, in my opinion: The rite belongs to a very deep and remote phylogenetic pattern to which the individual added very little. It is, therefore, very difficult to learn from the analysis of an individual what he feels when, as a member of the group, he conforms to the rite.

Children raised in a religious atmosphere make their own religious rites and ceremonies in the time when they need them most for the solution of their conflict; they abandon them when they can substitute them with other individual, neurotic means.

One of my patients, about ten years old, observed for two years most punctiliously and without any compulsion the strict Jewish dietary laws. He did it more rigorously than his environment because he needed them for the prevention of his incest-urges. He gave them up at the age of twelve when he got himself another mode of prevention, namely, he developed an extreme nausea bordering on fright, especially at meals, of the saliva of the mother and the others in the house.

Another patient of mine, in about her sixth year, began to observe most minutely all religious ceremonies. Frequent spyings at her parents' coitus engendered various conflicts in her that she tried to assuage by ritual observances. Later, when she developed different compulsion-neurotic symptoms, she abandoned them and lapsed into painful compulsatory doubts and hesitancies.

Freud sees similarity between religious ritualism and compulsion-neurosis. I see that the difference between the two is equally essential. A neurosis is the product of the individual himself. Religious observances seem to be imposed on man who, inclined to neurosis, escapes into religion when he is in need of it. He will give it up when he has found a substitute for it. He will repeatedly resort to it whenever he needs it again.

The normal man becomes religious according to the categories postulated by Freud of which he is not conscious. The neurotic, as a rule, can give reasons for his religiousness. Who is not neurotic has no reasons.

I chose for my object of investigation a rite of the synagogue that I experienced myself and by which I was deeply moved for a number of years. To refresh my memory of it, I visited an orthodox synagogue where they avidly preserve the old traditions and could rest assured that they observe the rite as it was done many centuries ago.

The rite is called "The Raising up of Hands" (Nesiath Kapayim) or "The Blessing of the Priests" (Birchath Kohanim). Its popular name is Duchan (Platform). It is done by the Kohenites, i.e., the reputed descendants of Aaron who, in the biblical narrative, is the high priest of the Hebrew tribes in the desert and a brother of Moses. The rite is traced back to the passage of Numbers vi. 22-27: "And the Lord spoke unto Moses, saying: Speak unto Aaron and unto his sons, saying: On this wise ye shall bless the children of Israel: ye shall say unto them: The Lord bless thee, and keep thee: the Lord make His face to shine upon thee and be gracious unto thee: the Lord lift up His countenance upon thee, and give thee peace. So shall they put My name upon the children of Israel, and I will bless them." The Kohenites stand up before the Ark, that, as a rule, is a platform (duchan) to which a few steps lead up, and which is the holiest place in the synagogue, and pronounce the blessing in a peculiar manner. The rite is done on all the festivals towards the end of the additional morning service (musaph). If the festival falls on a Sabbath, the rite is omitted, with the exception of the Day of Atonement (Yom Kippur) which is stronger than the Sabbath. But there are places when the rite is done even if a festival falls on a Sabbath. For long, in antiquity, the rite was performed daily and at every service. According to tradition (Tamid, v. 1), in the temple of Jerusalem the priests (kohanim) spoke the words of the blessing after the daily burnt-offering.

The minutiae of the rite are prescribed in the ritual code Shulchan Aruch Orach Chaim (128). Before the blessing the kohen must not drink wine or any other intoxicating beverage. Before he mounts the platform he shall wash his hands to the bones that connect them with the arm. It is thus that the priests did in the sancuary of yore. For this ablution no benediction is required, because the kohen washed already in the morning and pronounced the benediction.

The washing in the morning is, for all Jews, the most precisely prescribed in the same code: "He shall life up the vessel with the right hand and then put it into his left. First he must pour water on his right hand, then take the vessel in his right hand and pour on the left. He must do so three times alternating the hands. The water must reach the joint, in emergency to the end of the fingers. After the hands he must wash his face in honor of his Creator who, according to the Torah, made man in His image. He then rinses his mouth on account of the saliva accumulated therein, for the name of God must be pronounced in purity and sanctity. The water poured from a vessel must fall into a vessel. . . . The water of washing must not be used for any other purpose, for it became the water of the spirit of ununcleanliness. Before the washing he shall not touch with his hand his mouth, or his nose, or his eyes, or his ears, or any other opening. . . . Great care must be taken that the water come from a vessel drawn by human power. But in emergency . . . any fluid is permissible, even if it does not get on the hand by human act. The following must wash their hands: He who got up from bed, or comes from the lavatory or bath, or pared his nails, or had his hair cut, he who took off his shoes . . . cohabited sexually, cleaned his clothes, touched vermin, combed, touched covered parts of his body, came from the cemetery or from accompanying the dead to it. Lastly, one who let his blood."

Some of the precepts of the ablution of hands before meals, (if bread is eaten at it) are as follows: "All things must be removed from the hands that would not let water penetrate to his skin. One who has long nails must remove all dirt under them. Similarly, one must remove the rings, lest they be an obstacle to the water." On the hand of the Kohenite, before the rite of the blessing, the Levite pours the water. In the absence of Levites, the firstborn, "the opener of the womb," may do it. No one of the other Israelites may do it. Rather the Kohen shall do it himself, if a Levite or a firstborn is not present. "It is forbidden to the Kohen to mount the platform in shoes. He must remove them before the ablution."

The act is performed in the following way: The cantor calls aloud, "Kohenites," whereupon they, standing before the Holy Ark and facing it, pull their prayer-shawls (talith) over their heads, under which they stretch out their hands horizontally with the height of their shoulders, or a little above their head. The digits of the hands must be so arranged as to form five empty spaces. A space between the little and ring fingers and the middle and fore fingers; another one between the latter and the thumb; two other ones in the same way on the second hand. A fifth space is formed by bringing the two thumbs close to each other. There must be five spaces, as it is written: "Metzitz min ha'kerakim" ("He peereth through the lattice." Cant. ii. 9.) The numerical value of the Hebrew letter "h" that stands before "kerakim," is five[1]. In such a position the Kohenites repeat after the cantor every word of the blessing. I quote the whole verse of Canticles: "Hark! my beloved! behold, he cometh, leaping upon the mountains, skipping upon the hills. My beloved is like a gazelle or a young hart; behold, he standeth behind our wall, he looketh in through the windows, he peereth through the lattice."

"While the Kohenites bless the people they shall not look in any direction around them, that they shall divert not their attention from the blessing. They shall turn their gaze downwards. . . . The people shall hearken to the blessing with devotion, with their face turned towards the Kohenites. But they shall not look at the Kohenites, and the latter shall not look at their hands. The people also take the prayer-shawl over their face, that they look not there."

When the service approaches the rite of the blessing, commotion and excitement are noticeable in the worshippers. The Kohenites step out from their pews; they are in stockings, some also in slippers. They go through the ablution, and show that they are conscious of the solemnity and importance of their task. When I last saw the rite performed, the group of Kohenites consisted of three plain men, a private in the army, and a boy of fourteen. They didn't pay the slightest attention to the people. In such a great moment there exists no acquaintance, friend or relative. They are now Kohenites who at this moment stand far above the rabbi, even above the rich Jews in the front pews. They ascend the platform and face the Ark, and are soon wrapt in devout prayers prescribed to be said before the blessing. When the cantor exclaims: "Kohenim," they quickly turn to the public. One can see on the latter fear and utter devotion; many are all-covered with the prayer-shawals; others look aside, lest they be tempted to look at the Kohenites. On the right side of the platform stands the desk of the cantor, flanked by a number of singers of different ages, who are the closest to the Kohenim. They must be the most cautious not to look. They huddle together and look to the floor or aside. Two small boys stood before the platform. They were deeply touched; they gaped at the scene with open mouths and big eyes. After the blessing both the Kohenim and the people seem at rest; peace, joy, and satisfaction are reflected on their faces. The latter loudly and ostentatiously thank the former for the benefit bestowed upon them. With this the rite is concluded.

We cannot get a sufficient understaiding of the rite, unless we consider some particulars of it not mentioned in Scriptures.

In the temple of Jerusalem the Kohenites blessed the people every day, after the sacrifice of daily offering (tamid), from a platform in the hall of priests. This was an essential part of the service and concluded it. It is surprising that the priests were permitted to mount the platform on steps, as it is said to them: "Neither shalt thou go up by steps unto Mine altar, that thy nakedness be not uncovered thereon" (Gen. Ex. xx. 23). According to the commentators, the priest had to wear trousers while at the service, that his sex organ be covered. He had also to wear a girdle, that his heart see not his shame. The chassidim (pious) still use a girdle at the service; many do so the whole day. The idea is that the body consists of two parts: a pure upper one and a carnal lower one. A patient of mine suffering from claustrophobia was afraid that the buttons of his shorts might fall off and his pants slip down, and then. . . . To prevent the disaster, he fastened it to his shirt with a safety pin, or tied it with a cord to his body. He had a castration fear.

Before entering the sanctuary (Lev. x. 8), the priests were forbidden to take wine and strong drinks. Also today the Kohenites must not partake of any intoxicating fluid before the rite of the blessing. Frieda From-Reichmann pointed out that in the dietary ritual wine is a substitute for blood. The obsessional neurotic rite of ablution of hands and the prohibition of drinking of blood suggest a defense against murderous and cannibalistic urges, in short, against the temptation of the primal act. It is a defense against the wish to kill the faher and eat him. It is enjoined that the hands of the Kohen must be clean when the water is poured on them by a human act. It is to prevent self-deception that obsessional neurotics often do so. Let us not forget that the rite is performed before the Ark. There the Kohenites stand with their backs to the Ark and facing the public. It is significant that at the ablution only a Levite, who is inferior to the Kohen, may assist. The Kohen may do it himself, or a firstborn, "the opener of the womb."

The Kohen is the representative of God. He is that, among others, in the rite of the redemption of the firstborn (Numbers xviii. 14). Every "opener of the womb" belongs to God (Ex. xiii. 2), but he can be redeemed from a Kohen for five shekels. At the conclusion of the rite the Kohen pronounces the priestly blessing. In another Pentateuchal passage (Numbers iv. 13), it is said that the Levites are given to God and belong to Aaron and his sons. If the firstborn is the first only of the father, but he is not an "opener of the womb," no redemption is needed. The "opener of the womb" commits incest. He would also kill the father, as in the primal horde the firstborn must have been the ringleader in the doing away with the great father.

With the ablution the Kohen admits the primal sin and guards himself against its repetition. At the rite of the blessing the congregation identify themselves with the Kohenites who equally are of the people. No man was permitted to step on the threshold of the temple. It was the duty of the Kohenite keepers to prevent this. The taboo is sufficiently cleared up in two papers by Reik and Roheim. The latter proves that to tread on the threshold signifies a hostile intention against the master of the house and the wish to make the mistress of the house his own, sexually. According to Reik, it would indicate disrespect to the owner of the house by a displacement to the smallest. A survival of the keepers of the threshold might be the doorman before the mansions, and of the noble, the human and animal figures above gates, the cherubs of the Garden of Eden, and above the Ark in many a synagogue, the inscription on the door-post of the Jewish homes (mezuzah), the sphinxes, etc. The biblical book of Esther tells that when Esther wanted to approach the king in the interest of her people, she was afraid that the guard might kill her if she entered the king's room without being called by him, unless he held out to her his sceptre. This he fortunately did.

The injunction of taking off the shoes takes us further.

It is prescribed as follows:   "The Kohen is prohibited to go up with shoes to the platform where the blessing takes place.   He must remove his shoes before the ablution of the hands.   He must be careful that he put the shoes under the pew, that they be not seen.   Consideration for the public demands this."   Such is the rationalization of the theological commentators of tradition.   To remove the shoes is a very ancient custom.   Dr. G. Deutsch quotes the Talmud (Rosh Hashanah 31b), according to which the obligation of the Kohen to remove the shoes before the blessing remained in force after the destruction of the temple. No man was permitted to enter the temple with shoes.   This was not extended to the synagogues.   Till the present day a Jew is forbidden to wear shoes on the Day of Atonement, on the ninth of Ab. which is the traditional day of the destruction of the two temples, during the seven days of mourning (shivah), and on the seventh day of Tabernacles (Hoshanah Rabbah) at the morning service of the synagogue.   Footwear not made of leather has not been tabooed by Judaism.

A commentator of the Shulchan Aruch says that the reason for the prohibition of wearing shoes at the rite of the blessing is that the shoelaces might get loose, in which case the Kohen might be so busy with tying them again as to miss the rite, or a part of it.   The general opinion of the Jews is that the removal of the shoes is a sign of respect for the place.   The analytical investigation of the custom tells us something different and much more.   Analysts have tackled the theme already.   The investigation of shoe-fetishism enriched our knowledge in this matter with valuable material.

In the story of the thornbush God says to Moses: "Take off thy shoes from off thy feet, for the place whereon thou standest is holy ground" (Ex. iii. 5).   Joshua heard the same words when, after the crossing of the Jordan, he circumcised the Israelites with knives of flint at the "hill of prepuces" (Joshua v.).   From the occurrence of the two incidents, circumcision and the taking off the shoes, in the same passage, we may conclude that they stand in close relation to each other.   It is the acceptance of castration in order to demonstrate the giving up of incest.   Deutsch draws attention to an ancient Israelitish custom recorded in the book of Ruth (ch. v.): "Now this was the custom in former time in Israel concerning redeeming and concerning exchanging, to confirm all things: a man drew off his shoes and gave it to his neighbor: and this was the attestation in Israel" (v. 7).

Another ancient rite still practiced in Judaism, that of *chalitzah*, proves the castration-meaning of the removal of the shoes. The *chalitzah* rite is enjoined in Deuteronomy (xxv. 5) and is to absolve the elder brother, and also the other brothers, from marrying the wife of a brother who had died without an issue. "His brother's wife shall draw nigh unto him in presence of the elders and loose his shoe from off his foot and spit in his face and she shall answer and say: 'So shall it be done unto the man who doth not build up his brothers' House.' And his name shall be called in Israel The house of him that had his shoe loosed." Onan, though he performed the levirate marriage, had to die because he spilled the sperma on the ground and didn't want to build up his brother's house (Gen. xxxviii. 8). In the rite as it is done today a peculiar shoe is employed. The brother and the woman do as prescribed in the Bible.

Levy made the *chalitzah* the object of an analytical study[2]. He says, I believe very correctly, that the primary rite-object was the foot, from which the emphasis was later transferred to the shoe. Levy mentions that the shoes must be taken off in sacred places, on a fast-day, and in mourning. The defendant appears before the judge, the excommunicated and the prisoner must go, barefooted. The shoe, more correctly, the foot, is the symbol of power. To put the foot on something means ownership. Every place on which the Ottoman Sultans stepped belonged hypothetically to them. In a marriage custom the groom steps on the foot of the bride to signify that she is his property. Levy also mentions an ancient Jewish traditional rule that a buyer makes a field his own by walking the length and breadth of it. According to a Talmudic passage, the taking off of the shoe and handing it to the seller means to give up possession of something. Levy came to the conclusion that the foot symbolizes the penis and the shoe the vagina. By this he contradicts himself, as at the outset he says that the foot is the essential thing, and it was only later that the shoe took its place. In Levy's interpretation of the *chalitzah*-rite, the brother-in-law gives up his right to his sister-in-law, for which reason the latter pulls the shoe off the former's foot, that is, her vagina. As I see it, the taking off of the shoe is a castration symbol. The sister-in-law symbolically castrates the brother of her deceased husband, with the assistance and consent of the community. In the story of the adventure of the Argonauts the one-sandalled Jason loses his one sandal while he transports Hera, who is dressed as an old woman, over the river Enipeus. . . . Jason, the oracle says, will depose Pelias from his royal throne[3].

A patient of mine, who suffered from a foot-and-shoe fetishism, had an urge that he anxiously bid from all, namely, to polish the shoes of his father whenever he could get hold of them. Analysis showed that it was the condensed expression of coitus with the vagina of the mother and, at the same time, the veneration of the penis of the father. Another patient, the one who, as I told already, was afraid that his shorts would slip, and therefore tied them fast to his body, suffered from street phobia. Especially in wet weather and whenever his feet perspired, even slightly, his walk became faltering and if he forced it, he felt depressing anguish. In analysis it came out that the germ of his neurosis was an incident that he experienced once, or several times, when a child of three. He lay in bed between his parents. His mother noticed that he recoiled from her pubic hair, whereupon she teasingly drew his hand to her genital. The little boy feared that very much. Later, through his frequent walks with his mother, the infantile anguish was displaced to the shoe and foot, in fact, to the act of walking. As can be seen, the shoe symbolizes the vagina in relation to the foot, but in relation to the earth (mother) the shoe-foot symbolizes the penis. Robitsek equally recognized that the shoe may be a substitute both for the penis and for the vagina[4].

The *Politika*, a daily paper in Belgrade, Yugoslovia, in its issue of July 29, 1928, contained an illustrated article of a rare wedding custom still practiced in the Serbian village of Lavcani. After the wedding the bride and the mother-in-law go to a well where the former takes off one shoe and gives it to the latter. The old woman fills the shoe with water and hands it to the bride to drink. The village people interpret this really rare and strange custom to mean that the newest member of the family symbolically pledges obedience to her mother-in-law, and veritably humiliates herself before her.

All I said and quoted above confirms me in the opinion that

the Kohenites take off their shoes before going to the platform to bestow their blessing on the worshippers as a symbol of submission. This, in truth, means castration, the loss of the penis.

I quoted some of the precepts of the ablution of hands. The water must be poured on the hands by human act, either by the Kohen himself, or by a Levite, or by a firstborn, the "opener of the womb." By that the Kohenites manifest that they want to free themselves of and to keep from the primal sin, namely, the urge and wish to kill the father. Wine, as we know, is an old substitute for blood, for the blood of the father. It is for this reason that the priests must not partake of wine before the service.

But the killing of the father is not the only wish from which all must get away. They must equally guard themselves against incest. The injunction to take off the shoes demonstrates that they must submit to castration, in order that they become worthy to stand up before the Ark that contains the scroll of the Law, a representative of Jahweh, whom the Kohenites are to impersonate, and with whom they identify themselves in the rite of the blessing.

Reik says that "a blessing means to utter words that will take effect in the future. . . . In the ancient world a blessing is not a pious wish, but an act to become potent in reality[5]." In the Old Testament, blessings and curses occur very frequently. According to Reik, it is attested by the respective biblical texts that the essence of a blessing is a permit for the sex act, naturally only with persons permitted; moreover, the promise of the fertility of the womb and the possession of the land, in short, fertility and the mother-soil. The primary aim of the priestly blessing is to secure the grace of God. And the biblical blessing-texts evince that God manifests his grace by granting fertility and soil. In the course of time the aim extended to include also other boons: the cure and prevention of sickness and the non-fulfillment of malignant dreams. In old Jewish belief one-sixtieth of the dreams are true. The priests are regarded as prophets. The power of prophecy consists of sixty parts. In the blessing the Kohen represents God, is identical with Him, and the people become one with the divinity through the blessing. Great and saintly Jews bless their children, and the people, before their death. Thus, they transmit their power to others.    Extraordinary men, before their death, and but once only in life, can say words that are miracle working and bring blessing[6].    When Esau was cheated of his birthright by Jacob, he exclaimed despairingly:    "Hast thou but one blessing, O my father?"    (Gen. xxvii. 38).    Jacob doesn't bless Reuben, his eldest son, before his death, to punish him for cohabiting with Bilhah, his concubine.    (Gen. xxxv. 22).    He says to him: "Reuben, thou art my firstborn, my might, and the first-fruits of my strength; the excellency of dignity, and the excellency of power.    Unstable as water, have not thou excellency; because thou wentest up to thy father's bed; then defiledst thou it—he went up to my couch" (Gen. lxix. 2-4).

The rite of the Kohenites, however, is not exhausted by its two component elements discussed above.    The ritual code stipulates that the people must not look at the priests while the blessing is given, and even the priests themselves must not look at their hands while they are stretched out for the blessing.    A passage in the Talmud has it that one shouldn't look at the rainbow, at rulers, and at the Kohenites (Chagiga 16a). All three are father, respectively, god-symbols.    Behind the Kohenites is God; the Shechinah (divine glory) looks on the people, says the Midrash Rabbah.    A commentator of the Shulchan Aruch says that outside Palestine it would be permitted to look at the Kohenites, but it is not advisable to do so, because one might think not of the prayer, but of something else.

To look at somebody else means to desire and overpower him.    The look at God might arouse in one cravings for things that are due only to God.    He might want to get the better of God and have Him in his power.    We read in the scene at the thornbush:    "And Moses hid his face, for he was afraid to look upon God" (Ex. iii. 6).    The people were warned not to get close to Sinai, when God descended to the top to reveal the ten commandments.    As can be seen, the Bible affirms the primal fear of fiery looks and thundering voices that are mentioned by Hermann.    In the Sinai scene God is afraid lest the people get near the mountain and attack Him (Ex. xix).    To prevent this He overawes the people; there it is said:    "And all the people perceived the thunderings, and the lightning, and the voice of the horn, and the mountain smoking; and when the people saw it, they trembled and stood afar off" (Ex. xx. 15).    The prohibi-

tion of looking is connected with the primal scene. To this I
can adduce an experience of my own. In my childhood I looked
at the blessing priests, though I was warned not to do it, lest
I become blind. The general belief is that by looking one's vision
gets dimmed. A patient of mine, in whose neurosis the watching
of the primal scene played a great part, looked at the blessing
though he knew that blindness might be punishment. He did
it, which means that he protested against the prohibition of
looking. In his *Totem and Taboo*, Freud speaks of the fear of
looking at the primeval father. In my opinion, the taboo of
looking means that the son must not look when the father
cohabits with the mother, lest he desire her and feel hatred for
him. In this case the father will become angry and stare at him
with his awesome eyes, and shout at him thunderingly. According to Reik, the sound of the shofar (ram's horn) is the last
rattle of the murdered primeval father-totem animal that
frightens the people, because it reminds them of the primal sin,
the killing of the father, respectively, the urge to do so.

The peculiar division of the fingers at the blessing which
is a striking and essential feature of the rite, attracted attention
of many a scholar, as well as of two analysts. Even the
Kohenites themselves must not look at their own hands while
they give the blessing. We shall try to prove that the meaning
of this is that the hand is peculiarly God Himself. This explains
why neither the people, nor the priests, who represent God, must
not see God. In the view of Maimonides the looking disturbs
devotion. Rabbi Joseph says that it dims the eyesight. But
Rabbi Chagi says that he dared to look with no harm to him.
In the Midrash Rabbah can be read that the looking weakens
the eyes.

Through the lattice-like openings that the Kohenites form
with their fingers, God looks at the people. The gaze of the eyes
can be angry and frightening, but also loving, affectionate, and
sensuous. Ferenczi points out the identity of the eye and the
genital[7].

Of the position of the hands we find contradictory opinions
in Jewish tradition. The Shulchan Aruch makes it strictly obligatory, other authorities not. In view of the Shiboleth Hale-
keth the Kohenites tremble, for which reason they hold their
hands stretched out. It is evident to this commentator that the

position of the hands is not essential. Elia Gaon enjoins the stretching, but not the five spaces made with the fingers. Asherit is very particular about the spaces, as is the Shulchan Aruch. In the interpretation of the Midrash, God is behind the priests, through whose fingers He looks at the people. The latter wanted the blessing from God Himself, but He assured them that He stands behind the priests. It strikes one that those who stick to the five windows of the fingers motivate it by referring to "He peereth through the lattice" of Canticles, where in Hebrew there stands the letter "H," the numerical value of priests. Who is he that peers through the lattice? Presumably again God. According to the *Juedisches Lexicon*, Canticles consists of monologues and dialogues of two lovers who are happy in their union and long for each other sorrowfully when separated. When the biblical canon was made up there was much objection to taking it into Scriptures, but Rabbi Akiba prevailed. He interpreted it allegorically to mean a covenant of love between God and Israel; therefore it is the most holy. The Church takes it similarly as an allegory, but of Jesus and the Church, or of God and Mary. In Wetzstein's view, Canticles is a collection of wedding songs recited for seven days following the union. The text mentions King Solomon as the author, but this is wholly out of question. In the interpretation of modern scholars, it is a dialogue between the mother-goddess and her son-consort[8].

It is certain that the worshippers imagine behind the five-windowed lattice, made up by the fingers of the priests, God whom they love dearly, and who, in turn, looks at His people with extreme affection. Freud says, in his "Group-Psychology and Ego-Analysis": "We may, therefore, venture the hypothesis that love-relationships—expressed indifferently, ties of sentiment —make the essence also of the mass-soul." Here Freud, as Roheim[9] remarks, describes the libidinous structure of the mass. In the same place Freud continues: "A primary mass is an aggregate of individuals who put one and the same object in place of their Ego-Ideal and thereby bring about in their ego an identification among themselves." This sensuous bond is essentially homosexual. But a mass establishes a libidinous bond not only among themselves; they do so also with the leader. We saw in the Kohenite blessing that the priests are identical with God and the congregation both with God and the priests. Ferenczi says[10] that homosexuality is brought about, not only by a reaction to a very strong heterosexual urge, but also by way of regression, namely, by identification owing to object-love. A man gives up a woman as his outward object of love, and then sets her up in himself, puts her by identification in place of his ego-ideal. The man becomes feminine and wants a woman whereby he restores the heterosexual relationship. Roheim says[11] that "in many cases homosexuality develops when a man, instead of taking a mother-substitute for his love-object, identifies himself with her. On the other side, the consequence of this is the establishment of a paternal object relationship."

I proved that in the blessing of the Kohenites the congregation and the priests accept castration and give up their hostile attitude towards the father. This, as we see, has two consequences: on one side, identification with the father, the permission to become mature and a father, to possess the land and be fertile and to live a sexual life. On the other side, as it can be seen, the congregation thus establishes, in a homosexual form, the same relationship between itself and God that, as it observes, feels, and knows, only exists between father and mother.

The worshippers don't look at the priests and God, as Moses didn't look at God on Sinai. God Himself, as we know, warned the people not to get close to the mountain on which He dwells, lest He destroy them. One who sees the rite, or experiences it, gets the impression that in it the scene of Sinai is repeated on a small scale. The worshippers engage themselves out of fear in fervent and devout prayers, they huddle together, cover their faces, don't dare to look up, they, as it were, prostrate themselves before Yahweh. In return, the divinity promises to defend them. As in the Canticles, God and Israel become each other's lovers. There flashes through this homosexual tie the original Oedipus-situation, the dangers of which the rite was to abolish. The people get the original and forbidden incestuous pleasure, though in a different form. My investigations prove Reik[12] to be right according to whom the Sinai scene, and the blessing of the Kohenites which I regard as a repetition of it, is in its essence the repression of the urge to hate the father and to kill him, and the victory of the love and recognition of God over the unconscious hatred and anger. Reik[13] thinks that the masks of the savages serve magic purposes; they transform those who belong to the tribe into demonic creatures and totem-animals; they establish a primitive identification with the father. If I remember well, in another place Reik[14] says that the swaying of Jews at prayer, in certain times with phylacteries and prayer-shawl, corresponds to the dances of the savages which are the movements of the totem-animal with which the group and the individuals identify themselves.

Abraham[15] made use of Reik's paper on the Shofar in his interpretation of the priestly blessing and the position of the hands in it. He was equally struck by the prescribed spaces with the fingers, the right meaning of which, he believed, was not found yet. "The fourth and fifth fingers must be separated from the three others and they must remain in that forced position during the whole ceremony. The great significance attributed to the position of the fingers in both hands is evinced by the custom of having them engraved on the tombstone of a Kohenite as the emblem of priesthood. Taking into consideration the aversion of Judaism to pictoral representation[16] this exception must be meaningful." In the course of his investigations Abraham came to the conclusion that "in the priestly blessing the Kohenites (priests) imitate with the finger-spaces the cloven hoofs of the totem (ram). The prayer-shawl made of wool is a suitable substitute for the skin of the ram. The Kohenites, therefore, are in the blessing the totem, that is, like God." He says furthermore: "We have no other choice but to see in the priestly blessing . . . a totemistic rite." Frieda Fromm-Reichman[17] accepts Abraham's conclusions. The priest's task is to mediate between God and the people. He is the totem-animal, he is identical with God. Eder[18] similarly holds the same opinion.

As can be seen, I arrived at the same conclusion, with the difference that I did not contemplate any connection between the finger-spaces and the cloven hoofs of the totem-animal. The Kohen, when he stands on the platform wrapped in the prayer-shawl and his spaced hands stretched out for the blessing, is, indeed, an imitation of the totem-animal. It is true, the hoof of the totem-animal is cloven only into two parts, whereas the hand of the Kohen shows three parts in the blessing. As it is, Abraham arrived at the right conclusion, but in an erroneous way, at least, as far as the hands are concerned. I am afraid Abraham didn't know sufficiently the ancient sources relative to the priestly blessing. He should have delved into the meaning also of the "five windows."

The original biblical injunction that I quoted literally at the outset concludes with the words: "So shall they put My name upon the children of Israel, and I will bless them." Indeed, the essence of the blessing is that the Kohenites pronounce the proper name Yahweh in the blessing. The ineffable name was thus laid on the people who thereby became identical with God.

It is an everyday experience in the analysis of neuroses that what is the most essential to the understanding of the sickness is forgotten and lost in the course of time. The task of the analysis is to recover it and bring it to the surface, otherwise the solution of the problem cannot be a success scientifically and therapeutically. The same is true of the rite of the blessing.

For more than two thousand years the pronunciation of the name of YHVH has been omitted, but it has been done covertly, in a disguised form, in the blessing. I mean, the bearing of the hands. In the course of my investigations I found that most pious scholars, for obvious reasons, neglect this fact. The *Real-Encyklopedie*, edited by Hamburger, mentions that in the time of the second temple the most essential feature of the blessing was the pronunciation of the four-lettered name of God, namely, YHVH. In the time of the rule of the Syrians, after the death of Simon, the high priest, it was decreed not to pronounce any longer the tetragrammaton in the blessing. They might have done so out of fear that the rite might be misunderstood. Perhaps it had some resemblance to a pagan Greek rite. Some priests pronounced it, but in a manner that could not be discerned. They used a melody that enabled them to do so. This peculiar melody has been preserved to this day. The Kohenites still chant it when they utter the words of the blessing[19]. Rabbi Tarphon said that he listened so carefully to the words as to be able to get the true name out of them, despite the melody. Later they forbade saying the name even with the melody, for it must not be pronounced in any way outside Palestine. Commentators of the Old Testament say the pronunciation of the tetragrammaton as Jehovah originated with Luther and is totally false. No man knows how the name was pronounced. A great man and a miracle-doer is he who knows the mystery of the name of God (Bal Shem, The Master of the Name).   In common talk, when not praying, the Jews are still very careful not to utter even those names of God that are permissible to pronounce. Thus, they don't say Elohim, but Elokim.   They do so even in non-Hebrew languages.   In Hungarian, they don't write "Isten" (God) but Ist'n.   The third commandment forbids uttering of the divine name in vain.   According to Jewish tradition, God had a name consisting of 42 or 72 letters.

A rabbinical opinion advises that at the blessing the fingers be so placed as to form the divine name Shaday (SHDY).   This word is seen on the visible part of the Mezuza (amulet) placed on the door-post.   I hold that the position of the hands was one of the most essential features of the rite.   The Jewish theologians differ greatly in their prescriptions of the rite.   But all agree that every word of the biblical blessing has significance.   Some don't attribute any importance to the position of the fingers; others recommend that the fingers be held asunder: again others say that the right thing to do is to make five windows with them, etc.   I cannot enter here into a minute discussion of these opinions.   Rabbi Bachya, in his *Magen Abraham*, says what is most pertinent:   "The priests must firmly keep their hands outstretched, and must symbolize with their fingers the name of YHVH."   Rabbi Bachya, who was rabbi in Saragossa, Spain, and died in 1340, is the author of a mystic commentary to the Old Testament.   In his book, *H'Emuno*, the manuscript of which is kept in Oxford, he deals with the various names of God.   God (YHVH) has many additional names.   As to the first name, Bachya does not tell how it could be symbolized with the fingers. But he says that those who know Hebrew will find it out by themselves.   As to the name of Shaday, the method is known. In his *Magen Abraham*, Bachya says that the priests, when they lifted up their hands for the blessing, symbolized with their fingers the name of Yahweh.   Others believe that this refers to the name Shaday.   The thumb was the Daleth, the little finger denoted the Yod, and the three intermediate fingers the Shin.

We see Jewish tradition has two precepts in the position of the hands at the priestly blessing.   Firstly, the fingers must be so arranged that they form five windows through which God can look at the people.   Secondly, the fingers must denote the name of God. The divine name expressed with the fingers shall be laid upon the people.

All signs would indicate that the greatest importance is the letter "Shin" which has three stalks. The prescribed position of the hand clearly shows this letter. The straps of the phylacteries, both of the hand and of the head must be so placed that they delineate the letter. Reik and Langer discuss this in their papers[20]. Langer draws our attention to the three stalks of the letter and to the genital meaning of the number three. Spiez[21] does the same. Alexander and Graber[22] equally point to the genital meaning of the number. The strap of the phylacteries must be wound three times round the middle finger and then three times round the hand. The middle finger is called Ammah in Hebrew, which also denotes the penis. While the winding is done the worshipper recites a betrothal-formula which is taken from Hosea ii. 21-22. It ends with: "And I will betroth thee unto me forever . . . and thou shalt know the Lord." In Hebrew "to know" also means to cohabit. Langer, leaning on S. Schueck's *Sidur Rasban*, says: "The going of the bride around the groom three times at the Jewish wedding directly corresponds to the threefold winding of the hand-phylactery." Langer quotes Bachofen to the effect that the finger is to signify the creative and nutritive energy: "Isis gives the Malcanderson the finger instead of the breast for food." In mythological thinking the finger means the penis. Hermann equally points to the erotogenic role of the finger. Langer[23] does the same also in his "A Contribution to the Function of the Jewish Roll on the Doorpost."

There is a connection also between the finger and the name. Langer, taking his support from Mahler, mentions that "Egyptian dignitaries carried the initials of the royal name of the Pharaoh—who was the incarnation of God—on the left arm, that is, on the same spot where the pious Jews place the box of the hand-phylacteries that contain passages of the holy Torah."

In our days all kind of fun is made with the finger, which expresses persons, or as a rule, sexual acts. A prophet of Israel promises divine favor: "If thou take away from the midst of thee . . . the putting forth of the finger, and speaking vanity" (Isa. lviii. 9). Hermann[24] says that the fingers may mean the family.  The Hebrew letter Shin that the Kohenites imitate at the blessing signified teeth or the penis, according to Zoller[25] in the ancient Sinaitic script.  He shows that the shape of the same letter denoted the penis in the Egyptian hieroglyphs.  The meaning of the finger as the penis is evinced also by the "Wolfsmann," whose fantasy speaks of a finger-wound.  Freud[26] shows that this means fear of castration.  Marie Bonaparte[27] equally says that the finger may be equated with the penis.  She sets forth in her paper that on amulets there is found the outstretched arm, as *mano cornuta*, when the little and the forefingers are turned upwards and the other downwards, and as *mano fica*, when the thumb is put between the second and third fingers.  These three fingers signify protection from peril.

Name, hand, finger, and penis form a series.  In common life the penis is often called by different names.

Osterley[28], in his paper, "The Cult of Sabazios," says that long before the appearance of Christianity the cult of the Greek Sabazios was wide-spread among the Jews.  Sabazios was identified with Zeus, Mithra, and, especially, with Dionysos[29]. Sabazios was a god of agriculture, vegetation, and fertility.  He had many symbols, among others, the mouse and the serpent. In his cult the serpent played a great part, which, in the interpretation of scholars, means coitus between god and the worshippers[30].  The worshipper is the woman.  A prayer-overall of leather is used in the ritual.  This is explained by analysts as to signify rebirth.  The worshipper is the fetus, the leather the uterus.  The Jews wanted to imitate the cult and were angrily scored for it by rabbis of the Talmud.  The Sabazios-hand had a prominent role in the ritual.  In the hand the thumb and the first two fingers next to it stand upright, the two others are bent downwards.  The hand is always made of bronze.  It is, as a rule, hollow and placed on a stand.  The Sabazios hand had a votive and protective significance.  The three upright fingers probably mean a triad.  Many such hands were found.  On one the god is seen sitting between the thumb and the two other upright fingers, and underneath it a mother with her child is seen.  Here we have the trinity: father, mother, and child.  The Catholic church took over the Sabazios hand and made it a symbol of the trinity.  In ancient Christianity the priest held his hand in such a way when he blessed the people at the end of the mass. This was the Benedictio Latina. The Benedictio Graeca was different. In it the middle finger was bent downwards and the thumb crossed over it, and the three others were turned upwards.

I find that in the blessing the emphasis was transferred from the spoken word, namely, the name of God, to the written word. Zoller, in his study mentioned above, quotes Berthelet: "To the written words is perhaps attributed a greater power than to the spoken one. The cultural progress, manifested by the invention of the script, filled the naive man of antiquity with uneasy fear. To him peculiar forces must have been hidden behind the letters."

The uttered and written name means the penis in the unconscious. To the former I can quote examples from analytical practice. As to the written name, I make mention of two patients of mine who guarded themselves against signing their name when they wrote to a woman to whom they were or wanted to be bound by a love-relationship. In both the reluctance came from castration-fear.

In the blessing the fingers of the two hands form the word Shaday. The thumb and the four fingers adjoining it make the three-stalked "Shin." The right thumb makes a stalk, the second and third fingers make another stalk, the fourth and fifth ones the third stalk, of the three-stalked Hebrew letter "Shin." On the left hand an inverse "Daleth" is made up, as in a rectangle, by the thumb and the two adjoining fingers, and the "Yod" by the last two fingers.

In the week-day morning prayer, it is obligatory to the Jew to put on the phylacteries. With the strap, a "Shin" is made on the left hand to indicate the Shaday. The investigations of Abraham, Reik, and Langer, show that the worshippers, when wearing the phylacteries, identify themselves with the primeval totem-animal father. 1 compute that with the strap they, as it were, write the name of God upon their hands.

The biblical passage enjoins that the name of the divinity be put on the people of Israel. We have no idea of how the name of God was pronounced in the temple of Jerusalem. We equally don't know anything of how the Kohenites manipulated their fingers at the blessing there. All we know of all these things dates from the time of the Diaspora when the original pronunciation of the name was forgotten and supplementary names were used. In time the taboo of pronouncing the divine name was extended also to the supplementary names, for which reason they signified it with the fingers in the ritual of the synagogue.

In the center of the rite stood the pronunciation of the name. Only in it could the name be uttered and could the people hear it. The Kohenites were permitted to pronounce it, as they were consecrated for that purpose. Since in the Diaspora there is no recognized priesthood in the biblical sense, the consecration is done only on certain occasions and for temporary purposes, with the prohibition of wine, ablution of hands, and taking off of shoes. The meaning of these precepts we learned to understand.

The fact that the tetragrammaton could be pronounced only in certain circumstances and with certain ceremonies, shows clearly that the name could not be pronounced and heard otherwise. Why did God so zealously guard His name? In all probability, because the name is identical with God Himself to whom no mortal must get near. To utter a name means, as Reik proved, to exercise power over its bearer. In the Bible it occurs several times that God, as a reward and for protection, changes names. So Jacob was named Israel, Saray was made Sarah, Abram was called Abraham. In the analytical literature the problem received already some attention, among others, by Abraham and Stekel. May I mention here an interesting Jewish custom that is still widely practiced among the pious. A critically sick child is given an additional name, to save him from death decreed for him. If he is called Shalom, another name, let us say, Jacob, is added. Shalom was sentenced to die, not Shalom Jacob. By that God is given a loophole to exercise mercy He is asked for by special prayers.

In our analytical practice we can often hear from patients that when they are introduced and their name is mentioned, they feel anxiety. An old patient of mine who consulted me said that he stutters when he tells his name. An impotent patient of mine, now in analysis, gets frightened whenever he hears his name mentioned behind him. I explain this to be a castration anxiety, that with his name, his genitals, his life, might be taken. I observed in two children that they say the name of the father with fear mixed with shyness. To pronounce a name means: to unite with its bearer, to overwhelm him, to attack him. The great significance of the name is evinced by the saying "nomen est omen"; by the experience that many hold in it high or in low estimation, or are ashamed of it; by the care with which it is chosen; by the wish to change it; by the belief that with it the ancestors are kept alive; by the custom to give the child an ancient name; to give a maiden a name by marrying her; by such sayings as: "he bears my name," "he brought shame on my name," "he besmirched my name," "I forbid that he bear my name," "don't take my name into your mouth," etc.

Summing up, I see in the rite of the blessing of the Kohenites a Freudian phylogenetic pattern that symbolically reflects several stages in the sexual development of man and in the unfolding of the Super-Ego.

The father, with his fiery and fearful eyes, deters and overawes the youth about to turn against him. The aim of the youth is to make an end to the physical and sexual power of the father and to commit incest. For fear of punishment they must constrain themselves and rather acquire the love of the father. By means well known from obsessional neurosis, by not drinking wine and with the ablution of hands, they ward off the parricidal and cannibalistic urges; by the acceptance of castration, by taking off the shoes, they give up incest. By this they win the love of the father, even his amorous love, and between the two there is established a homosexual bond that unites them. The father's overawing and threatening eyes, even his penis, are turned into loving eyes, into a loving penis, and through the lattice made with the fingers God looks affectionately at his people, Israel. He appoints his priests, the Kohenites, who with the rite made themselves fit for the task, as His representatives to bless the people. The blessing is done in such a way that with the hand that symbolizes the paternal penis the Kohenites put upon the people the divine name that equally symbolizes the paternal penis. The god-father and the people with the penis thus joined together, as it were, establish a friendship, I may say, conclude a blood-covenant.

The blessing is given by the divine hand that, as a protecting and defending phallus, rises over the people. With the putting on of the hand-phallus, that is, the divine name, of god-father upon the people, the latter's penis becomes identical with that of the father. By the castration inflicted upon it the people didn't suffer any loss (only pain); it rather won by it. Like the paternal penis, also, that of the people can now live its sexual life without any threats and danger; through the land given to its possession it gets back the lost mother, the castrated penis reaches the size of that of the father, and both the land and the people are blessed. Blessed, therefore, is he who renounces the repetition of the primal sin and incest. And cursed is he who sticks to them.

In the course of our investigations we familiarized ourselves with the Sabazios-hand. The book by Seligman gives a fine illustration of it. Between the thumb and the adjoining two fingers held together sits the father, and in the palm, as in a cave, the mother with the infant.

We saw the connection of the oath with begetting, the position of the hand at the oath, with which a man proves that the child is his child. Finally, we got the impression that the three fingers are a trinity, that of the father-mother-child.

It is my opinion that the original and deep meaning of the blessing takes us to this trinity, on which the rest is only layers. Again we get an excellent example of the "series-formation" that was discovered by Freud, and that occurs often in mental life. With the finding of a drive to hold onto and to run away, Hermann took us a decisive step forward. He points out very emphatically that in it can be seen the great significance of the mother-child relation in life and neurosis of the adult. This circumstance plays an important part also in the blessing; it is complemented and made perfect by the addition of the father. Blessed is the condition in which father, mother, and child remained together, were together, in perfect harmony.

The development of the libido disturbs this happiness. The described complications prove this sufficiently. The aim of the ritual is to eliminate the complications that arise in the course of the sexual development and hinder the permanency of the happy trinity.

In the last analysis, the blessing wants to say: "I, the father, who begot you, demand that you renounce your urge of parricide, your desire to cohabit with my wife, your mother, and that you assure me that I haven't to fear you, that you subject yourself to my authority. If you fulfill all these requirements you become worthy of my blessing, that is, to get back to the infantile situation in which we three, I, mother, and you, lived in an undisturbed union and happiness. As a token of this I put on your head three fingers of my hand, that is the symbol of the trinity."

I am aware of the incompleteness and deficiencies of my paper. But a more exhaustive discussion of the subject, its comparison with the puberty rites and other phenomena, transcends my ability and knowledge.

# References

1.  The Hebrew letter "h" has a great mystic meaning in Judaism: The four lettered name of God is Yahweh (YHWH). The name was originally Yahu (YHU), to which a second H was added. Abraham's name was changed from Abram to Abraham, Saray's to Sarah, Joshua to Johoshua. In a few places in the Bible Jehoseph occurs instead of Joseph, etc.

2.  Die Schuhsymbolik im juedischen Ritus, in the *Monatsschrift für die Wissenschaft des Judentum,* vol. 62.

3.  O. Rank. Beitraege zur Mythenforschung, p. 399. Medea is a mother-symbol. The passage across the river expresses the coitus, respectively, incest. The loss of one sandal means castration. That Jason kills his father and cohabits with the mother, as told, stands in the middle of the story, but belongs to the end of it.

4.  Der Kotillon. Intern. Psychoanalyt. Verlag.

5.  Psychoanalytische Studien zur Bibelexegese. Jakobs Kamf, *Imago.* 1919, 5.

6.  Juedisches Lexikon, article "Jakobsegen."

7.  Ferenczi, Zur Augensymbolik, *Intern. Zeitschrift*, i. 1913, and *Ibid.* his "Reiben der Augen ein Onanicersatz," where he points to the identity of the eye and the genital. Reitler, Zur Augensymbolik, *Ibid.* See also Hollos, *Int. Zeitschr.* ix. The penetrating eye threatens with castration those who touch it. The loving eye protects from evil. It is evident that in the blessing the divine eyes are a penis-symbol. On the harmful effect of the eye much material is found in Seligmann's "Der Boese Blick."

8.  Hide and seek is a much-liked play between mother and child. The five fingers of the hand are spread over the face in a way that allows the eyes to see. The players thus hide, yet see.

9.  "Voelkerpsychologisches," that is also a review of Freud's Group-Psychology. *Intn. Zeitschr.* viii.

10. In a review of the same book and in the same issue.

11. *l. c.*

12. Reik in *Das Ritual.*

13. "Die Pubertatsriten der Wilden," in *Das Ritual.*

14. Die Gebetmantel und Gebetriten der Juden. Cf. Langer, Die Jüdischen Gebetriemen. Both in *Imago,* 1930.

15. Der Versöhnungstag. *Imago,* 1920.

16. Judaism forbids only representations of human and animal figures, not of hands.

17. *Imago* i. 27.

18. *Imago,* 1933.

19. Following Reik, the tune in the blessing might be reminiscent of the last growling of the "Urvater."

20. Reik, Gebetmantel und Gebetriemen der Juden. Langer, Die jüdischen Gebetriemen. Both in *Imago* xvi.

21. Zwei Kapitel ueber Kulturelle Entwicklung. *Imago,* 1924.

22. *Imago* ix.
23. *Imago* xiv.
24. To the sphere of such notions belongs the so-called long nose, the making of a long nose by extending its size with the hand. The penis-meaning of the hand is obvious here. The meaning of the jeering is, according to Fenichel (Die Lange Nase, *Imago* 1928, 1), that though it be that long, yet, I am not afraid; or, more correctly, it is a representation by the opposite. At the same place Fenichel discusses the custom of ascertaining whether or not one told the truth by investigating whether the nose is soft or hard. This would lead to the problem of the oath. One had to prove with an oath. The original form of the oath was the laying of the hand on the penis. The two testicles are the two witnesses; hence, in Latin, the witness is called testis. Well known is the custom of "giving one the fig." This is also a kind of jeering, and means the coitus itself, or only the vagina. This is the so-called mano fica that was widely used as an amulet. A goodly number of figures of it can be found in Seligmann's book, *Der Boese Blik*. He gives also the explanation. Fig in Greek is "ficon," in Italian, "fica." But fica means also cunnus, the sex-organ of the woman. King Victor Emanuel made a mano fica at Solferino, that the battle turn in his favor. With the Romans and Greeks the middle finger was called "unchaste." They apologized if they happened to utter it in company. Homosexuality is indicated by tickling the palm of a fellow when shaking hands with him. Caligula, so Seligmann quotes, pointed with his middle finger to his palm towards Cassius Caerea, to jeer at his femininity. The Talmud, as Seligmann says, counsels against the evil eye by putting of the right thumb into the left hand, and vice versa.

I draw attention to the custom of the "beating down" by a third person on two hands, put into each other by wagerers. In my opinion, this means the contact of the three penes, the value of which is like a blood-covenant. It is like several boys who cross their urine in an arc.

Here I mention the Nazi, Fascist, Albanian and Communist salute, the Hungarian Holy Right Hand; furthermore, the hand in Daniel, that wrote on the wall the fatal words. Seligmann says and shows a figure of a hand which hung over the entrance of homes in very many places in olden times. The fingerprint is nowadays used as the surest proof of identification. In Seligmann's book can be seen various hand amulets. One amulet shows the identity of the hand and the penis, another, a mano fica, is put into the middle of fertility (vagina), a third is a Roman legion-sign, another is a hand-sign with the shield of David on a Tunisian drum. Others are: a hand with the divine name Shaday, an oath-formula with three hands, a hand that unifies the hand and the eye, above between fingers a man and beneath on the palm is a mother with an infant.

To this I got the very interesting information from a patient of mine. In the center of her neurosis was the compulsion-thought that her parents cohabit for the sole aim of begetting her. She imagined in her phantasy that she will write a diary in which her daughter will read that she is not the product only of a chance-coitus done for pleasure, but done with the intention of begetting her. She was jealous and envious of those encounters that her parents had before she was born. For many months, and in every hour of them, without exception, she carried out the following play: She pulled her handkerchief upwards between her first and second fingers and wound it once around the forefinger and twice around the middle finger, then she turned it back between the first and second fingers. The rest of it that was hanging down she forced down with her thumb. The other end of the handkerchief she wound through the back of the hand around the joint and held it fast. She unwound what she did and repeated it. This resembles strikingly the 169th figure in Seligmann's book. The thumb is the patient who stands apart and wants to separate the parents united in sexual embrace.

"The hand here is the lord of death." This we read in Hermann's paper, Regression in Goethe's Drawing Expression (*Imago* x). Mrs. Hermann equally points to the erotogenic significance of the hand (The Foundation of Marie Bashkirtseff's Drawing Genius. *Imago* x). Of the genital significance of the hand speak also Ferenczi and Rank (Uber Verschaemte Hande. Intern. Zeitschr. ii). Also Daly proves on excellent clinical material the penis-meaning of the hand (Hindu-Mythologie und Kastration-komplex. *Imago* xiii). Very plastic is the figure of the goddess Kali-ma.

Hermann directed my attention to the Hungarian book of Maria Medvei (*Az Egyptomiak halottas tisztelete es halottas szobrocskai. Srtekezesek a kelet okori nepeinek tortenetebol.* Budapest, 1917). There I read the following interesting passage: "In the between-the-five-and-six-hour-room Osiris holds judgment, and there, together with the other gods who belong to his court, he judges the dead." The numeral "5" is striking.

25. Alphabetstudien. *Imago* 1931.
26. Zur Geschich einer infantilen Neurose.
27. Uber die Symbolik der Kopftrophaen, *Imago*, 1924.
28. In *The Labyrinth*, edited by S. H. Hooke, London, 1935. I got the material about the god from my brother, Dr. Arthur Feldmann, Hamilton, Ontario, Canada.
29. He is equated by some scholars quoted in the Labyrinth, also with Yahweh Sabaoth (The Lord of Hosts) of the Old Testament.
30. In the prophetic books of the Old Testament the relationship between God and Israel in many passages is imagined as a marriage between Yahweh and Israel, Israel being the female partner. Hosea ii. 18; Isaiah xxiv. 13; lvii. 5. In Isaiah liv. 5 we read: "For thy maker is thy husband, Yahweh Sabaoth is his name."

# A Selected Bibliography on Psychology and Judaism

## ADOLESCENCE

Anisfeld, M., Munoz, S.R., & Lambert, W.E. The structure and dynamics of the ethnic attitudes of Jewish adolescents. *Journal of Abnormal and Social Psychology,* 1963, 66:31-36.

Anon. The neurotic personality of the marginal man. By a college student. *Reconstructionist,* 1950, 15(18):20-23.

Baggaley, Andrew R. Comparison of temperament scores of Jewish and Gentile male students. *Psychological Reports,* 1963, 13(2):598.

Bernard, Jessie. Biculturality: a study in social schizophrenia. In Graeber, I., & Britt, S. (eds.), *Jews in a Gentile World.* NY: Macmillan, 1942.

Boroff, David. The Jewish college student. *Reconstructionist,* 1959, 25(4):3-7.

————. Jewish teen-age culture. *Annals of the American Academy of Political & Social Science,* 1961, 338:79-90.

Budick, Isadore. Jewish college youth. *Jewish Education,* 1955, 26(2):52-56.

Clark, E. Motivation of Jewish students. *Journal of Social Psychology,* 1949, 39:113-117.

Eckstein, Rudolph. A clinical note on the therapeutic use of a quasi-religious experience. *Journal of the American Psychoanalytic Association,* 1956, 4(2):304-313.

Elkind, David, & Elkind, Sally. Varieties of religious experience in young adolescents. *Journal for the Scientific Study of Religion,* 1962, 2(1):102-112.

Franzblau, Abraham N. *Religious Beliefs and Character Among Jewish Adolescents.* NY: Harper, 1934.

Glad, D. D. Attitudes and experience of American-Jewish and American-Irish male youth as related to differences in adult rates of inebriety. *Quarterly Journal of Studies in Alcoholism,* 1947, 8:406-472.

Glustrom, Simon. *Living with Your Teenager; A Guide for Jewish Parents.* NY: Bloch, 1961, 175p.

Goldberg, Nathan. Religious and social attitudes of Jewish youth in the U.S.A. *Jewish Review,* 1943, 1:135-168.

Goldsmith, Jerome M., & Berman, Irwin.  Middleclass Jewish delinquency.  *Journal of Jewish Communal Service*, 1962, 39(2):192-196.

Greenberg, Meyer.  The Jewish student at Yale: his attitude toward Judaism.  *Yivo Annual of Jewish Social Science,* 1946, 1:217-240; In Rose, Arnold (ed.), *Race Prejudice and Discrimination.*  NY: Knopf, 1951.

————.  Social characteristics of the Jewish students at the University of Maryland.  *Jewish Social Studies,* 1961, 23:21-37.

Havens, Joseph.  The changing climate of research on the college student and his religion.  *Journal for the Scientific Study of Religion,* 1963, 3:52-69.

Herman, S. N.  American Jewish students in Israel: a social psychological study in cross cultural education.  *Jewish Social Studies,* 1962, 24:3-29.

Kuhlen, Raymond G., & Arnold, Martha.  Age differences in religious beliefs and problems during adolescence.  *Journal of Genetic Psychology,* 1944, 65:291-299.

Levinson, Boris M.  The problems of freshmen in Yeshiva College and Stern College.  *Yeshiva Education,* 1958, 2:13-25, 45.

————.  The problems of Jewish religious youth.  *Genetic & Psychological Monographs,* 1959, 60:309-348.

————.  The vocational interests of Yeshiva College freshmen.  *Journal of Genetic Psychology,* 99:235-244.

————.  Yeshiva College subcultural scale: an experimental attempt at devising a scale of internationalization of Jewish traditional values.  *Journal of Genetic Psychology,* 1962, 101:375-399.

Nathan, M.  *The Attitude of the Jewish Student in the Colleges and Universities Toward His Religion.*  NY: Bloch, 1932.

Robison, Sophia M.  A study of delinquency among Jewish children in New York City.  In Sklare, Marshall (ed.), *The Jews: Social Patterns of an American Group.*  Glencoe, Ill.: Free Press, 1958, 535-541.

Rosen, Bernard C.  Adolescence and Religion. The Jewish Teenager in American Society.  Cambridge, Mass.: Schenkman, 1965, 218 p.

————.  Minority group in transition: a study of adolescent religious conviction and conduct. In Sklare, Marshall (ed.), *The Jews: Social Patterns of an American Group.* Glencoe, Ill.: Free Press, 1958, 336-346.

Sanua, Victor D. Differences in personality adjustment among different generations of Jews and non-Jews. In Opler, Marvin K., (ed.), *Culture and Mental Health.* NY: Macmillan, 1959, 443-466.

Sovin, Aaron. Self-acceptance of Jewishness by young Jewish people. *Jewish Education*, 1955, 26(1):22-31.

Sukov, May, & Williamson, E. G. Personality traits and attitudes of Jewish and non-Jewish students. *Journal of Applied Psychology*, 1938, 22:487-492.

Swerdloff, Sol, & Rosen, Howard. *The College and Career Plans of Jewish High School Youth.* Washington, D.C.: B'nai B'rith Vocational Service, 1964, 64 p.

Van Dyke, Paul, & Pierce-Jones, John. The psychology of religion of middle and late adolescence: a review of empirical research, 1950-1960. *Religious Education*, 1963, 58(6): 529-537.

## AGED

Levinson, Boris M. Jewish subculture and WAIS performance among Jewish aged. *Journal of Genetic Psychology*, 1962, 100:55-68.

————. A research note on subcultural differences in WAIS between aged Italians and Jews. *Journal of Gerontology,* 1960, 15:197-198.

Linden, Maurice E. Emotional problems in aging. *Jewish Social Service Quarterly*, 1954, 31:80-89.

## THE AMERICAN SCENE

Barron, M. L. The incidence of Jewish intermarriage in Europe and America. *American Sociological Review*, 1946, 11:6-13.

Brill, Abraham A. Adjustment of the Jew to the American environment. *Mental Hygiene*, 1918, 2:219-231.

Cahman, Werner J. *Intermarriage and Jewish Life.* NY: Herzl Press, 1963, 212 p.

Chein, Isadore. The problem of Jewish identification. *Jewish Social Studies*, 1955, 17:219-222.

Clark, Kenneth B. Jews in contemporary America. Problems

in identification. *Jewish Social Service Quarterly,* 1954, 31:12-22.

Davidson, Alice, & Weber, Mary. *A Comparison of Irish Catholics and Jewish Families Coming to a Child Guidance Clinic.* Boston: Simmons College School of Social Work, 1960.

Dreikurs, Rudolph. The Jewish family: a psychiatrist looks at Jewish family life. *New Currents,* 1944, 2:28-31.

Duker, A. G. Socio-psychological trends in the American Jewish community since 1900. *Yivo Annual,* 1954, 9:166-178.

Franzblau, Abraham N. A new look at the psychodynamics of Jewish family living. *Journal of Jewish Communal Service,* 1958, 35:57-71.

Gersh, H. New suburbanites of the 50's; Jewish division. *Commentary,* 1954, 17:209-221.

Golner, Joseph H. Dilemma of the American Jew. *Jewish Social Service Quarterly,* 1954, 31:165-172.

Gordon, Albert I. *Jews in Suburbia.* Boston: Beacon Press, 1959, 264 p.

Gordon, Milton M. *Assimilation in American Life. The Role of Race, Religion, and National Origin.* NY: Oxford University Press, 1965, 276 p.

Grinstein, Alexander. Profile of a "doll"—a female character type. *Psychoanalytic Review,* 1963, 50(2):161-174.

Hanawalt, Nelson G. Feelings of security and of self-esteem in relation to religious belief. *Journal of Social Psychology,* 1963, 59(2):347-353.

Heiss, Jerold S. Premarital characteristics of the religiously inter-married in an urban area. *American Sociological Review,* 1960, 25:47-55.

Kramer, Judith, & Leventman, Seymour. *Children of the Gilded Ghetto; Conflict Resolutions of Three Generations of American Jews.* New Haven: Yale University Press, 1961, 228 p.

Lourié, Anton. The Jew as a psychological type. *American Imago,* 1949, 6:119-155.

MacCrone, I. D. A note on the attitude of Jewish subjects towards intermarriage. *Proceedings of the South African Psychological Association,* 1952, No. 3, 19.

Mace, David R. *Hebrew Marriage; A Sociological Study:* NY: Philosophical Library, 1953, 271 p.

Mayer, John E. *Jewish-Gentile Courtships; An Exploratory*

*Study of a Social Process.* NY: Free Press, 1961, 240 p.

Nardi, Noah. Studies in Jewish home environment. Abstract. *American Psychologist,* 1946, 1:258.

O'Brien, Robert W. Some socio-economic comparisons of six Seattle Jewish congregations. *Journal of Human Relations,* 1954, 2(3):39-47.

Orlansky, Harold. The Jews of Yankee City. *Commentary,* 1946, 1(3):77-85.

Peto, Andrew. The demonic mother image in the Jewish religion. In Muensterberger, Warner, & Axelrad, Sidney (eds.), *Psychoanalysis and the Social Sciences.* Vol. V. NY: International Universities Press, 1958.

Poll, Solomon. *The Hasidic Community of Williamsburg.* NY: Free Press, 1962, 308 p.

Resnick, Reuben R. Some sociological aspects of intermarriage of Jews and non-Jews. *Social Forces,* 1933, 12:94-102.

Rudavsky, D. Religion and religiosity in American Jewish life. *Journal of Educational Sociology,* 1960, 33:314-320.

Shoulson, Abraham B. (ed.). *Marriage and Family Life; A Jewish View.* NY: Twayne, 1959, 299 p.

Sklare, Marshall. Assimilation and the sociologists. *Commentary,* 1965, 39:63-67.

Sklare, Marshall (ed.). *The Jews. Social Patterns of an American Group.* Glencoe, Ill.: Free Press, 1958, 669 p.

Sklare, Marshall, & Vosk, M. *The Riverton Study: How Jews Look at Themselves and Their Neighbors.* NY: American Jewish Committee, 1957.

Slotkin, J. S. Jewish-gentile intermarriage in Chicago. *American Sociological Review,* 1942, 7:34-39.

Tennenbaum, Ruth. Jewish parents in a child guidance clinic: A study of culture and personality. *Smith College Studies in Social Work,* 1939, 10:50-76.

Wolfenstein, Martha. Two types of Jewish mothers. In Mead, Margaret, & Wolfenstein, Martha (eds.), *Childhood in Contemporary Cultures.* Chicago: University of Chicago Press, 1955; In Sklare, Marshall (ed.), *The Jews. Social Patterns of an American Group.* Glencoe, Ill.: Free Press, 1958, 520-534.

ANTI-SEMITISM

Ackerman, Nathan W.    Antisemitic motivation in a psychopathic personality; a case study. *Psychoanalytic Review,* 1947, 34:76-101.

Ackerman, Nathan W., & Jahoda, Marie. *Antisemitism and Emotional Disorder. A Psychoanalytic Interpretation.* NY: Harper, 1950, 135 p.

——— & ———. The dynamic basis of anti-Semitic attitudes. *Psychoanalytic Quarterly,* 1948, 17:240-260.

——— & ———. Towards a dynamic interpretation of anti-Semitic attitudes. *American Journal of Orthopsychiatry,* 1948, 18:163-173.

Adorno, T. W., *et al.* Prejudice in the interview material. In *The Authoritarian Personality.* NY: Wiley Science Editions, 1964, 603-653.

Berkowitz, Leonard. *Anti-Semitism and the displacement of aggression.* Bobbs-Merrill's Reprint Series in Social Sciences. Indianaopolis: Bobbs-Merrill, 1965.

Bettelheim, Bruno. The dynamism of anti-Semitism in Gentile and Jew. *Journal of Abnormal & Social Psychology* 1947, 42:153-169.

———. *The Informed Heart; Autonomy in a Mass Age.* Glencoe, Ill.: Free Press, 1960, 309 p.

Bonaparte, Marie. Des causes psychologiques de l'antisémitisme. *Revue français de Psychanalyse,* 1951, 15:479-491.

———. Psychanalyse de l'antisémitisme. *Evidence* 1952, 25:5-10.

Brenner, Arthur B. Some psychoanalytic speculations on anti-Semitism. *Psychoanalytic Review,* 1948, 35:20-32.

Cohen, E. H. *Human Behavior in the Concentration Camp.* NY: Norton, 1953.

Engel, W. Reflections on the psychiatric consequences of persecution. *American Journal of Psychotherapy,* 1962, 2:191-203.

Fenichel, Otto. Elements of a psychoanalytic theory of anti-Semitism. In *Collected Papers,* 2d Series. NY: Norton, 1954.

———. A psychoanalytical approach to anti-Semitism. *Commentary,* 1946, 2(1):36-44.

Frankl, Victor E. Experiences in a concentration camp. In

*Man's Search for Meaning.* Part I. Boston: Beacon Press, 1963; NY: Washington Square Press, 1965.

―――. Psychologie und Psychiatrie des Konzentrationslagers. *Psychiatrie der Gegenwart,* 1961, Bd. 3, 743.

Freud, Sigmund. A note on anti-semitism. *Standard Edition,* 23.

Glenn, Judes. Circumcision and anti-semitism. *Psychoanalytic Quarterly,* 1960, 29:395-399.

Grunberger, Bela. The anti-Semite and the oedipal conflict. *International Journal of Psycho-Analysis,* 1964, 45(2):380-385.

―――. Circoncision et l'antisémitisme. *Psyché-Paris,* 1947, 2:1221-1228.

Jones, Ernest. The psychology of the Jewish question. Contribution to a symposium: Gentile and Jew. In *Essays in Applied Psycho-Analysis,* Vol. I. London: Hogarth Press, 1951, 284-300.

Kagan, Henry E. *Changing the Attitude of Christian toward Jews: A Psychological Approach through Religion.* NY: Columbia University Press, 1952, 155 p.

Kurth, Gertrud M. The Jew and Adolph Hitler. *Psychoanalytic Quarterly,* 1947, 16:11-32.

Levinson, Daniel J. The study of anti-Semitic ideology. In Adorno, T. W., *et al., The Authoritarian Personality.* NY: Wiley Science Editions, 1964, 57-150.

Lewin, Kurt. Psycho-sociological problems of a minority group. *Character & Personality,* 1935, 3:175-187.

―――. Self-hatred among Jews. *Contemporary Jewish Record,* 1941, 4:219-232; In *Resolving Social Conflicts.* NY: Harper, 1948, 186-200.

Liefmann, Else. Mittelalterliche Überlieferungen und Antisemitismus; ein tiefenpsychologischer Beitrag zu seinem Verständnis. *Psyche-Stuttgart,* 1951, 5(9):481-496.

Loeblowitz-Leonard, Henry. The Jew as symbol. II. Anti-Semitism and transference. *Psychiatric Quarterly,* 1947, 21:253-260.

―――. A psychoanalutic contribution to the problem of anti-Semitism. *Psychoanalytic Review,* 1945, 32:359-361.

Loewenstein, Rudolph M. *Christians and Jews: A Psychoanalytic study.* NY: International Universities Press, 1951, 224p.

————. The historical and cultural roots of anti-Semitism. In *Psychoanalysis and the Social Sciences,* Vol. I. NY: International Universities Press, 1947, 313-356; In *Yearbook of Psychoanalysis,* Vol. IV. NY: International Universities Press, 1948, 226-262.

————. *Psychanalyse de l'Antisémitisme.* Paris: Presses de l'Universitaires Français, 1952.

Maranz, Georges.   Les conséquences de la circoncision.   Essai d'explication psychanalytique de l'antisémitisme.   *Psyché-Paris,* 1947, 2:731-745.

Meyer, Herschel.   Nationalism and Jewish self-hatred.   *Medical Leaves,* 1941, 3.

Pedersen, Stefi.   Unconscious motives in pro-semitic attitudes. *Psychoanalytic Review,* 1951, 38:361-373.

Sacher, Harry.   Revenge on the prophets: a psychoanalysis of antisemitism.   *Menorah Journal,* 1942, 28(3):243.

Sanua, Victor D.   Minority status and psychological adjustment.   *Jewish Journal of Sociology,* 1962, 4:241-253.

Sarnoff, I.   Identification with the aggressor: some personality correlates of anti-semitism among Jews.   *Journal of Personality,* 1951-52, 20:199-218.

Schindler, Walter.   The sexual aspects of anti-semitism. *International Journal of Sexology,* 1949, 2:239-246.

Secord, P. F., & Saumer, E.   Identifying Jewish names: does prejudice increase accordingly?   *Journal of Abnormal & Social Psychology,* 1960, 61:144-145.

Simmel, Ernst (ed.).   *Anti-Semitism. A Social Disease.* NY: International Universities Press, 1946.

Sullivan, Harry Stack.   Anti-Semitism.   In *The Fusion of Psychiatry and Social Science.*   NY: Norton, 1965.

Trautman, Edgar C.   Fear and panic in Nazi concentration camps: a biosocial evaluation of the chronic anxiety syndrome.   *International Journal of Social Psychiatry,* 1965, 11:134-141.

————. Psychiatrische Untersuchungen an Überlebenden der National-sozialistischen Vernichtungslager 15 Jahre nach der Befreiung.   *Nervenarzt,* 1961, 32:545-551.

Wangh, Martin.   National socialism and the genocide of the Jews.   A psychoanalytic study of a historical event.   *International Journal of Psycho-Analysis,* 1964, 45(2):386-398.

————. A psychoanalytic study of anti-semitism. *Psychoanalytic Quarterly*, 1963, 32:299-301.

Weissberg, N. C., & Proshansky, Harold M. The Jewish anti-semite's perceptions of fellow Jews. *Journal of Social Psychology*, 1963, 60:139-151.

Winkler, G. E. Neuropsychiatric symptoms in survivors of concentration camps. *Journal of Social Therapy*, 1959, 5(4).

### CHILDREN

Brown, Sheldon S. A guidance experiment in the religious school. *Jewish Education*, 1962, 33:52-57.

Chein, Isador, & Hurwitz, J. *A Study of Minority Group Membership: The Reactions of Jewish Boys to Various Aspects of Being Jewish.* NY: Jewish Welfare Board, 1950. Mimeographed.

Dinin, Samuel. The contribution of Jewish education to the development of the American Jewish personality. *Jewish Education*, 1951, 22:19-23.

Elkind, David. The child's conception of his religious determination. I. The Jewish child. *Journal of Genetic Psychology*, 1961, 99:209-225.

Esman, Aaron H. (ed.). *New Frontiers in Child Guidance.* NY: International Universities Press, 1958, 218 p.

Fishman, Joshua A. Patterns of American self-identification among children of a minority group. *Yivo Annual for Jewish Social Science*, 1955, 10:212-266.

————. Social science research relevant to American Jewish education. *Jewish Education*, 1957/58, 28:49-60; 1959, 29:64-71; 1960, 30:35-45.

Flowerman, Samuel H. Psychological effects upon pupils of religious instruction in the schools. *Jewish Education*, 1952, 23(3):29-33, 48.

Fusswerk Fursay, Joseph. Le test de Rorschach chez les enfants Juifs, victims des lois raciales. In Minkowska, F. (ed.). *Le Rorschach.* Paris: Desclee & Brouwer, 1956, 193-207.

Hamilton, Gordon. *Psychotherapy in Child Guidance.* NY: Columbia University Press, 1947, 340 p.

Hartley, E. L. Children's use of ethnic frames of reference.

*Journal of Psychology*, 1948, 26:367-386.

Henoch, C. *Dynamics of Anxiety in Two Culturally Different Groups.* Doctoral Dissertation. Yeshiva University, 1961.

Jewish Board of Guardians. *Primary Behavior Disorder in Children; Two Case Studies*, by Staff Members of the Jewish Board of Guardians. NY: Family Welfare Association of America, 1945, 1947, 59 p.

Lehrer, L. 'Jewishness' in the psyche of the American Jewish child. *Yivo Bleter*, 1942, 4.

Levinson, Boris M. A comparative study of the intelligence of Jewish preschool boys and girls of orthodox parentage. *Journal of Genetic Psychology*, 1957, 90:17-22.

————. The MMPI in a Jewish traditional setting. *Journal of Genetic Psychology*, 1962, 101:25-42.

————. (Psychological effect of the all-day school.) *Shevilay Hachinuch*, 1955, 15:163-168.

————. Some research findings with Jewish subjects of traditional background. *Mental Hygiene,* 1963, 47:129-134.

————. Subcultural values and I.Q. stability. *Journal of Genetic Psychology*, 1961, 98:69-82.

————. Subcultural variations in verbal and performance ability at the elementary school level. *Journal of Genetic Psychology*, 1960, 97:149-160.

————. Traditional Jewish cultural values and performance on the Wechsler tests. *Journal of Educational Psychology*, 1959, 50:177-181.

Lewin, Kurt. Bringing up the Jewish child. *Menorah Journal*, 1940, 28:29-45; In *Resolving Social Conflicts*. NY: Harper, 1948, 169-185.

M'rom. M. (Studying the personality of Jewish children in the U.S.A.) *Hahinukh*, 1952/53, 25:24-43.

Nardi, Noah. Studies in intelligence of Jewish children. *Jewish Education*, 1948, 20:41-50.

Revitch, Eugene. *The Mental Hygiene Value of Jewish Education.* Your Child and You Pamphlet Series, No. 2. NY: United Synagogue Commission on Jewish Education, 1954.

Sanua, Victor D. Social science research relevant to American Jewish education. *Jewish Education*, 1962, 32:99-114; 1963, 33:163-175; 1964, 34:187-202.

## FREUD AND JUDAISM

Aron, Willy. *Freudiana Judaica.* Jewish Forum, 1956, June: 98-99; Aug:104-105; Sept:138-139.

——. Notes on Sigmund Freud's ancestry and Jewish contacts. *Yivo Annual of Jewish Social Science,* 1956-57, 11:286-296.

——. (Notes on Freud's ancestry and his Jewishness.) *Yivo Bletter,* 1956, 40:166-174.

Bakan, David. *Sigmund Freud and the Jewish Mystical Tradition.* Princeton, N.J.: Van Nostrand, 1958, 326 p.

Bernfeld, Siegfried, & Bernfeld, Suzanne C. Freud's early childhood. *Bulletin of the Menninger Clinic,* 1944, 8:107-115.

Feldman, A. Bronson. Freud and God. *Critic & Guide,* 1951, 5:100-111.

Freud, Sigmund. On being of the B'nai Brith. An address to the society in Vienna. *Commentary,* 1946, 1(5):23-24; *Standard Edition,* 20.

Gilbert, Arthur. Freud and his Jewishness. *Reconstructionist,* 1954, 19(17):7-11.

Goldhammer, Leo. Herzl and Freud. In Patai, R. (ed.). *Herzl Year Book,* Vol. I. NY: Herzl Press, 1958, 194-196.

Grollman, Earl A. *Judaism in Sigmund Freud's World.* N.Y.: Appleton-Century, 1966.

Kagan, Henry E. *Six Who Changed the World: Moses, Jesus, Paul, Marx, Freud, Einstein.* NY: Yoseloff, 1963, 278 p.

Philp, H. L. *Freud and Religious Belief.* NY: Pitman, 1956.

Sachs, Hanns. The man Moses and the man Freud. *Psychoanalytic Review,* 1941, 28:156-162.

## ISRAEL

Bloch, Gottfried. Remarks on psychotherapeutic activities in Israel. *International Journal of Group Psychotherapy,* 1959, 9:303-307.

Blumenthal, H. E. *Psychological Problems of the Adolescent Immigrant in Israel of Today.* Jerusalem: Ministry of Labour, Department for Vocational Education, 1958, 154 p.

Caplan, Gerald. Clinical observations on the emotional life of children in the communal settlements in Israel. In Senn, Milton J. E. (ed.). *Problems of Infancy and Childhood.* NY: Josiah Macy, Jr. Foundation, 1954, 196 p.

Davies, A.  Michael, & Kaplan-Dinur, Atara.  Suicide in Israel: an epidemological study.  *International Journal of Social Psychiatry*, 1961/62, 8(1):32-44.

Diamond, Stanley.  Kibbutz and shtetl: the history of an idea. *Social Problems*, 1957, 5:71-99.

Duker, Abraham G.  Some aspects of Israel's impact on identification and cultural patterns.  *Jewish Social Studies*, 1959, 21:25-45.

Friedjung, Josef K.  Five years psychoanalytic educational work among Jewish youth immigrants.  In *Max Eitingon in Memoriam*.  Jerusalem: Israel Psychoanalytic Society, 1951, 256-267.

Freud, Sigmund.  To the opening of the Hebrew University. *Standard Edition*, 19.

Gabriel, K. R.  Nuptiality and fertility of origin groups in Israel. *Jewish Journal of Sociology*, 1960, 2:74-97.

Geismar, Ludwig L.  Ideology and the adjustment of immigrants.  *Jewish Social Studies*, 1959, 21:155-164.

Golan, Shmuel.  Collective education in the kibbutz.  *Psychiatry*, 1959, 22:167-177.

Hes, J. P.  Attitudes toward mental illness in Israel.  *Israel Annals of Psychiatry & Related Disciplines*, 1963, 1(1):112.

————.  Hypochondriasis in oriental Jewish immigrants. *International Journal of Social Psychiatry*, 1958, 4(1):18-23.

Kafman, Mordekhay.  (Inquiry about behavior of 403 kibbutz children.)  *Ofakim*, 1957, 11:339-367.

Kalmus, Ernst E.  (On manic-depressive psychosis in Israel.) *Harefuah*, 1957, 52:150-151.

Lev, Yehudat, *et al.*  (Emotional adjustment questionnaire: psychology of youth in Israel.)  *Hahinukh*, 1956/57, 29:146-155.

Levinger, L.  Psychatrische Untersuchungen in Israel an 800 Fällen mit Gesundheitsschaden-Forderungen wagen Nazi-Verfolgung.  *Nervenarzt*, 1962, 33:75-80.

Miller, Louis.  An approach to psychiatric and mental health research in Israel.  *Israel Annals of Psychitary and Related Disciplines*, 1963, 1(1):3-10.

Neubauer, Peter B. (ed.).  *Children in Collectives: Child-Rearing Aims and Practices in the Kibbutz*.  Springfield, Ill.: C. C. Thomas, 1965, 420 p.

Palgi, Phyllis. Immigrants, psychiatrists, and culture. *Israel Annals of Psychiatry & Related Disciplines*, 1963, 1(1): 43-58.

Rabin, Albert I. Attitudes of kibbutz children to family and parents. *American Journal of Orthopsychiatry*, 1959, 29: 172-179.

————. Comparison of American and Israeli children by means of a sentence completion technique. *Journal of Social Psychology*, 1959, 49:3-12.

————. The Israeli kibbutz as a "laboratory" for testing psychodynamic hypotheses. *Psychological Record*, 1957, 7:111-115.

————. Kibbutz children: research findings to date. *Children*, 1958, 5:179-184.

Spiro, Melford E. *Kibbutz: Venture in Utopia.* Cambridge: Harvard University Press, 1956, 266 p.

————. The Sabras and Zionism: a study in personality and ideology. *Social Problems*, 1957, 5:100-109.

Talmon-Garber, Yonina. The family in Israel. *Marriage & Family Living*, 1954, 16:343-349.

————. Social change and family structure. *International Social Science Journal*, 1962, 14(3):468-487.

Weinberg, Abraham A. Mental health aspects of voluntary immigration. *Mental Hygiene*, 1955, 39:450-464.

Winnick, H. Z. (Psychological problems of immigrants' absorption.) *Ofakim*, 1957, 11:138-144.

## JEWISH WIT AND HUMOR

Hes, J. P., & Levine, J. Kibbutz humor. *Journal of Nervous & Mental Diseases*, 1962, 135:327-331.

Hitschmann, Edward. Zur Psychologie des jüdischen Witzes. *Psychoanalytische Bewegung*, 1930, 2:580-586.

Reik, Theodor. Freud and Jewish wit *Psychoanalysis*, 1954, 2(3):12-20.

————. *Jewish Wit.* NY: Gamut Press, 1962, 246 p.

————. Vom Wesen des jüdischen Witzes. *Almanach*, 1937, 71-81.

————. Zur Psychoanalyse des jüdischen Witzes. *Imago*, 1929, 15:63-88.

Roback, Abraham A. Humor in Jewish folklore. *Chicago Jewish Forum*, 1948, 6:167-173.

## MENTAL HEALTH

Abrahams, Gerald. *The Jewish Mind.* Boston: Beacon Press, 1961, 420 p.

Bacon, S. D., *et al. Studies of Drinking in Jewish Culture.* New Haven: Yale University Press, 1951.

Brill, Abraham A., & Karpas, M. Insanity among Jews. *Medical Record,* 1914, 86:578-579.

———— & ————. Insanity among Jews: is the Jew disproportionately insane? *Journal of Nervous and Mental Diseases,* 1914, 41:512-517.

———— & ————. Is the Jew disproportionately insane? *New York Medical Journal,* 1914, 100:739-741.

Franzblau, Abraham N. Psychotherapy and the ministry. *International Record of Medicine,* 1955, 168:793-797.

Gittelsohn, Roland B. Judaism and mental health. *Judaism,* 1959, 8:323-328.

Glasner, Samuel. Judaism and its therapeutic applications. *Annals of Psychotherapy,* 1959, 1(2):40-46.

Gold, Henry R. Can we speak of Jewish neuroses? In Noveck, Simon (ed.), *Judaism and Psychiatry.* NY: United Synagogue of America, 1956, 155-160.

Goldberg, Jacob A., & Malzberg, B. Mental disease among Jews. *Psychiatric Quarterly,* 1928, 2:194-213.

Hirsch, W. *Rabbinic Psychology.* London: Goldston, 1947.

Kagan, Henry E. The rabbi, his family, and the community. *Jewish Religious Health,* 1962, 1:350-361.

Keith, Seward, & Freedman, Meyer. Jewish temperament. *Journal of Applied Psychology,* 1935, 19:70-84.

Malzberg Benjamin. *Mental Disease Among Jews in New York State.* NY: International Medical Book Corp., 1960, 140 p.

————. The prevalence of mental disease among Jews. *Mental Hygiene* (NY), 1930, 14:926.

Myers, Jerome K., & Roberts, Bertram H. Some relationships between religion, ethnic origin and mental illness. In Sklare, Marshall (ed.), *The Jews: Social Patterns of an American Group.* Glencoe, Ill.: Free Press, 1958, 551-559.

Myerson,A. Neuroses and alcoholism among Jews. *Medical*

*Leaves,* 1941, 3:104-107.

Noveck, Simon (ed.). *Judaism and Psychiatry; Two Approaches to the Personal Problems and Needs of Modern Man.* NY: United Synagogue of America, 1956, 197 p.

Orlansky, Harold. The study of man. Jewish personality traits. A review of studies on an elusive problem. *Commentary,* 1946, 2:377-383.

Rinder, Irwin D. Mental health of American Jewish urbanites: a review of literature and predictions. *International Journal of Social Psychiatry,* 1963, 9:104-109.

————. Polarities in Jewish identification: the personality of ideological extremity. In Sklare, Marshall (ed.), *The Jews: Social Patterns of an American Group.* Glencoe, Ill.: Free Press, 1958, 493-504.

Rosenbloom, C. R. Notes on Jewish drug addicts. *Psychological Reprints,* 1959, 5:769-772.

Sanua, Victor D. Comparison of Jewish and Protestant paranoid and catatonic patients. *Diseases of the Nervous System,* 1962, 23:320-326.

————. The socio-cultural aspects of schizophrenia: a comparison of Protestant and Jewish schizophrenics. *International Journal of Social Psychiatry,* 1963, 9:27-36.

Snyder, Charles R. *Alcohol and the Jews; A Cultural Study of Drinking and Sobriety.* Glencoe, Ill.: Free Press, 1958, 226 p.

Sperling, Abraham P. A comparison between Jews and non-Jews. *Journal of Applied Psychology,* 1942, 26:828-840.

Whitlock, G. E. Structure of personality in Hebrew psychology. *Interpretation,* 1960, 14:3-13.

Yarrow, Marian Radke. Personality development and minority group membership. In Sklare, Marshall (ed.), *The Jews: Social Patterns of an American Group.* Glencoe, Ill: Free Press, 1958, 451-474.

### THE OLD TESTAMENT

Arlow, Jacob A. The consecration of the prophet. *Psychoanalytic Quarterly,* 1951, 20:374-397.

Beck, Samuel J. Abraham's ordeal: creation of a new reality. *Psychoanalytic Review,* 1963, 50:175-189.

Bellak, Leopold. A note about Adam's apple. *Psychoanalytic*

*Review*, 1942, 29:300-302.

Brenner, Arthur B.   The covenant with Abraham.   *Psychoanalytic Review*, 1952, 39:34-52.

————.   The great mother goddess: puberty initiation rites and the covenant of Abraham.   *Psychoanalytic Review*, 1950, 37:320-340.

Choisy, Maryse.   Quelques réflexions sur une psychologie de Cain.   *Psyché-Paris*, 1953, 8:88-95.

Daur, R.   Biblische Besinnung.   In Bitter, W. (ed.), *Angst und Schuld*.   Stuttgart: Klette, 1959.

Desmonde, William H.   The murder of Moses.   *American Imago,* 1950, 7:351-367.

Eckstein, Rudolf.   The Tower of Babel in psychology and in psychiatry.   *American Imago*, 1950, 7:77-141.

Feldman, Arthur A.   The Davidic dynasty and the Davidic messiah.   *American Imago*, 1960, 17:163-178.

Feldman, Sandor S.   The sin of Reuben, firstborn son of Jacob.   In Muensterberger, W., & Axelrad, S. (eds.), *Psychoanalysis and the Social Sciences,* Vol. IV.   NY: International Universities Press, 1955, 282-287.

Fingert, Hyman H.   Psychoanalytic study of the minor prophet, Jonah.   *Psychoanalytic Review*, 1954, 41:55-65.

Fishman, Joshua A.   Psychology and Bible stories.   B.   How safe is psychoanalysis.   *Jewish Education*, 1952, 23:45-48.

Fodor, A.   The fall of man of the book of Genesis.   *American Imago*, 1954, 11:203-231.

Fortune, R. F.   The symbolism of the serpent.   *International Journal of Psycho-Analysis*, 1926, 7:237-243.

Freud, Sigmund.   Moses an Egyptian.   *International Journal of Psycho-Analysis*, 1938, 19:291-298.

Gagern, Friedrich Ernst von.   Réalisation de soi et névrose et la lumière des 10 commandements.   *Psyché-Paris*, 1954, 9:403-432.

Gerber, Israel J.   *Immortal Rebels: Freedom for the Individual in the Bible*.   NY: Jonathan David, 1964.

Godin, André.   Isaac "at the stake": a psychological enquiry into the manner of presenting a Biblical episode to children.   *Lumen Vitae*, 1955, 10:65-92.

Goitein, Lionel.   Green pastures: Psalm 23.   *American Imago,* 1956, 13:409-414.

————. The importance of the Book of Job for analytic thought. *American Imago*, 1954, 11:407-415.

Gordon, Hirsch L. Psychiatry in Bible, Talmud and Zohar. In *Jews in the Arts and Sciences*. Jubilee Volume, Jewish Academy of Arts and Sciences. NY: Herald Square Press, 1955.

Jones, Ernest. The birth and death of Moses. *International Journel of Psycho-Analysis*, 1958, 39:1-14.

Katz, Joseph. The Joseph dreams anew. *Psychoanalytic Review*, 1963, 50(2):92-118.

Laughlin, Henry P. King David's anger. *Psychoanalytic Quarterly*, 1954, 23:87-95.

Levin, A. J. Oedipus and Sampson, the rejected hero-child. *International Journal of Psycho-Analysis*, 1957, 38:105-116.

Levy, Ludwig. Ist das Kainszeichen die Beschneidung? Ein kritischer Beitrag zur Bibelexegese. *Imago*, 1919, 5:290-293.

————. Die Kastration in der Bibel. *Imago*, 1920, 6:393-397.

————. Die Sexualsymbolik des Ackerbaus in Bibel und Talmud. *Zeitschrift für Sexualwissenschaft*, 1916, 2:437-444.

————. Die Sexualsymbolik der Bibel und des Talmuds. *Zeitschrift für Sexualwissenschaft*, 1914, 1:274-279, 318-326.

————. Sexualsymbolik in der biblischen Paradiesgeschichte. *Imago*, 1917, 3:16-30.

————. Sexualsymbolik in der Samsonsage. *Zeitschrift für Sexualwissenschaft*, 1916, 3:256-271.

Rautman, Arthur L. A tale of Moses: post-doctoral interlude. *Mental Health* (NY), 1964, 48:455-462.

Reik, Theodor. *Mystery on the Mountain; the Drama of the Sinai Revelation*. NY: Harper, 1959, 210 p.

————. Psychoanalytische Studien zur Bibelexegese. Jacobs Kampf. *Imago*, 1919, 5.

————. *The Temptation*. NY: Braziller, 1961, 256 p.

Revitch, Eugene. Psychology and Bible stories. A. How dangerous is the apple? *Jewish Education*, 1952, 23:43-44.

Róheim, Géza. The covenant of Abraham. *International Journal of Psycho-Analysis*, 1939, 20:452-459.

————. The garden of Eden. *Psychoanalytic Review*, 1940, 27:1-26, 177-199.

————. The passage of the Red Sea. *Man*, 1923, 23:152-155.

Rosenberg, Stuart E. *More Loves Than One: The Bible Confronts Psychiatry.* NY: Ungar, 1965.

Rosenzweig, Efraim M. Some notes, historical and psychoanalytical, on the people of Israel and the land of Israel with special reference to Deuteronomy. *American Imago,* 1940, 1(4):50-64.

Rubenstein, Richard L. The significance of castration anxiety in rabbinic mythology. *Psychoanalytic Review,* 1963, 50(2): 129-152.

Schindler, Walter. Depth psychology and dream interpretation in the Bible. *International Journal of Sexology,* 1954, 8:77-82.

Schroeder, Theodore. Mathias the prophet. *Journal of Religious Psychology,* 1913, 6:59-65.

Singer, Richard E. *Job's Encounter.* NY: Bookman, 1963, 276 p.

Slap, Joseph W. The genesis of Moses. *Psychoanalytic Quarterly,* 1958, 27:400-402.

Weiss, Samuel A. The biblical story of Ruth: analytic implications of the Hebrew Masoretic text. *American Imago,* 1959, 16:195-209.

Wellisch, Erich. *Isaac and Oedipus. A Study in Biblical Psychology.* NY: Humanities Press, 1955, 131 p.

Zeligs, Dorothy F. Abraham and the covenant of the pieces. *American Imago,* 1961, 18:173-186.

————. Abraham and monotheism. *American Imago,* 1954, 11(3):293-315.

————. A character study of Samuel. *American Imago,* 1955, 12:355-386.

————. The personality of Joseph. *American Imago,* 1955, 12:47-69.

————. *Psychoanalysis and the Bible: A Study of Seven Personalities in the Old Testament.* NY: Abelard-Schuman, 1965.

————. A psychoanalytic note on the function of the Bible. *American Imago,* 1957, 14:57-60.

————. Psychological factors in the teaching of Bible stories. *Jewish Education,* 1951, 22:24-28.

————. Saul, the tragic king. Part 1 & 2. *American Imago,* 1957, 14:61-85, 165-189.

————. Solomon: man and myth. *Psychoanalysis*, 1961, 48(1): 77-103, 48(2):91-110.

————. A study of King David. *American Imago*, 1960, 17:179-200.

————. Two episodes in the life of Jacob. *American Imago*, 1953, 10:181-203.

Zimmerman, Frank. The book of Ecclesiastes in the light of some psychoanalytic observations. *American Imago*, 1948, 5:301-305.

RELIGION

Barag, Gerda. The question of Jewish monotheism. *American Imago*, 1947, 4:8-25.

Feldman, Arthur A. Freud's *Moses and Monotheism* and the three stages of Israelitish religion. *Psychoanalytic Review*, 1944, 31:361-418.

Freud, Sigmund. *Civilization and Its Discontents*. London: Hogarth Press, 1946.

————. *The Future of an Illusion*. NY: Liveright, 1928.

————. *Moses and Monotheism*. NY: Knopf, 1939, 218 p.

————. *Psychoanalysis and Faith: Dialogue with the Reverend Oskar Pfister*. NY: Basic Books, 1963, 152 p.

Ginsburg, Sol W. Concerning religion and psychiatry. *Child Study*, 1953, 30:12-20.

————. *Man's Place in God's World: A Psychiatrist's Evaluation*. NY: Hebrew Union College—Jewish Institute of Religion, 1948.

Gold, Henry R. The psychological approach to Judaism. In Jung, Leo (ed.), *Judaism in a Changing World*. NY: Oxford University Press, 1939.

Hirschberg, H. H. 1800 years before Freud; a re-evaluation of the term Yetzer ha-ra. *Judaism*, 1961, 10:129-141.

Kristol, Irving. God and the psychoanalysts. Can Freud and religion be reconciled? *Commentary*, 1949, 8:434-443.

Liebman, Joshua Loth (ed). *Psychiatry and Religion. A Symposium*. Boston: Beacon Press, 1948.

Maslow, Abraham H. *Religion, Values, and Peak-Experiences*. Columbus: Ohio State University Press, 1964, 123 p.

Ramnoux, Clémence. Sur une page de "Moïse et le monothéisme." *Psychanalyse*, 1957, 3:165-187.

Reik, Theodor.  *Dogma and Compulsion; Psychoanalytic Studies of Myths and Religions.*  NY: International Universities Press, 1951.

Róheim, Géza.  Some aspects of semitic monotheism.  In Muensterberger, Warner, & Axelrad, Sidney (eds.), *Psychoanalysis and the Social Sciences.*  Vol. IV.  NY: International Universities Press, 1955.

Steindletz, E.  Hasidism and psychoanalysis.  *Judaism,* 1960, 9:222-228.

Velikovsky, Immanuel.  Psychoanalytische Ahnungen in der Traumdeutungskunst der alten Hebräer nach dem Traktat Brachoth.  *Psychoanalytische Bewegung,* 1933, 5:66-69; Abstract in *International Journal of Psycho-Analysis,* 1933, 14:507.

Weinstein, Jacab S.  Religion looks at psychiatry.  *Central Conference of American Rabbi's Journal,* 1954.

Weiss, M. D.  Repression and monotheism.  *Judaism,* 1961, 10:217-226.

Zilboorg, Gregory.  Psychoanalysis and religion.  Catholic, Protestant and Jewish attitudes to Freudianism.  *Pastoral Psychology,* 1959, 10:41-48.

### RITUAL

Almansi, Renato J.   A further contribution to the psychoanalytic interpretation of the Menorah.  *Journal of the Hillside Hospital,* 1954, 3:3-18.

————.  A psychoanalytic interpretation of the Menorah.  *Journal of the Hillside Hospital,* 1953, 2:80-95.

Arlow, Jacob A.   A psychoanalytic study of a religious initiation rite, Bar Mitzvah.   In Eissler, Ruth K., *et al.* (eds.), *The Psychoanalytic Study of the Child.*  Vol. VI.  NY: International Universities Press, 1951.

Barag, Gerda C.  The mother in the religious concepts of Judaism.  *American Imago,* 1946, 4:32-53.

Eder, Montague D.  The Jewish phylacteries and other Jewish ritual observances.  *International Journal of Psycho-Analysis,* 1933, 14:341-375.

Feldman, Sandor S.  The blessing of the Kohenites.  *American Imago,* 1941, 2:269-322.

————.  Notes on some religious rites and ceremonies.  *Journal* of the *Hillside Hospital*, 1959, 8:36-41.

Foa, V. G. An equal interval scale for the measurement of Sabbath observance. *Journal of Social Psychology*, 1948, 27:273-276.

Fodor, A. The origin of the Mosaic prohibition against cooking the suckling in its mother's milk. *International Journal of Psycho-Analysis*, 1946, 27:140-144.

Freud, Sigmund. Obsessive acts and religious ceremonies. In *Collected Papers*, Vol. 2. NY: Basic Books, 1955.

————. *Totem and Taboo*. NY: Modern Library, 1960, 207 p.

Fromm, Erich. Der Sabbath. *Imago*, 1927, 13:223-234.

Fromm-Reichmann, Frieda. Das Jüdische Speiseritual. *Imago*, 1927, 13:235-246.

Götz, Berndt. Die Passahfeier und ihre ethnopsychologische Verwandtschaft mit den Initiationsriten. *Zeitschrift für Sexualwissenschaft*, 1930, 17:232-244.

Hanauer, W. Das rituelle Tauchbad (Mikve) der jüdischen Frauen. *Sexualprobleme*, 1913, July.

Langer, Georg. Zur Funktion der jüdischen Türpfostenrolle. *Imago*, 1928, 14:457-468.

————. *Die jüdsichen Gebetsriemen. Mit Anhang: Verwandtschaft mit afrikanischen Kulturkriesen. Des Feuer. Die Schlange.* Vienna: Internationale Psychoanlytischer Verlag, 1953, 53 p; *Imago*, 1930, 16:435-486.

Levy, Ludwig. Die Schuhsymbolik in jüdischen Ritus. *Monatschrift für Geschichte und Wissenschaft des Judentums*, 1918, 62:178-185.

Marcuse, Max. Penisstrangulation bei den Ghetto-Juden. *Zeitschrift für Sexualwissenschaft*, 1926, 13:31-32.

Reik, Theodor. A booth away from the house. *Psychoanalytic Review*, 1963, 50(2):7-26.

————. *Pagan Rites in Judaism*. NY: Farrar, Straus, 1963.

————. The prayer shawl and the phylacteries of the Jews. A psychoanalytic contribution to Hebrew archaeology. In *Dogma and Compulsion, Psychoanalytic Studies of Myths and Religions*. NY: International Universities Press, 1951, 181-228.

————. *Ritual; The Psychological Problems of Religion*. NY: Farrar, Straus, 1946, 221-261.

Róheim, Géza. Passover and initiation. *Man*, 1923, 23:178.

Woolf, M. Prohibitions against simultaneous consumption of milk and flesh in orthodox Jewish law. *International Journal of Psycho-Analysis*, 1945, 26:169-177.

## MISCELLANEOUS

Cronbach, Abraham. New studies in the psychology of Judaism. *Hebrew Union College Annual*, 1946, 19:205-273.
————. The psychoanalytic study of Judaism. *Hebrew Union College Annual*, 1931/32, 8-9:608-740.
————. The psychology of religion. A bibliographic survey. *Psychological Bulletin*, 1928, 25:701-719.
Freehof, Solomon W. Three psychiatric stories from rabbinic lore. *Psychoanalytic Review*, 1942, 29:185-187.
Frumkin, Robert M. The Jewish intellectual and his Jewishness: a social psychological analysis. *Ethos*, 1958, 3:7-9.
————. The Jewish passion for social justice: a social psychological analysis. *Ethos*, 1957, 2:40-42.
Gilbert, Arthur. A rabbinic theory of instincts. *Psychoanalysis*, 1955, 3(3):36-43.
Gold, Henry R. (Jewish contribution to the development of medical psychology.) *Harofe Haivri*, 1951, 24:94-105.
Isaac-Edersheim, E. Messias, Golem, Ahasver; drei mythische Gestalten des Judentums. *Internationale Zeitschrift für Psychoanalyse*, 1941, 26:50-80, 179-213, 286-315.
Kaplan, Leo. The Baalshem legend. *Psyche & Eros*, 1921, 2:173-183.
Landes, Ruth, & Zborowski, M. Hypotheses concerning the Eastern European Jewish family. *Psychiatry*, 1950, 13:447-464.
Levin, Max. Psychoanalytic interpretation of two statements from the Talmud. *International Journal of Psycho-Analysis*, 1930, 11:94-95.
Levinson, Boris M. The socioeconomic status, intelligence and personality traits of Jewish homeless men. *Yivo Annual of Jewish Social Science*, 1956/57, 11:122-141.
Lorand, Sandor. Dream interpretation in the Talmud. *International Journal of Psycho-Analysis*, 1957, 38:92-97.
Meadow, Arnold, & Vetter, Harold J. Freudian theory and the Judaic value system. *International Journal of Social Psychiatry*, 1959, 5(3):197-207.

Meissner, William W. *Annotated Bibliography in Religion and Psychology.* NY: Academy of Religion & Mental Health, 1961, 235 p.

Menninger, Karl A. The genius of the Jew in psychiatry. *Medical Leaves,* 1937, 1:127-132.

Nardi, Noah. (*Psychology and Education.*) Tel Aviv: Chachik Publishing House, 1955, 400 p.

Patai, Raphael (ed.). *Current Jewish Social Research.* NY: Herzl Foundation, 1958, 102 p.

Roback, Abraham A. The euphemism in Yiddish. A study in folk psychology and philology. *Jewish Forum,* 1921, 4:736-744.

Sanua, Victor D. A survey of the needs of Jewish social science research. *Journal of Jewish Communal Service,* 1963, 40(1):48-57.

# Index

Religion, evolution, of, 60-61; primitive, 61-62; primitive and diet, 298-99, 302-04; primitive and ritual, 279
Rites. *See* Ritual
Ritual, *Mezuzah* as, 310-11, 313-14, 321-22; number 7 as, 371-73, 382-86; phylacteries as, 307-41; primitive religions and, 279; psychoanalysis and, 275-77; shoe removal as, 409-13; spitting and, 282; *Talith* as, 310, 313, 318-21; *Tsitsith* as, 309-10, 317-18
*Rosh Chodesh,* 352-53

Sabbath, 292, 345, 353, 356, 386-89
Schizophrenia, among Jews, 169-80
Security, of college girls, 183-89
Self-esteem, in college girls, 183-89
Self-hatred, 134, 194
Senility, 269-70
Seven, as ritualistic number, 371-73, 382-86
Sex, Christian attitude to, 64-65; Jewish attitude to, 65-66, 75; in primitive religion, 62
Shoes, removal of, 409-13
*Shtetl,* life in, 23-55
Sibling rivalry, 135
Siblings, in American-Jewish culture,

87-88; in *shtetl,* 28-29, 32, 37-38, 42, 48
*Simchat Torah,* 351, 357
Social mobility, 125, 241; neuroses and, 147
Son, attitude of mother to, 87-88; in *shtetl* life, 27, 45-46
Son-in-law, in *shtetl,* 40-42
Spitting, 411; as ritual, 282
Stereotyping, of Jews, 123-25
*Sukkot,* 348, 350-51, 357

*Talith,* 310, 313, 318-21, 418
*Talmud,* psychological heritage of, 266; compared to psychoanalysis, 157-61
*Tefillin. See* Phylacteries
*Torah,* 357-58
Totem, Jewish, 324, 415, 418
*Tsitsith,* 309-10, 317-18

Values, Jewish, 154-55
Vocations, of college males, 239-42

Washing, of hands, 405-06, 408-09, 413
Wife, role of, in *shtetl,* 26

Youth, college, religious, 219-52